Current Cases in Public Administration

edited by

Marc Holzer and Ellen Doree Rosen

John Jay College of Criminal Justice
The City University of New York

1817

HARPER & ROW, PUBLISHERS, New York
Cambridge, Hagerstown, Philadelphia, San Francisco,
London, Mexico City, São Paulo, Sydney

for Madeleine and Milton

Sponsoring Editor: John L. Michel
Project Editor: Pamela Landau
Senior Production Manager: Willie Lane
Compositor: Maryland Linotype Composition Co., Inc.
Printer and Binder: The Maple Press Company

Current Cases in Public Administration

Library of Congress Cataloging in Publication Data
Main entry under title:

Current cases in public administration.

  1. United States—Politics and government—1971–
—Case studies.   2.   Bureaucracy—United States—Case studies.   3.   Public administration—Case studies.
I.   Holzer, Marc.   II.   Rosen, Ellen Doree, 1924–
JK424.C86   353'.00092'6   80–25652
ISBN 0–06–042879–1

CONTENTS

Businesslike Government 95

Section III: POLITICS AND POLICY-MAKING 107

The Swine Flu Affair 112

All the President's Women 124

Deciding the Budget 134

An Empty Building 146

Going Nowhere: A Story of Transitory Madness 150

PREFACE

Textbooks on public administration provide valuable generalizations about the functioning of public sector organizations. All too frequently, however, the relevance of those generalizations for solving practical, day-to-day problems has been limited because these books tend to be unappealingly dry and abstract.

One way to close the gap between the theory and practice of public administration is to integrate case studies into basic introductory courses. Since the 1930s public administration faculty (especially part-time appointees with full-time administrative positions) have utilized the case approach to supplement more formal course material and teaching methodologies. Use of cases has helped develop an awareness —often implicit rather than explicit—that cases can provide an interesting and effective approach; it is growing. Whereas texts present classification systems and causal relationships, cases engage the emotions and thus heighten interest, insight, and awareness that administrative theory is germane to real life.

Our goal is a relevant, lively book in which the commentaries implicit in each case approach administration from a fresh, unorthodox perspective. The cases we have chosen are not only "real world" but often controversial or newsworthy in nature, being drawn from material across a varied spectrum, without weighting toward any particular philosophy. Cases have been selected for the critiques of public administration that they represent and the problems that they highlight. They confront the many criticisms of the public administrative performance. Today governmental administrative agencies—federal, state, and local —are under fire from all sides. From the right, they are perceived as intrusive, overly regulatory, undertaking activities and making decisions that should properly be left to individual initiative. From the middle, they are seen as wasteful of the tax dollar, inefficient, inconsiderate of the citizen-client, and possibly corrupt. From the left, they are viewed as unjust and inattentive to the needs of the politically weak. Contemporary students of public administration are aware of these perceptions and probably share many of them; this is as true of undergraduate Inner City or Sun Belt youths as of bureaucrats pursuing the Master of Public Administration degree. It is our intention to use these familiar and specific perceptions as a basis from which to develop wider, more general, and theoretically sounder understanding. Throughout, our objective is to implant an awareness that the real world and public administration *are* joined in theory and practice.

With students uppermost in mind, we have chosen cases that are:

1. Relatively succinct in order to retain student interest.
2. Entirely current—1976 to the present. We find that students relate best to those cases that evoke familiar names or dramatic events.
3. Readable. Students today are accustomed to lively, pithy reportage from television, newspapers, or newsmagazines. They are alienated, if not confused, by lengthy, detailed, academic presentations, such as tables, model forms, and charts so characteristic of other casebooks. We rely most heavily on materials written by investigative journalists and other professionals.

The cases in this book are drawn primarily from news media, including newspaper and newsmagazine feature articles, magazines, interest group publications, journals of controversy and critique, interviews, and excerpts from popular books.

Some of the "cases" contain more than one "reading." Each case is preceded by an introduction, intended to guide students to major case points in the context of an established public administration framework.

Each introduction is followed by questions for discussion. The casebook is accompanied by a short instructor's guide which contains suggestions as to the most effective use of cases, in general, and of these, in particular. The guide also poses questions and suggests exercises beyond those detailed in the casebook.

The organization of the casebook is based on a specific, comprehensive conceptual framework which we have developed and tested. On one level the framework helps to build a grasp of the field historically; each case is related, in terms of contemporary problem solving, to the principle or issue dominating a major "stage" in the development of public administration. Five central "approximations" to effective public administration form the structure of the framework.

1. Reform and the civil service: The concept that a neutral civil service, free from political influence, is more likely to be efficient; graft and corruption must be controlled.

2. Management models: A search for orderly administration in which scientific sense would replace common sense.
3. Politics and policymaking: The realization that values and responsiveness must be considered, in addition to efficiency.
4. Human behavior: The views of workers as motivated by complicated social and psychological forces rather than merely economic incentives.
5. Program effectiveness: The reemphasis on output and outcomes as well as on process, on effective goal accomplishment as the object of activity.

This book would not have been possible without the assistance of Doris DeVito, who typed the bulk of the manuscript, and Joseph Rauen, who managed the correspondence for permissions. Typing was also provided by Chaki Najarian and research assistance by Philip Budne and Charles Fishman. The assistance of research librarians at the Croton Free Library, the Ossining Public Library, the Great Neck Public Library, the John Jay College of Criminal Justice Library and the Newspaper Collection in the Annex, the New York Public Library, as well as the assistance of Joan Stephens of the Center for Productive Public Management, was crucial to securing citations and materials. John Michel of Harper & Row, who more than encouraged us by his confidence and constructive criticism, deserves greater credit than we can express here.

M.H.
E.D.R.

The following matrix is provided as a guide to the use of this book with eight popular public administration textbooks. Opposite the title of each reading are the chapter numbers for which it is most appropriate.

	N&N	B&O	B	McC	M	S	H	D
Section I: Reform and the Civil Service								
Hiring and Firing in the Civil Service	4 14	6	5	1	8	5	5 8	5 9 15
The Bureaucrats and Mr. 1069	6	2 14	2	3	1		2	Epilogue
The "Jungle" Revisited	20	6	11	5		4	2	11
Reflections on Gift-Giving	4	6	11	6	2 8	5	1 2	11
The Energy Hustle	1 2 4		11	4		4	2	11 15
Cold-Shower Time at the Smithsonian	1	9	1 2	4	6	4 9	7	1 10
Carter's Cactus Flower at HUD	4 13 14	6 8	5 12	4	5 6 8	5 7	5 8	5

Key: N&N = Nigro, Felix A. and Nigro, Lloyd G., *Modern Public Administration*, 5th Ed. (New York: Harper & Row, 1980).

B&O = Bernstein, Samuel J. and O'Hara, Patrick, *Public Administration: Organizations, People and Public Policy* (New York: Harper & Row, 1979).

B = Berkley, George E., *The Craft of Public Administration* (Boston: Allyn & Bacon, 1975).

McC = McCurdy, Howard E., *Public Administration: A Synthesis* (Reading, Mass.: Cummings Publishing Co., 1977).

M = Morrow, William L., *Public Administration: Politics, Policy, and the Political System*, 2nd Ed. (New York: Random House, 1980).

S = Sharkansky, Ira, *Public Administration: Policy-Making in Government Agencies*, 4th Ed. (Chicago: Rand McNally, 1978).

H = Henry, Nicholas, *Public Administration and Public Affairs* (Englewood Cliffs, N.J.: Prentice-Hall, 1975).

D = Davis, James W., Jr., *An Introduction to Public Administration: Politics, Policy, and Bureaucracy* (New York: The Free Press, 1974).

	N&N	B&O	B	McC	M	S	H	D
The Privileged Civil Servant	4 6 11 14 15 17	5 6 7	4 5 11	2 8 10	8 11	5	2 5 8	5 6

Section II: Management Models

	N&N	B&O	B	McC	M	S	H	D
Bureaucracy as a Dirty Word	10 20	11	1	3 9	1	2	2 6	14
The Great Asphalt Bungle	1 17		11	6	2	4	1 6 10	14
Letter from Washington	17	14	11	7		4 6	2	14
Bureaucratic Blackout	11	4	5 7	7		3 6	6	Epilogue
When Washington Tries to Build a Railroad	6 10	1 12 13	3	1	3	6 11	1	12 14
Businesslike Government	1 6	3	1 10	4 7	2	3	1 6 9	9 15

Section III: Politics and Policy-Making

	N&N	B&O	B	McC	M	S	H	D
Warning: National Security May Be Hazardous to Your Health	3 4	8		5		3	2 9 12	1
The Swine Flu Affair	3 10	6 8		5	1	3	4 9	3 12
All the President's Women	4 10	8		4	4 10	5	5 8	5 9
Deciding the Budget	4 9 15 16	7 8 9	8 12	3 6	10	3 8 9	7 9 10	2 13

	N&N	B&O	B	McC	M	S	H	D
An Empty Building	10		12	5	1	3 8	2 4 9	11
A Story of Transitory Madness	3 8 10	10 12		4 5	7	3 8 10	7 9 10 11	2 11 12 14
The Assassins	4 20	8 11	11	6	1	4 11	4 6	1 8 9
Section IV: Human Behavior								
My Brief Career as a Bureaucrat	4	5	5	8	8	5	2 4 5 8	6
Balancing Ideals and Frustration in the Bureaucracy	4 13	5	5	8	8	5 7	8	6
The Reward System	1 2 3 13 14 20	6 8 9	4 5 11	8	8	5 6	4 5	6
The City Manager Builds a New Life	13	5	4	8	3	5	3 5	6
The City's Biggest Landlord	13	5	4 6	6 8	6	5	2 3 5 10	6
Neil Welch, Boat Rocker	13	3 5	4 6	2	11	6	5	6
Snow Report	6	5	4	2 8	3	6	4	6

	N&N	B&O	B	McC	M	S	H	D
The Rise and Fall of Richard Helms	4 20	8	4 11	1 3 6	8	5	4 5	5 8 9 10
Businessmen in the Bureaucracy	1	1 3	1	1 3	8	5 7	5 8	6
Professionals Can Buck the Boss, If They Know the Ropes	4	3 6	4	4 6 10	8	3 4 5	4 5 9 12	6 8
Inside Outsiders	4 5 8	6 8	12	4 10	6 9	5 8	5 8 12	5 8

Section V: Program Effectiveness

	N&N	B&O	B	McC	M	S	H	D
Grim Legacy of Nuclear Testing	12	13	11	5		3 6 11	2 12	10 12 14
A City Speaks Its Mind About Federal Red Tape	5	8	11	3	7	6 10	9 11	11 14 Epilogue
Doing Business with the Government	5 20	8 11	11 12	5	5	8 11	9	14 Epilogue
Tower Warning Was Ignored, Group Charges	20	11	12	10		6	2	14
Field & Stream Annual Dumb-Dumb Award	4	4	4	3	1	3 8 11	2 9 12	12 14
The FBI	4 11 20	4 8 11	7 12	3	5	6 11	2 4	9 14

	N&N	B&O	B	McC	M	S	H	D
The Tax Revolt	16	9 10	8	5	10	3 8	7	13
Dealing with Fraud and Waste in Government	17 20		11	4 7	3	4 6 9	6 9	
Regulate the Regulators	20	9 13	11	10	6	4 9	9	10 15
Power on the Potomac: Whistle Blowing in the Plutonium	4 20	6	11	5 6 10	5	6	2 5	10 11
The Price of Blowing the Whistle	4 20	6 11	11	6	8	6 8	2 5	14

Section I
REFORM AND THE CIVIL SERVICE

One of the continuing tug-of-wars in American public administration
has been competence versus responsiveness. Even in the relatively
small bureaucracies presided over by presidents from Washington to
John Quincy Adams, competence and qualification were relatively
highly valued. But in 1828 the elevation of Andrew Jackson to the
presidency initiated a new administrative philosophy—"spoils." As
opposed to government by an "elite," that system emphasized
rotation in office as a means to achieving politically responsive
administration. According to Jackson, almost any citizen was fit to
carry out the "simple" duties of public management which was, after
all, just a matter of common sense.

Unfortunately, the price of responsiveness was high. Inefficiency
became endemic, graft widespread, scandals frequent—not only at the
federal level but also at the state and municipal levels where the spoils
system prevailed. But a large, increasingly industrialized and therefore
more complex nation could not tolerate such poor public service
administration. The reaction was a reform movement that appealed for
efficiency and honesty in government, often drawing a dichotomy
between (1) policy *determination,* to be achieved via politics, and (2)
policy *implementation,* to be achieved via nonpolitical administration.

The Pendleton Civil Service Act of 1883 created a neutral,
bipartisan Civil Service Commission—the beginning of the system
that now covers 90 percent of public employees. But many critics now
argue that the price of a "merit" system, insulated from politics, has
been too high. Mediocrity and incompetence are so pervasive that the
system does not work much better than its predecessors. Other critics
add that graft and corruption have not, in fact, been eliminated;
although we have done away with their most obvious forms, they
persist in subtle ways—friendly ties, collusion, deferred favors—
occasionally in blatantly illegal instances.

1

2 REFORM AND THE CIVIL SERVICE

The cases in this section are current examples of the tension between competence and responsiveness and of the unintended side effects of the civil service "medicine" that we prescribed to improve government.

Hiring and Firing in the Civil Service

No public agency is without its tales of incompetent bureaucrats. It is generally recognized that although there are many dedicated and competent civil servants, there are also many civil service "workers" who are literally cheating the taxpayers. One of the chief problems has been that it is almost impossible to fire an incompetent employee. With the exception of employees who "blew the whistle" on irresponsible activities, almost no one used to be fired. Another complaint is that the veterans' preference system for hiring results in eliminating many higher-scoring candidates from the bureaucratic work force. Until very recently it has been difficult to reward excellent service; everyone at the same grade level received the same raises. President Carter's 1978 reform of the Civil Service system confronted these problems. Although Congress refused to abolish veterans' preference, the act modified the old Civil Service system in other ways. Raises can now be earned on an individual basis. Special procedures protect whistle blowers, whereas firing for incompetence is being speeded up.

The following cases exemplify personnel problems in government. Such problems are still apparent at the state and local levels and to some degree at the federal level as well. Isn't a "clerk-typist's" demonstrated inability to clerk or to type grounds for ready dismissal? Not according to "It isn't Easy to Fire a Bureaucrat." Surely, shooting a co-worker or throwing your work away is grounds? Not according to "The Battle over Bureaucracy." A 99.99 examination score earns selection for hiring in a merit system? Not according to "Civil Service: A Battle Lost."

QUESTIONS FOR DISCUSSION

Will President Carter's Civil Service reform program have a long-term impact?

Should government bureaucrats be subject to the same hiring/firing procedures as those that pertain in the private sector?
Why do bureaucrats need protection from political influence?
Why do the courts make it so difficult to fire government employees?
Why would Congress refuse to curtail the veterans' preference system?

IT ISN'T EASY TO FIRE
A BUREAUCRAT

The 21-foot chart zigzagging across the office of Harrison Wellford, the Carter administration's reorganization director, shows how the dismissal of an incompetent federal worker can drag on and on.

In this case, according to Wellford's office, a supervisor who followed all the proper steps needed more than 18 months to fire a clerk-typist who "couldn't clerk or type." Failure to "go by the book" results in the overturning of nearly a third of government firings.

"Agency management alone caused 15 months of delay," says the reorganization office. "The supervisor had to break every logjam."

The case history shows how paper work, investigations and conferences stretched out the process.

January, 1975, through June, 1975—New supervisor realizes employee is never around when work is needed. He documents her failure to perform required work. He tells her that her work is deficient. He keeps track of her absences and tardiness. He holds several meetings with her and with agency officials to discuss her work.

July, 1975, through December, 1975—Supervisor asks employee to provide doctor's certificates after any future absences. He holds several more meetings with her and with agency officials.

January, 1976, through July, 1976—Supervisor writes to employee, telling her that her record is poor. He checks with her doctor, who says his signature was forged on medical certificates excusing employees' absences. Supervisor asks personnel officials to investigate. More meetings are held. Employee is notified that she will be dismissed in 30 days. Finally, the employee resigns, citing health reasons.

The supervisor's feeling of accomplishment was short-lived. He had spent so much time on the case that his own supervisor reprimanded him for neglecting his other duties.

THE BATTLE OVER BUREAUCRACY

. . . If an employee cannot be fired, what about shifting him out of the department? A request for such a transfer must be submitted to the Civil Service Commission, where it often sinks out of sight. To get rid of incompetents, managers steer them to what are called "turkey farms," offices where nothing much is required and little damage can be done. The bureaucracy is studded with these farms, which a HUD analyst claims can be spotted on sight. "Just walk down the halls," he says. "You'll see lots of zombies."

Many employees openly admit to doing nothing to earn their pay. For a year and a half a statistician at HUD earning $13,000 a year, and four equally idle co-workers, drank coffee, pondered crossword puzzles and listened to the radio. "Our supervisors were always telling us to look busy," she says. "But there's only so much you can pretend when you haven't got a damn thing to do." . . .

The most promising people are often mangled by the Government machinery. Harold Hodgkinson, director of HEW's National Institute of Education during the Ford Administration, wanted to promote a talented secretary but was unable to get her reclassified, in a better job. The Civil Service Commission said that if she were reclassified, every other secretary in the agency would have to be reclassified. "There is almost no ability to promote able people from secretarial and clerical positions into leadership posts," he says. "Once people are on a track, you can't get them switched to another." . . .

A Department of Housing and Urban Development field office got 25 names through the Civil Service roster to fill several temporary clerk-typist positions for a year. The office superintendent, a white man, selected seven people (four women and three men) from nine applicants, all of whom were black. One of the rejected applicants, Mr. F., on probation for assault, complained to the Equal Employment Opportunity Office that he had been the victim of race and sex discrimination. The superintendent admitted that he had rejected F. because of his criminal record. F. was given one year's employment retroactively because, it was reasoned, blacks are arrested for assault more often than whites, so F. was discriminated against because of race. . . .

Beaman Hysmith, a mail carrier, shot a co-worker in the chest. While he was serving his sentence, the Postal Service dismissed him.

Reprinted by permission from TIME, The Weekly Newsmagazine; Copyright Time Inc. 1978.

Hysmith appealed his dismissal and won reinstatement because of a procedural flaw; the same person who proposed Hysmith's ouster had reviewed the case. The Post Office had to shell out approximately $5,000 in back pay for the time Hysmith was out of work pending his appeal, but with proper paper work it finally axed him permanently. . . .

On receiving persistent reports that orders for Government Printing Office publications were not being filled, the GPO secretly marked some fake order forms and tracked down the culprit, a 33-year-old worker who had pitched the marked forms into a wastepaper basket. The GPO removed him, a decision upheld by the Civil Service Commission, but the employee persuaded the commission's Appeals Review Board to reinstate him on the grounds that he could not be sacked for something no one had seen him do. The clerk got almost full back pay. The GPO then installed TV monitors to spy on the form filers, and now complaints about nonfulfillment have practically disappeared.

CIVIL SERVICE: A BATTLE LOST

Martin Waldron

About three years ago, Ruth Ballou took the state Civil Service test for a job she had created—coordinator of Federal and local programs in the Division of Consumer Affairs—and made a perfect score of 99.999.

But the job didn't go to Mrs. Ballou. A male colleague also took the test and scored 82.5.

Since that was a passing grade and one of the top three scores, and because the colleague had served in the United States military during wartime and Mrs. Ballou had not, the job, under New Jersey law, went to him.

Mrs. Ballou appealed to the state's Civil Service Commission, and when she lost there, she retained a lawyer and went to court.

Last Monday, after two years and considerable legal expense, the State Supreme Court upheld the law and the Civil Service Commission and said that Mrs. Ballou was not entitled to the job.

The New Jersey veteran's preference law gives veterans an "absolute" preference over nonveterans in hiring and promotion, a measure that has proved popular with elected officials.

The Supreme Court did not pass on the wisdom of having such a system; it said that the "sensible" thing to do might be to give veterans extra points on Civil Service tests. But that, the court added, is a decision for the Legislature to make.

Mrs. Ballou said that she was not against giving some preference to wartime veterans, but that an "absolute" and neverending preference somehow seemed unfair to others, especially women.

However, she said that she now planned to let the matter drop. Her husband has been patient enough, she added.

Mrs. Ballou is 69 years old, and pretty soon would be too old to hold the job—even if she got it.

"I was doing it for the principle of the thing, and for the generations to come, not for myself," Mrs. Ballou said, adding that she found the Supreme Court's decision "incredible."

Even though the State Constitution of 1947 provided that the Legislature could adopt a veteran's preference law, the one that the Legislature did adopt seemed to Mrs. Ballou to go too far.

Under the New Jersey system, a wartime veteran can use his or her "preference" repeatedly.

When she filed her suit, Mrs. Ballou made three major arguments against the present preference system:

It is unconstitutional because it is "absolute, permanent and inexhaustible."

It violates the due-process-of-law clause of the 14th Amendment to the United States Constitution.

It is unconstitutional in that it discriminates against women as a class.

The veterans' preference system in New Jersey is "sex-neutral," the court said, and thus is not "invidious or unreasonable discrimination" even though it "disfavors women to a substantially greater degree than other nonveterans."

No one knows how many wartime veterans are working in state Civil Service jobs. The Civil Service Commission tried to find out in 1975, and concluded that about 12,000 of the 60,000 merit-system posts were held by veterans.

A study showed that 78 percent of them had obtained their jobs in the first place because of the preference system and not because they scored highest on Civil Services tests.

In addition to the state Civil Service jobs, there are about 145,000 such positions in local governments in the state; veterans also have preference there.

A recent study of New Jersey's Civil Service system by private consultants showed that the veteran's preference setup is "one of the major impediments to management accountability."

"The impact of veterans' preference is to deny appointing authorities any discretion in the selection of new employees," the report said. "On a purely theoretical basis, a recommendation for the complete abolition of veteran's preference could be supported."

Almost every administrator is against the system privately, the report said, and 88 percent of them asserted that it had hurt their agencies.

In addition, the report continued, the veterans' preference system denies the state an opportunity to get the most qualified employees and discriminates against women.

However, the report went on to note that, since many states give some sort of preference to veterans—mostly by adding points to their test scores—it did not seem reasonable to expect the Legislature to do away with the system altogether.

The study group suggested that veterans be accorded extra points when taking tests to get a job, but that promotional preference be done away with. It added:

> While it is irrelevant to this study, it should be kept in mind, when considering the treatment of veterans, that New Jersey provides other benefits for veterans: certain reduced taxes, educational opportunities, and the like. The state will not be mistreating its veterans if it modifies a benefit relating to employment. . . .

Introduction
The Bureaucrats and Mr. 1069

A negative image of rigid, self-serving organizations is often born of routine contacts with public bureaucracies. Consider the example of a typical city dweller. He or she may take public transportation to work, all the while reading about newsworthy administrative failures (local welfare fraud, state laxity in inspecting nursing homes, CIA surveillance of private citizens; administrative success is rarely reported). When he or she is driving to work, listening to much the same news, seat belts are a reminder of federal safety regulations and low gas mileage serves as a reminder of antipollution agencies. Each week the family depends on the public sanitation department to pick up refuse, on the police department to patrol streets, and on the school system to transport and educate children. The weekly paycheck suffers heavy deductions for federal, state, local, and social security taxes. But if the services for which he or she has prepaid are not provided as our citizen expects—if the garbage is not picked up on time, if the police treat him rudely or if her child is bused past the neighborhood school to one more distant—they will probably become angry at "bureaucracies." Anger will intensify if complaints are not promptly considered. And frustration with large organizations may grow even more intense as they become enmeshed in impersonal, complex procedures throughout the year—waiting on a series of lines to renew license plates, spending hours "deciphering" intricate income tax forms and regulations. A citizen is asked so often for his or her social security, credit card, or account numbers that he or she complains of feeling less than human, an anonymous being virtually undifferentiated from others.

Michael Herbert Dengler's case, presented in "The Bureaucrats and Mr. 1069," epitomizes those frustrations. If government bureaucrats (as well as their private counterparts) treated him as impersonally as a number, why not call attention to that process of dehumanization by changing his name to a number? To the extent that Dengler

9

intended to underscore an issue, rather than actually to change his name, he and the editors of the *Saturday Review* agree on the major points: An unintended consequence of bureaucracy is dehumanization. And in treating us impersonally, bureaucracy is not even accomplishing its major objective of treating us rationally.

QUESTIONS FOR DISCUSSION

How many identification numbers have you been assigned by bureaucracies: social security, college, motor vehicle, hospital, postal service, and so on?
How many organizations recognize you only by your social security number?
What rules and regulations could we drop—and what would be the consequences of this?
Are we better or worse off because organizations treat us in an impersonal manner that is intended to assure fairness?
If a bus stops again for passengers who have reached the door just as it closes but falls behind schedule because of that, would you praise or criticize the driver? What principles should guide such decisions?

THE BUREAUCRATS AND MR. 1069

Norman Cousins

A recent newspaper item reports that a Minnesota citizen has applied to the court for authorization to change his name to the number 1069. The case has raised all sorts of fascinating questions, and so we were pleasantly surprised to receive a telephone call about it from Donald T. Barbeau, Chief Judge of the District Court in Minneapolis, who will have to decide whether to grant Michael Herbert Dengler's request. Judge Barbeau said he was consulting students of history, philosophy, and human rights because the law books offered little precedent for a case of this kind.

The judge had heard from a number of sources that *SR* had been waging a war against the increasing depersonalization of human beings and that in this connection, we regularly ran spoofing advertisements in the magazine's classified columns in which we concocted whopping

Reprinted by permission of Saturday Review, "The Bureaucrats and Mr. 1069" by Norman Cousins, January 21, 1978.

computer errors that were supposed to have resulted in all sorts of horrendous mix-ups. Judge Barbeau had been told that SR's reason for the spoofs was that we thought society had gone much too far in the direction of a computerized and numbered humanity. He wondered whether we had any thoughts to offer on the case before him.

We asked the judge to tell us about Michael Dengler. We learned that Mr. Dengler, 32, had held a variety of jobs, including teacher and short-order cook. To all intents and purposes he is a solid citizen with nothing in his background to indicate instability or eccentricity. . . . He insists that society has the obligation to respect his right to be known by four digits of his choosing rather than by the name given him by his parents.

After listening to Judge Barbeau, my first impulse was to side with Mr. Dengler. If his way of asserting his individuality was to be called by a number, that was his privilege and his problem. The fact that a digital moniker runs against convention—Mr. Dengler would probably be the only one so designated of 4 billion human beings—did not seem to me to be an argument against him.

Yet, after thinking about it, I wasn't so sure I was right. I realized that the cause of individuality was not likely to be served by a legal decision enabling Mr. Dengler to be known as Mr. 1069. The essential issue was whether a decision in his favor would accelerate a process of dehumanization that has already gone much too far.

The most serious battle being waged in the world today is not between conflicting political systems but between number-prone bureaucracies and individual citizens. Everywhere in the world, whatever the ideology, people are being encumbered and entangled by functionaries who hold sway through triplicate paper forms. Their questions are often as incomprehensible and impenetrable as their underlying purpose is obscure. No sooner are the conditions they impose met than are new obfuscations raised. The functionaries are as obsessive as they are implacable. They are not confrontable, they are gray figures lost in a landscape of long corridors and an infinity of filing cabinets bulging with regulations.

The bureaucrats may speak in different tongues in different parts of the world, but they are equally misunderstood everywhere. Their officialese comes as naturally to its perpetrators as their administrative fines. The tax form alone makes everyone in the world kin. Nothing is more universally recognizable or poignant than the baffled look on the faces of decent but helpless citizens, whether their native habitat is Chile, Chad, or Chicago, when confronted by the need to compute their taxes according to a series of questions whose only object, seemingly, is to provide the final triumph of numbers over logic.

The American farmer who wants authorization to shift his crop from soybeans to grain; the Muscovite manager of a bakery who needs approval before he can swap apartments with a bus driver so that both can live nearer to their jobs; the young Rumanian language specialist who needs permission before leaving her job as a tourist guide in order to teach at the university; the British dentist who finds it easier to fill teeth than government forms after he has done so; the Italian grocer who has prudently put his money in a savings bank, only to have the funds impounded because he forgot to submit the bankbook for interest computation—all these are citizens battered and beleaguered by the bureaucrats. They are victims of a monumental numbers game in which the deck is stacked in favor of the state. Every time people have to queue up somewhere, the bureaucrats score a point against the human race.

In the best of all possible worlds, there might be no harm in allowing Michael Herbert Dengler to be known by a number. But in a world overrun by bureaucrats, replacing even a single human name with a number is like throwing raw meat to lions or a hanging curve to Reggie Jackson. Can anyone imagine anything riskier than fortifying the natural tendency of bureaucrats to forget faces and remember numbers?

The bureaucrats are impelled by a dream of a soulless world in which everything will be known about everyone and in which digits are supreme. The individual's secrets will become as extinct as gracious letters written in artistic longhand. But secrets are precious. They have to do with human failings. They must not be entrusted to computers.

Give the blasted bureaucrats more numbers to play with? Never. Michael Herbert Dengler should be consoled, and his assertion of individuality should be redirected. The court could sympathize with him if what he really wanted was to put more distance between himself and the bureaucracy; but it would be a mistake to expect the law to set a precedent that could be seized upon by all those in public agencies who think computerese rather than humanese.

There is something unholy and inhuman about digits when they are used as identifiers, whether on a Buchenwald registry or a Minnesota court order. Far better to let Mr. Dengler be renamed Mr. Emperor or Mr. Majesty or Mr. Monarch of All He Surveys than Mr. 1069. Far better, too, to sustain and even encourage the illusion that a man is a mighty potentate than to permit him to be a perforation on a computer card.

The Jungle Revisited

In 1906 Upton Sinclair's *The Jungle* so vividly dramatized deadly abuses in the meat-packing industry that it helped gain close federal regulation. We have now institutionalized federal, state, or city oversight in many industries. But effective regulation depends directly on the integrity of regulators—the "imperfect" human beings who carry out our "perfect" laws. The conflict is between private profit and public good—as it has been since Boss Tweed was paid $13 million for a $1 million courthouse, or the Collector of the Port of New York skimmed off $10 million during the 1840s.

Bribery of meat inspectors is profitable to the packing company, but costs the public millions in overpricing. Similarly, a bribe to a building inspector profits the construction company but may create dangerous conditions for building tenants for years. Paying off a fire inspector may profit a homeowner who does not comply with codes but may create a fire hazard, and so on.

Corruption in the meat-packing industry is an unfortunate "by-product" of the regulation Sinclair helped win. As John Coplin's case indicates, its pervasiveness reflects the system's willingness to overlook and tolerate bribery. Despite Coplin's exoneration, he is probably a pariah to his fellow workers. Part of the problem is, as Sheets indicates, there is "a feeling among grades that they work for the industry, not the government."

QUESTIONS FOR DISCUSSION

Are you personally aware of similar cases of corruption?

Are public officials paid enough to help them resist bribes?

If a bribe is offered and accepted, and that action is discovered, is the organization/individual offering the bribe likely to be punished to the extent the acceptor is?

Is corruption more common now?

If an employee "blows the whistle" on corruption, will he or she be cold-shouldered by other colleagues? Will it end the employee's career?

What policies or procedures might discourage corruption like this?

HOW CORRUPTION PADS YOUR MEAT BILL

America's meat industry, the target of muckraking investigations since the early 1900s, is under attack again.

Amid great secrecy, Justice Department investigators are zeroing in on allegations that bribery, fraud and extortion are widespread in the 38-billion-dollar-a-year industry. . . .

Some critics of the industry allege that corruption—ranging from fraudulently upgrading the quality of meat to price manipulation to extortion by federal meat inspectors—adds as much as 10 cents a pound to the real price of beef and is a major reason for consumers' rising food bills.

Richard Lyng, president of the American Meat Institute, acknowledges that some shady business practices may occasionally occur on the fringes of the industry, but he denies that corruption is prevalent among meat companies. He calls for the quick prosecution of meat-company officials involved in illegal business dealings.

Federal investigators say that only a small percentage of the nation's 6,337 federally inspected meatpacking and processing firms engage in wrongdoing, but cite these incidents as proof that the problem is not an isolated one:

> After pleading "no contest" to price-fixing charges in federal court, 12 Los Angeles area meat companies on July 24 were fined a total of $540,000. Eight company officials got jail sentences ranging from 10 to 30 days. Charges against another company and two officers are pending.

> Indictments against Agriculture Department meat inspectors in 1977 led to 33 convictions for bribery and other violations of U.S. meat regulations. Fifty-three company officers and 15 employees were convicted.

   A California-based consumer organization received $300,000 in
settlement of a class-action suit against a San Diego meatpacking firm. A second suit, seeking up to 6 billion dollars in
damages, has been filed against some Southern California
packers and processors, alleging mislabeling, bribing government meat inspectors and manipulating beef prices. "Ten cents
per pound is tacked onto the price of meat in Southern California
due to illegal practices," claims George Schultz, an attorney
who represents the consumer organization CALPIRG (California Public Interest Research Group).
The president of an Oklahoma meat firm was fined $2,000 and
given six months' probation last April for adding soy-protein
extender to about 40,000 pounds of meat and labeling it "ground
beef." The firm got a $4,000 fine and one year's probation.

   It was three quarters of a century ago that Upton Sinclair's book,
The Jungle, exposed unsanitary conditions in the nation's meatpacking
plants. Today, while sanitary conditions have greatly improved, critics
contend that there's still something rotten about the meat business. "A
lot of people are wondering why beef prices are so high, and a big
part of it is corruption," says Schultz, the public-interest lawyer.
   Industry experts claim that its very nature—and regulations
themselves—make the industry vulnerable to corruption and attractive
to criminals.
   Two practices by the government are considered especially subject
to manipulation.
   One is the requirement that meat crossing state lines into interstate
commerce must be inspected by federal employees; the other is the
voluntary meat-grading program under which the packer pays for
federal employes to grade the meat and stamp it for yield and quality
so that consumers know whether cuts are "good," "choice" or "prime,"
and priced accordingly.
   Just a little bit of cheating can make a lot of money illegally, says
Carol Tucker Foreman, Assistant Secretary of Agriculture: "If a grader
dishonestly upgrades just 1 out of every 10 carcasses from good to
choice, the packer could gain $30 a carcass, or $300 an hour, or $2,400
a day, or $12,000 a week—all at the expense of consumers and pro-
ducers."
   Fraudulent grading is difficult to prove, she adds. "A government
beef grader examines about 100 carcasses every hour. Many of his
decisions are close judgment calls, and every call means money to the
meatpacker."
   In the Southern California case involving the $300,000 class-action
settlement, Hugo Ralph Lueck, a former federal meat grader, confessed

in a sworn deposition that he received weekly bribes of $100 from officers of a meatpacking company to upgrade their beef from good to choice quality. He said he was also treated to free lunches, tickets to sporting events, and meat and liquor.

Agriculture Department supervisors make random checks on the work of federal graders, but Lueck's testimony indicates that the system breaks down. He said the plant owners always told him when his supervisor was approaching so that he could adjust his grading.

In a similar case, owners and three employes of meatpacking plants in Massachusetts and Connecticut were convicted in 1977 for conspiring to sell the Defense Department more than 500,000 pounds of inferior beef. A jury found that to accomplish this, defendants bribed military meat inspectors.

Meatpackers and processors indirectly pay the salaries of meat graders. Reason: In return for the Agriculture Department guarantee of quality, meat firms contribute to a government-controlled trust fund from which graders are reimbursed. That, Foreman charges, creates "a feeling among graders that they work for the industry, not the government."

Because federal meat inspectors have the authority to close down a plant or production line temporarily if they detect unsanitary conditions, they, too, are the targets of corporate bribery—and sometimes the initiators of extortion from meat companies.

Federal investigators two years ago uncovered evidence in the New York City area that led to the conviction of 31 inspectors for receiving bribes from meatpackers.

Company officials who admitted making payments of up to $125,000 said they did so to prevent "costly harassment" by inspectors who can halt or delay plant operations at a cost to the company of up to $5,000 a day.

The payments varied from $10 to $100 weekly in either money or gifts, including meat products—and "one inspector was taking enough meat each week to stock a wholesale butcher shop," says one investigator.

Investigators also have discovered counterfeits of blue-ink stamps used by inspectors and graders to certify the safety and quality of meat. Carol Seymour, a compliance officer with the Agriculture Department's food-safety and quality services, said there have been cases where meat was fraudulently stamped by "dipping a Coke bottle into blue ink." The blurred blue-ink stamp, she said, led many people to believe that the meat had been inspected by the Agriculture Department. One department official says that while only 33 of its 9,000 inspectors were convicted of wrongdoing in 1977, the situation is much more serious than that, adding: "There is a lot of money involved and it's only a rare case that comes to trial."

The department is having problems in cleaning up the inspection-and-grading system, says Assistant Secretary Foreman. "It is hard to get the U.S. attorney to go after someone taking a few pounds of meat in exchange for favors. We need to punish both companies and inspectors." . . .

The Agriculture Department, in an effort to crack down on abuses, has increased the number of supervisors who review the work of each grader. "Their presence reduces the opportunities for bribery," says Foreman.

But because of its inexact nature, experts say the meat-inspection and grading system will be hard to reform. Federal officials trying to enforce the regulations say they need more cooperation from the Justice Department and more enforcement tools.

Although the Agriculture Department has the authority to withdraw inspection from meatpacking and processing plants involved in illegal practices, Foreman says the rule is difficult to enforce.

"Withdrawal requires an extensive hearing process than can go on for years," she adds. "Realistically, we don't have the ability to close plants."

L. L. Gast, deputy administrator of the Agriculture Department's food-safety and quality services, echoes the need for new enforcement tools. At present, he says, the penalties range from a warning—"a slap on the wrist"—to criminal prosecution. Once a criminal proceeding has started, the government cannot shut down a plant until the case is settled.

Between these extremes, Gast contends, is the need for civil penalties that would allow the government to levy heavy fines against corporate malefactors.

At the moment, however, Foreman admits that "there is something inadequate about the system."

Congressional hearings and investigations into the meat industry are expected to continue well into 1979 before specific recommendations and charges are made—and meanwhile, financially squeezed Americans will be watching the outcome as the price of meat keeps rising in the stores.

LABELING MEAT

John Coplin[1]

John Coplin joined the U.S. Department of Agriculture in 1946, and in 1955 he became the main station supervisor in Philadelphia. "Almost immediately," he said, "I uncovered irregularities in the station's activities."

Among the illegal practices he discovered, Coplin was particularly outraged by a grading system which allowed meat to be labelled as "choice" in Philadelphia when that same meat did not qualify for that grade in the Midwest. Although Coplin notified his Washington bureau chiefs of these findings, no action was taken.

Coplin transferred to Chicago, as a main station supervisor, where he again found many irregularities. These included misgrading meat for commercial and military use; certifying inferior meats for city, county, federal, and state institutions; and conflicts of interest among packers, meat graders, and meat grading supervisors.

Coplin reported these findings to the director and deputy director of the USDA Meat Grading Service. Told by the supervisors that he should "soft pedal" any remedial action, Coplin then felt compelled to take his discoveries to the FBI. The FBI investigation concluded that most, perhaps all, of the assistant supervisors and many of the meat graders were receiving gratuities in the form of free meat, money, auto repairs, and gift certificates. Approximately 70 percent of the employees at the Chicago Station accepted resignation or dismissal, rather than face charges.

Among other discoveries, Coplin also found that between 1958 and 1963, approximately 15.5 million pounds of beef which only qualified as U.S. "good" in the Midwest, were graded as "choice" at one Baltimore company. Coplin decided to report this illegality to USDA's inspector general. As a result, no beef has been labelled "choice" at this plant since September 1963.

However, Coplin was never commended for his good work. On the contrary, Washington supervisors began cutting back Coplin's personnel just when work was piling up higher than ever. Frequently,

Published by permission of Transaction, Inc. from THE BUREAUCRAT, Vol. 6, No. 4 Copyright © 1977 by The Bureaucrat, Inc.
[1] This case summary is based on the testimony of John Coplin before the Subcommittee on Federal Spending Practices, Efficiency, and Open Government of the Committee on Government Operation, September 23, 1976.

Coplin would hire and train assistant supervisors, only to have his own trainees replaced once they became valuable.

In December 1963, Coplin and an assistant supervisor were victims of a suspicious auto accident in the Chicago Packing House district. What appeared to be a meat truck forced Coplin's car into a railroad support abutment. The car was demolished, and Coplin wound up in the hospital with several broken bones and lacerations.

But Coplin stayed in Chicago even though his conscientious anti-corruption campaign went unrecognized and unrewarded by the Department of Agriculture. The reason, in Coplin's view, was that the meat grading staff at Washington headquarters is riddled with ineptitude, political motivations, and cover-ups, as were the corrupt Chicago-based officials whom he had forced out of the department.

In July 1976, for example, a meat grader detailed to the Los Angeles station told Coplin of a colleague who would begin grading beef carcasses only after picking up $200 placed inside an envelope behind the men's room mirror. This was part of the grader's daily preclean-up routine.

One national supervisor still openly admits to Coplin that as a meat grader he was expected to pick up meat gifts from a packer for his supervisor when that official was away on field trips. He then delivered the meat and even placed it in the freezer, so that his boss' family would have free beef while he was away.

In July 1975, Senator Lawton Chiles of Florida asked Coplin to testify before his Subcommittee on Federal Spending Practices, of the Committee on Government Operations, about irregularities in military meat inspection and procurement practices. Upon arriving in Washington, Coplin was told by his superiors that he must be accompanied to the hearings by a Washington official of the USDA, Mr. David Hallet.

After the two arrived at the hearing room, the chief of the subcommittee staff contacted Senator Chiles, who informed Mr. Hallet that Coplin would be testifying alone. Before leaving the room, according to Coplin and several witnesses from the committee staff, Hallet warned Coplin that this action could adversely affect Coplin's career. The Department of Justice later investigated this claim and reported no basis for the allegation. However, following Coplin's testimony, he was notified that he would be suspended for five days without pay for "neglect of duty and failure to follow instructions." This was based on a misunderstanding which had developed eight months earlier concerning a request by Coplin that he be reimbursed for using his car on government time. . . .

On a more hopeful note, however, Carol Tucker Foreman, assistant secretary for food and consumer services of the Department of Agriculture, recently rescinded the five-day suspension against Coplin. She ordered all references to the suspension removed from Mr. Coplin's personnel file, and awarded him back pay for the penalty period. As Ms. Foreman stated in a letter dated June 24, 1977 to Senator Lawton Chiles: "I am convinced that, despite the absence of specific evidence to this effect, the timing of these events might give rise to the appearance of retaliatory action against employees who cooperate with congressional oversight of department operations. This department will not permit even the appearance of such motivation, for we recognize the valid and necessary role such cooperation performs in our system of checks and balances."

Introduction
Reflections on Gift-Giving

The giving of a gift is a time-honored sign of friendship. But the offering of gifts as corrupting bribes is a practice that probably dates back to the establishment of the first public organizations. It was particularly rampant under President Andrew Jackson's spoils system. During much of the nineteenth century, at all levels of government, graft was widespread, scandals frequent. It was not unusual for a public official to receive very large sums for reasons of influence, not friendship. Such behavior is still not unusual in many developing societies.

William Simon wants to buy some of the "gifts" that he had received while in office. The laws written to counter graft and scandals are clear: Gifts valued at more than $50 are the government's property. But Buckley questions whether the law is unnecessarily suspicious of true friendship tokens. On the other hand, perhaps Senator Douglas's position better serves the public, presuming that the important point is to avoid even the appearance of impropriety.

QUESTIONS FOR DISCUSSION

Were the gifts Mr. Simon received intended to influence him as to policy?
Were such "gifts" paid for by foreign governments or by individual leaders?
If gifts were paid for by government, does that indicate policy intent?
Is gift-giving from an official of one country to another, or from a governor
   to a president, important in building personal working relationships?
   Should we expect them to deal fairly with each other without such tokens?
Is a strict law regarding gift-giving necessary as a "signal" to bureaucrats
   that improper behavior of any type will not be tolerated?

REFLECTIONS ON GIFT-GIVING

William F. Buckley, Jr.

Guess what Shirley Temple is doing right now? As chief of protocol, she has to decide whether William Simon should be permitted to buy from the United States Government some of the gifts he was given while Secretary of the Treasury, or whether that would be opposed to the "spirit" of the law. The gifts Mr. Simon desires to hang on to are those that "mean something special" to him, namely, a Russian shotgun, a cigarette box from Saudi Arabia, two silver-colored necklaces from Israel, a set of matched pistols from Argentina, a wristwatch from Leonid Brezhnev with Brezhnev's name engraved on it, and a porcelain sculpture from Spain. The law says that any gifts from foreign officials worth more than $50 must be turned over to the United States Government. What then happens to them, if you were President of the United States, is that they end up decorating those shrines ex-Presidents and their friends build to preserve their sacred memory; or, if you were a lesser light they are quietly auctioned off a few years down the line by the General Services Administration.

Mr. Simon is a gun collector, which explains in part why he wants to hang on to the shotgun and to the pistols. The silver necklaces apparently have sentimental value (they alone are valued at less than $50, so there is no problem there). The porcelain sculpture from Spain presumably has nostalgic as well as artistic value. It isn't plain why he wants to hang on to the watch. The only gift I would accept from Brezhnev is an urn containing the ashes of the Brezhnev Doctrine. On the other hand, if every time you look at your watch you see Brezhnev's name, that's not a bad idea either, since it is good to remind ourselves that life is nasty, brutish, and short, thanks substantially to Brezhnev. Furthermore, William Simon being one of the world's exemplary libertarians, there are no grounds for suspecting any alienation of affection. If Mr. Simon goes back to Wall Street, he will no doubt want to be the only guy in the board room who tells the time by looking at Brezhnev's watch.

When I was a little boy, though not so little I shouldn't have known better, a lady at a souvenir shop in Stratford-On-Avon gave me, after my sisters and I had loaded up on Shakespeareana, a miniature *Hamlet*—the whole play, reduced to a book the size of a passport photograph. I was delighted, and fished out of my grubby pocket a

Reprinted by permission of National Review. *National Review*, Vol. 29, January 21, 1977.

shilling, which I, in turn, insisted on giving the lady. With us was an old friend who taught me music, but has had no other failure during her lifetime, and later she told me I must learn to accept gifts, any methodical attempt to requite which has the effect of squirting cold water on acts of spontaneous generosity.

One supposes that the law binding William Simon was written on the assumption that foreign officials are not engaged in acts of spontaneous generosity, but rather in formalities, or even cynicism. The exchange of gifts between heads of state is a ritual that began with the beginning of history. The question arises whether it is possible for a foreign leader to make a spontaneous gift. Sadat, for instance, is clearly attached to Henry Kissinger, not to the Secretary of State. Will he wait until Mr. Kissinger is out of office, and then make him a gift? Not to Be Opened until after Your Resignation?

It is one of the uglier aspects of public service that such spontaneities are forbidden because they are presumptively suspect. The next man who takes you to lunch may turn out to be the Korean ambassador. The late Democratic Senator Paul Douglas once wrote on the subject, laying down the law that $7 was the maximum value for an acceptable gift to an elected official, $7 being, in those days, the price of the most expensive book. A few Democratic Congresses later, you need to pay twice $7 to buy even a socialist primer to give to your local congressman.

I hope Mr. Simon gets to keep his presents, and if he doesn't, I'm going to send him two silver-colored necklaces, and pretend they came from Israel.

Introduction
The Energy Hustle

Under the spoils system, inefficiency was endemic and profiteering commonplace. But the growing, industrializing, complex America could not continue to tolerate poor public service administration. Waste and dishonesty had to be curbed. In the post-Civil War period, reform movements appealed directly to the public for efficiency and honesty in both politics and administration. Reformers did succeed in defining "conflict of interest" as an immoral situation. It is now common to find such constraints on officials as the prohibition against having a financial interest in any company that their agency regulates or has commercial dealings with.

Similar situations that are considered ethical within the "letter of the law" are increasingly coming into question on moral grounds. Daniel Guttman's investigation of the Department of Energy (DOE) finds that its consultants are often former officials, that its contractors are heavily influenced by the private energy corporations that DOE is mandated to oversee, and that firms that are substantially involved in the energy field are asked to provide "studies" for DOE decision makers. Guttman's analysis underscores a basic question: Is government run by business?

QUESTIONS FOR DISCUSSION

Are guidelines covering conflict of interest for consultants strict enough?
Should many tasks performed by consultants have been carried out by DOE itself, instead?
Could DOE operate without the expertise consultants provide?
Can conflicts of interest be avoided in a field such as energy where private and public sector experts train in the same specialized schools?
What problems result for us when experts move between employment in the public and private sectors?

How does the consultant firm, as an entity exempt from many conflict of interest laws and which serves both government and industry, complicate control over conflict of interest?

THE ENERGY HUSTLE

Daniel Guttman

It is against the law, of course, for any high official of the new Department of Energy to have a financial connection with the private companies DOE deals with and regulates. The 1977 legislation creating DOE bristles with post-Watergate morality. The financial disclosure requirements for DOE employees are so stringent that they had to be pruned back by a federal judge who found them to be unconstitutional invasions of privacy. DOE employees must make do on their civil service salaries, and are subject to rules limiting the extent to which they can work for industry even after leaving the Department.

Yet metropolitan Washington hosts a growing number of people who are not so constrained. They are lavishly reimbursed by the Energy Department for services allegedly rendered in helping to create and manage our national energy policy; and simultaneously they hold themselves out for hire to private energy companies, offering to explain the government's policy to them. What service they actually provide to either side is something of a mystery.

This prosperous enterprise is made possible because the DOE conflict-of-interest rules and salary limits, like others throughout the government, do not apply to private *contractors* hired by the department, as opposed to its own employees. The Energy Department has quickly settled into the comfortable habit, developed by other federal agencies since World War II, of contracting out great chunks of its responsibilities. For those with energy expertise to offer for sale, and for established consulting firms on the lookout for new markets, DOE has become a gold mine.

At 10 cents a page (for copying), the most recent computer printout of Energy Department consulting contracts may be obtained by any citizen willing to pay $91. Sprinkled throughout are the names of familiar giants of free enterprise. The research and development arms of oil companies like Exxon, Gulf and Mobil are in for millions of dollars. There are awards to General Electric. Almost three billion dollars of public funds have been committed to Westinghouse over 30 years of the atomic energy program. But most of the contracts are with lesser known companies that are not primarily manufacturers or "producers," but rather are set up specifically as wholesalers of planning and management "expertise."

One such company that has turned the energy crisis into a booming consulting business calls itself Energy and Environmental Analysis, Inc. (EEA). EEA has at least 11 different contracts with the Energy Department. For example, EEA received more than $200,000 for "technical assistance" to "support" the National Energy Plan, and $75,000 for "analysis related to formulation and assessment of policy options and legislative proposals in energy, supply, demand, and regulatory programs." The largest award to EEA was $1,681,225.

Meanwhile, EEA also offers its services to private enterprise. A brochure states, "EEA economists and energy experts have been involved in the formulation and initiation of many major U.S. energy programs. . . . EEA can aid government clients in administering energy policies and private clients in responding to them." Among the services offered to private clients are "representation with state, Federal, and local environmental agencies," "assistance in bringing special industry problems to the attention of regulatory agencies in rulemaking and other proceedings," "analysis and representation in rate-making procedures," and "fuel price forecasts."

The brochure brags that EEA's staff includes former employees of the Environmental Protection Agency who wrote a particular set of regulations, and it says these experts are now available to help private clients to "minimize adverse effects arising from" these regulations. Shell Oil, Exxon and Standard Oil of California, says EEA, are among the companies it assisted in "coping" with these particular regulations. The brochure lists other private clients, including the National Parking Association. It also boasts of having advised EPA about "parking management." The DOE printout reports a $125,000 award to EEA to study "Federal parking pricing options." You get the picture.

EEA's founder and president is Robert Sansom who served the Nixon-Ford administration as an environmental administrator. According to EEA's brochure, Sansom was a "member of William Simon's 1973 'kitchen cabinet.'" He started EEA after leaving the government. Sansom said the EEA brochure is out-of-date, and the firm now works almost exclusively for the government. Nevertheless, he declined to provide a current list of his private contracts. As a contractor rather than a government employee, he is under no obligation to do so. Nor need he reveal how much profit he and his associates make from their government work.

Arthur D. Little, Inc. is a large, established, consulting firm that has plunged into the energy market. ADL's 1976 annual report boasts of a "major project" for the Energy Research and Development Administration on commercial possibilities of new energy technologies through the year 2025. According to the report, "[We] are exploring efforts that could be undertaken by government agencies to expedite the commercialization of the most promising new energy technologies." The same annual report reveals that ADL is providing a "significant" amount of assistance to "present and potential" coal producers, conducting solar research for the government and the utility industry and offering "specialized consulting services for nuclear development." When the Justice Department and the Atomic Energy Commission wanted to study the competitive structure of the atomic energy industry—an industry created by public funds—they hired ADL to do the work. ADL's report explained that "industry cooperation was enhanced by assurances" that information they supplied would remain in private hands and would not be used by government agencies "to enforce laws subject to their jurisdiction." It must indeed have been reassuring to these companies to know the information they supplied was being kept and analyzed by an organization that regularly solicits business from companies in the energy field.

In the battle for the control of the nation's energy future, the prize territory is the Energy Department's multibillion-dollar research and development budget. It may surprise devotees of oil industry advertising, but these giants of the private energy industry provide scandalously little support for R&D. A *Business Week* survey shows that R&D expenditures by the "natural resources" industry equalled 7.6 percent of profits. By comparison, the automobile industry spent 57.8 percent, the chemical industry spent 39.7 percent, the drug industry spent 52.1 percent and even the leisure time industry spent 58.4 percent. Indeed, General Motors alone spent considerably more than all 18 major oil companies in the survey. The billions of taxpayer dollars spent on energy research and development will determine the shape of the energy industry in the future. It is therefore the industry's good fortune that the government is determined to rely on those experts that the industry also calls its own.

In 1974, for example, the American Gas Association, the natural gas industry's trade association, published a wish list of R&D projects, entitled "Gas Industry Research Plan 1974–2000." The contractors hired by the AGA—including Arthur D. Little, Battelle Columbus Laboratory, Stanford Research Institute, the Institute for Gas Technology and the Mitre Corporation, all have multiple contracts with the Energy Department as well.

Mitre Corporation, which was hired to "coordinate" the AGA study, appears to have cornered the "coordination" business at DOE too. (DOE deputy secretary John O'Leary is a Mitre alumnus. Secretary James Schlesinger himself prepped at Rand.) Mitre was created in 1958 to supervise the Air Force's electronics technology spending. It now wins contracts to supervise other contractors throughout the federal government.

Is the nation interested in geothermal energy? Mitre is scheduled for $587,137 to "provide the nation with an acceptable option which if exercised would permit the timely exploration of our geothermal resources." Mitre apparently found the option it was looking for, because it later got $649,969 for "support services for the division of geothermal energy." What about solar energy? Mitre received $1,464,406 to "develop a set of utilization scenarios for each of the solar technologies included in the national solar energy R&D program," another $200,000 for work on "solar technology transfer," and a further award to create a Solar Energy Research Institute. Coal is a more likely candidate for short-term relief than solar or geothermal energy. As for coal, Mitre has received $2,459,944 for planning assistance to the Office of Coal Research and another $501,615 to prepare the environmental impact statement for the coal R&D program. Mitre also supervised a report on nuclear power for the Ford Foundation and, according to its latest annual report, is "currently developing a plan [under Federal contract] to stimulate the commercial use of wind energy."

In addition to these fairly specific assignments, Mitre has received $1,357,278 for "ERDA environmental analysis of the National Energy R&D plan," another $4,690,087 "to provide planning, analytical, technical and other required services to the staff functions within ERDA/CCU," and another $377,411 for an analysis of ERDA demonstration programs. And for good measure, Mitre is scheduled to receive $513,223 to "develop scenarios to incorporate uncontrollable factors, the results shall provide the over-all framework for the conduct and evaluation of the study," and $184,842 for "seven tasks to perform technical support."

Mitre's chairman of the board is Dr. Robert A. Charpie, president of Cabot Corporation. Cabot Corporation's activities include oil and gas production, natural gas processing and distribution and the importing of liquified natural gas. Another Mitre board member is Dr. Raymond L. Bisplighoff, vice president of Tyco Laboratories, which has received government dollars for solar energy research and has engaged in a joint venture, with the Mobil Oil Corporation, to develop silicon solar cells. Mitre's board also includes Dr. Teddy F. Walkowicz, chairman of the National Aviation Corporation, an investment company with extensive holdings of energy industry stock.

Compared to some other DOE contractors, Mitre has only a modest network of interlocks with the energy industry. Take Stanford Research Institute, for example. The DOE printout lists more than 30 SRI contracts, including studies of synthetic fuel, markets for coal technology, energy shortage contingency planning and solar program evaluation. Typically, SRI also works for private clients including oil companies, utilities, coal companies and equipment manufacturers. Its governing boards include top executives of utilities (Pacific Gas and Electric, Southern California Edison, Montana Power, Tenneco), oil companies (Standard Oil of California, Union Oil), owners of coal resources (Utah International, Armco Steel, US Steel), energy industry suppliers, engineers, consultants, law firms and banks that manage large blocs of stock in energy companies.

Contractors are exempt from the conflict-of-interest laws that apply to federal employees. The only restraint on their behavior is a loose doctrine called "organizational conflict of interest" that is supposed to prevent contractors from bidding on hardware that they themselves recommend. In 1975 it was discovered that the Interior Department and ERDA (the Energy Research and Development Agency, now part of DOE) had hired Bechtel Corporation to compare slurry pipelines and railroads as methods of transporting coal, just as Bechtel was preparing to enter the coal slurry pipeline business. There was a great to-do in Congress, but the executive branch explained that the Bechtel contract violated no prevailing government policy. Under pressure, however, the Energy Department has begun to write conflict-of-interest regulations that require contractors to disclose information relating to potential conflicts.

The question of gross conflicts of interest somewhat obscures the more fundamental issue of who runs the government. A longstanding Budget Bureau directive provides that ". . . executive agencies will perform for themselves those basic functions of management which they must perform in order to retain essential control over the conduct of their programs. These functions include . . . planning of programs, establishment of performance goals and pursuits and evaluation of performance." It is hard to tell from the printout of the Energy Department's contracts with consulting firms whether this standard is being violated. Who knows what it means when, for example, DOE pays a company called Booz Allen Applied Research $256,620 to "develop a program to implement a plan for the federal energy management program multiyear action plan"? But there are only two possibilities. Either the legal standard for delegation of government policymaking to private individuals is being violated, or the taxpayers are paying millions of dollars for palaver. Probably it is some combination of the two.

Introduction
Cold-Shower Time at
the Smithsonian

In 1921, administrative reform and management advocates accomplished the passage of the Government Budget and Accounting Act. The act significantly professionalized both the executive and congressional oversight of management, centralizing the federal budget process in a new Bureau of the Budget and establishing a General Accounting Office to help legislators monitor the actual expenditure of appropriations.

The case of the Smithsonian, or precisely of S. Dillon Ripley, its secretary, highlights legislative–executive relationships. Although the Smithsonian is technically not a part of the executive branch, it acts very much as executive offices do. Ripley's actions exemplify the executive official's impatience with restraints. Legislators, on the other hand, are particularly upset at being "confronted with a fait accompli," such as the Smithsonian's funding of the Cooper-Hewitt Museum. The hidden contingency fund calls into question the meaningfulness of budgets submitted to appropriations committees, if such budgets are not really adhered to. Similarly, the Smithsonian Research Foundation was "designed to get around some tiresome restrictions on the use of appropriated money." As a whole, such actions—which are paralleled in other agencies at the federal, state, and municipal levels—tend to weaken the role of elected officials in determining and controlling how public funds are spent.

In the last decade, through the Congressional Budget and Impoundment Control Act of 1974 and the Congressional Budget Office it established, Congress has assumed a stronger role in budgetary oversight and accountability. And the Smithsonian, recognizing the power of the purse, has learned not to flout its major funding source.

QUESTIONS FOR DISCUSSION

Would tighter congressional control inhibit the Smithsonian's ability to develop new ideas?

Are budgets merely charades that neither legislators nor bureaucrats are really expected to follow?

Can clever administrators always find ways around legislative oversight?

How much flexibility should an agency have in spending budgeted funds?

Should administrators who ignore budgets be dismissed?

COLD-SHOWER TIME AT THE SMITHSONIAN

Irwin Ross

It is one of the glories of the American democracy that no institution is immune from critical assault. Still, admirers of the Smithsonian Institution are appalled these days by the variety of offenses charged to that venerable body by Congress, the General Accounting Office, the *Washington Post,* and a claque of lesser critics.

The Smithsonian, after all, has long been regarded as a national treasure, ranking with the Washington Monument and the Lincoln Memorial. It has been extraordinarily popular both with museum-goers (over 20.4 million visits last year) and donors, who have bestowed on it everything from the Spirit of St. Louis to the Hope diamond. It is unrivaled as a museum complex, with ten museums and galleries in Washington alone, offering everything from Oriental art to a space capsule. It is also a scientific institution of considerable renown, especially in the fields of theoretical astrophysics and evolutionary biology.

And yet, within the last eighteen months, the Smithsonian and its long-time chief executive, S. Dillon Ripley, have been taken to task by members of the House and Senate Appropriations committees, who curbed some of his activities. It has been the subject of an exhaustive inquiry by the General Accounting Office, which turned in a negative report on certain of its fiscal practices. It currently faces three more inquiries—by investigators of the House Appropriations Committee, by a House Administration subcommittee, which is planning a round of public hearings next fall, and by an "audit review committee" of its own board of regents.

Reprinted from the November 6 issue of FORTUNE Magazine by special permission; © 1978 Time Inc.

The staff of the Smithsonian has been alternately shocked and bemused by all the attention. "After Watergate, everyone is suspicious of everyone," says Treasurer T. Ames Wheeler. "Times have changed so quickly. Everybody loved the Smithsonian, then—whammo!—cold-shower time. Maybe we were naive, but we had 130 years of love and affection."

Indeed, Smithsonian critics are crawling out of the woodwork. Since charges of dubious practices first hit the Washington papers, Capitol Hill staffers have been deluged with tips, many of which arrive anonymously by mail. One persistent tipster signs himself "Birdwatcher" a whimsical allusion to Ripley's renown as an ornithologist. Charles A. Krause, who wrote a number of critical pieces in the *Washington Post,* reports that frequently some unknown voice would ring him up saying, "This is your deep throat at the Smithsonian. Did you look into the matter I phoned you about last week?" Krause would then have to elicit details about the prior conversation in order to figure out whom he was talking to; the fact is, he was in contact with several people referring to themselves as his Smithsonian deep throat.

The major charges against the Smithsonian all come down to disregard of the prerogatives and sensibilities of its congressional paymasters; no illegal misuse of money has been alleged by Congress. The federal government provides close to 90 percent of the Smithsonian's annual budget of nearly $127 million, yet the institution has at times been dismayingly slipshod about keeping Congress informed as to how it was spending the taxpayers' money.

"The simplest way to put the problem," says Dwight E. Dyer, staff member of the Senate Appropriations subcommittee that deals with Ripley, "is that the Smithsonian would like the federal money, like any federal agency, but they don't like the restrictions that apply to it."

Dillon Ripley has inevitably become the focus of the criticism, both because he has been chief executive (his formal title is Secretary) since 1964, and because he has been accused of a variety of personal delinquencies. The charges, widely publicized by the *Washington Post,* range from conflicts of interest to spending too much time away from his Washington desk.

Ripley's style and personality rub many people the wrong way. His critics often accuse him of being aristocratic and snobbish. In this egalitarian age, many of them start out being bothered by his name—S. Dillon Ripley II. (The S. is for Sidney, which Ripley says he long ago dropped to avoid confusion with a cousin.)

There is also something faintly patrician about his appearance. At sixty-three, he is a tall, bald-headed, angular man, erect in carriage, and courtly and even elegant in demeanor. His elegance is hardly a matter of dress: he often wears the narrow lapels and ties of a dozen years ago. The elegance comes rather from his graceful use of language and the habit of speaking in whole sentences, with an occasional archness of expression or whimsical allusion. There is a certain professorial air about him—he was indeed a Yale professor for many years—and occasionally a bit of pedantry shows through. He will compliment an acquaintance, for example, for referring correctly to the Court of St. James's—not overlooking the "s."

Ripley is aware of the impression he creates in some circles, and he is pained by it. "I may look snobbish because I wear the Yale Club tie symbolically," he sadly confides to a visitor, "but I'm not a snobbish person in the sense of how I feel about people."

Indeed, Ripley likes to characterize himself as a "populist." The tag, which does not refer to his politics (he calls himself an independent), is not altogether inappropriate; for no other Secretary has done more to make the average person feel at home at the Smithsonian. It was Ripley who put the carousel and the gaily decorated popcorn wagons on the Mall and who produced the open-air summer Festival of American Folklife, celebrating the diversity of America's ethnic heritage in song and dance, arts and crafts. Under his administration, exhibits have become "people-oriented" in an imaginative way, with small fry provided with a model of a dinosaur to climb over and a hunk of real dinosaur bone to pat. Visitors really smell spices when they pause at the display of an Italian kitchen in an exhibit of the Museum of History and Technology.

Ripley is especially fond of the carousel. Mary Lynne McElroy recalls that when she first came to work for him as a secretary, ten years ago, he suddenly halted his dictation one fine morning. "Come with me," he proposed, then shed his jacket and led her down the staircase and out the door to the carousel, where they mounted horses and rode a few times around. It is an annual spring ritual for him.

There is an amiable bit of ham in him that he has no hesitancy showing. Last year, when the Smithsonian opened a small-scale replica of the Centennial Exhibition in Philadelphia in 1876, Ripley got General Grant's carriage out of storage, borrowed a team of horses, and drove up to open the exhibition together with Chief Justice Warren Burger, both dressed in top hats. Recently, when Ripley came to Louisville to deliver a speech at the opening of a new museum, he was asked whether he'd take a ride in a balloon gondola with the city's mayor. "Oh, yes," said Ripley. "Haven't been up in a balloon since I played Phineas Fogg for the Yale Dramat." And up they went, toward the roof of the atrium.

The ultimate source of Ripley's troubles is his executive style. He is a strong executive, with a stiff-necked sense of independence and a certainty of his own rectitude that have allowed him to disregard appearances to a degree that he would doubtless deplore in others. Despite its federal funding, Ripley has sought to run the Smithsonian with minimal accountability to Congress. . . .

Until recently, Ripley had no reason to think that he should operate with the circumspection of a government bureaucrat. The Smithsonian has never, of course, been a government bureau. Its unusual status derives directly from the manner of its founding.

The story is a familiar one. The English scientist James Smithson, an illegitimate son of the Duke of Northumberland, left an estate later valued at over $540,000 to the U.S., a country he never visited, "to found at Washington, under the name to [sic] the Smithsonian institution, an establishment for the increase and diffusion of knowledge among men." In 1836, Congress voted to accept the bequest, with its conditions, and ten years later, after endless debate as to whether the institution should be a university, a library, a national observatory, a museum of arts and sciences, or something else, set up the Smithsonian as a combination museum, library, and embryonic research center. A few years later, the library was dropped.

The mission to increase the diffuse knowledge among men was put in the hands of a Secretary and a board of regents consisting of the Vice President of the U.S., the Chief Justice, three Senators, three members of the House of Representatives, and six other citizens. By a tradition early established, the Chief Justice is elected Chancellor (or chairman) of the board of regents. The board has total control of the institution though it is obligated to report each year to the Congress on operations and expenditures. Thus from the outset the Smithsonian was what lawyers call a "trust instrumentality" of the U.S. The U.S. government was the trustee, the beneficiary being nothing less than all of mankind—an awesome concept, particularly when extended into perpetuity.

For its first ten years, the Smithsonian was able to finance itself solely out of its own resources. Its trust funds were on deposit at the Treasury, drawing 6 percent interest, an arrangement that over a period of years generated enough cash to construct the first building in 1855—the many-towered "castle" that is now the administration building—as well as run the institution.

Then Congress pressed the board of regents to take over the nation's modest natural-history and scientific collections, a responsibility that entailed additional expense and resulted in appropriations each year. In 1879, Congress voted $250,000 to construct a second building, now known as the Arts and Industries Building, and by 1882 the Smithsonian was dependent on congressional appropriations for more than 80 percent of its operating expenditures, a condition that has continued to this day. . . .

Little wonder, then, that Congressmen are unwilling to regard the Smithsonian as merely "a private institution under the guardianship of the government," a characterization made by Chief Justice Taft, speaking as Chancellor, back in 1927 and quoted approvingly by Ripley earlier this year. But if it's not that, what is it? Some members of the Smithsonian staff are occasionally at a loss to answer the question. "We're not a private institution," John F. Jameson, assistant secretary for administration, informed some visitors recently. Confronted with the Taft quote, Jameson retreated. "You're seeing Peter Powers [the general counsel]. He'll give you the latest word on what we are." Powers then explained that the Smithsonian was a private body in the sense of being nongovernmental; it was not private in the sense of being nonpublic; and it was assuredly accountable to Congress. . . .

Another anomaly: while the Smithsonian is a nongovernmental body, 3,500 of its employees are federal civil servants because they are paid from federal appropriations. The 1,300 employees on the private roll have an identical salary scale. Both kinds of employees often work side by side in the same offices, often without having the faintest clue as to why their status is different. At the apex of the structure, Ripley is on the private roll (earning $66,000, the same as a Cabinet Secretary), as are the treasurer and general counsel.

Through most of its existence, the anomalies of the Smithsonian's status caused few difficulties, for Congress paid little attention to the institution. The first general oversight hearings in more than 100 years were held during a fortnight in July, 1970, by a subcommittee of the House Administration Committee, headed by Frank Thompson Jr., a New Jersey Democrat. The subcommittee's report was favorable, although it questioned the wisdom of putting the Hirshhorn museum on the Mall and reproved the Smithsonian for poor employee relations and slipshod purchasing practices.

After the Thompson hearings, all was quiet for a few years. Rumbles began on the Senate side in 1975, when Appropriations Committee staffers discovered that the Smithsonian was requesting over $500,000 in operating expenses for the Cooper-Hewitt Museum of Decorative Arts and Design in New York. At issue was not the merits of Cooper-Hewitt, or the reasonableness of that expense bill, but the fact that Congress was being asked to pay it without ever having been informed of the Smithsonian's decision to take over the museum from its former sponsors.

The board of regents had been within its rights to make the

commitment (it did so in 1967), and initially it had sufficient private funds to cover the great bulk of the costs of the project. But when it turned to Congress for substantial help, the Appropriations committees felt victimized. "We were confronted with a fait accompli," says Dwight Dyer. If Congress refused to vote the money, the blame for the collapse of the museum would be on its head. The Smithsonian got its money, but at some cost to damaged relations on the Hill.

Then there was the matter of the contingency fund. The Senate subcommittee began to pick up complaints from Smithsonian bureaucrats annoyed at having their budgets "skimmed" to build up something called the "Secretary's reserve fund" to meet unexpected expenses during the year. A merchant marine officer and art collector named Robert Hilton Simmons, who had been waging a highly vocal, one-man crusade against Ripley since 1969, appeared before the Senate subcommittee to testify that the contingency fund involved a 7 percent tax on the Smithsonian's varied activities. The actual figure turned out to be 1 to 2 percent—amounting to some $1 million a year—for the programs covered (and some were exempt). But Simmons had the satisfaction of causing Ripley a measure of embarrassment.

The matter of the contingency fund figured for two years in a row before the Senate subcommittee. "Why didn't you just ask for a discretionary fund?" Senator Ted Stevens of Alaska demanded. "We give several agencies discretionary funds and they report to us on their use. . . . Why didn't you do that?" There was no adequate answer. Later, Treasurer Wheeler came up with a justification. The contingency fund had been mentioned, along with other matters relating to the 1972 budget, in a letter to the House and Senate subcommittees in September, 1971. No one had objected then, and the Smithsonian regarded silence as approval—apparently for the indefinite future. Meanwhile, however, the staffs and membership of both of the subcommittees had changed, and no one at the Smithsonian brought up the matter of the fund again. Last year, however, Congress ended it.

Cooper-Hewitt and the contingency fund figured prominently in the investigation of the Smithsonian that the Senate asked the General Accounting Office to undertake last year. Another issue tackled by the GAO involved the Smithsonian Research Foundation. This organization was established in 1966 after Congress decreed that federal employees, including Smithsonian scientists, could in most cases no longer receive research grants from the National Science Foundation. Instead, Congress gave the Smithsonian an appropriation for research, both in dollars and in blocked foreign currencies held by the U.S. abroad. The Smithsonian then proceeded to set up its own wholly controlled foundation to dole out these funds.

There is no doubt that the foundation was designed to get around some tiresome restrictions on the use of appropriated money. Normally, an appropriation has to be spent in a designated fiscal year, and it can pay only the salaries of federal employees. Through the device of the foundation, money earmarked for a particular year was converted to "no year" money; the requirement that research assistants be federal employees was also circumvented. Both kinds of flexibility are doubt-less desirable in the case of research projects. The trouble was that the Smithsonian had never received congressional approval for the founda-tion, or even informed Congress how it operated. The GAO urged that the foundation be abolished and it is now being phased out, with Congress providing only enough money to enable it to complete existing projects.

Despite his sometimes high-handed management, Ripley's con-tributions to the Smithsonian have been sizable, a point conceded by most of his detractors. Before he came to the Smithsonian, he had spent nearly two decades at Yale, where he had been both a professor of biology and director of the Peabody Museum of National History. During his Yale years, he had developed a strong belief in the need to bring museums to the people, to make them exciting and accessible rather than remote marble palaces. "I dread the idea of museums being mausoleums," he says. "It's fine for an individual to go and have a lovely reflective time in the Freer Gallery, but for 20 million people you must have the Hope diamond, you must have dinosaurs." . . .

Ripley's proudest achievement in museum-building is the National Air and Space Museum, which opened on July 1, 1976. In 1966, Congress had authorized $40 million for the construction of the build-ing, with the proviso that the appropriations should not be requested until the Vietnam war was wound down.

When the time came to start construction, inflation had bumped up the cost of the structure to $70 million. Ripley decided that Congress would never go for that sum, and instructed the architect to redesign the building so that it cost no more than 40 million. In the end, the building came in $500,000 under budget and a few days earlier than planned—an achievement about which the Smithsonian, understandably, has not ceased to boast. In its first year, 10 million people visited it, making it by far the most popular museum in the world.

From the outset, Ripley was not satisfied with enhancing the Smithsonian's public appeal in Washington, but has sought a broader national constituency. In his view, a museum needs public members, for, unlike a university, it has no alumni to support it. He started the "associates" program in the Washington area in 1965, offering a variety of lectures and concerts and gradually building up a membership of 43,500.

Then, in 1970, he launched the *Smithsonian* magazine, a handsome, lavishly illustrated monthly covering the Smithsonian's varied fields of interest, under the editorship of Edward K. Thompson, a longtime managing editor and editor of *Life*. Associate membership, which now costs $12 a year, brings a subscription to the magazine—the big draw. The *Smithsonian* has been astonishingly successful. In fiscal 1976, it earned $2,928,300, after setting aside a reserve of $480,000 in case IRS decides it has to pay tax on its advertising revenue. These profits go to swell the institution's trust funds.

Ripley has been successful in almost everything he has set his hand to at the Smithsonian—with the exception of congressional relations and press relations. He is now making efforts to mend both, and he has been uttering the appropriate pieties about Congress. "After all," he says, with an air of infinite patience, "Congress is the boss. We won't fly in the face of congressional will." . . .

Introduction
Carter's Cactus Flower at HUD

Most of the jobs in federal agencies are filled under the Civil Service system. The posts at the top, however, are filled by political appointees. In this way the president can exert control. The administrators ultimately responsible for running things are chosen for their commitment to the president's programs and policies. They are also subject to dismissal at the will of the president. However, under the Constitution, their appointments require the consent of the Senate. Confirmation hearings often constitute a grilling of the nominee, and approval is far from automatic. At this level, it is important to be as good at politics as it is to be good at administration.

When Patricia Roberts Harris appeared for confirmation as Secretary of Housing and Urban Development, Senator Proxmire questioned her qualifications and voted against her appointment. She won approval despite this and went on to win over the Senator by her performance.

QUESTIONS FOR DISCUSSION

Should top posts go only to people who are experts in the fields that they will administer?

Does Senate confirmation make the appointment process more rational? Or is it just a political football?

Why is the good will of the Congress important for the head of an executive agency?

Why is the good will of his/her own Civil Service staff important for the head of an executive agency?

CARTER'S CACTUS FLOWER AT HUD

Herman Nickel

As a black and a woman, Patricia Roberts Harris, Jimmy Carter's choice for Secretary of Housing and Urban Development, looked like the typical token "two-fer." Senate Banking Committee Chairman William Proxmire was quick to point out during her confirmation hearings that she lacked the one qualification he thought the job required: a track record in the housing field.

True, she was known as a party loyalist in the Hubert Humphrey tradition, had served as ambassador to Luxembourg under Lyndon Johnson (1965–67), and was at the time a partner in a well-known Washington law firm. But neither this background nor her impressive list of directorships—Chase Manhattan, I.B.M., Scott Paper—swayed Proxmire; in fact they added to his reservations. Facing the immaculately dressed matron in the witness chair, he wondered aloud whether she was "sufficiently by, of, and for the people" to be attuned to the needs of the poor. Harris pierced him with a steely stare and delivered a memorable rebuke.

"Senator," she shot back, "I am one of them, you do not seem to understand who I am. I'm a black woman, the daughter of a dining-car waiter . . . Senator, to say I am not by, and of, and for the people is to show a lack of understanding of who I am and where I came from . . . [If] my life has any meaning at all, it is that those who start out as outcasts may end up being part of the system . . . I assure you that while there may be others who forget what it meant to be excluded from the dining room of this very building, I shall never forget it."

The exchange didn't stop Proxmire from casting the lone vote against her confirmation, but it put Washington on notice that Pat Harris is a fighter. Having made her way to the top as a black woman in a white man's world, she has always had to scrap—at least from the day when, as a six-year-old, she whacked a fellow first-grader over the head with her umbrella for making slurring remarks about her race.

Her gutsy qualities are being directed these days toward reactivating one of the big-spending departments of the welfare state, while serving a President who seems to be getting serious about cutting

Reprinted from the November 6 issue of FORTUNE Magazine by special permission; © 1978 Time Inc.

the federal deficit. At a time when the political clout has been shifting to the suburbs, she is trampling on some congressional toes to channel more housing money to the central cities and the lower- and moderate-income sectors of the market. Perhaps her toughest job, and one she has so far made very little progress on, is convincing the taxpayers that they are getting their money's worth from an agency that has had a reputation for waste and even scandal.

Her manner of addressing these problems has not made Pat Harris the easiest member of the Administration to get on with. Self-righteous, brittle, excessively partisan, quick to read racist motives into honest policy differences—these are some of the qualities that have made her the cactus flower of the Carter Cabinet. There are those who argue, however, that some of the same combative traits may prove to be useful in reordering a department that, in Proxmire's phrase, had become a "basket case."

Established in 1965 amidst the optimism of Lyndon Johnson's "Great Society," HUD has hardly had a happy history. Its urban renewal program, an early effort to revive inner cities, became almost synonymous with wholesale demolition of homes to make way for offices and public buildings. George Romney later got the subsidized-housing boom going, but his record was marred by rampant fore-closures and corruption. In 1973 Richard Nixon put HUD on "hold." His two-year moratorium on new subsidized housing deprived the department of its major program. Under Gerald Ford, Secretary Carla Hills fought through authorization for 406,000 units and achieved some 40,000 starts in 1976, but she was out of office before she could reap some of the credit Pat Harris has since been claiming for herself.

Even though Jimmy Carter won a lot of urban votes, he did not come through with the kind of handsome funding for HUD that Pat Harris had hoped for. The fiscal-1979 budget ceilings originally pro-posed by the Office of Management and Budget were so low that some HUD officials fumed that their colleagues in the Executive Office Building must have slept through the election. Harris fought back with an optimal list of programs that would have totaled $54 billion. All things considered, she did well to land the $38.4 billion dollars Congress eventually approved.

In the eyes of HUD's constituency, which includes such disparate groups as builders, mayors, and spokesmen for the poor, the most telling measure of the Secretary's performance is HUD-subsidized housing starts. The total of 155,000 units started this year falls way short of the record of 367,000 units set by Romney in 1971, but is nearly four times her predecessor's 1976 total. Over 200,000 units are forecast for 1979.

Harris's broader constituency, the general public, may remember her in the long run for the impetus she has given to rehabilitation, an unexciting but cost-effective approach that has been neglected for years. She has spent $264 million to upgrade older, blighted public-housing projects, pushed a Neighborhood Strategy Program that subsidizes renovation of Apartment buildings in distressed areas, and expanded the Urban Homesteading plan, through which do-it-your-selfers can buy abandoned homes at minimal cost.

To get businesses to move into blighted areas, Harris has instituted Urban Development Action Grants. The $456 million made available thus far has attracted $2.7 billion in private capital and, by HUD's estimate, has created or saved 117,000 jobs.

Harris recognizes that unless a slum neighborhood discovers its own stake in rehabilitation and participates in the process, pouring federal money into it is like pouring water into a leaky bucket. That is why she has assigned the task of working with inner-city groups to a remarkable ghetto priest, Father Geno Baroni, who as an assistant secretary of HUD is now applying on a national scale some of the lessons he learned as a pastor in one of the toughest areas in Washington, D.C.

Such programs have won her the respect of Proxmire, now her most powerful backer in her attempt to channel housing funds to the poor, and of House Banking Committee Chairman Henry Reuss, who has effusively called her "the best HUD Secretary ever." Key members of the U.S. Conference of Mayors, which had seen her nomination as a sign of President Carter's "striking insensitivity to the problems of the city," are now high on her performance too.

Harris arrives at her wood-paneled modern office by 7:30 in the morning and leaves, her briefcase bulging, some eleven hours later. More often than not, she is picked up by her husband, an administrative judge with the Federal Maritime Commission. (They are childless.) The couple live in a comfortable home in an integrated middle-class section of northwest Washington.

Her fighting qualities have helped restore morale among the 16,000 HUD employees even though she is known as a very demanding boss. Two high-level black political appointees left the department after Harris let it be known that their performance didn't measure up to her stiff standards.

She has surrounded herself with a triumvirate of experienced housing experts who help her run the department. Under Secretary Jay Janis, forty-five, is a successful builder-developer who was executive assistant to Secretary Robert Weaver from 1966 to 1968. He is the department's chief operating officer. The two assistant secretaries who run the bulk of HUD's programs are Robert C. Embry Jr., forty-one, who came to his job as assistant secretary for community planning and development after a brilliant record as Baltimore's housing commissioner, and Assistant Secretary for Housing Lawrence B. Simons, fifty-one, a lawyer turned real-estate and construction entrepreneur. Their experience helps offset Harris's lack of any, and she has proved, they say, to be a quick study.

Where Pat Harris has run into her greatest trouble is with her bold assertion of regulatory power over how housing money should be used and where. This has been the common denominator in her battles to gain control over the operations of the Federal National Mortgage Association, a shareholder-owned corporation better known as Fannie Mae, and to impose stricter conditions on how local authorities may spend Community Development Block Grants. In both cases, Harris has insisted that she is merely trying to meet her statutory responsibility to make sure that enough funds go where they are most needed— i.e., to the central cities and the low- and moderate-income sectors. But her opponents have claimed just as adamantly that she is after more power than Congress ever intended to give the HUD secretary.

Harris has pushed her point with more valor than discretion. The White House still shudders about her war with Fannie Mae. In January she launched a salvo in the form of a memo arguing that President Carter had the power to fire Fannie Mae's chairman and president, Oakley Hunter, a former Republican Congressman, Harris presented Carter with a legal brief, commissioned for about $16,000 contending that Hunter's obstinacy in cooperating with HUD made him subject to dismissal. She even appended a draft letter of dismissal for Carter's signature.

The proposal set off alarm bells on Stuart E. Eizenstat's Domestic Affairs and Policy staff, which, rightly, smelled trouble. The Justice Department, giving the HUD brief a rather contemptuous back of the hand, expressed grave doubts that firing Hunter would stand up in court. On top of that, Carter had just replaced David Marston, the Republican U.S. attorney in Philadelphia, amid a storm of controversy. The last thing the President needed was yet another charge that he was engaging in a politically motivated purge. But the White House was prepared to explore whether Hunter could be induced to step aside voluntarily. The Administration's ubiquitous Mr. Fixit, Robert Strauss, was assigned this delicate mission. Strauss found Hunter unwilling to budge, and there the matter was dropped. "I think all I did was to take some of the heat off it," Strauss says now.

But Harris continued to battle on another front. Parallel to her attempt to get rid of Hunter, she had ordered the drafting of regulations to ensure that Fannie Mae lives up to the "public purposes" laid down in its 1968 charter. Her Republican predecessors had never written such regulations though the charter gave HUD the statutory authority to issue them. In fact, Fannie Mae, with a $39-billion mortgage portfolio, has been uniquely free from regulation. Although only about half a dozen U.S. corporations are larger, Fannie Mae is exempt even from the scrutiny of the Securities and Exchange Commission.

The proposed regulations, which Harris published for comment on February 23, created an uproar. They sought to compel Fannie Mae to invest 30 percent of its mortgage portfolio in central cities and 30 percent in low- and moderate-income housing. (The two categories naturally overlap.) Fannie Mae retorted that the idea of mandatory credit allocation violated the autonomy guaranteed in the corporation's charter, and also jeopardized the rights of its shareholders to a "reasonable return" on their investment. The comments by interested parties, which have to be given some weight in this sort of proceeding, were negative by a lopsided margin, with mortgage bankers, security analysts, realtors, and builders coming down heavily on Fannie Mae's side of the argument. Even the U.S. Conference of Mayors was critical. Fannie Mae put the White House on notice that it was risking an embarrassing court battle if the regulations were not substantially altered.

When the final regulations were promulgated on August 15, the mandatory credit allocations were gone and had been replaced with mere "goals." In effect, Harris had beat a retreat, which was clearly a relief to the White House.

Harris still insists that her final regulations are not "substantially changed" from her original propoals and that, in any case, she reserves the power to try for mandatory allocations if Fannie Mae falls behind the goals. But the inevitable outcome would be a court test, and there is no sign that the White House has got any keener about that kind of passage at arms.

In her parallel battle with the House of Representatives over closer control of Community Development Block Grants, Pat Harris again met stiff resistance to the mandatory-quota approach. She first proposed that in order for projects to qualify, communities would have to show that 75 percent of the funds would benefit low- and moderate-income citizens. In this, she won enthusiastic backing from Senator Proxmire, who has long felt that the program had degenerated into a version of general revenue sharing that channeled more money into prosperous than into poor neighborhoods.

Harris's attempt to correct this situation ran into highly effective opposition from Representative Garry Brown, the Michigan Republican who is the ranking minority member of the House subcommittee on housing and community development. Brown works very closely with Subcommittee Chairman Thomas "Lud" Ashley, on the theory that housing bills need a bipartisan base to become law. With Brown,

Ashley had agreed on the wording of the 1974 Housing Act, which allowed HUD to turn down applications for program grants only if they were "plainly inappropriate."

Bowing to political reality, HUD later dropped the 75 percent requirement. But under the rules that have gone into effect, any application that cannot demonstrate that 51 percent of the grant would benefit low- and moderate-income people will be rejected as "plainly inappropriate"—unless the local authority can somehow prove otherwise. Even this toned-down language was too much for Representative Brown, who saw it as increased HUD meddling with local development plans. On June 29, by a surprising vote of 244 to 140, the House voted to block the HUD authorization bill unless the regulations are changed. Now there are signs that HUD may be prepared to show further "flexibility" to prevent a prolonged House-Senate deadlock and get the authorization bill passed.

As Harris sees it, her problems have arisen out of "ten years of slander of programs for the poor." Whether that charge is true or not, there does seem to have been some erosion of political support for such measures. Representative Brown says: "A Secretary of HUD will have a problem unless he or she recognizes that political phenomenon and appreciates the political clout of the suburbs." And power politics are bound to govern programs like subsidized housing that dispense large benefits to only a fraction of the people who are theoretically eligible to participate.

Starting with the assumption that the majority still wants to do the "decent thing," Harris is convinced that she can turn the tide by making her programs work and proving that they are not "pork barrel for the poor." While her stress on rehabilitation is a big improvement over the old liberal reflex of simply adding new housing projects when the existing ones are blighted, she clearly has a long way to go to restore public confidence in HUD.

Her faith in the effectiveness of government will leave skeptics with a sense of deja vu, for there is little evidence that federal dollars can have more than a marginal effect on the economic and demographic trends that are at the root of urban decay. But it reflects Pat Harris's belief that as the system worked for her, so it can also work for the ghetto poor. She has no thought of quitting. For one thing, as she told Senator Daniel Patrick Moynihan, "it would make too many people happy."

The Privileged Civil Servant

President Andrew Jackson emphasized rotation in office as a means to politically responsive administration. Almost any citizen was considered fit to carry out the "simple" duties of public management. In Jackson's own words:

> The duties of all public offices are . . . so plain and simple that men of intelligence may readily qualify themselves for their performance; and I cannot but believe that more is lost by the long continuance of men in office than is generally to be gained by their experience. They are apt to acquire a habit of looking with indifference upon the public interest.

Jackson's concern is still valid today. Is our government by the *people* or by an *elite for* the people? In our society, esteem and financial rewards go, not to workers in basic industry, but to those who analyze, plan, and administer—solving problems on paper. As the author of this case puts it, "People who work on docks, farms, and oil wells are simply not 'comparable' to the people in Washington, who work on paper." Has the Civil Service system that supplanted spoils led inadvertently to a class of government employees who are out of touch with the problems they are supposed to solve?

Washington, D.C., is the epitomy of this problem. Peopled almost entirely by government employees or employees of organizations that work closely with the government, it is the richest area in the country. Not only is federal pay at least comparable to the private sector, but fringe benefits are not trifling. In addition to permanent job security, there are unpublicized "opportunities" many of us do not enjoy: low cost parking, access to free long distance lines, copying machines, and so on.

Bureaucrats enjoying such privileges can come to lose all sense of what they cost. They don't know, or care, that ultimately someone must pay for everything, as Charles found out in "Adding the Crat to the Bureau."

Tom Bethell, a Washington editor of *Harper's,* set out to discover how this came to pass. Bethell argues in "The Wealth of Washington" that federal employment is so attractive that bureaucrats lose touch with the real world. There is no incentive to leave, to compete in the marketplace. Washington is a "Paper city where paper problems are confronted, ultimately being provided with paper solutions."

QUESTIONS FOR DISCUSSION

Why is Washington called a "privileged ghetto"?

What was the purpose of establishing pay comparability? How has it operated in practice?

What is the federal triangle? What groups compose it? How does it work?

Are our bureaucrats so content as to be out of touch with common problems?

Is it just Washington bureaucrats who are overpaid, or does the problem of being out of touch extend to federal employees outside Washington, as well as to state and local employees?

In attempting to stamp out political influence in government administration, have we lost sight of Jackson's argument that rotation in office is necessary to maintain vitality in government?

ADDING THE CRAT TO THE BUREAU

Tim James

Austerity is very much in fashion these days among our political leaders. Political columnists tell us that this means the politicians have finally gotten the message from the people. Perhaps, but they certainly have not conveyed it to those who work in the Federal bureaucracy beneath them.

My friend Charles, a law student, learned this firsthand when he spent the summer working for the Labor Department in Washington.

Along about his third day on the job, Charles recalled recently, a female co-worker explained that "now that you have your own desk, you can fix it up any way you want." What that meant, Charles soon learned, was that they were about to go on a shopping spree on Charles' behalf, to refurbish his fully furnished desk.

So Charles and his mentor went downstairs to the General Services Administrative store, armed with the department's G.S.A. charge card and—believe it or not—a shopping cart.

"I was perfectly content with what I had," Charles emphasized. The purchases he was to make were "just to get a new look—anything I wanted."

His companion insisted that once he had replaced some items on his desk he had to replace them all: desk mat, note-holder, pencil-holder, in-and-out trays—the works.

To "color-coordinate" them. ("I'm not kidding," Charles assured me when he saw the incredulity on my face.)

After the normal desk paraphernalia had been picked out, Charles's mentor realized that there was still something missing. "Do you want an ashtray?"

"I don't smoke."

"Well, get one anyway."

So Charles bought an ashtray (color-coordinated, of course).

All the while, Charles recalled, his companion was " 'bragging' about previous purchases she had made in the hundreds of dollars. . . . It was like she was proud of it, like it was her own charge card."

When they returned with Charles's cartload, his desk top had to be cleared of the old to make room for the new. So the perfectly good "old" furnishings were deposited in a closet whose contents gave evidence that "this type of stuff had gone on before," Charles said. The closet was overflowing with discarded equipment, "stuff that could be used by anybody—it wasn't as if it was worn out or what-ever."

Equally appalling was the fact that "there was no real accounting." He said, "As far as I know, she didn't turn in a list of what she got."

After finishing the story of the shopping spree, Charles reflected a bit on the significance of his own participation, or at least acqui-escence. "I was just as appalled as a lot of people . . . taxpayers . . . might be," he recalled.

Then why did he take part? A peculiar sort of peer pressure. "It's kind of a team-player concept. . . . It seemed like if I . . . said no to a lot of things . . . it would seem like I was strange," Charles explained. "It was sort of as if everybody was watching me," he added.

But Charles's scruples did force him to draw the line: "I still staunchly refused to get a nameplate," Charles said proudly, explaining that not only was he just a summer employee but also that his desk faced the wall, making a nameplate ludicrous. Nevertheless, "I was asked if I wanted one," he recalled.

The alarming thing about Charles's story is not, of course, the amount of waste involved in his own experience, but rather the fact that this was apparently business-as-usual. How does one explain such wastefulness in an era of concern over Government spending? In part it is probably the inability of Government workers to imagine such petty indulgences amounting to any significant dent in a budget measured in hundreds of billions of dollars. Perhaps more importantly, however, the recent "Proposition 13 fever" has often taken the form of hostility to Government employees—whose mid-sections have generally been the first to be pinched by Government "belt-tightening." In such times, living well at the office may be the public employee's best revenge.

THE WEALTH OF WASHINGTON

Tom Bethell

. . . The prospect is good for Washington. All the indicators are up. Government salaries are up; employment is up; rented office space is up; and real estate values are up, up, and up. Property is the most engrossing topic of conversation at those famous Georgetown dinner parties, people blushing slightly about what a killing they have made. . . .

Washington has now become the richest metropolitan area in the United States, according to figures compiled by Marketing Economics Institute, Ltd.

. . . Two Washington suburban counties lead the list of the "50 Richest Counties" as measured by the 1970 Census.

. . . I could provide more figures for the Washington area, but they would be superfluous. Suffice it to say that 25 percent of the area's employees are on the federal payroll. These people have managed, over the years, to evolve a system whereby they pay themselves well. As a result, *Time* magazine recently noted, Washington has become a "privileged ghetto, home of a pampered class all but immune to the disheartening tantrums of the economic weather." During the 1974 recession, unemployment in the capital was 30 percent below the national average.

The laws of supply and demand not only do not apply to Washington, they are turned inside out. Problems elsewhere in the country merely contribute to the wealth of Washington. The fuel crisis takes the shape of a new Department of Energy, where 19,000 bureaucrats under Dr. James Schlesinger's command will have $10 billion to play with—roughly equal to the total profits of all the oil companies. Figures such as these are enough to make one wonder if the energy crisis can't be traced to some action originally taken in Washington; the recent history of price controls does nothing to allay this suspicion.

When considering the economic success of Washington, an innocent might conclude that this is indeed surprising, bearing in mind that those who come here to work in the government are mostly compassionate, public-spirited people—admirers of Franklin D. Roosevelt and his wife. So one surmises that it must be just an accident that they ended up doing so well. These were people who wanted to do good; who saw poverty and wanted to stamp it out; saw discrimination and determined to end it; saw slums and dreamed of humane dwelling spaces. . . . They saw all this opportunity for doing good, and yet, somehow, a good many of them ended up sipping French wines in the quiet of their pocket-sized Georgetown backyards, discussing real estate investments before retiring early to bed because they had next day an urgent "report" to write on the sad state of the economy. . . .

The wealth of Washington derives primarily from federal pay, which is high and keeps getting higher all the time. Federal pay is a complex subject, but worth trying to simplify.

. . . The gentleman explaining the intricacies of federal pay to me was Ed Preston, an assistant director of the OMB and plainly a veteran of bureaucratic wars. Having listened to him, I pointed out that the problem with "comparability" was all the evidence that government workers earn more than those in the private sector. I cited some figures put out by the Advisory Commission on Intergovernmental Relations that especially indicated this. Preston's reply suggested that if the government were an army it would be deficient in privates and corporals. More and more, the jobs government workers do are being defined in such a way that they correspond to upper-level jobs in the private sector. Here is what Preston said: "The federal government has shifted to an increasingly professional, technical, and scientific work force. Twenty or thirty years ago we had essentially a government of clerks. But now, with moonshots, the space program, and so on, all that has changed." . . .

I called Dr. John Shannon at the Commission on Intergovernmental Relations, the little-known commission that had innocently contrasted civilian and government pay. I told Shannon that I had found his figures very revealing. "We got a real nasty letter from the head of the Civil Service Commission about that," he said. "They claim that the government is now made up mostly of atomic physicists and people like that."

It is, in fact, an extremely difficult matter to ascertain whether the correct functioning of government now really does demand the skills of highly qualified scientists and managers, or whether job descriptions have merely been inflated to give this impression: no doubt partly both. I spent an afternoon phoning the Civil Service Commission, being routed from one office to the next, but made little headway.

There is not even a simple answer to the question: What kind of work does, say, a GS-5 do? . . . In response to this question, Eugene Dahlman, assistant chief of the Standards Division, told me: "It varies from occupation to occupation. You can have a grade 5 engineer or a grade 5 secretary. The grade 5 engineer would be just out of school, of course."

This was peculiar, surely, because a grade 5 engineer is paid the same as a grade 5 secretary, on a scale of pay assumed to be "comparable" to that for work done in the private sector, and yet clearly engineering work is in no way comparable to secretarial work. How, then, can they be lumped together and be called comparable to anything?

Robert W. Hartman, an economist with the Brookings Institute, has pointed out that it is precisely this lumping together of various private-sector jobs into one pay rate that results in federal pay nosing ahead as it does. In March, 1977, a GS-clerical worker was paid $10,677 annually, Hartman writes. At that time BLS investigators returned from their travels and reported their findings: The salary for comparable jobs in the private sector was $10,100.

Hartman comments as follows: "This finding—which a hard-nosed type might regard as an excuse for a pay reduction—was transformed into a pay raise under what is called the government comparability method." How was this achieved? "At GS-5, the private-sector secretarial wage was combined with technical jobs paying $11,700, administrative posts at $12,346, and professional slots at $13,439 to reach an average survey salary for GS-5 of $10,736."

This means, of course, that a GS-5 employee doing "technical" work (the recent engineering graduate, no doubt) would be slightly *underpaid* at this grade, but then he will soon be promoted to GS-7 (even-numbered grades are skipped by many employees at this level). Salary inflation in the government has been partly caused by grade inflation. . . .

I later called the Civil Service Commission, and the information it provided suggests that government pay increases could very easily be halted completely for a number of years. (Carter might also consider that such a public-sector pay freeze would undoubtedly do wonders for inflation. The pressure that would be generated within the federal bureaucracy to cut back on federal spending as a way of bringing inflation under control would be something wonderful to see. Alas, it is a pipe dream.)

It is a remarkable fact that in 1977 the equivalent of the entire population of Texas inquired about the possibility of a job with the federal government. And, as Mike Causey noted in his "Federal Diary" column in the *Washington Post*, these statistics "represent only people who got through. Nobody knows how many job hunters have been frustrated by long lines or seemingly forever busy telephone numbers, and have given up. They aren't counted in the statistics."

. . . I had a drink with a friend of mine at one of those subterranean Washington bars that somehow contrive to be full of people already well into their second cocktail at five minutes past five. My friend landed a good job with the Carter Administration a little more than a year ago. He ordered a Bass ale and began: "A fourfold increase in salary does wonders, I'll admit." He told me that his job is to manipulate the press so that his boss, a Cabinet member, comes out looking good. It turns out to be easier to do this than he thought it would be. The daily press is the easiest, he said. "If someone writes something I don't like, then I don't return his phone calls for a week. They're always on deadline, so they need me." He then began to talk about the fringe benefits of government.

"The per diem travel allowance is generous," he admitted. "Seventy-five dollars a day in Paris. Forty to fifty dollars a day in the U.S. I bet not many people lose money on that. Then there's parking. It costs us $5 a month, although normal Washington rates are $4 a day. All the top people get parking spaces—in other words, just the people who could afford to pay the going rate. Then there are the federal credit unions. I can get 7 percent on a savings account, and if I want to get a loan to buy a car, I pay 8 percent on the loan."

He thought for a moment and lit a cigarette. "We get no expenses for lunch," he said. "That's one of the drawbacks. Why do you think there has been all this fuss about the three-martini lunch? It's one of the few fringes enjoyed by the private sector but not by us. And according to the new conflict-of-interest laws I am not allowed to be taken out to lunch by someone who does business with the department. Luckily, the *New York Times* has no business dealings with us."

He ordered another beer. "Oh," he said. "Many hotels have government rates. Everyone tries to get into the Essex House in New

York because it gives government rates—about $35 for a double. It's very hard to get in at weekends."

I asked him why hotels had lower rates for government employees. (Essex House's standard rate is $70–$90 for a double.)

"It's a tradition in the hotel going back to World War II," he said. "Government per diem used to be very low then. But to justify higher per diems today, I notice, the employee unions talk about the high cost of staying in hotels."

"Anything else you can think of."

"Sabbaticals," he said. "I know it sounds crazy. But the government is more and more filling up with professors and more and more seems to resemble a university. I have a friend at the Law Enforcement Assistance Administration who applied for and was granted a sabbatical to work on a dissertation."

My friend turned next to the complex subject of pensions and retirement benefits. "Basically," he said, "we pay 7 percent of our gross income instead of paying into Social Security." (Which is 6.05 percent at present and will rise to 7.05 percent by 1985. But then most private-sector employees also contribute to pension plans in addition to paying social security.) A recent change in the law raised the retirement age in the private sector from 65 to 70, but federal employees were exempted from any compulsory retirement due to age. This raises the specter of ending up with a government of octogenarians, or would if there were not several inducements built into the pension structure to encourage relatively early retirement. (Pensions, unlike salaries, do get an annual cost-of-living adjustment.)

"Oh, the biggie—I nearly forgot it," my friend continued. "The WATS line. There's no excuse for anyone above about GS-11 level having a long-distance phone bill, because you can call from the office. All you have to do is dial 8. . . . It's a wonderful freebie. I'm involved with a girl in Boston right now and my phone calls would normally be costing me about $500 a month. It's better to call early in the day, I've found, because after 4:00 p.m. everybody suddenly realizes the day has gone by and they haven't called their mother yet. Nobody minds. It's not anybody's money. . . ."

With that appropriate "bottom line" it seemed time to go. As we were getting into his car my friend told me: "I'm seeing a psychiatrist at the moment because I don't know when I'll be able to afford it again."

"How does the health plan work?" I asked.

"First of all, every government employee has a choice of about ten health plans to choose from," he said. "So you can figure out the one that best works in your favor. I'm on Blue Cross High Option, for which I pay $9.50 every two weeks plus 20 percent of the shrink's fee, plus $100 deductible."

He dropped me at my door and said he was going on to a function somewhere. "If you get on the White House invite circuit you never have to pay for dinner all the time you're in Washington. Ciao."

One fringe benefit he didn't mention was the near impossibility of getting fired, although this did not apply to him and the approximately 2,000 others whose jobs are classified as "Schedule C," meaning that they are political appointees. But for the vast majority there are now so many grievance procedures and courts of higher appeal that the story is told of the supervisor who, in trying to fire an insolent and indolent underling, spent so much time filling out forms and meeting with adjudicators over a period of eighteen months that he ended up himself receiving an unfavorable performance rating for neglecting his regular work. . . .

By the time I went to see Carter's top reorganization man, Richard A. Pettigrew, and his assistant, Chris Matthews, I was beginning to appreciate the magnitude of the problem facing them. It was paradoxical that this should be so, however, because there could be no doubt that Carter and his reorganization team had the support of a large majority of Americans—perhaps as many as 80 percent of the voters. Certainly they had the conservatives behind them, and an increasing number of disaffected liberals. This was, after all, the issue above all others that had propelled Carter-the-Outsider into office.

Who, then, was against him on the issue? The answer can best be described as a "federal triangle." The term "federal triangle" in Washington refers to nine square blocks of government buildings lying between Pennsylvania Avenue and Constitution Avenue, but there is also a conceptual federal triangle, and it is important to understand, because the wealth of Washington essentially derives from it. Its three vertices are: Congress, the Executive departments and agencies, and the federal employee unions. . . .

In the first place, federal employees in the various Executive departments band together into unions. Skillfully appropriating the terminology of trade unionism, they dub themselves "labor" at this moment, thus again revealing the chameleon-like nature of the beast we are dealing with. These employee unions then "bargain" on such matters as fringe benefits, hours of work, grievance procedures. Just a minute, you may be wondering. With whom do they bargain? I wondered this myself and phoned the American Federation of Government Employees, by far the largest federal employee union, and I was routed to a Mr. Dick Calistri. I asked him how this "bargaining" worked.

"Well," he said, "we sit down and we have a give-and-take. Maybe we're bargaining on working conditions. . . ."

"Who's on the other side of the bargaining table?" I asked.

"Management!" Calistri said, in a tone indicating he was surprised that I could ask so stupid a question.

What is this "management"? Everyone involved is on the federal payroll, after all. The bifurcation of government into labor and management is surely a sleight of hand intended to conjure up a vision of dark satanic mills, robber barons, and child labor.

I asked Calistri who actually represented "management" at the bargaining table. Maybe it was the political appointees. As these people really do come and go from government, that would at least set them apart from the permanent civil service labor force.

"They're not necessarily political appointees," Calistri said. "They may be high-level civil service people."

That was what I had been afraid of. In other words, the difference between labor and management in government is one of degree (seniority), not kind. It was all beginning to look more and more like a shell game to me. No wonder government ends up winning no matter what.

The next "side" of the triangle is particularly important: the lobbying of Congress. As Calistri told me: "That's our bag, really."

The question in my mind was, how important is the federal employee vote to the average Congressman? Ten percent of his constituency (approximately) may be on the federal payroll—which means that 90 percent is not. Therefore he shouldn't have to worry too much about the federal vote, should he?

"Yes, he should, and will," Chris Matthews told me in the Old Executive Office Building, next to the White House. Before coming to work for the Carter Administration, Matthews, who is young and commendably enthusiastic about the daunting topic of government reorganization (second only to "budget" in its lack of reader appeal, he feels), worked for three years on Capitol Hill, and so is familiar with Congressional sentiment on the subject.

"Federal employees are a vocal, high-intensity group," he said. "Government change affects them directly. They know exactly who to call on the Hill, and their voice is heard in the media if they decide to make a fuss."

At that point his boss, Richard Pettigrew, stuck his head in the door to ask about the progress of a memo. Pettigrew was Speaker of the Florida House of Representatives and helped organize Carter's Florida primary. Now he has been "rewarded" with this Sisyphean task. Matthews told him what we were discussing.

"All it takes is a well-organized group of voters who are all going to vote the same way on one issue—their own self-interest—and the Congressman will respond," Pettigrew said. "Especially when they are as well-organized a network as federal workers."

After Pettigrew left, Matthews said: "You've also got to bear in mind that all the relevant legislation goes through the House Civil Service and Post Office Committee, and the Congressmen with high percentages of federal employees in their districts—such as Herb Harris of Virginia and Gladys Spellman of Maryland—always gravitate to that committee. And they shape that legislation. Same with the comparable committee in the Senate, which is where I worked for three years. All of those Senators had close ties to the federal employee unions." Once it emerges from these committees, such legislation is only amended on the floor in the most minor ways, if it is amended at all.

And this brings us to the third side of the triangle. Because they want to be reelected, Congressmen are generally on the lookout for ways in which to increase government programs. This is because enlarged federal programs enlarge the number of constituents that a Congressman can "service," thus adding to the number of voters who will be suitably grateful on election day. The result is a powerful ratchet effect, with federal programs and expenditures getting larger, but almost never smaller. To make matters worse, Congressman who routinely oppose this trend on fiscal grounds have been very successfully packaged by opinion makers, and labeled Neanderthal: Heartless. Their concern about abstractions like the soaring national debt has made it easy to dismiss them as "uncompassionate."

Congressmen are therefore ever on the alert for ways in which to expand government beneficence, and the precise ways in which they do this involve, as one might guess, expanding the definition of people who are alleged to be "deprived" by handicaps, minority status, shortage of money, or by broadening the boundaries of poverty, and so on. Public service job creation, such as the Comprehensive Employment and Training Act, is an example. The upshot is that as government programs expand, the Executive departments' budgets increase, and so do the number of federal employees needed to administer them. This increases the number of people putting pressure on Congress to increase their pay and benefits. And so on. . . .

These unwelcome developments have come about little by little— so slowly that hardly any audible objection has been heard. The *Washington Post* will roar its thunder at transient Washington—the Presidents and their entourages who come and go at regular intervals —but on the subject of permanent Washington, the entrenched civil servants and their increasingly lavish emoluments, the *Post* has preserved a dignified editorial silence. One appreciates that they do not wish to offend the main body of their readers. Nor, indeed, would the many *Post* reporters who rely on the bureaucracy for their stories want to offend their sources. Perhaps this is why the *Post's* front page so often seems to end up looking like a hearty endorsement of greater government in the guise of news. . . .

For a final opinion about the wealth of Washington, I drove out to Rockville in Montgomery County, Maryland, where I had a lunch appointment with James P. Gleason, the Montgomery County Executive —a position comparable to that of mayor. I drove out Wisconsin Avenue, past the white marble Mazza Galleria housing Neiman-Marcus and satellite boutiques (it opened in November and is now almost fully rented), past Lord & Taylor, Saks Fifth Avenue, out farther beyond the beltway and past the White Flint Mall, which also opened last year and has as its principal attraction Washington's second Bloomingdale's, and a few minutes later arrived at the County Office Building in Rockville. . . .

Gleason sitting alone, vaguely senatorial looking, seemed to be weary of government and its works. At the end of this year he retires, having been County Executive for eight years.

. . . He said . . . "One out of five people in the U.S. is now working for government. And government is getting so big that it is getting harder and harder for it to do anything effective. The tragedy of our times is that no one is really thinking about what is going on. That's the sin of it. . . ." He thought ahead to his retirement, when he hoped to do some writing, and then back to the time when he worked for Senator Knowland. After Knowland had retired he came back to Washington once and Gleason met him. "Remember," Knowland warned, "don't stay around here too long. It's not the real world. . . ."

This is the oldest and most tired of Washington clichés—not the real world—but there is surely an important element of truth to it. Bloomingdale's, Mazza Galleria, Saks, the Palm Restaurant, Sans Souci, all the private-sector enterprise that feeds on the huge volume of tax dollars pouring into Washington is real enough, but what contribution to productive endeavor do the government toilers themselves really make?

Contemplating bureaucracy, C. Northcote Parkinson enunciated his famous law, that work expands to fill the time available for its completion, with its important corollary, that "an official wants to multiply subordinates, not rivals."

All perfectly true, but it seems to me that government activity today is increasingly dominated by one of the most ominous trends of our time (and is no doubt responsible for it in large measure): A person in our society will be paid more money, and be more highly esteemed, if instead of solving a problem materially he solves it on paper.

Don't work for an oil company—you might get your hands dirty. Work for the Department of Energy and ponder energy "policy." This is much more prestigious. You are a nurse? The pay is low and you change bedpans. Better try and get on a health "task force" and write a memo on "health care delivery systems." You want to paint a picture? Hard work. Better go to work for the National Endowment and talk about creative partnerships at a meeting. Your salary is assured.

At some point in the complex Washington scheme, the problems jump across from real life onto a piece of paper. At that point they become much more pliable, remunerative, and status-laden. . . . And that is the sense in which Washington is not the real world. It is Paper City, where paper problems are confronted, ultimately being provided with paper solutions. The more of these problems it can lay its hands on, the richer the city gets—rich with paper money, that is.

Section II
MANAGEMENT
MODELS

The establishment of a Civil Service system amid a prevailing atmosphere of reform provided both the means and the impetus for more "businesslike" government. The dominant ideal became machinelike efficiency in getting the job done with a minimum of wasted energy. But "common sense" was not an adequate guide in these complex matters. Guidelines were needed.

Studies of the business organization had given rise to a number of supposedly universal "laws" or "principles" of administration and to a procedure, scientific management, by which optimum efficiency could be achieved. It was no more than logical to borrow these discoveries for application to the management of public sector organizations.

Building on the work of Henri Fayol, Gulick and Urwick identified a set of processes that take place in every organization and gave us the acronym POSDCORB for them. Among the principles were some rules for the healthy conduct of these processes. For example, organizations should always adhere to the (scalar) principle of a chain of command with unity of command. The work of Frederick Taylor and his followers demonstrated the efficiencies in having management study, identify, and then teach workers the "one best way" of performing each task.

These management theories proved in the long run to be inadequate for explaining organizations satisfactorily. They failed to account for the complexity of human nature or for the impact of an uncertain and changing environment. But if they omitted the muscle and the flesh, they did provide an understanding of the skeleton: Organizations are made up of certain parts and processes that have to be "managed."

The cases in this section are designed to illustrate the management model today: What happens when key processes do break down; how the search for more efficient procedures goes on; and some of the stupidities that result when the blindly "programmed" bureaucratic machine operates without concern for its members or for its impact on society.

Bureaucracy as a Dirty Word

The term *bureaucracy* is double edged—it is described as an advantage, and criticized as a problem. Max Weber's "ideal type" or model of bureaucracy describes an arrangement of positions that he considered to be the "most rational known means" of accomplishing objectives. The chief characteristics of the Weberian model include: universal rules impersonally carried out, use of written records, division of duties into spheres of competence, training for each position, selection on the basis of competence, hierarchical arrangement of offices, salary based on position, and tenure of office. These characteristics make for an enduring, predictable, efficient "machine." But, like a machine, such an organization can be inhumane, just functioning blindly.

In "Tales from the Bureaucratic Woods" James Boren, a prominent Washington gadfly, summarizes humorously what we all suspect: beneath the calm façade of rules and regulations, a hidden cost of equity and order can be gross inefficiency, marked by a smoke screen of paperwork in undecipherable language, rules without reason, and employment without output.

"The Little Things that Bring Big Government Under Fire" features such bureaucratic stupidities as the shuffling of sand dunes and mandated bilingual instruction of English-speaking people.

And just to show that bureaucratic machinery can grind on blindly in other parts of the world as well, "Speaking of Red Tape, Soviet Labels in Fertilizer and Coffee Got Mixed" describes what happened when some shipping documents got confused in the USSR.

QUESTIONS FOR DISCUSSION

Is Boren fair?
Would you rather be a Boren or a bureaucrat?

Is there a workable alternative to Weber's ideal type?
How could each of the "stupidities" have been prevented?
What bureaucratic "horror stories" have you heard recently?

TALES FROM THE BUREAUCRATIC WOODS

Next to golf stories, the tales businessmen tell each other these days are apt to be inside jokes about the excesses and absurdities of the bureaucracy in Washington. Rare is the top executive who cannot relate a painfully funny account of bureaucratic harassment—like the time a company was ordered to show cause, through endless forms and correspondence, why it should not be denied a government research grant for which it had not applied. Because the anecdotes are true, they often hurt too much for executives to laugh.

But such stories are the laughingstock-in-trade of bureaucracy's own Baedeker, James H. Boren, who has amassed more howling tales from the bureaucratic woods than Henny Youngman has one-liners. Item: Governor Dolph Briscoe of Texas last year nominated to a state job a man who had been dead for two years. Item: A Master Charge bank spent 13 cents in postage to bill an Oklahoma card holder for exactly 1 cent.

A familiar Washington gadfly, Jim Boren is a kind of Puck of the Potomac who smokes crooked Philippine cigars and carries a pencil with an eraser at both ends as emblems of the "dynamic inaction, bold irresolution and creative nonresponsiveness" of the Capitol's self-perpetuating bureaucracy. As President of the International Association of Professional Bureaucrats (INATAPROBU), a pseudo-organization that claims 970 members and 29 coordinating committees, Boren travels 160,000 miles a year lecturing groups ranging from the American Bankers Association to the Ski Clubs of America. Although Boren makes his living this way, his tilting at bureaucratic windmills appears to strike a responsive chord in audiences.

A onetime special assistant to the U.S. coordinator of the Alliance for Progress, Boren is a genuine former bureaucrat who holds five degrees. But in the ten years that he has presided over INATAPROBU, his act has been one of Washington's biggest put-ons. He once appeared as an expert witness before a Congressional committee on public works, and refused to take the oath. To give a direct yes or no, Boren protested, would be highly unprofessional in a career bureaucrat.

In 1972, Boren dramatized the Post Office Department's slipshod delivery performance by carrying a saddlebag of mail by horseback 170 miles from Philadelphia to Washington. Boren's private Pony Express beat some of the test mail by as much as eight days. To this day, mail addressed simply to James Boren, Washington, D.C., is promptly delivered since every letter carrier in the capital knows who, what and where he is.

Ostensibly, Boren celebrates the survival instinct and enduring growth of the bureaucracy, whose credo he describes as, "When in charge, ponder. When in trouble, delegate. When in doubt, mumble." But in fact he uses biting satire to expose bureaucratic waste and inefficiency. In his role as bureaucracy's selfappointed watchdog, Boren keeps extensive files. "To deny paper to a bureaucrat is to deny canvas to an artist," he explains. INATAPROBU's files are filled with examples of bureaucratic boondoggling that make for the kind of stories businessmen tell in golf club locker rooms. Among Boren's best worst-case instances of the bungled government bureaucracy:

> One large drug company spends $15 million a year filling out 27,000 government forms, thus adding about 50 cents to the price of each prescription.
>
> The 4,100 government regulations on ground beef result in a hidden hamburger tax of about 4 cents-to-5 cents per pound.
>
> The Food and Drug Administration took eleven years to decide how many peanuts should be required in peanut butter.
>
> An oil lease proposal off the New Jersey coast recently required 4,043 pages of environmental paperwork. The lease was voided when a federal judge ruled that the proposal had inadequate documentation.
>
> The University of Maryland was obliged to turn down a government grant because the estimated cost of processing the federally mandated paperwork would be greater than the grant. "To a bureaucrat, pornography is a blank sheet of paper," Boren says.
>
> Since the U.S. Postal Service became a private—and presumably more efficient—organization, the number of assistant postmasters has swelled from six to 36. At the same time, according to a

Boren sampling of postal performance, 25.5% of special-delivery letters get to their destination after regular mail.

To protect workers constructing a high bridge in New Orleans, the Occupational Safety and Health Administration (OSHA) ordered all hands to wear life preservers on the job. The bridge workers went to court to have the order set aside. In the event a worker fell from such a height, the bridge builders protested, the prescribed life preserver could break his neck.

Secretary Joseph Califano of the Department of Health, Education and Welfare last year issued a 402-word job description for a chef to staff HEW's executive dining room and never once mentioned cooking skill.

Due to the foresight of the Board of Education of financially strapped New York City, at the current rate of consumption the city's schools have enough rubber softballs in warehouses to last students 23 years, enough magnets on hand for 32 years and wooden beads sufficient to outfit kindergartens until the year 2626.

The Pittsburgh office of the Pennsylvania Cigarette Tax Bureau runs on a $300,000 annual budget. Last year, its seventeen full-time investigators managed to confiscate a grand total of 400 cartons of contraband cigarettes worth $225. Assuming that the bureau sold the contraband smokes and collected the $1.80 in taxes on each carton, the Pittsburgh office showed a net operating loss of $299,775.

When the town of South Lake, Texas, applied to the Farmers Home Administration for financial aid in constructing a water sewage system, the FHA, after considerable study, advised the community that it was too large for its program, and recommended that South Lake apply to the Department of Housing and Urban Development. HUD, in turn, ruled that the town was not big enough for its aid. After some five years passed, during which South Lake enjoyed a modicum of growth, it applied anew to HUD. This time the agency soberly informed town officials that South Lake was still not big enough to qualify for HUD aid—and never would be until it got a proper sewage system. Such "collaborative orbital referrals prove a basic bureaucratic principle," says Boren. "If you study a problem long enough, it may go away."

But government bureaucrats are not the only masters of "articulate waffling and finger-tapping interdigitation," Boren points out. There is plenty of glorified gobbledygook to go around in the private sector as well. He cites one trade association that was recently queried by a magazine writer for basic statistical information on its industry. The association supplied the information all right, but two weeks after the writer's deadline. Then it submitted a bill to the publication for $24 to help defray the cost of research.

Boren reserves some of his sharpest cudgels for bureaucrats in the communications industry, whose careers depend upon the Federal Communications Commission renewing the licenses of their respective radio and TV stations. Since renewal is partly based on a station's community involvement, Boren explains, many stations host luncheons with community leaders as a means of showing that a dialogue exists.

At one such pre-renewal function tendered by the Metromedia station in Washington last year, Boren delivered a speech as vice president of Amalgamated Fat Trimmers International, a fictional union with 364,000 nonexistent members. But the audience, including meatpacking executives and the chairman of a House committee on small business, had no trouble believing Boren when he explained that his union members specialized in "slant trimming" of beef in order to expose the visual impact of the lean "while being honest with the consumer."

There is no such thing as slant trimming, Boren points out. But every bureaucrat can relate to the INATAPROBU principle: "If you're going to be a phony, be sincere about it."

Before Boren was done, he had convinced the luncheon guests that any causal relationship between cholesterol and heart attack was "a stupid use of statistics." He even interested the station program manager in the need for a documentary on "the importance of fat in the American diet." When the news director advised the audience that they had been had, says Boren, "I got out of there fast."

For outstanding examples of bureaucratic mumbling, Boren each year awards perpetators with the "Order of the Bird." He has presented 36 of the pot-bellied, featherless statuettes thus far, along with a number of "rejection scrolls." Chairman Alfred Kahn of the Civil Aeronautics Board, for instance, was denied INATAPROBU member-ship for directing his people to write in simple language. "A very subversive activity in a bureaucrat," Boren clucks. This year he expects to give the bird to a dozen recipients—among them, the White House "for its ability to answer letters to the President without reading them."

The Administration's award stems from correspondence that Boren initiated last April, when he wrote to President Carter volunteering to serve as an unpaid adviser on reducing the flow of government paper by "orchestrating paper proliferation in order that bureaucrats can meet their shufflistic responsibilities." A Presidential assistant duly replied that "you may be certain that we will make every effort to relate your background and experience to vacancies that occur on boards and commissions."

Not content with such White House waffling, Boren penned a follow-up letter noting his dedication to "maximizing institutional quibbility" and citing his qualifications as a "regulator of the bureaucracy." This time the White House replied: "You may be certain that you will receive every consideration." So despite President Carter's vow to eliminate waste and inefficiency in government, Boren believes that 1978 should be a banner year for bureaucrats. "The state of the bureaucracy has never been better," he advises.

THE LITTLE THINGS THAT BRING BIG GOVERNMENT UNDER FIRE

When President-elect Carter begins to cope with the nation's anti-Big Government mood in the months ahead, he will find this:

It is the petty provocations of bureaucratic nitpicking rather than major policy blunders that really irritate people.

To more and more Americans, rules, regulations and red tape often going beyond the bounds of common sense seem to be the three R's of everyday life.

Intervention by federal, State and local officials is viewed in State after State as strangling private and personal rights.

Wrath exploded earlier this year, for instance, when federal bureaucrats banned father-son events in public schools as discrimination against girls. They backed away from their ruling after the public let out a loud cry.

So much ire has been aroused over nitpicking that 24 State legislatures have set up machinery to review and overturn rules and regulations considered, in the words of Iowa's law, "unreasonable, arbitrary, capricious, or beyond the scope of agency authority."

Talk with citizens across the nation and examples flood in. As reported by news bureaus of *U.S. News & World Report:*

• *Korean Tempest.* School officials in Cumberland County, N.C., detail what they regard as a classic case of federal nitpicking.

Last May, the Department of Health, Education and Welfare blocked a $350,000 federal grant to the tax-poor county until it arranged to provide bilingual teaching for 25 children of South Korean military personnel stationed temporarily at Fort Bragg, a nearby U.S. Army post.

Federal officials told the county it would have to hire enough certified bilingual teachers within the next three years to give the Koreans special instruction in their native tongue.

This was agreed to, local officials say, even though none of the children's parents requested any changes, none planned to stay in the country longer than 18 months, and several said they had placed their children in public schools to give them a complete immersion in American language and culture.

Martin Gerry, director of HEW's Office for Civil Rights, concedes that the Cumberland case is a "tempest in a teapot" that "never would have happened except for a statistical accident."

Earlier, the same county had been questioned by the federal authorities because it didn't provide bilingual instruction for 700 Lumbee Indian pupils in the schools.

The school system had to spend time convincing Washington that the Lumbees are English-speaking people who, says School Superintendent C. Wayne Collier, "lost their tribal language long before this nation was a nation."

• *Hassle Over Scales.* Consider "the great pizza row." Owners of the Chicago Pizza & Oven Grinder Company are arguing with officials over a matter of city-registered scales. A Chicago ordinance says that when food is sold by the pound, a city-registered scale must be in view of customers.

Chicago Pizza's menu offers "pizza by the pound," a 1-pounder for one price and a 2-pounder for a higher price. Actually, the 1-pounder weighs about 1 pound, 10 ounces, and the 2-pounder is much heavier than that.

Recently, the city sent two inspectors to Chicago Pizza. They ordered 1-pounders and then demanded to use a scale to weigh their meals.

Charles Smital, co-owner of the restaurant, says he led the inspectors to the back of his kitchen and let them put their pies on an unregistered scale he used for weighing dough. The inspector hit Mr. Smital with a $25 fine and ordered him to buy and display a city-registered scale.

Mr. Smital and his partner, a lawyer, were enraged. Other fast-food restaurants, they say, don't have scales for weighing their quarter-pounder hamburgers and 12-ounce sirloin steaks.

Nevertheless, a jury found the owner guilty of violating the ordinance.

· *Smelly Situation.* Residents of neighborhoods surrounding a new Atlanta sewage-treatment plant complained for some weeks that the stench in the area had become unbearable.

Finally, they demanded that the city do something about it.

The problem, it turned out, was this:

An engine used to drive blowers that kept down the smell had broken and workmen had requested the city to order a replacement. After more than six months, the city still had not done so. Reason: The engine's manufacturer had failed to submit a contract-employment report showing the racial breakdown of its work force. By then, the part was no longer being manufactured by the company and was available only from an out-of-State supplier.

After the neighbor's protest, the city relented and ordered the $10,000 part. "We probably paid about 15 per cent premium because we had to get it right away and it came by air freight," says a sanitation official.

Citizens of Midland, Tex., saw the price of land for a senior citizens' housing project go up by 20 per cent when one federal agency involved couldn't decide whether it should be located east or west of a particular street. The sites were within a block of each other.

"The site finally chosen was not as well located and cost 20 per cent more," says Mayor Ernest Angelo, Jr. "We ended up with no choice because, through all the delays, we lost our option on the other property."

· *"Let 'em Eat Cake."* At Fort Vancouver in Washington State, the National Park Service is restoring an old fur-trading fort, once a part of the Hudson's Bay Company's operations.

In the project, a replica of the fort's kitchen was built with two large brick ovens like those of pioneer days.

When the Park Service decided to make bread the way the fort's occupants did, the bureaucrats put their feet down. Dan Gillespie, superintendent of Fort Vancouver Historical Site, says he was told by the Southwest Washington Air Pollution Control Authority that the wood-burning ovens could not be used because they would put too many contaminants into the air.

The authority said the fort could make bread on occasion as long as it was not sold commercially. If bread was sold on a regular basis, the oven's chimneys would have to be equipped with smoke scrubbers, the authority ruled.

Mr. Gillespie protests that the situation is "silly," because not that much smoke would be released even in commercial bread baking. . . .

• *Choir Boys.* In Wethersfield, Conn., a sex-discrimination ruling may mean that its all-boy choir from elementary schools will never sing again. Robert Zysk, choral director, says the group has been disbanded until the Department of Health, Education and Welfare rules on the issue of whether the choir discriminates against girls. He says many of the boys would have been too embarrassed to sing in a coeducational group.

Mr. Zysk volunteers his time, so there is no cost to the community. But the choir was cut off when HEW advised the town fathers that the school system might lose federal funding by operating a discriminatory choir.

Regulations of the Government's Occupational Safety and Health Administration are specially annoying to many businesses. Construction of a proposed highway overpass in Indiana was vetoed by OSHA, for example, because the State had failed to conduct a noise-abatement study of how the project would disrupt the quietude of a cemetery that is a quarter of a mile away.

Businessmen guffawed, therefore, when word got out that OSHA itself had run afoul of the law. OSHA ordered that vehicles at construction sites must use back-up beepers that warn pedestrians and workers. But now the Environmental Protection Agency has told OSHA that some of the beepers are too noisy for EPA's noise standards.

• *Dune Trouble.* In some cases, officials try to reach Solomon-type decisions in order to clear up conflicts. Example:

One of the regional boards of the California coastal zone conservation commission, which is charged with protecting California beachlands, turned its attention to a strip of shoreland in Marin County, north of San Francisco.

Three home-owners who had leveled sand dunes in front of their homes so as to get a better view of the Pacific Ocean were granted permits retroactively to do just that. But a condition was that the three property owners first restore the dunes to their original condition—and then relevel them.

Who rates the blame for what's seen by the public as nitpicking? Many officials contend they don't. Says Gary Holloway, a senior planner for the California coastal commission: "This organization has to be nitpicking because of the strict definitions in the Coastal Protection Act" approved by voters.

Whoever is at fault, however, millions of people want government to change its ways.

SPEAKING OF RED TAPE, SOVIET LABELS ON FERTILIZER AND COFFEE GOT MIXED

Hedrick Smith

MOSCOW, Oct. 24—People the world over fall victim to the power of paper and the rigidity of bureaucracy. But rarely have the awe of documents and the iron hand of the Soviet bureaucracy been more simply captured than in the great fertilizer foul-up.

As *Izvestia,* the Government newspaper, told the story, a railroad car full of bagged fertilizer was being shipped to Terbuny, a town about 250 miles south of Moscow, and at the same time a shipment of 728 jute bags full of top-grade coffee beans was being sent to Yelets, 33 miles from Terbuny.

At the New Proletariat Railroad Station near Moscow, railroad workers accidentally put the shipping documents for the coffee on the fertilizer and vice versa, sending each to the wrong destination.

At Terbuny there was consternation at the unusual appearance of the "fertilizer." "The granules, although similar to the expected color and form, failed to dissolve in water," Izvestia reported. Moreover, the cargo was in jute bags instead of plastic as expected.

The workmen, concluding that there had been an error, reported it to the stationmaster in Birkin, but he was a man with unflagging faith in documents. "Don't make up new tales of the thousand and one nights," he retorted. "Send the railroad car to the distribution point of the agricultural Technical Agency for unloading."

There too doubts arose, but the stationmaster was in no mood for trifling when they called him. "Unload your car quickly or else I will fine you for idling the railroad car," he ordered.

An agronomist who was summoned took a handful of bagged beans over to the local agricultural administration. Leading specialists there decided it must be coffee, but they could not summon the courage to overrule the documents.

"Since it is fertilizer, according to the papers, you should unload the shipment quickly," the farm administration ordered.

Izvestia, incensed by what it called the "mindless routine" work of all concerned, observed that this was in violation of standing instructions to agronomists that in cases of doubt all material should be kept in one storehouse.

Nonetheless, the unloading and distribution to state and collective farms went full speed ahead. Some farms stored the coffee beans under sheds. At other places they were simply dumped to await use as fertilizer.

Meanwhile, the agronomist called on a chemist for a scientific test. The chemist put a pound or two in a jar, but he forgot to take it to his laboratory, *Izvestia* noted sarcastically, and even now "the sample" stands at the agricultural administration.

Izvestia reported that an order eventually went out to all Terbuny farms: "Immediately gather all the material, down to the last bean, and bring it back to the station." Three months later, the paper lamented, nine bags of first-grade coffee are still missing—worth "a sizable sum."

Izvestia did not choose to describe how far the other shipment went before people who were expecting coffee discovered that they were using fertilizer instead.

Introduction
The Great Asphalt Bungle

The clear separation between politics and administration was demanded by reformers such as Woodrow Wilson, who suggested a dichotomy between (1) policy determination via politics and (2) policy implementation via nonpolitical administration. Later, Frank Goodnow interpreted the Constitution as a statement of "two distinct functions of government." Policy centered in the legislative and then judicial branches and was only to be administered by the executive. Policy was an expression of state will, depoliticized administration the execution of that will. The thrust of the reform movement was captured in the saying, "There is neither a Democratic nor a Republican way to build a road, just the right way."

But governments are still plagued daily with costly mismanagement. Contractors incur "cost overruns." Supplies are lost. Funds are not placed in interest-bearing accounts. Excess employees are maintained on the payroll. Reporters often suspect that such errors are an indication that, despite the movement to make administration a neutral tool of government, political influence is still rampant.

The "Great Asphalt Bungle" argues that without strict adherence to the principles of management—in this case the independent audit—corruption is tempting. "Invisible middle-level bureaucrats and publicity-shy businessmen" certainly can use intricate rules and regulations to their own advantage. Political ties and economic self-interest sometimes overcome ethics. But it is important to underscore Pileggi's statement that "Most of the 40,000 companies that do business with the city are reasonably honest and provide the city with the necessities of municipal life." It would be irresponsible to label the vast majority of civil servants as dishonest, or most businesspeople as greedy and collusive.

QUESTIONS FOR DISCUSSION

Does industry also suffer from the type of mismanagement apparent in this case?

Is collusion a problem that management can normally detect, or is that the function of law enforcement authorities?

To what extent could government expenses be cut, but services maintained at the same level?

To what extent does the asphalt situation reflect simple mismanagement?

To what extent does it reflect the politicization of administration?

THE GREAT ASPHALT BUNGLE

Nicholas Pileggi

On February 15, the Jet Asphalt Corporation, of 32-02 College Point Boulevard, Flushing, Queens, was sent two checks totaling $7,865 by the comptroller of the city of New York.

The checks attracted very little attention around the Municipal Building, since they were only two of approximately 800 checks mailed out by the city that day and represented only a fraction of the $8.3 million the city paid for asphalt last year.

They didn't even attract much attention across the street at City Hall, where Assemblyman Charles Schumer and General Services Commissioner Peter P. Smith III had been issuing press releases and conducting news conferences in the Blue Room and charging that a small group of asphalt companies, including Jet, may have overcharged the city $5 million over the last three years.

The fact that the Municipal Building's check-writing apparatus could have continued to send money to a company under investigation by both city and state officials is indicative of the fact that there are really two governments in New York. One is the elected officials at City Hall. The other is in the Municipal Building across the street. The government in City Hall spends most of its time in office trying to find out what is going on in the other government across the street. The permanent government in the Municipal Building couldn't care less. Even today, while stringent austerity measures are being publicized at City Hall, across the street in the uncharted cubicles of the Municipal Building, where the checks are written, arcane contracts that cost the city $1.7 billion a year are being drawn between invisible middle-level bureaucrats and publicity-shy businessmen with unlisted telephone numbers.

Most of the 40,000 companies that do business with the city are reasonably honest and provide the city with the necessities of municipal life. There are other companies, however, that are still selling goods and services to the city long after they have been caught padding their bills, providing shoddy merchandise, rigging their prices, and bribing city inspectors. Some of these companies change their corporate names after they are caught, others hide behind trade associations, and a few have even "fired" or retired the rare executive who was caught gypping the city. But the companies themselves continue their collusive ways and the city continues to hemorrhage hundreds of millions of dollars every year through a totally inefficient purchasing system.

Until July 1, 1977, the comptroller's office pre-audited at random a small percentage of the city's purchases to make sure it was getting the quality and quantity of goods and services for which it was about to pay. Since then, however, even that minimal safeguard has been abandoned. As a result of the city's charter reform, which went into effect July 1, 1977, the pre-auditing powers have been taken away from the comptroller's office and turned over to the same agencies that make the purchases. The comptroller's office, therefore, is now essentially in the checkwriting business, and, as long as the city's computer indicates that there is money in an agency's budget, any bill the agency submits is paid.

"We still do post audits, some at random," says a spokesman for Comptroller Harrison J. Goldin, "but we do most of them after a complaint that something has gone wrong. Then we send a letter out to the agencies involved requesting that they send us the pertinent vouchers. That usually takes about two weeks. If we find that there has been something wrong, we will either refer the entire matter to the district attorney or just deduct what we feel is owed the city from the agency's budget."

In spite of the fact that 450,000 checks for goods and services are being mailed out by the comptroller's office every year, outsiders rarely get a look at the way the city makes most of its purchases. On the surface the system looks foolproof. There are elaborate public bidding procedures, and competing companies must often submit hundreds of thousands of dollars in bonds to ensure their good intent. There are contract specifications drawn up in great detail by city officials, there are line-by-line inspections by city engineers and experts at almost every step, and there is overall monitoring by the city agencies' accountants and lawyers.

But beneath the surface, for those contractors familiar with the terrain and who have a pal or two in the bureaucracy, every regulation has a loophole and every ironclad specification has a hairline flaw. Companies experienced in dealing with the city know exactly how the machinery works and are adept at manipulating it. They can assure that bid requirements are tailored so as to exclude competition. They get paid on time. They know which of the "mandatory" city requirements they have to observe, and which they can forget. They join forces with like-minded firms to rig the bidding and then take turns submitting the "low" bid. But, most important, the owners of these companies have become extraordinarily chummy with the supervisors, foremen, and deputy commissioners who are supposed to be safeguarding the interests of the city. They buy seats for their civil-service pals and middle-level bureaucrats at political fund-raising dinners. They remember birthdays and sometimes they even employ the friends and relatives of city employees and local pols. They have managed to prosper under several mayors and any number of austerity programs, because the decisions that affect their profits are not made by City Hall, but rather by the anonymous borough-bound department supervisors, deputy commissioners, and 30-year civil-service veterans who really run New York. The price to the taxpayers of this chumminess between the city's vendors and the bureaucrats who are supposed to be monitoring costs is hundreds of millions of dollars every year.

"Our pre-audits did have a useful purpose in keeping agencies in line," says Deputy Comptroller Paul O'Brien. "The city employees sometimes get very close to the companies they are supposed to be watching. They often socialize. They develop very cooperative relationships. We have found them to be members of the same local political clubs. There is an accommodation that begins to develop between the two parties, and the city usually winds up footing the bill. The old pre-audit system may not have been perfect and it may have caused delays, but we did look at checks before they were mailed out, and our auditors became very skillful at spotting potential trouble."

Now, with the comptroller's office out of the picture, any civil-service clerk worth his pension can easily befuddle a nosy outsider with statistics, studies, engineering reports, shoe boxes filled with vouchers, invoices, and affidavits.

Today, one of the few inquiries being directed at the corridors of the Municipal Building is being made by Charles Schumer, the chairman of the Assembly Subcommittee on City Management and Governance. Schumer is looking into several little-known, though costly, scams that snaked their way through the bureaucracy. It was Schumer who discovered that many of the city's most flagrant real-estate-tax evaders were buying deteriorated tax-defaulted properties at city auctions and allowing them to deteriorate even further while at the same time collecting the guaranteed rent checks of welfare tenants. Schumer spotted a drug program that cost $750,000 to treat three patients. He made inquiries into tax assessments, fee juggling, and the monopoly of a few real-estate appraisers.

But of all these investigations, the most interesting involves the multimillion-dollar asphalt game. Recently Schumer, who was joined by General Services Commissioner Smith, began looking into the possibility that a small clique of closely connected asphalt suppliers may have been overcharging the city by at least $5 million over the last three years. It is an investigation still in progress, but so far it has provided the city with a fascinating and rare glimpse of the Municipal Building's government in action.

The inquiry started when Schumer and Smith realized that the city was paying between 30 and 35 percent more for its asphalt than did either Con Edison, the Port Authority, or any of the other large-volume users of pothole filler and paving materials. Smith became aware of the problem because one of his first tasks in office was to purchase 524,000 tons of asphalt. Schumer, on the other hand, began looking into asphalt when his office received a confidential report that he says revealed possible collusion among the dealers to jack up their prices.

"The more I looked, the deeper it got," says Schumer.

> It has been a quiet and very profitable operation. It looks like the companies would pretend to bid against each other. Sometimes, it seems, one company would act as a 'front' for the others and purposely submit a totally unrealistic high bid, so that the high bids of their 'competitors' would look more legitimate and create the illusion of competitive bidding.
>
> I am beginning to realize that much of this has gone on because of the impenetrable gobbledygook in the way contracts were written and the specifications drawn up. There were complicated zoning requirements and mileage restrictions and mechanical-equipment demands and other irrelevant contractual details to knock companies out of the bidding.

Recently it looked like a Jersey company was going to underbid the locals by about $6 a ton. The Jersey company was within the mileage specifications. It had the right zone requirements. Then somebody changed the rules. Suddenly asphalt trucks were arbitrarily prohibited by the Transportation Department from using tunnels when delivering city asphalt. City engineers had apparently made studies showing that there were more traffic delays in tunnels than on bridges and therefore, the city-bought asphalt might fall below the required 300-degree temperature. The fact that the city need not accept cold asphalt, even if it is delivered, was apparently overlooked.

The real reason for the sudden restriction on the use of tunnels, some observers suspected, was to kill off the Jersey bidder by forcing him to use the George Washington Bridge and thus go beyond the required six-mile travel limit.

"The coziness between these companies was obvious, but no one seemed to be watching," says Schumer. "One of the contract specifications for selling asphalt to the city is that you have a backup supplier, in case you temporarily run out. Well, over the last three years, whenever the Mascali or Willets Point asphalt companies won a contract, Jet Asphalt would be named as their backup supplier, and whenever Jet won the city contract, then Mascali was Jet's backup.

"The Willets Point and Mascali firms seem to have even more than a backup relationship," says Schumer. "According to the Queens telephone directory, there is a listing for 'Willets Point & F. Mascali,' although the number has been changed and is now unlisted. A trip out to their yards shows them to be within 4,000 feet of each other, and according to various public records relating to the companies, they appear to share officers and to have different corporate names listed at the same address."

"The city has been ripped off," says Schumer. "Last year the city paid $19.50 a ton for 432,000 tons of asphalt, while the Port Authority paid $17.05 a ton for smaller quantities, a hundred times smaller, and for any grade they wanted."

Asphalt has always been big business in New York. It has been an even bigger business since 1973, when the city decided to close down its last asphalt-producing plant. Since then, the city has been totally dependent upon the very companies Assemblyman Schumer's subcommittee is investigating. Exactly why the city should have closed its last asphalt plant is not known. There were many reasons put forward by city officials at the time, including a cost-accounting rationale about how much money the city was going to save by buying its asphalt on the open market. What happened, of course, was that the "open market" suddenly shrank and companies such as Jet Asphalt Corp., Mascali & Sons, and the Willets Point Asphalt Co., all of Flushing, Queens; and the Asphalt Road Products Company of Brooklyn, as well as others, became part of a multimillion-dollar monopoly at the city's expense.

And there have, of course, been any number of investigations into the asphalt business over the years. There have been repeated charges of collusive bidding; there have been suspended jail terms and fines meted out in federal court to some of the asphalt suppliers after they pleaded guilty to antitrust violations; there have been accusations by outsiders that the Metropolitan Asphalt Paving Association is made up of sixteen companies with interlocking ownerships, and that they get about 98 percent of the city's asphalt business. James Comyns, the owner of the Erie Conduit Company, a Long Island asphalt dealer who has managed to get some city bids, accused the members of the Metropolitan Association of sabotaging his work for the city, burning his trucks, and getting city inspectors to harass him and his workers with violation citations and various other administrative punishments.

What Assemblyman Schumer and Commissioner Smith were actually beginning to learn was the extent of the political and civil-service connections of the asphalt companies. It was nothing new. In 1973, the officers of one of the companies they were investigating had been questioned by a federal grand jury looking into illegal campaign contributions in connection with the 1972 presidential campaign. While nothing came of the federal inquiry, the testimony of asphalt executives, city officials, and politicians revealed an uneasy camaraderie.

In 1973, Frank Castiglione, an official in the Jet Asphalt Company, and Frank LoCurto, an officer of Mascali & Sons, both testified before the Senate Watergate Committee and said that they had donated $10,000 in cash to John V. Lindsay's presidential campaign. At the time of their contributions both companies, as well as their various contracting subsidiaries, had several contracts with the city, especially in Queens, where the company officials had been regulars at Democratic-party fund-raising dinners as far back as 1966.

During his testimony, Castiglione said that he, along with Fred Durante, the president of Durante Brothers, Inc., (a company listed at the same address as Jet Asphalt), and Louis Durante, the company's treasurer, had joined in a $5,000 contribution to the Lindsay campaign. Frank LoCurto, of Mascali & Sons, gave the other $5,000. Castiglione said that all of the money had been turned over to Peter Jordan, a general superintendent with the Highways Department in Queens. Castiglione told investigators that he and his colleagues felt "no pressure" to contribute to the campaign, even though they had been given at least 28 contracts by the city to build playgrounds, pave streets, and sell asphalt. He also saw nothing unusual in contributing $10,000 in May to a presidential campaign that had been disbanded in early April. According to an investigator familiar with the case, the asphalt men were told the money was to help pay off a campaign debt, not to pave their way to the White House.

Peter Jordan, the general superintendent of the Highway Department's Queens plant, is typical of the kind of bureaucrat who is also half a politician. Jordan's name pops up at fund-raising dinners for the Queens County Democratic Committee as far back as 1966. He was an active member of the Jefferson Democratic Club in Queens and earned $18,120 from the city as a general superintendent, even though his payroll record listed him as a "gasoline-roller operator." He was well enough known in Queens political circles for his boss, Deputy Commissioner of Highways David W. Keiper, to ask him to help raise money for Lindsay's waning presidential campaign.

Deputy Commissioner Keiper told investigators that even though no one in the Lindsay camp had asked him to raise money for the campaign, he had seen an article in a newspaper that said Lindsay still owed $100,000. Keiper claimed that on his own initiative in May of 1972, he talked with his subordinate, Peter Jordan, and "advised" him of the Lindsay debt. Keiper denied that he had specifically suggested to Jordan the soliciting of contractors or suppliers of goods to the city.

Jordan testified that he contacted Castiglione and LoCurto at least twice within the next week and that, just possibly, he might have mentioned the amount of money that he was seeking. Within a week, Jordan said, he met Keiper and handed over an envelope containing $10,000 in $20 bills.

Keiper, in turn, told the investigators that he had never counted the money but had merely delivered the envelope to Richard Aurelio, Lindsay's campaign manager and a former deputy mayor, at the Lexington Avenue Lindsay headquarters. Keiper also said that Jordan had written the names of the contributors on the inside of the envelope and that he had never even looked to see who the Lindsay benefactors were.

Whether this was the only campaign contribution from asphalt dealers is not known, and whether or not any of these contributions was ever reported by the campaign officials is uncertain. What is known, however, is that in June of 1972, barely a month after Castiglione and LoCurto contributed the $10,000, their companies submitted joint bids for $1.7 million in city asphalt contracts and their bids were accepted. It was also at this time that officials were making up their minds about whether or not to close down the last city-owned asphalt plant. Anthony Ameruso, who is now the city's transportation administrator, but was then a divisional director for Highway Planning, had argued strenuously for retaining city-owned asphalt plants. The last plant, incidentally, was in Flushing, Queens, and Peter Jordan was in charge of its maintenance. Ameruso warned that the city would be totally dependent upon outside suppliers for its asphalt and even cautioned that the city would have no recourse if the private asphalt dealers should begin to escalate their prices. Ameruso's suggestions went unheeded and by 1975, as Schumer's investigation reveals,

Castiglione and LoCurto's companies were charging the city between 30 and 35 percent more for its asphalt than they were charging their other customers.

The wrinkles are endless. The 127-50 Northern Boulevard address of the Willets Point asphalt company, for instance, turns out to be the same as that of a Department of Sanitation facility. The Department of Sanitation leased (for seven years at $95,000 a year) a garage and 76,000 square feet of space on June 1, 1972 shortly after Castiglione's campaign contributions. The curious leasing arrangements—which has the Department of Sanitation and the Willets Point asphalt company occupying the same address—did not attract attention at the time, since the lease had been drawn in the name of the Columbia Asphalt Company, which *also* has the same address.

But then, of course, Municipal Building politics never do attract attention. That is one of the main reasons why they continue, immune to new mayors, cost-conscious control boards, and even nosy assembly-men like Schumer.

Introduction
Letter from Washington

A basic premise of the management model—applied to public or private organizations—is control, "seeing that everything is accomplished in conformity with the established plan and command." Yet complete control is, in reality, elusive. The ease with which William Sibert diverted almost a million dollars from UMTA underscores the limits of control.

The letter overstates the case: "no one really knows what goes on in the bureaucracy on the day-to-day operational level." It does, however, raise a fundamental question: Can even well-intentioned management anticipate every contingency—anticipate errors, consequences, and loopholes?—or must we learn largely through mistakes? The same type of problem confronts the nuclear power industry (the Three Mile Island accident was due to unanticipated breakdowns), the space program (the Apollo fire that killed three astronauts was due to unrecognized flammability of materials) or the airlines (the DC-10 crash that killed 274 people in Chicago was due to incorrect maintenance).

In the less dramatic instance of Medicare income, the letter's argument is more acceptable. He suggests that HEW's programs are *chronically* mismanaged, that one of our largest bureaucracies does not learn from its mistakes. Perhaps this is because the consequences of their actions never directly hurt the individual employees or officials who fail to do their best; losing at Medicare affects them no more than losing at Monopoly.

QUESTIONS FOR DISCUSSION

How large are the undetected loopholes in government programs?
Can we "tighten up" management, or should we expect to learn primarily through mistakes?

Do officials personally suffer the consequences of their mistakes?

In what ways are the Sibert and Califano stories related? In what ways do they differ?

Could the two problems have been equally predicted or anticipated?

How would you prevent recurrences of these particular problems?

LETTER FROM WASHINGTON

Cato

What do Joseph Califano and William Sibert have in common? Until Sibert was put in the pokey last year, both worked in the federal bureaucracy, Califano as HEW chief and Sibert as an analyst in the Transportation Department's Urban Mass Transportation Administration (UMTA). Califano is still on the job; Sibert won't be back. But during the past year, each in his own way helped to confirm a long-standing suspicion: no one really knows what goes on in the bureaucracy on the day-to-day operational level—least of all the people who ostensibly run it—and until something sufficiently embarrassing to be newsworthy happens, no one much gives a hoot.

Sibert, you'll recall, was the Walter Mittyish fellow—bearing a striking resemblance to Billy Carter—who like many other men his age suddenly seemed to realize that the good things in life were never to be his. But unlike most of the rest of us, he decided to do something about it, by rigging a Transportation Department computer to issue $857,000 in UMTA funds to William Sibert. And then, public monies in hand, he proceeded to do what millions of American males secretly yearn to do: he bought a new home; he bought a fleet of cars; he bought a yacht. He showered his womenfolk with gifts; he laid on a Las Vegas junket; and he bought his very own topless go-go bar, which is now the property of the Federal Government, and perhaps the only federal operation ever to run in the black.

It is difficult to resist liking Sibert, especially when he smiled that sly little Billy Carterish smile as they hauled him off. Nor is his contribution to the understanding of how our government works insignificant. For the fact is that had his bankers not grown suspicious, no one would have missed that $857,000 at all. The concept of accountability

Reprinted by permission of National Review. *National Review* Vol. 30, April 14, 1978.

is nearly nonexistent in the federal bureaucracy, and a million dollars of public money is just computer paper.

This is nowhere more true than at HEW, where Joseph Califano presides over the nation's biggest business, with a proposed FY 1979 budget that is larger then the total combined assets of the nation's twenty largest oil companies. The suspicion here has long been that various welfare and health-care programs are so loosely and badly administered that HEW seldom can tell precisely how much has been spent for what by whom and when. And frequently, when it does attempt to account for the expenditures of public monies, HEW blunders so badly that it confirms that suspicion, in spades.

The most recent case in point is HEW's hit list of $100,000-per-year Medicare doctors. The emphasis in Califano's HEW is on proving that everything in the health-care system except federal intervention drives up medical costs. Hospitals are one prime target; the other is doctors, who present a very special political problem. Doctors remain among the most highly respected people in America—much more respected than government officials. Thus, government officials who want to take over the nation's health-care system feel that first they must destroy the credibility of doctors, especially those who insist on practicing privately. One way to do this is periodically to issue a list of physicians who seem to be growing fat by bilking the government under the Medicare program.

But the problem is that this list is generally so laced with errors, that it defeats its own purpose. The 1977 list, for instance, which cost $136,000 to work up, has been investigated by Congress and found to be poorly prepared, mistake-riddled, excessively costly, and badly managed. Among the more egregious of the 450 errors, individual physicians and group practices were confused; the list contained names of dead or retired doctors; many reported dollar amounts were inaccurate. One Michigan doctor listed as receiving $115,000 actually received $15,000. His comment: "My wife must think I have an apartment on the side and a mistress as well."

HEW's foulups on its $136,000 report on $100,000 Medicare doctors were so flagrant that Califano actually issued a somewhat qualified apology, something he seldom does. But there was no apology for the misuse of public money, nor will there ever be. True, some of the more bitter critics here continue to carp, asserting that bureaucratic maladministration of the funds the Feds collect from us is a national scandal. But they just don't seem to understand that whether it's Califano misusing it for libelous lists or Sibert misusing it just as honestly for go-go bars, in Washington it's little more than computer money. And who can get excited about that?

Bureaucratic Blackout: The Control Room That Didn't Control

Without the communication of information an organization cannot function. Internal continuity and coordination depend on the exchange of information—via meetings, directives, bulletins, reports, files, training instruction, telephone calls, casual conversations, and so on. And an organization's ability to cope effectively with circumstances and to succeed in its mission depends, likewise, on the receipt of accurate information and on the successful transmittal of messages. When significant facts are unknown, activities are likely to be inappropriate. One important managerial task, then, is to ensure that appropriate communications channels exist and also that members of the organization make effective use of them, because communication is a psychological—as well as a physical—process. People say, and hear, only what they are prepared to.

On July 13, 1977, New York City suffered a lengthy blackout which, among its other deleterious effects, gave rise to looting. The electric system collapsed because personnel lacked information—on events, on system capacity, and on procedures. They lacked the information for a variety of reasons: They were not told, they didn't pay attention, they didn't want to hear, or they had forgotten.

QUESTIONS FOR DISCUSSION

How does the expression, "there are none so blind as those who will not see" fit this case?

What were barriers to horizontal, vertical, and lateral communication in this case?

How can situations such as this be avoided or at least minimized?

Where do managers in the public sector learn about the communication process and how to manage it?

CON ED'S PRE-BLACKOUT CALLS PUNCTUATED BY WORRIES

Victor K. McElheny

"You've got to shed load immediately or you're going to go right down the pipe with everything," the dispatcher in the New York Pool control center shouted to the man running the Consolidated Edison Company's power control center, as systems strained shortly before the city was plunged into blackness on July 13.

The Con Ed man apparently did not respond fast enough.

Within minutes, the system failed and New York City was without electricity.

The worried exchanges as the crisis was building have been made public by Con Ed as part of a report by the utility's engineers and consultants analyzing the causes of the blackout.

Among those talking were the senior pool dispatcher of the New York Power Pool control center at Guilderland, N.Y., the system operator on duty in Con Edison's energy control center at West End Avenue and 65th Street, and that operator's supervisor, Charles J. Durkin Jr., Con Edison's chief system operator.

For many minutes during the crisis, the Con Ed system operator thought erroneously that he could still use a feeder line through Westchester County, while the New York Power Pool dispatcher thought erroneously for a time that a tie between Long Island Lighting Company and Con Edison had been interrupted.

Because of misunderstanding the status of the Westchester line, W 93, the Con Edison system operator concentrated at first on having an overload on a north-south line called 80 reduced by cutting the output of a power plant at Roseton, near Newburgh, on the west side of the Hudson River.

The Con Edison report said: "Although the New York Power Pool operator and the system operator discussed this strategy from their respective viewpoints, the discussion never focused on whether feeder W 93 was, or was not, in service. This question "was critical to the effectiveness of the strategy."

Excerpts from the tapes—each representing a separate call—follow.

8:56 P.M.

POOL: Bill, you better shed some load until you can get down below this thing because I can't pick up anything from the north, see?

CON EDISON: Yeah.

POOL: So you better do something to get rid of that until you get yourself straightened out.

CON EDISON: I'm trying. I'm trying.

8:59 P.M.

POOL: Bill, I hate to bother you, but you'd better shed about 400 megawatts of load or you're going to lose everything down there.

CON EDISON: Bill, I'm trying to.

POOL: You're trying to. All you have to do is hit the button to shed it and then we'll worry about it afterwards. But you got to do something or they're going to open the Linden [N.J.] tie on you.

CON EDISON: Yeah, right. Yeah, fine.

9:02 P.M.

POOL: Hello.

CON EDISON: Look any better?

POOL: No, You still got to get rid of about 400, Bill, because you're 400 over the short-time emergency on that 80 line.

CON EDISON: Yeah, that's what I'm saying. Can you help me out with that?

POOL: I can't do nothing because it's got to come from the lower part of the state and there's nothing there to help you with. You got to do it in. . . .

CON EDISON: There's no G.T. [gas turbine] because they went home.

POOL: O.K. Then you're going to have to shed load because that's the only way that things is going to save you 'till you get them [deleted] things on, because I told Long Island to pick up everything he had and that's the only place that I can get in to you.

CON EDISON: Can you help me?

POOL: There's no way I can help you, see? O.K. Will?

9:05 P.M.

CON EDISON: Bill, I'm going to cut feeder 80. I've no way of deloading it right now.

POOL: Can't you shed load and relieve it? If you cut feeder 80 then you are really going to be in trouble. . . .

CON EDISON: Can't Roseton back off?

POOL: I can have Roseton back off but that's not going to help your 80 line. . . .

CON EDISON: It should be able to help me if he backs off on those Roseton machines.

POOL: Yeah, but you got nothing to pick up. See what I'm saying? You need something in the south to ease it off, and there's nothing you can do but shed load down there. You can't get your turbines on.

CON EDISON: It's just the idea. I was figuring on going ahead of the game and letting them go naturally. I'm getting the Narrows put on and the Astoria.

POOL: Yeah. If you get them on, then I can back off stuff from the north, see?

CON EDISON: Right.

9:06 P.M.

DURKIN: You got some problems, huh?

CON EDISON: Yeah, Charlie, just one moment, huh? I got, I lost Y 88 and W 98 and it looks like W 97 is alive back on one breaker from Millwood, Indian Point. Then I got overload and I got 81 taken down. But it must have been struck by lightning. Because 81 went out. I'm overloaded on 80 by 1430 megawatts. I'm trying to get everybody back up, but I have no G.T.'s. I had Ravenswood [Queens] G.T.'s go home.

9:10 P.M.

DURKIN: Pick up at least 100, pick up 150 if you can [on the feeder from Linden]. Tell Cockerham to tell New Jersey that we're in danger of shutting down all of New York.

CON EDISON: Yeah.

DURKIN: O.K. We've got to take some power in.

CON EDISON: Tell Linden I got to take some more power in. We're in danger of losing it. Everything's cascaded around here.

9:20 P.M.

CON EDISON: Yes, Willie.

POOL: You got to shed load immediately or you're going to go right down the pipe with everything. You've lost that 80 line there now.

CON EDISON: He lost the 80 line?

POOL: Yeah, you'd better shed load immediately.

CON EDISON: Oh.

POOL: At least 600 megawatts anyway.

CON EDISON: Yep, O.K.

9:22 P.M.

POOL: John [addressing Con Edison power dispatcher]. Will you shed load down there immediately.

CON EDISON POWER DISPATCHER: Yeah.

POOL: At least 1,000 megawatts or you're going to go right down the pipe.

CON EDISON POWER DISPATCHER: All right, pal.

9:27 P.M.

POOL: O.K. I'm going to tell you one more time. If you don't shed about 600 MW of load immediately.

CON EDISON POWER DISPATCHER: He's doing it as fast as he can, pal.

POOL: All you got to do is push a button to get rid of it.

CON EDISON DISPATCHER: That's what he is doing right now.

POOL: Shed 600 MW immediately or you'll lose that Linden and you're out of business. That's the only thing you have left, John.

Two minutes later, as the Con Edison system controller was making a second attempt to operate the manual load-shedding equipment to the left of his console, the tie to Linden failed. By 9:36 P.M., the entire system had collapsed.

NEW YORK TIMES EDITORIAL: THE CONTROL ROOM THAT DIDN'T CONTROL

If, in the critical hour or so before the July 13 blackout, key personnel in Con Edison's control center had taken correct action promptly, they might well have averted complete collapse of the system. Instead, they bumbled. Whatever larger verdicts are ultimately reached in the several continuing investigations of the blackout, it is now clear from Con Edison's second blackout report and hearings before a special mayoral commission that the utility left the public in the care of a control room whose personnel and equipment were not prepared to handle the emergency.

The bumbling began with the Con Edison system operator's initial strategy. It was based on the belief that a particular feeder line from the north was still in service, when he should have known it was not. For one thing, he failed to read a teletype machine which indicated the line was down. The system contained a more dramatic indicator—a flashing screen with a high-pitched alarm. But where was it? In another room. Personnel there knew the line was out but failed to tell the system operator. Thus uninformed, he ignored increasingly urgent entreaties from the New York Power Pool to disconnect some customers in order to save the whole system.

As the situation deteriorated, the harassed operator virtually yielded command to his boss, the chief system operator, who sat in his by-now darkened house reading diagrams by a kerosene lantern and issuing orders by phone. When he finally ordered that customers be disconnected, the system operator pushed the disconnect buttons, but nothing happened. Apparently, he didn't operate the equipment properly. The operator had not practiced load-shedding since the equipment was installed years ago; the utility industry has no simulators for such practice.

Others in the control center also behaved erratically. One deputy assured the New York Power Pool that Con Edison was shedding load when it wasn't—just to "get rid of" the nagging caller. Another, who was supposed to alert police and other public officials, failed to do so— even when the police, seeing lights go out, called for information.

All of these individuals bear some responsibility for the control room's performance. But they must not be made scapegoats. Con Edison management selected and trained them. It also designed the control center whose layout contributed to the confusion. Con Edison is now studying ways to improve its training, operating procedures, and the design of its control center. Inevitably, in times of crisis, the security of the city's electrical lifeline must be left to the judgment of a few key individuals. But there is no excuse for sending them into action ill-prepared or ill-equipped.

Introduction
When Washington Tries to
Build a Railroad

Management of a project involves the technical questions of planning, organizing, staffing, directing, coordinating, reporting, and budgeting. In public sector projects, each of these processes is hedged about by rules, regulations, and crosschecks that serve to control illegal or unnecessary expenditures but which also serve to create paperwork and delays. The "Principles of Management" suggest that there should be a hierarchy of authority with unity of command so that all activities can be dovetailed and controlled.

The project of transforming the Boston-Washington rail line into a high-speed corridor failed all along the line—a late start, inexperienced personnel, missing or worn-out equipment, and interminable delays—due primarily to a "mind-boggling, top-heavy administrative structure." Decision making was divided up among three organizations, none of which had full authority or a view of the entire picture.

QUESTIONS FOR DISCUSSION

Could AMTRAK's management have foreseen its problems?
Would a comprehensive project management system have helped?
Should the job have been given over entirely to private industry?
Would the public have tolerated some corruption as the price of less red tape
   in the interests of speeding up the project?

WHEN WASHINGTON TRIES TO BUILD A RAILROAD

Fred W. Frailey

On May 1, 1977, Transportation Secretary Brock Adams turned the first, symbolic spadeful of dirt to mark the official start of the most ambitious project for high-speed passenger trains this country has ever seen.

Today, scarcely two years later, the timetable for creating a "superrailroad" between Boston and Washington already is two to three years off target and costing hundreds of millions of dollars more than expected.

A mind-boggling, top-heavy administrative structure is often blamed for the delays and cost overruns. Other causes: inexperienced designers, untrained workers, scant supervision and an overambitious construction schedule. Even the Federal Bureau of Investigation is involved, to probe possible ripoffs by subcontractors.

In short, the federal government's Northeast Corridor Project has turned into a textbook example of how not to build a railroad.

Now Secretary Adams is asking Congress to extend the official completion time of the project from 1981 to 1984, and to increase funding by one third—from 1.75 to 2.5 billion dollars.

Even that much added time and money may not be enough to complete the venture. "It's entirely possible in 1981–1982 we'll be back and say, 'Hey, this thing just didn't pan out,'" Amtrak President Alan Boyd told a congressional hearing in March. Adds his chief engineer, Robert F. Lawson: "We can't keep going this way and never finish." Louis Thompson, the man who directs the entire undertaking for the Department of Transportation's Federal Railroad Administration, admits, "The one big problem this project has had is people promising things they can't deliver."

A lot was promised in February, 1976, when Congress passed legislation to turn the Penn Central's run-down line from Boston to New York, Philadelphia, Baltimore and Washington into the most up-to-date, high-speed railroad in the U.S.

Passenger trains would zip along at speeds of up to 120 miles an hour. Schedules for the 224-mile trip from New York to Washington would be slashed from 3 hours, 15 minutes or longer to 2 hours, 40 minutes. Fifty minutes would be taken off today's 4-hour-30-minute timing from New York to Boston. Over a billion dollars' worth of postponed maintenance work on track and facilities would be done. The electric-power system would be modernized and overhead wires extended from New Haven, Conn., to Boston, so electric locomotives could be used for the entire 456 miles. Stations would be rebuilt, curves eased, signals modernized and highway crossings eliminated.

But the project, no matter how well administered, may have been under-financed from the beginning. Congress ordered engineering studies begun in 1973. Those studies indicated that to complete a New York-Washington trip in 2 hours, 30 minutes with five intermediate stops, or a New York-Boston journey in 3 hours, would require speeds of up to 150 miles an hour and cost 4.3 billion dollars.

When Congress got around to authorizing the work in 1976, President Ford threatened to veto even a much less expensive project. A last-minute compromise put the cost at 1.75 billion and trimmed the ambitious trip-time goals to reflect the smaller price tag.

Thomas Allison, then chief counsel of the Senate Commerce Committee, says the Department of Transportation "came up with a new estimate very hastily to justify that figure." He adds: "I thought at that time it wasn't enough money. But, faced with a veto, we felt it was better to agree on 1.75 billion, and to take another look later."

The law specified that trains were to begin operating on the faster schedules by February, 1981.

Delays began at once. Amtrak and William T. Coleman, President Ford's Secretary of Transportation, fought over whether the government-subsidized passenger-train company should own the Boston-to-Washington tracks. The alternative: let the line be run by Conrail, the company Congress set up to succeed the bankrupt Penn Central. Not until August, 1976, did Coleman release money for Amtrak to buy it. An entire work season was thus lost. "If we had started that first year," says Paul Reistrup, Amtrak's president at the time, "we could have gotten people trained for the hard work that lay ahead."

Rather than give Amtrak prime responsibility to carry out the enormous rebuilding job, Secretary Coleman insisted it be managed directly by DOT's Federal Railroad Administration. FRA set up a Northeast Corridor Improvement Project Office. But few of its people had actual railroad experience, and nobody there had the expertise necessary to design bridges, stations, new track layouts and signal installations, or to supervise the rebuilding. Amtrak employees or subcontractors were to do most of the actual work.

In late October, 1976, FRA selected DeLeuw, Cather/Parsons & Associates to design the improvements and oversee the work. In so doing, claims Amtrak's Reistrup, the Federal Railroad Administration set up "a three-headed monster" that kept tripping over itself.

The problem, as viewed by Amtrak people, was that FRA wanted to make every decision, including unimportant ones. "Even the Federal Highway Administration doesn't build the highways itself," says Reistrup. One Senate aide recalls that his phone conversation with an FRA official in Washington, D.C., was interrupted while the official scurried about arranging for a piece of work equipment to be unloaded from a truck hundreds of miles away.

Organizational problems abounded. Amtrak was to furnish the construction work force and operate the rebuilt railroad, but could not design it. DeLeuw, Cather was to design the improvements and inspect the work as it was performed, but lacked authority to order Amtrak to correct construction errors. Amtrak and DeLeuw, Cather dealt with each other through FRA's Northeast Corridor Improvement Project staff, which functioned like most bureaucracies—slowly, amid tons of paper work. Reistrup had an organizational chart of the corridor program drawn for him once, and says it looked "like the wiring diagram of a B-29."

Amtrak's Lawson describes how the system worked in practice: "We would decide we needed a piece of work equipment. DeLeuw, Cather would come up with a package of design specifications and a cost estimate, and write it out. We would go through a series of reviews of those specifications, writing letters back and forth. Hopefully, we'd agree. Then FRA would look at it, and its lawyers and procurement people, too. That meant more back-and-forth letter writing. Finally, it would go out for bids, which would come in for evaluation and review by everyone. Six or seven months after it all began, we could order the equipment, and eight or nine months after that, we might get it."

When it became owner of the line in August, 1976, Amtrak found few experienced track and engineering supervisors left— most had taken jobs elsewhere with Conrail. "We had pieces of track-work equipment assigned to us in the takeover that hadn't been used in years," says Lawson. "A lot of it was stripped. Good pieces had disappeared, and many of the machines we never did find. So we got mostly junk."

Without good machines or a crop of supervisors, Amtrak failed dismally to meet 1977 goals for track upgrading. According to congressional testimony, Amtrak spent 104 percent of the money budgeted for track upgrading in 1977—but accomplished only 63 percent of the work. In 1978, Amtrak's efficiency improved by roughly 25 percent, but it still fell short of the rebuilding goals and spent more money than expected.

Amtrak blames some of its problems on delays in receiving

designs. As late as February, 1979, Lawson was still awaiting designs from DeLeuw, Cather for work that was to have been done in 1978. "If plans don't come forth," he says, "you can't accomplish the work."

Amtrak has been criticized for administration laxity. An audit of purchasing records could not identify 63 percent of the equipment listed as having been bought. The FBI was called in when it appeared that subcontracts had been awarded to at least one company with a fictitious address.

By January, 1978, people involved in the project were aware that even the scaled-down list of improvements could not be finished by 1981, and that the mandated trip times could not be achieved with the 1.75 billion dollars. Secretary Adams then ordered a "redirection study" of the program.

That study took a full year, and led to Adam's recommendation that Congress allow three more years and another 750 million dollars.

In addition, Thompson was hired last May from a consulting firm to run FRA's Northeast Corridor Improvement Project office. "I've tried," he says, "to ignore the sins of the past, to streamline the whole operation and get everyone headed in the same direction." By almost everyone's account, Thompson has succeeded in cutting through some of the red tape.

Right now, he and Alan Boyd, Amtrak's current president, are negotiating changes in the working relationships between Amtrak and FRA.

Boyd expects one result to be that Amtrak will not have to follow the federal government's time-consuming and unwieldy purchasing procedures.

As for the 120-mile-an-hour passenger trains, the first ones may appear in the faster, 2-hour-40-minute New York-Washington schedules in 1981. But full high-speed service won't go into effect south of New York until 1983 or north of New York until 1984.

"Only by . . . hindsight could you say we should have done it differently," contends Thompson. "There's no precedent for the Northeast Corridor Project. It took experience to convince everybody there was a better way."

Lawson, who as Amtrak's chief engineering officer has struggled through the program from its inception, can only conclude: "This is one of the most frustrating jobs I've ever had. People wonder why I stay here. I can only reply that it's a challenge."

Businesslike Government

The business sector is often pointed to by government's critics as a model of efficiency. A century ago, Woodrow Wilson and other reformers suggested that the running of government needed to be made more businesslike. In the intervening decades various management models, under such rubrics as "scientific management," "POSDCORB," and "Auditing," have been used to apply business principles to the functions that government is charged with performing. The applied study of administration did not, however, satisfy the public's demands that its employees be smarter and work harder. Despite a hundred years of civil service improvement, government's continued insufficiency was clearly reflected in a Harris Poll performed for the National Commission on Productivity in the early 1970s; the public perceived government workers as far less productive than almost any other work group. Could the quality of the government work force have been viewed any more negatively in the 1870s? Today, candidates for political office and businesspeople continue to echo the demand for a more efficient work force.

One reason for continued dissatisfaction is the fact that disparity in public–private salaries at the upper levels has often discouraged the very best managerial talent from entering or remaining in government. As "They're Trimming the Fat from State Government" shows, Ohio's experiment with full-time volunteers (on leave from their companies and still on company salaries) is an innovative program to overcome salary differences and to provide fresh perspectives as to efficiency. The result is an annual saving of many millions of dollars.

"Point Man for the Carter Reorganization" illustrates how, on a larger scale—billions of dollars—a federal government team in the Office of Management and Budget is using business principles and businesspeople on loan to ferret out federal mismanagement and inefficiency.

Robert W. Poole Jr. describes an alternative means of making city governments more businesslike: "contracting out." The premise of that arrangement, which Camden, New Jersey, and Lafayette, California, have adopted, is that contractors are more innovative and frugal than government; they have greater incentives and fewer obstacles to delivering services.

QUESTIONS FOR DISCUSSION

Why could not public employees make the same suggestions as business-people do? Is it that businesspeople are so much more competent? Is it just that they bring fresh perspectives to governments' problems and ask questions that almost any outsider might ask?

Do suggestions receive readier acceptance or greater recognition if they come from prestigious private sector executives rather than from middle- or lower-level government bureaucrats?

Do such suggestions have a lasting impact, once the borrowed executive leaves?

When services are contracted out, will citizens be served as well? Will officials be as responsive to their needs and special problems?

What services in your community could be contracted out?

THEY'RE TRIMMING THE FAT FROM STATE GOVERNMENT

Trevor Armbrister

By December 1974, Wisconsin's Division of Motor Vehicles (DMV) was disastrously behind in its work, and citizen complaints were mounting. It took eight weeks to process auto-title registration with a backlog of more than 50,000. Gov. Patrick J. Lucey decided to call for help from the business community. Allen A. Sieczkowski, a 28-year-old budget manager for the J. C. Penney Co. in Milwaukee, accepted the challenge.

Studying procedures at the DMV main office in Madison, Sieczkowski found administrative disorder and a crying need for modernization: "They had buried themselves under a mountain of red tape." Drawing from his own experience, the young businessman recommended solutions. There were far too many steps in the processing; cut some of them out. Applications were processed manually; a computer could do the work more efficiently. Job assignments should be more clearly defined; DMV employes agreed. By December 1975, the office work load had been substantially reduced, the backlog had disappeared, and processing time had been slashed to ten days.

Quietly, without fanfare, businessmen all across America are volunteering their skills to help state governments cut costs and perform more efficiently. The names of these programs, and their accomplishments, vary from state to state. Yet, over the past dozen years, they've saved taxpayers an estimated $5.5 *billion*. The contribution has been costly to the firms which pay the salaries of businessmen spending time away from their own jobs. But by helping state governments function more smoothly, they've created a healthier business climate, and that in the long run has been a more than adequate reward. As Dr. Richard L. Lesher, president of the U.S. Chamber of Commerce, stresses, "Businessmen have a big stake in helping governments get along on less."

The 1960s witnessed a disturbing, accelerating trend all across the United States. While state populations increased only slightly—most by less than 15 percent—state payrolls ballooned. Government at the state and local level became one of the fastest growing "industries" in the country, and, as demands for services multiplied, expenditures began climbing out of sight. Raising taxes provided only temporary relief.

When James A. Rhodes took office as governor of Ohio in 1963, the state, despite increased taxes, had unpaid bills of more than $100 million. Unemployment was high and rising rapidly; corporations were moving out of state. What was needed was a total reorganization of Ohio's state government.

State finance director Richard Krabach remembered how a blue-ribbon commission headed by former President Herbert Hoover had once probed the federal government's efficiency. Couldn't similar scrutiny be directed at state government? Krabach consulted with Hoover in New York, then sought further advice from Warren J. King, president of Warren King and Associates, a Chicago-based consulting firm. Quickly, the two men drew up ground rules: It would not suffice to "borrow" executives one or two days a week. They would have to recruit the best talent in the state, on a full-time volunteer basis, until the job was done. Governor Rhodes enthusiastically issued an executive order establishing the Council for the Reorganization of Ohio State Government.

At a meeting of the top executives of two dozen Ohio firms,

Krabach called for volunteers. "We're not looking for checkbook patriotism. What we want from your companies is talent. And not just anyone; we need the people you can't spare."

"Who do you want from me?" asked Alfred S. Glossbrenner, then president of Youngstown Sheet & Tube Company.

"Howard Bishop, your chief industrial engineer."

With Bishop as their chairman, 94 Ohio businessmen studied every department of state government. Three months later, they presented 511 recommendations—to save Ohio taxpayers $50 million a year. Reforms included abolition of specific jobs, such as that of the employe whose duty it was to measure the depth of the Toledo-Cincinnati canal—which had been closed for 63 years. Other recommendations called for application of modern business techniques, and even consolidation of whole overlapping agencies. Rhodes implemented nearly 75 percent of the recommendations. Actual annual savings were $60 million—or $10 million above the estimate—and for the next five years Ohio led the United States in its rate of industrial growth.

Encouraged, consultant King took the idea to other states' chief executives. In 1965, Gov. Dan Evans of Washington agreed to give the concept a try. Ninety of that state's top business executives hammered out a report with 670 recommendations. Two-thirds of these were implemented, to save some $20 million per year. Oklahoma businessmen suggested 399 ways to streamline their state's government; 250 of them were okayed, for annual savings of $15 million.

Then, in 1967, Gov. Ronald Reagan of California asked King to coordinate a study in his state. The 252 "loaned executives," divided into seven teams, weighed in with 2000 suggestions. These enabled Reagan to cut spending by $175 million a year.

By 1976, some 20 states had asked King to coordinate management reviews of their governments. More than 1500 businessmen had participated. They offered 14,500 suggestions which could, if put into action, save taxpayers a monster $4.8 billion. (Encouragingly, a large number of those suggestions came from state employes themselves.) Meanwhile, other states—including Missouri, Minnesota and Wisconsin —had instituted programs of their own, and savings there over the years had run into the hundreds of millions.

In almost every state, cost-cutters discovered that government could become more efficient by:

• *Restructuring Agencies to Provide Services More Efficiently.* During the 1960s, West Virginia's welfare rolls had increased dramatically. Thus, when Gov. Arch A. Moore, Jr., took office in 1969, one of his first acts was to ask state businessmen for recommendations to "help bust the welfare cycle." Accepting their suggestions, he merged the state's Welfare and Employment Security departments. He expedited welfare applications by reducing the number of offices—county, district and state—through which they had to make their way, and by installing computer terminals in the county offices.

Moore added refinements of his own. At his instigation, West Virginia became the first state to require that recipients, if able to work, accept appropriate employment. Before, 14,000 welfare fathers had received benefits. Today fewer than 1000 do. Recipients used to average 20 months on the rolls. Today they average seven. The six-week processing time for new applicants has been cut to one. Saving thus far: $60 million. Between 1970 and 1974, the nation's welfare rolls increased by 36.2 percent; in West Virginia, the rolls dropped by 32.4 percent.

Reorganizations and consolidations haven't been limited to welfare departments. Inspired by businessmen's recommendations, Florida is working on the development of a "one-stop" automotive services system to replace its 690 locations for such services as driver's licenses, vehicle inspection, license-plate sales, and processing of titles.

In Connecticut, alarmed by the high cost of maintenance at state buildings in Hartford, businessmen discovered that a private firm would do the job for one-third the price. The saving: $760,000 per year.

• *Insisting on Tighter Money Management.* In Minnesota, members of Gov. Wendell Anderson's volunteer task force found that it took Revenue Department employes an average of 4.5 days to process each incoming check. By depositing checks the day they arrived, the department could reap additional interest of nearly $700,000 per year. In New Jersey, businessmen recommended saving $1.5 million by reducing the amount the state kept in checking accounts and investing the money in securities. Another $4 million could be realized simply by improving the investment portfolio of state pension funds.

• *Stopping Unnecessary Purchasing.* Almost everywhere, businessmen have found, states are buying items they don't need, paying more than they should, and keeping excessive supplies in inventory. Simply by purchasing compact cars instead of standard-size vehicles, businessmen discovered, North Carolina could save $265,000 per year. In Ohio, businessmen learned that one state hospital had bought enough sugar to last it for 16 years.

In Minnesota, executives found that the highway department had enough supplies for 18 months. Their recommendation: keep on hand only enough for three to four months. The department agreed. The $5 million that had formerly been funneled into excess inventory every year was poured instead into concrete, asphalt and blacktop. Result: the state has been able to continue its highway construction program, while some states—because of reduced gasoline-tax revenues and heavy inflation—have had to shut down their programs.

· *Charging Users Fair Fees for State Services.* Copies of birth certificates, professional licenses, driving permits—the list of services that citizens expect from state government is varied and long. Often, states don't charge enough to defray the costs. Ever since 1927, for example, New Jersey had charged a constant $5 fee for issuing teaching certificates—though in the interim teachers' salaries had increased by 700 percent, and the Department of Education was losing money. The businessmen's suggestion: raise the certificate fee to $20, and glean an additional $600,000 per year.

In Alabama, the Governor's Cost Control Survey discovered that the Alcoholic Beverage Control Board was spending $75 to process each annual license renewal for retail beer outlets, but charging just $10. Raise the fee, the businessmen said. (This has not yet been done, as of this writing.) In Iowa, executives concluded that the state could earn $1.4 million by increasing its charges for hunting and fishing licenses and boat registrations. (This was one of the minor recommendations by a blue-ribbon Economy Committee, which has helped Gov. Robert D. Ray cut taxes, expand services, and establish a substantial surplus in the state treasury.)

The mere establishment of a businessmen's task force is, of course, no panacea for the problems that plague state government. Without a determination by the governor to recruit the best talent available, without his firm commitment to implement as many of the recommendations as possible, without follow-through by the businessmen themselves, the effort can fail. Some suggestions may prove impracticable; legislatures may stall others for reasons of their own. Yet, in all but a few of the states which have attempted to improve their management functions, the result has been more efficient, more economical government. And that is what taxpayers want.

Recently, Ohio and Pennsylvania invited businessmen back to study their operations for a second time. One executive involved in the Pennsylvania study—Otto Ehrsam of Bethlehem Steel—was visiting a correctional facility with other members of his team. Invited for lunch, they discovered to their surprise that they did not have to pay. Checking further, they discovered that the state provided free meals to 2700 correctional-bureau employes every day. Annual cost: $745,000. "We decided that this ought to stop," Ehrsam recalls. "We said that there should be no such thing as a free lunch in state government."

POINT MAN FOR THE CARTER REORGANIZATION

If William Harrison Wellford can persuade the federal government to pay its utility bills on time, he will have earned his salary several hundred times over.

This dereliction is now costing the government about $25 million a year in late-payment fees.

Mr. Wellford might be called an efficiency expert, but on the federal payroll he is listed as executive associate director for reorganization and management in the Office of Management and Budget. . . .

Every modern President has taken office determined to improve governmental efficiency and reduce waste. President Carter is no different. How well he succeeds will depend on people like William Harrison Wellford.

To help him ferret out federal mismanagement on many fronts, Mr. Wellford has a small army of experts—130 full-time professionals such as lawyers, accountants and engineers, plus another 200 on loan from other agencies. Additionally, several American companies have donated the services of some of their top management people.

The $25 million for delinquent payment of utility bills turned up by the Wellford sleuths may be only the tip of an iceberg that juts out of a sea of weak federal management. Take the telephone system, for example.

"For the past 10 years the government's use of telephones has been going up by about 16 percent annually," Mr. Wellford says. "In private business the increase has been only nine percent. Why the difference? The federal work force has not grown. I was amazed to learn that no one is really managing this telephone system. No one even knows how many phones are in use by the government. This area could involve the waste of many millions of dollars." . . .

Cash management is a phrase that crops up frequently in any discussion of government reorganization. Every major corporation, and smaller businesses as well, learned a long time ago that every idle dollar is a wasted dollar. The government is just getting around to learning that axiom. By putting new cash-management techniques into play, the government is expected to save $125 million in 1978 and 1979.

Paying and collecting bills on time will account for a large part of these savings. By simply issuing letters of credit instead of lump

Reprinted by permission of Nation's Business. Nation's Business Vol. 66, October 1978.

sum grants, the government will save $41 million this year. For example, if a university has been approved for a $10 million grant to be spent over three years, it will draw funds as they are needed instead of getting the $10 million all at once. The money which remains behind will earn interest for Uncle Sam.

If the government isn't frittering money away by paying its utility bill late, it is wasting money by paying other bills too early. A General Accounting Office study found that the government, in one recent year, paid $118 million more in interest than was necessary on money borrowed to pay bills well before they fell due.

"We have brought in a number of business executives who are experts in cash management, and that is beginning to pay off handsomely," says Mr. Wellford. "Before they are finished, they will have set into motion some simple cash management practices that will save the taxpayers many millions of dollars."

Business has given the Wellford investigators many examples of governmental inefficiency. One glaring case is the paperwork and red tape confronting companies trying to meet the requirements of the Employee Retirement Income Security Act administered by both the Treasury and Labor departments.

"In response to an enormous amount of comment from business people, we have been pushing these two departments to get together and sort out their differences," says Mr. Wellford.

The effort may be paying off. Under a paperwork reduction proposal before Congress, the estimated nine million man-hours spent annually by business filling out ERISA forms would be halved, saving an estimated $25 million. . . .

The expertise of private business has been welcomed by the reorganizers who say they recognize the need to impose business methods of operation on government.

"We get these experts from the larger corporations, but I would like to see more brought in from the smaller companies." Mr. Wellford says. "They have much to offer."

Unfortunately, he says, most of these volunteers are available for only three to six months.

"This does not give them the time they would like to stay with a problem until it is solved," he says.

"Bringing reform to government is a tedious process. These people bring not only their special expertise but also their outside views on everything that is going on. They challenge us."

The government has a multimillion-dollar investment in computers that not only help in running the day-to-day operations, but also play an important part in the conduct of national security. The Wellford investigators found the federal computer system lagging behind private industry's. The hardware was not always right for the particular job, and computer personnel were poorly or inadequately trained.

"We would have liked to have gone outside for the experts that could have straightened us out, but there are strong conflict-of-interest regulations which held us back," Mr. Wellford explains. "Anyone directly associated with the computer industry could not get in the door."

The government did get help, however, from computer personnel with Coca-Cola and several other large corporations where conflict of interest was not a problem. . . .

CITIES DISCOVERING MERITS OF PRIVATE CONTRACTING FOR SERVICES

Robert W. Poole, Jr.

Four years ago Camden, N.J., had 90 garbage collectors operating 16 trucks. Today Camden's garbage is being picked up by a private firm using only 35 employees and nine trucks. The same firm—O'Connor Corp.—took over trash collection in Collingswood, N.J., in January, replacing 12 city workers with one man and a modern side-loading truck. In nearby Pitman Borough the conversion to private enterprise occurred February 1. Three men and one truck replaced 14 city employes and five trucks.

What's happening in southern New Jersey trash collection is no fluke. All across the country budget-conscious city officials are discovering the merits of private contracting.

Because they're in business to make money, private firms are more cost-conscious than city agencies. They seek out modern, automated equipment that can be operated by fewer employees. They analyze the work to develop more efficient methods. And they're better labor bargainers, paying competitive wages but avoiding over-generous pensions and fringe benefits that are bankrupting some cities.

Best of all, from an administrator's standpoint, contracting minimizes bureaucracy and red tape. The company is fully responsible for

Reprinted with permission by Human Events. Human Events Vol. 38, June 17, 1978.

doing the job—and can be held accountable by contract. No longer need the department head or city council fight endless battles over work rules or modernization. "The headaches are what you really get rid of," says Collingswood Mayor Michael G. Brennan.

While Eastern cities are replacing inefficient municipal departments with private contractors, many Western cities have avoided ever setting up the departments. In California some 35 cities which have incorporated since 1958 belong to the California Contract Cities Association. These cities rely on contracts for a substantial portion of their public services. Typically, their suppliers include the county government and a number of private firms; occasionally, a larger adjacent city may also supply a service by contract.

Altogether, there are 36 different kinds of services being obtained by contract in these cities, under a total of 401 different contracts. The county government is the principal contract supplier of law enforcement services and supplies a portion of many of the others—such as engineering and street maintenance. But private firms provide a great variety of services, including tree trimming, park maintenance, street sweeping, traffic signal maintenance, and pavement striping.

Santa Fe Springs found that it could cut its tree trimming budget by 36 per cent by contracting with a private firm instead of using city crews. A survey by the association found that for engineering contracts in excess of $5,000, cities could get faster and cheaper service from private firms, despite the wide range of specialists available on the county engineer's staff.

A good example of a contract city is Lafayette, Calif. Incorporated in 1968, Lafayette is a mostly residential suburb of Oakland and Berkeley, with 13 square miles and about 20,000 people. In deciding to incorporate, the voters aimed at making maximum use of contracting services, in order to avoid entirely the need for a city property tax and keep city employes to a bare minimum. So far, they have succeeded.

Lafayette's 1977–78 city budget totals only $2.1 million—about $105 per capita. The city has only six full-time employes, supplemented by two part-timers and eight federally funded CETA workers. Many of the public services in Lafayette are provided by other public entities, via special districts. This includes water, sewers, transit and schools. But most other services are provided by contract, either with Contra Costa County or with private firms. And recently the trend has been to shift from county services to private contractors.

Last August Lafayette switched its public works contract from the county to a private firm—RJA Maintenance Contractors, a subsidiary of Maryland-based Roy Jorgensen & Associates, a large management consulting firm. The city expects to save money under the new contract—its first-year cost of $398,645 is only a 4 per cent increase over last year. The county would have charged 10 per cent more.

Bigger savings are expected in the future because of the contractor's flexibility. RJA operates with a single full-time manager, hiring subcontractors as needed for specific street and storm drain maintenance projects. Without a full-time crew to keep busy, it can concentrate on doing only the jobs the city really wants done.

"Contracting of work has a tremendous advantage during slack periods," reports RJA manager Maynard Crowther. "You don't have to find work for employes. And there's an advantage to not having to negotiate with unions or be strapped with the civil service system, which at times is not very flexible." Further, the city doesn't have to buy a lot of specialized equipment that would end up sitting around most of the time.

The ability of contracting to save taxpayers money has been verified by independent studies. Last year economist Robert Deacon of the University of California at Santa Barbara carried out a statistical analysis of contract versus non-contract cities in Los Angeles County.

Comparing 23 contract cities with 41 non-contract cities in a sophisticated computer model, Deacon focused on police protection and street maintenance, the two most frequently contracted services there. He found, on the average, that street maintenance cost 43 per cent more in the non-contract cities, police protection 72 per cent more.

Deacon identified several reasons for the lower cost of contract services. One is what economists call "economies of scale"—i.e., that there is generally a most efficient size for an enterprise producing a good or service. It is quite unlikely that the area and population of a city define the optimum size for each of its many different public services.

Contracting permits a city to select a supplier that is more likely to be an efficient size. Secondly, enterprises are more efficient when they face competition. When suppliers are selected by contract, they must compete instead of acting like monopolists. Third, city departments tend to overproduce services, due to the natural tendency of civil service employes to feather their own nests. Contract suppliers can't afford this expensive tendency.

These facts account for the boom in municipal contracting. Whether replacing age-encrusted bureaucracies or giving new cities a lean, flexible start, contracting clearly represents a break for the taxpayer.

Section III
POLITICS AND
POLICY MAKING

Section I emphasized neutrality and Section II, models of efficiency. Inflexible adherence to supposed management "truths" or "the one best way" leaves little room for compromise between competing values. But a major trend in public administration has been based on recognizing that the dichotomy between politics and administration is not realistic. Major appointed administrative officials often take the lead in making policy, and officials at lower levels must be involved in interpreting policies. A more realistic concept is: public administration = politics + management.

The "politics" emphasis argues that in a political system in which many groups have a voice (pluralism), bureaucrats with substantial expertise play key roles. Indeed, legislation is written as often by bureaucrats as by legislators. The bureaucracy is as capable as any other participant in the political process of mobilizing support for its interests, as likely as any to become part of a policy-making coalition.

Once a law has been enacted, it is interpreted administratively in its execution. Thus, as the final step in the policy-making process, administration is the "last chance" to influence policy. Laws written in only a few pages must be interpreted in many and often unanticipated specific cases. With such discretion, agencies become the objects of policy preferences from external sources—interest groups, legislators, the media, individuals, and so on. Internally, within an agency, officials often become advocates for the external pressures to which the organization is subjected—arguing for or against certain positions and interpretations.

One way to make the policy-making process more objective is to make it more logical. The rational-comprehensive school argues that the best made decisions are logically made. Alternatively, incrementalists defend the present "muddling through" process as realistic, as being able to respond to the interests of many groups without freezing any out, as being able to respond to crisis pressures and deadlines, and as not requiring the massive investments of time and effort that "logical" decisions necessitate.

The cases in this section stress the interaction of political values and administration: the exercise of administrative discretion in interpreting policy directives, the need to decide between countervailing values and interests, and the relation between external and administrative advocates of policies. This section also illustrates the policy process: the need to decide, the need for information and the role of the expert, and the rational and incremental decision styles.

Introduction
Warning—National Security May
Be Hazardous to Your Health

Laws are administratively interpreted in their execution. As the final step in the policy-making process, administration is the ultimate focal point of the process. It is the "last chance" to influence policy. Laws written in only a few pages must be interpreted in many and often unanticipated specific cases. Administrative discretion, then, is a fact necessitated, rather than precluded, by the law. Administrative agencies are the objects of outside pressures, often by interest groups and legislators, because administrative initiative in drafting policy and administrative discretion in interpreting policy inherently include value preferences. Even so-called "technical" decisions are actually value laden.

Interest pressure fields are also to be found inside public organizations. Officials often become advocates for the external pressures to which the organization is subjected—arguing for or against strict automobile exhaust standards, advocating or disparaging the necessity for nuclear-generating plant cooling towers.

The Beryllium case illustrates both facets of policymaking—external and internal. After an initial decision by OSHA to tighten standards, industrialists placed direct pressure to reverse the decision. And, within the bureaucracy, cabinet level officials reflected those arguments.

QUESTIONS FOR DISCUSSION

Was OSHA's decision a reasonable one, or should worker exposure have been cut to almost zero micrograms?

Why would Califano and Schlesinger have sided with industry? because of political pressure from the White House? because of personal gain? because of concerns over national security?

Who should make such value decisions as balancing national security against the health of workers?

Were pressures by industrialists unethical?

WARNING—NATIONAL SECURITY MAY BE HAZARDOUS TO YOUR HEALTH

Edward Sorel

In 1968, Health, Education and Welfare officials were informed by private research sources that exposure to the metal beryllium could cause fatal respiratory disease and cancer. After months went by without government actions (beryllium is a critical component in aerospace and nuclear industries), a Massachusetts researcher threatened to make her findings public. At that point, a senior HEW official wrote a memo, warning: "This would be a bombshell if her views would ever get into print." To avoid such a bombshell, the government initiated its own tests, and when they found strong evidence of the metal's danger as a human poison and carcinogen, they did the only thing possible under the circumstances: They ordered more tests.

Finally, in 1976, the Labor Department's Occupational Safety and Health Administration (OSHA) finished adding up the corpses and concluded that perhaps the 30,000 workers who are exposed to beryllium dust and fumes *should* have a bit more protection. They proposed new regulations cutting worker exposure from two micrograms to one microgram per cubic meter of air.

The two companies that produce beryllium insisted that they could not meet the proposed standard with current technology. Suddenly, HEW started getting a lot of phone calls from industrial fat cats and capital politicos strongly suggesting the proposed new standards were ill-advised. Senator John Glenn, whose home state of Ohio manufactures the stuff, went straight to the top and began badgering Joseph A. Califano Jr., HEW Secretary, for an independent review of the whole issue. At this point, Mr. Califano, whose concern with preventing lung cancer from cigarettes is well publicized, decided to take a more tolerant attitude toward cancer from beryllium. He wrote a letter to Glenn promising that yet another review of the beryllium matter would be undertaken.

Here the matter might have disappeared for another ten years had not the bullheaded James R. Schlesinger entered the china shop. Mr. S., who had previously served his country as head of the CIA and

By Edward Sorel from Esquire magazine (November 7, 1978). © 1978 by Esquire Magazine Inc.

Defense, is now, as all the world knows, head of the Energy Department. On August 30, he wrote Ray Marshall, Secretary of Labor, saying that a study by his department concluded that the cost of meeting the proposed exposure standards for beryllium would drive the only two non-Communist producers of the metal out of business and cut off the U.S. supply. "The loss of beryllium production capability," he wrote, "would seriously impact our ability to develop and produce weapons for the nuclear stockpile and consequently, adversely affect our national security."

In other words, the national security of this nation depends on us not doing anything to protect the lives of 30,000 Americans.

If this is patriotism, I'll take subversion.

The Swine Flu Affair

MEMORANDUM TO THE SECRETARY

The top positions in administrative agencies are characteristically filled by political appointment. Executives are chosen for their administrative ability and for their commitment to carrying out the kinds of policies that the particular leadership favors. Such people often move from post to post. They are seldom experts in the subject with which the agency deals. In making important decisions, then, they are influenced to a great extent by the way in which the "experts" within the agency present the problems and possible alternatives to them.

Although such policymakers rarely make an effort to analyze their own experiences as lessons for future policymaking, Secretary of the Department of Health, Education, and Welfare, Joseph Califano made that effort after the decision on the swine flu vaccine. The reasons for pursuing that analysis are best put in his own words:

> As a lawyer and former special assistant to former Secretary of Defense Robert S. McNamara and President Lyndon Johnson, I had frequently faced situations with little or no initial knowledge of the complex substance of the events or subject matter involved. This swine flu situation surprised and bedeviled me, however, because I knew so little that it was difficult even to determine *the questions to ask* in an attempt to reach an intelligent decision.
>
> During this experience—and the review of the swine flu program it occasioned—I was struck that those who might find themselves facing sensitive health policy decisions could benefit greatly from a careful study of that program.
>
> If the swine flu experience had any lessons to teach, it was important that we learn them. If there had been mistakes or missteps—however well-intentioned—it was important to learn what they were so we might

not repeat them, either in immunization policy or in other, similar decision-making contexts.*

One of the documents appended to the study that Califano commissioned was a memorandum, prepared to acquaint the secretary with the facts and with the pro's and con's of possible courses of action to meet the anticipated swine flu epidemic. But one piece of information was not included: the strong opinion of government virologist Anthony Morris that the vaccine should not be used because it was ineffective and perhaps dangerous.

The impetus for making a crucial decision is often so strong that individual warnings are ignored without careful consideration of their validity. Employees who sound embarrassing warnings are often silenced. They are fired, demoted, reassigned, or left in place without meaningful responsibility. In a brief alternative to HEW's account, *The Bureaucrat* questions whether Dr. J. Anthony Morris was unconscionably ignored, resulting in deaths, paralysis, and costly waste. The fact that dissents, such as that of Dr. Morris, have often proven valid has led to new, recent policies of protecting the employee who calls outside attention to problems. The suggestion has also been offered that provision should be made for presenting any dissenting "minority opinions" along with the prevailing opinion and policy recommendations.

QUESTIONS FOR DISCUSSION

Secretary Califano himself raised the following questions in his introduction to the swine flu study that he had commissioned:

"First, how shall top lay officials, who are not themselves expert, deal with fundamental policy questions that are based, in part, on highly technical and complex expert knowledge—especially when that knowledge is speculative, or hotly debated, or when 'the facts' are so uncertain?"

"When such questions arise, with how much deference and how much skepticism should those whose business is doing things and making policy view those whose business is knowing things—the scientists and the experts?"

"How should policymakers—and their expert advisers—seek to involve and to educate the public and relevant parties on such complicated and technical issues? To what extent can there be informed and robust public debate before the decision is reached?"

What percentage of current policymakers in HEW or other agencies, do you think, have bothered to read *The Swine Flu Affair* or any similar analysis of how policy is made?

* Richard E. Neustadt and Harvey V. Fineberg, M.D., *The Swine Flu Affair: Decision-Making on a Slippery Disease* (Washington, D.C.: U.S. Government Printing Office, 1978), p. iv.

MEMORANDUM

Department of Health, Education, and Welfare
Office of the Assistant Secretary for Health

TO: The Secretary   Date: Mar 18 1976
           Through: ES MK 3/18
FROM: Assistant Secretary for Health
SUBJECT: Swine Influenza—Action

ISSUE

How should the Federal Government respond to the influenza problem caused by a new virus?

FACTS

1. In February 1976 a new strain of influenza virus, designated as influenza A/New Jersey/76 (Hsw1N1), was isolated from an outbreak of disease among recruits in training at Fort Dix, New Jersey.
2. The virus is antigenically related to the influenza virus which has been implicated as the cause of the 1918–1919 pandemic which has killed 450,000 people—more than 400 of every 100,000 Americans.
3. The entire U.S. population under the age of 50 is probably susceptible to this new strain.
4. Prior to 1930, this strain was the predominate cause of human influenza in the U.S. Since 1930, the virus has been limited to transmission among swine with only occasional transmission from swine to man—with no secondary person-to-person transmission
5. In an average year, influenza causes about 17,000 deaths (9 per 100,000 population) and costs the nation approximately $500 million.
6. Severe epidemics, or pandemics, of influenza occur at approximately 10 year intervals. In 1968–69, influenza struck 20 percent of our population, causing more than 33,000 deaths (14 per 100,000) and cost an estimated $3.2 billion.
7. A vaccine to protect against swine influenza can be developed before the next flu season; however, the production of large

quantities would require extraordinary efforts by drug manufacturers.

ASSUMPTIONS

1. Although there has been only one outbreak of A/swine influenza, person-to-person spread has been proven and additional
   outbreaks cannot be ruled out. Present evidence and past
   experience indicate a strong possibility that this country will
   experience widespread A/swine influenza in 1976–77. Swine flu
   represents a major antigenic shift from recent viruses and the
   population under 50 is almost universally susceptible. These
   are the ingredients for a pandemic.
2. Routine public health influenza recommendations (immuniza-
   tions of the population at high risk—elderly and chronically ill
   persons) would not forestall a flu pandemic. Routine actions
   would have to be supplemented.
3. The situation is one of "go or no go." If extraordinary measures
   are to be undertaken there is barely enough time to assure
   adequate vaccine production and to mobilize the nation's health
   care delivery system. Any extensive immunization program
   would have to be in full scale operation by the beginning of
   September and should not last beyond the end of November
   1976. A decision must be made now.
4. There is no medical epidemiologic basis for excluding any
   part of the population—swine flu vaccine will be recommended
   for the total population except in individual cases. Similarly
   there is no public health or epidemiologic rationale for narrow-
   ing down the targeted population. Further, it is assumed that
   it would be socially and politically unacceptable to *plan* for less
   than 100 percent coverage. Therefore, it is assumed that any
   recommendations for action must be directed toward the goal
   of immunizing 213 million people in three months (September
   through November 1976). The nation has never attempted an
   immunization program of such scope and intensity.
5. A public health undertaking of this magnitude cannot succeed
   without Federal leadership, sponsorship, and some level of
   financial support.
6. The vaccine when purchased in large quantities will cost
   around 50 cents per dose. Nationally, the vaccine will cost in
   excess of $100 million. To this total must be added delivery
   costs, as well as costs related to surveillance and monitoring.
   Part, but not all, of the costs can be considered sunk costs, or as

non-additive. Regardless of what strategy is adopted, it will be extremely difficult to estimate the amount of additional costs that will result from a crash influenza immunization program.

7. The Advisory Committee on Immunization Practices will recommend formally and publicly, the immunization of the total U.S. population against A/swine influenza.

8. Any recommended course of action, other than no action, must assure:

that a supply of vaccine is produced which is adequate to immunize the whole population.

that adequate supplies of vaccine are available as needed at health care delivery points.

that the American people are made aware of the need for immunization against this flu virus.

that the population systematically reach or be reached by the health system.

that the Public Health Service maintain epidemiologic, laboratory, and immunization surveillance of the population for complications of vaccination, for influenza morbidity and mortality, and for vaccine effectiveness and efficacy.

that the unique research opportunities be maximized.

that evaluation of the effectiveness of the efforts is conducted.

ALTERNATIVE COURSES OF ACTION

1. No Action

An argument can be made for taking no extraordinary action beyond what would normally be recommended. To date there has been only one outbreak. The swine flu virus has been around, but has not caused a problem among humans since 1930.

PRO

The market place would prevail—private industry (drug manufacturers) would produce in accordance with its estimate of demand and the consumers would make their own decisions. Similarly, States would respond in accordance with their own sets of priorities.

The "pandemic" might not occur and the Department would have avoided unnecessary health expenditures.

Any real action would require direct Federal intervention which is contrary to current administration philosophy.

CON

Congress, the media, and the American people will expect some action.

The Administration can tolerate unnecessary health expenditures better than unnecessary death and illness, particularly if a flu pandemic should occur.

In all likelihood, Congress will act on its own initiative.

2. Minimum Response

Under this option there would be a limited Federal role with primary reliance on delivery systems now in place and on spontaneous, nongovernmental action.

   a. The Federal Government would advise the drug industry to develop and produce A/swine vaccine sufficient to immunize the general population. The Federal Government would underwrite this effort by promising to purchase vaccine for the 58 million Federal beneficiaries.

   b. A nationwide public awareness program would be undertaken to serve as general backdrop for local programs.

   c. The Public Health Service would stimulate community programs sponsored by local organizations (medical societies, associations, industries, etc.).

   d. The Center for Disease Control would maintain epidemiologic and laboratory surveillance of the population.

   e. The National Institutes of Health would conduct studies and investigations, particularly on new and improved vaccines.

PRO

The approach is characterized by high visibility, minimum Federal intervention, and diffused liability and responsibility. It is a partnership with the private sector that relies on Federal stimulation of nongovernmental action.

The burden on the Federal budget would be minimal. Assuming purchase of vaccines for 58 million beneficiaries, plus additional costs related to c., d., and e., above the total new obligational authority requirement would not exceed $40 million ($32 million for vaccine; plus 8 million for surveillance, monitoring, evaluation, and research).

Success would depend upon widespread voluntary action—in terms of individual choice to seek immunization and in terms of voluntary community programs not unlike the polio programs of the past.

CON

There is little assurance that vaccine manufacturers will undertake the massive production effort that would be required to assure availability of vaccine for the entire nation.

There would be no control over the distribution of vaccines to the extent that they are available; the poor, the near poor, and the aging usually get left out. Even under routine flu recommendations in which the elderly are a primary target, only about half the high risk population gets immunized against flu.

Probably only about half the population would get immunized.

3. Government Program

This alternative is based on virtually total government responsibility for the nationwide immunization program.

   a. The Federal Government would advise vaccine manufacturers to embark on full scale production of vaccine with the expectation of Federal purchase of up to 200 million doses.
   b. The Public Health Service, through the CDC would purchase the vaccines for distribution to State Health Departments.
   c. In each State the health department would organize and carry out an immunization program designed to reach 100 percent of the State's population. Vaccine would be available only through programs carried out under aegis of the State health department (or the Federal Government for direct Federal beneficiaries).
   d. Primary reliance would be placed on systematic, planned delivery of vaccine in such a way as to make maximum use of intensive, high volume immunization techniques and procedures—particularly the use of jet-injector guns.
   e. In addition to a general nationwide awareness program, intensive promotion and outreach activities would be carried out at the local level. Maximum use would be made of temporary employment of unemployed workers, high school and college students, housewives, and retired people as outreach workers and for jobs requiring no special health skills.
   f. The Center for Disease Control would maintain epidemiologic and laboratory surveillance of the population.
   g. The National Institutes of Health would conduct studies and investigations, particularly on new and improved vaccines.
   h. The program would be evaluated to assess the effectiveness of the effort in reducing influenza associated morbidity, hospitalization, and mortality in a pandemic period.

PRO

Under this alternative adequate availability of vaccine would be closest to certainty, and the vaccine would be distributed throughout the nation most equitably.

There would be greater certainty of participation of all States as well as a predictably more uniform level of intensity across the nation.

Accessibility to immunization services would not depend upon economic status.

This approach would provide the framework for better planning— for example, the use of travelling immunization teams which could take the vaccine to the people; and greater use of the jet injector, and other mass immunization techniques.

The Federal and State governments traditionally have been responsible for the control of communicable diseases; therefore, the strategy relies upon government action in an area of public health where the States are strong and where basic operating mechanisms exist.

CON

This alternative would be very costly and given the timing, the magnitude of the problem, and the status of State fiscal health, the costs would have to be borne by the Federal Government. The impact on the Federal budget would be an increase of $190 million in new obligational authority.

The approach is inefficient to the extent that it fails to take advantage of the private sector health delivery system, placing too much reliance on public clinics and government action.

While this approach would undoubtedly result in a higher percentage of the population being immunized than would be the case with the *Minimum Response* strategy (alternative 2); it is unlikely that the public sector could achieve uniform high levels of protection. Although socioeconomic barriers to immunization services would be virtually eliminated, breakdowns would occur because the program is beyond the scope of official agencies.

A totally "public" program is contrary to the spirit and custom of health care delivery in this country and should only be considered if it is clearly the most effective approach.

4. Combined Approach

A program based on this strategy would take advantage of the strengths and resources of both the public and private sectors. Successful immunization of our population in three months' time can be accomplished only in this manner in this country. In essence, the plan would rely on: the Federal Government for its technical leadership and coordination, and its purchase power; State health agencies for their experience in conducting immunization programs and as logical distribution centers for vacine; and on the private sector for its medical and other resources which must be mobilized.

   a. The Federal Government would advise vaccine manufacturers to embark on full scale production of enough vaccine to immunize the American people. The Public Health Service would contract for 200 million doses of vaccine which would be made available at no cost through State Health agencies.
   b. State health agencies would develop plans to immunize the people in their States through a combination of official and voluntary action—travelling immunization teams, community programs, private physician practices, as examples.
   c. The strategy would be to tailor the approach to the situation or opportunity—using mass immunization techniques where appropriate, but also using delivery points already in place such as: physicians' offices, health department clinics, community health centers—any place with the competence to perform immunization services.
   d. Awareness campaigns would be carried out at the local level against a broader, generalized nationwide effort. Use would be made of unemployed workers, students, etc., for certain jobs.
   e. The Center for Disease Control would maintain epidemiologic and laboratory surveillance of the population.
   f. The National Institutes of Health would conduct studies and investigations of vaccine effectiveness and efficacy.
   g. The program would be evaluated to assess the effectiveness of the effort in reducing influenza associated morbidity, hospitalization, and mortality in a pandemic period.

PRO

   Under this alternative adequate availability of vaccine would be closest to certainty, and the vaccine would be distributed throughout the nation most equitably.

   There would be greater certainty of participation of all States as well as a predictably more uniform level of intensity across the nation.

   Accessibility to immunization services would not depend upon socioeconomic factors.

   Making use of all delivery points better assures that the vaccine will get to more people.

The approach provides the framework for planning and expands the scope of resources which can be applied.

Undertaking the program in this manner provides a practical, contemporary example of government, industry, and private citizens cooperating to serve a common cause.

CON

This strategy would require substantial Federal expenditures. A supplemental request of approximately $134 million would be needed.

Under this alternative there is the greatest possibility of some people being needlessly reimmunized.

DISCUSSION

Any of the courses of action would raise budgetary and authorization questions and these will be discussed later. More important is the question of what the Federal Government is willing to invest if some action is deemed necessary to avert a possible influenza pandemic. We have not undertaken a health program of this scope and intensity before in our history. There are no precedents, nor mechanisms in place that are suited to an endeavor of this magnitude. Given this situation, can we afford the administrative and programmatic inflexibility that would result from normal considerations about duplicative costs, third party reimbursements, and Federal-State or public-private relationships and responsibilities? The magnitude of the challenge suggests that the Department must either be willing to take extraordinary steps or be willing to accept an approach to the problem that cannot succeed.

It is recommended that the Department, through the Public Health Service and the Center for Disease Control, undertake an influenza immunization campaign as outlined in alternative 4, "Combined Approach." This alternative best satisfies all of the minimum program requirements outlined earlier and more importantly, it is the most likely to succeed—more people would be protected.

The question of legislative authorization is not entirely clear. It would appear that Section 311 a. of the Public Health Service Act contains adequate authority to implement the recommended program. If 311 a. cannot be used, then it will be necessary to seek "point of order" authority in the supplemental appropriation act. It is anticipated that Congress would be receptive to "point of order" language in this instance.

It will be necessary to seek a supplemental appropriation so that all parties can begin to mobilize for the big push in the fall. It will also be necessary for the funds to be available until expended because the program, although time-limited, falls into fiscal year 1976, the transition quarter, and fiscal year 1977. In general terms the request would be for approximately $134 million made up as follows:

Immunization Programs	
(vaccines, supplies, temporary personnel, awareness)	$126 million
Surveillance and Research	8 million

RECOMMENDATION

It is recommended that the Secretary adopt alternative 4 as the Department's strategy and that the Public Service be given responsibility for the program and be directed to begin immediate implementation.

(signed) James F. Dickson
for Theodore Cooper, M.D.

SWINE FLU

Dr. J. Anthony Morris

Dr. J. Anthony Morris, a government virologist, took on an entire administration over the swine flu vaccination program—and paid with his job. But Morris' firing is only the latest episode in a struggle that stretches back over a decade.

During the late 1960s, Morris' experiments with flu vaccines led him to conclude that the vaccines were ineffective and perhaps dangerous. Among the vaccine-related risks he encountered were muscle aches and pains; headaches, from mild to acute, which might persist from a few hours to weeks; and paralysis, from tingling fingers and arms, to nerve damage. Finally, swine flu can cause Guillain-Barré syndrome, a disease which leads to paralysis and death. Morris felt that the mass inoculation program was particularly dangerous because of the difficulty involved in accurately measuring the vaccine's potency.

After reporting his findings to superiors at the National Institutes

Published by permission of Transaction, Inc. from THE BUREAUCRAT, Vol. 6, No. 4. Copyright © 1977 by The Bureaucrat, Inc.

of Health, Morris was moved into a small office with no phone and his reports were ignored. Valuable research animals were killed. Morris later testified before a congressional committee looking into mismanagement at NIH.

A General Accounting Office inquiry confirmed many of Morris' allegations, and his program was shifted to the Food and Drug Administration. Morris' responsibility at the FDA was to examine vaccines for hazards posed by slow, latent, and temperate viruses. Meanwhile, in 1972, a three-member grievance panel agreed that Morris had indeed been harassed for his outspoken opposition to many vaccine programs.

Morris kept an eye on the vaccines in his new job, and when a Fort Dix flu-related death caused the government to launch its massive vaccination program, the outspoken virologist began a one-man program to publicize the risks of taking the swine flu shots.

After President Ford ordered the inoculation program, Morris gave a series of seminars at NIH, and wrote letters to the *New York Times* and the heads of NIH and FDA. Federal health experts were embarrassed by Morris' actions and allegations, particularly since he discovered that live flu vaccines might be carcinogenic. Despite Morris' objections, the vaccine, tested on human subjects and approved by Congress as a potential cure-all for the flu, was ready for mass dissemination.

Six days after Morris sent his letter opposing the program to FDA commissioner Alexander M. Schmidt, he was fired on the grounds of "insubordination and inefficiency." Morris responded to the insubordination charges by saying, "When the president tells me to buy 12 chairs, I will buy 12 chairs. But when the president tells me to vaccinate every man, woman, and child against swine flu, I will refuse because it is dangerous and a nonaccomplishable goal."

The Civil Service Commission ruled in Dr. Morris' favor on the scientific merits of his case (except for one minor exception), but ruled against him because he refused to carry out orders—orders which Dr. Morris felt had perilous public consequences. He will now bring his case to federal court.

Meanwhile, the swine flu epidemic never came, and in its place came the Guillain-Barré syndrome. By the time the swine flu vaccinations were halted in December of 1976, 12 Americans had died of Guillain-Barré, and more than 250 had been paralyzed. Outbreaks of the disease were seven times greater among the vaccinated than the unvaccinated.

As a result of the program, $400 million in claims have been filed against the government, and the Justice Department has already hired 25 lawyers to assist in the defense.

Introduction
All the President's Women

After a policy is formulated, its implementation is far from assured. Each year the federal government fails to spend some of its appropriations. Each year many groups in our society doubt that governments at all levels are really committed to implementing policies; they object that job training programs lag, that safety regulations are not enforced, that housing discrimination is not effectively combatted, and so on. Having won policy victories in the legislatures and the courts, representatives of those groups have shifted their efforts and tactics to the less glamorous bureaucracy in order to achieve effective policy implementation.

The case of women appointed to the Carter Administration highlights a particularly organized and effective campaign to win implementation of a specific electoral promise as well as legislation prohibiting discrimination on the basis of sex. But even in an arena where the failure to keep such promises is very visible (the media kept a running tally of appointments of females), obstacles were substantial: difficulty of access to the president, negative attitudes among his advisers, personality conflicts, scarcity of "qualified" women. Yet the woman's groups were sophisticated enough to appreciate the need for political support—the need to mobilize external forces for supposedly "internal" decisions.

QUESTIONS FOR DISCUSSION

Can you cite examples of other policies or laws that are made with great "commitment" and fanfare but which "wither away" when it comes to implementation?

Were middle-class women's groups more effective in their efforts than groups of poor people would be in battling the bureaucracy? Why?

What attitudes do people generally hold about the bureaucracy's commitment to implementing policies?

Do bureaucrats tend to think "safely" of reasons not to carry out policies—rather than reasons to implement them?

ALL THE PRESIDENT'S WOMEN

Helen Dimos Schwindt

If you had asked any politically savvy feminist a year ago how much she expected Jimmy Carter to do for women, she might well have answered that she had high hopes and low expectations. He had, after all, promised during the campaign to "tear down the walls" that kept women out of the decision- and policy-making processes in government. But then other Presidential candidates had promised women some part of the moon. Now, a year into the new Administration and many months after the frenzied appointments process was basically completed, if you asked that same woman to assess the Administration's effort, she would be likely to reply: "Less than I hoped for; far, far less than women needed; but more than I expected."

Taking into account a fierce lobbying effort mounted by women last year, the resulting 12 percent of Presidential appointments looks terrible. But inside Carter's Administration, the women themselves tend to rate the efforts with qualified approval. As Carol Tucker Foreman, a new Assistant Secretary in the Department of Agriculture, put it: "Women until now have been systematically excluded from government. Now they're being systematically included. That makes a big difference."

Jimmy Carter can boast of appointing more women to high office than any President before him. There are two female Cabinet members, Patricia Roberts Harris at the Department of Housing and Urban Development (HUD) and Juanita Kreps at the Department of Commerce. (The Roosevelt, Eisenhower, and Ford administrations had one woman Cabinet member each.) And there are two women Under Secretaries: Lucy Wilson Benson at the State Department, and Bette Anderson at Treasury. There are also at this writing two women Assistant Attorneys General, 10 Assistant Secretaries, and women heading the National Highway Traffic Safety Administration and the Equal Employment Opportunity Commission. There is even the first woman on the Securities and Exchange Commission, which oversees one of the last strongholds of male exclusiveness, Wall Street.

Still, the actual number of appointments was disappointing, and even many Administration officials expected the figures to be higher.

But, as Carol Foreman points out: "Percentages don't tell the whole story. You have to look at the quality of the positions." And the caliber of the women appointees is certainly impressive. Most have strong feminist leanings even if they lack public activist credentials. . . .

Reprinted with permission by Ms. Magazine. Ms Vol. 6, January 1978.

In many cases, they had cultivated broad support networks before coming into government. Some come from consumer advocacy organizations—Foreman was co-opted from her very successful Consumer Federation of America, for instance, to run Agriculture's Food and Consumer Services. And Joan Claybrook, who is Administrator of the National Highway Safety Administration, was chief lobbyist for Ralph Nader's Congress Watch.

Two outstanding public interest lawyers have gone to the Justice Department as Assistant Attorneys General. Barbara Babcock, a Stanford law professor who founded a San Francisco organization called Equal Rights Advocates, now heads the Civil Division. And Patricia Wald, a former legal services attorney and Director of Litigation for the Mental Health Law Project in Washington, is heading the Office of Legislative Affairs.

Many of the appointees also bring political expertise to their new jobs. At State, for example, there is Patt Derian, a former Democratic National Committeewoman from Mississippi and a long-time political worker with roots in the Southern civil rights movement. She's now Coordinator of Human Rights and Humanitarian Affairs. Patsy T. Mink's committee work on the Hill when she was Representative from Hawaii made her one of Washington's most knowledgeable experts on environments and natural resources—an expertise she'll be able to use as Assistant Secretary for Oceans and International Environment and Scientific Affairs. A resolute feminist, she was an early supporter of the National Women's Political Caucus, and coauthored the legislation that mandated the National Women's Conference in Houston and the 50 state conferences that preceded it.

Carter should also be given some credit for appointing women with enough conviction and strength to disagree with him, sometimes even in public. A sign that he could tolerate public dissent gracefully occurred at the press conference to announce Juanita Krep's appointment in December, 1976. After he remarked to reporters that it was difficult to find qualified women, Kreps stepped forward to assert that she thought "it would be hard to defend the proposition that there are not a great many qualified women." As all faces turned toward him, he retorted mildly, "I think she said she disagrees with me!" Try to imagine Presidents Johnson or Nixon doing that.

Last but hardly not least, the Carter Administration has named women to the kinds of positions that can in no way be construed as "women's jobs." Note the assignment given to Lucy Wilson Benson, former president of the League of Women Voters and administrator of the Massachusetts human services agency: as Under Secretary of State for Security Assistance, she has the fifth-ranking job in the department and the highest-ranking job at State ever to be held by a woman. Her position includes responsibility for limiting the spread of nuclear weapons as well as heading up a new interagency Arms Export Control Board to review all arms transfers abroad to see if they conform to Carter's arms reduction policy.

Whatever the sincerity of Carter's intentions regarding the hiring of more women and minorities, an organized women's lobby has to be given the lion's share of the credit for the gains of 1977. For the first time in a Presidential election period, politically active women who had sought and won verbal promises during the campaign stayed with the fight long after the inaugural bunting was put away. Coordinated by Jane McMichael, the director of the National Women's Political Caucus, and legislative director Ann Kolker, and other NWPC staffers, women organized into a cohesive pressure group; they cataloged literally thousands of highly qualified women candidates for various levels of appointments; they found influential allies to ratify their choices; and most important, they kept up the pressure.

The work progressed in several stages. In the fall of 1976, before Election Day, the Caucus sent to Jimmy Carter and Gerald Ford a list of some 60 top positions in government that were considered vital to women's concerns. After the election, the Caucus began suggesting names of women for Carter's Transition team, and submitted a list of 40 prominent women who could serve in the Cabinet. "Our basic operating assumption," said Ann Kolker, "was that everything had to be done in a dozen different ways to be effective."

Under Caucus auspices, the leaders of some 40 women's organizations collaborated to form the Coalition for Women's Appointments. The Coalition secured interviews with the President and Vice-President, with Cabinet members, and with other key Administration people. They talked not only about more jobs for women and, in some cases, about individual candidates; they also followed up later as jobs were filled by visiting the new appointees to press positions on issues of paramount importance to women. In fact, some of these second-round delegations were in the happy position of paying visits to new Administration representatives who owed their jobs at least partly to the Coalition's efforts.

There were times, however, when women felt they were taking one step forward, then two steps back. They were particularly unhappy when some of the younger White House aides—Hamilton Jordan, in particular, who made many of the critical job decisions—didn't seem to take women in general very seriously. Women from the campaign, who complained bitterly about Jordan and Press Secretary Jody Powell, were especially disgruntled after two of their most prominent colleagues, Barbara Blum, a deputy campaign director, and Mary King, Carter's campaign adviser on women's affairs, were given second-string jobs in the Administration. (Hamilton Jordan summoned them separately to his White House office to tell them they were not qualified for top-level jobs. Blum ended up with the Number Two spot at the Environmental Protection Agency, and King became second in command at the volunteer agency, ACTION.) At one point, when Carter was assembling his new Administration in Georgia and prospects seemed particularly bleak for women, representatives traveled to Atlanta to lay out their lists before the President's old friend and adviser, Charles Kirbo. Parting on a conciliatory note, they told Kirbo they were pleased with appointments of the caliber of Juanita Kreps. At that point, Kirbo thrust his hands down into the pockets of his country plaid suit and protested: "But we found her; we didn't get her from your lists!"

Many of the successful women's appointments did come from the Caucus lists. The appointment of former New York City Human Rights Commissioner Eleanor Holmes Norton to head the Equal Employment Opportunities Commission is a good example.

First, the Caucus set about identifying her competition. Ronald H. Brown (Director of the Washington Urban League) soon emerged as the AFL-CIO's candidate and Norton's strongest competitor.

Those involved in the effort to get Norton appointed disagree as to just how opposed labor was to her candidacy. Some believe that at least the conservative wing of the labor movement was adamantly opposed because of certain alternatives she had proposed to job layoffs —alternatives that would not penalize the recently hired groups in which women and blacks tend to cluster. Organized labor, of course, has traditionally supported a strict seniority system. Others maintain that labor was not opposed to Norton *per se*, but had already committed its support to Brown. In any case, while the White House was offering no concrete objections to Norton nor proposing other willing candidates, her appointment was held up for some three months.

The women's network just turned up the pressure. For example, Gloria Steinhem recalls: "Someone in the White House would say, 'She doesn't have any labor support,' or 'If she had a little business support, that would help'; then we'd run out and get some labor leaders or some businessmen to endorse her candidacy. First you have to get all the natural constituency; then you get the unnatural!" At one point, the White House apparently decided to break the stalemate with a third candidate who'd be acceptable to the women's lobby. But they ran up against what must have seemed to them to be the unorthodox behavior of women. Carter approached Bella Abzug, whom the appointments coalition was vigorously supporting for a Cabinet post. But when he asked her if she would like the EEOC job, Bella is reported to have replied: "That's Eleanor's job, and I'm not going to take it."

Finally, the Administration gave up, and put Eleanor Norton's name through for an FBI check.

Bella Abzug's case was not so successful—even with the vigorous endorsement of New York's Mayor Abraham Beame, who must have wanted her exit from New York before she decided to challenge his mayoral seat. (Abzug was eventually appointed presiding officer of the National Commission on the Observance of International Women's Year.) As far back as December, 1976, NWPC Advisory Board Chair Sissy Farenthold and Gloria Steinem were pressing Bella's case as a candidate for Secretary of Transportation—a post for which she has superb credentials from her work on transportation problems in Congress. But rumors started coming from the White House by January that she was not a good administrator, or that she was too abrasive.

"That was the technique," said Congresswoman Barbara Mikulski (D.-Md.). "The rumors would float out of Hamilton Jordan's office. . . . Take Barbara Jordan, for example. There were rumors floated that she wasn't a great lawyer. Now you know as well as I do, she's an excellent lawyer."

Jordan herself was at one point rumored to be on the President's "short list" of Cabinet possibilities. And her former associates were said to be fielding queries from Carter people about her understanding of the law. Jordan, who had let it be known that the only executive branch job she was interested in was Attorney General, was invited to meet with Carter in December. But the President-elect apparently tried to see if she had any interest in Housing and Urban Development or Health, Education, and Welfare. In any case, the meeting was not a happy one. Barbara Jordan left Blair House under a full head of steam and refused to comment on what happened.

Arvonne Fraser, through her own hard work, is one woman from the campaign who landed on her feet in the new Administration with a job heading the Women in Development Office at the Agency for International Development (AID). "I was one of the old hands in Washington," she explained. (She had helped to organize both the NWPC and the Women's Equity Action League, and she worked on many legislative projects for women.) She also ran the Congressional office of her husband, Donald Fraser (D.-Minn.), for years as a volunteer. "The campaign people knew me. [They did indeed: she was regional coordinator for the Carter campaign in three Midwestern states, winning two of them.] Also, I am a motherly figure. [She has a warm, generous manner and a smile that puts one instantly at ease.] I can give people bad news and not make them feel too bad. I think they thought that would be useful!"

In the job she took after the White House assignment, she is reviewing all U.S. AID programs around the world to make sure they include and benefit women. Though Fraser is happy with the job, it was not her first choice. She first conducted a quiet, careful campaign for the head of the Women's Bureau in the Labor Department by asking all the right people, including the President, to give her the job; by lining up important supporters; and by taking care to thank all those who were helpful. At the same time, she told the President that she would be willing to consider other assignments if that post was not available. In sum, she had proven capabilities; made herself useful during the campaign; she knew some of the right people; and she was flexible—a combination that any politician would find attractive.

Inside the Carter camp, the effort to include women started before the election with the 51.3 Percent Committee in Atlanta, which began to funnel resumes of highly skilled women to the Democratic National Committee's (DNC) Talentbank '77 office. After the election, the spotlight shifted quickly to Transition headquarters in Washington, where two separate, but definitely not equal, personnel groups went into operation. In the more public effort, the Talent Inventory Program (TIP) under Transition director Jack Watson assigned campaign workers and short-term appointees to find lists of potential nominees including women, blacks, and various ethnic minority members and to sort out the thousands of resumes gathered from the DNC, the NWPC, and other organizations and individuals across the country. TIP did the legwork while a second high-powered "Personnel Advisory Group" operated under Hamilton Jordan. The consensus is that no major appointment was made without Jordan's approval.

Even though their input may have eventually paid off for some sub-Cabinet posts, many in TIP were disillusioned. "I thought it was an effort in futility," said Nancy Payan Dolen, a volunteer on TIP's "hispanic desk." "We prepared lists and lists—and then when the Cabinet was appointed, the lists were thrown out. Many Mexican-Americans I knew said, 'Why bother: he is not going to appoint one of our top people to a Cabinet post.'"

The lists may have been discarded, but the actual resumes weren't. After the inauguration, they were all shipped in boxes over to the old Executive Office Building next to the White House where they were taken over by a huge, affable man from Massachusetts named Jim King—a former Ted Kennedy aide and Carter advance man who became a new director of White House personnel. There the resumes were all refiled, recoded, "prioritized" with an emphasis accorded to talented women and minority group members, and punched into a streamlined new computer system through which, for any imaginable job, the vital statistics of a series of candidates could be instantly called up on a small television screen. It was an impressive gadget— the envy of any headhunter with a shopping list for private industry.

But it was grossly underutilized. One reason is that once the Cabinet was chosen, the President really did turn over to the Secretaries complete responsibility for picking their aides; and naturally, rather than consulting the White House computer, they tended to bring in their own people. (The White House did reserve the right of veto on these appointments, but, by all accounts, it was rarely used.)

For women, this hands-off approach had uneven results. In some departments, like Agriculture or Defense, there were very few women placed at high levels. At Commerce, it was a different story: 48.4 percent of Secretary Juanita Kreps's appointments were women. As one of her aides said: "We have an old girl network in operation here!" King did his best to let the other departments know about his trove: "I have really pushed the agencies," he said. "I thought we could structure an opportunity to make a basic institutional change. . . . I've suggested to people at HEW, for example, 'Send your people up here and use our files.' But they'd say to themselves, 'Where did this guy come from.' "

King believes the President supported his mission as an advocate for underrepresented groups. Indeed, Carter did reiterate his commitment in Cabinet meetings, and he sent the following handwritten memo to Cabinet officers and agency heads on March 25, soon after he met with a Women's Coalition delegation: "We are all committed to a continuing effort to hire strongly representative numbers of women and minority citizens. Please be prepared when asked to give me a report on this at all pay levels above GS 15. Jimmy Carter."

Reordering the priorities of an administration's hiring procedures was tricky—particularly in dealing with a Congress prickly about its ancient patronage rights. "Just to show you how difficult it is to buck tradition in Washington," King recalled, "I deliberately picked two men to act as receptionists in this office—they're the ones who answer the phones. And I have three women who handle all the personnel work. Well, I've had several complaints from Congressional offices about our turning their calls over to women. Their attitude is that they're not being given high enough priority if women are handling their requests." (To be completely accurate, the predominantly Democratic Congress probably wouldn't have cared if tape recordings had been taking the phone calls if its patronage requests had been successful.)

In retrospect, it seems obvious that the President, if not some of his principal aides, tried very hard to hire women and minorities and to urge his Cabinet members and agency heads to do so. If the whole appointments phase took longer than usual—at one point Hamilton Jordan and Jim King attributed the delays partly to the search for women and minority members—it was probably substantially due to the confusion that reigned during the Transition period. It was a decentralized procedure, and each department went about the task somewhat differently. Thanks to the efforts of the women's lobby, some especially talented women, often through no special efforts of their own, made it onto many of the lists circulating around the Capital. One New York business executive who got Washington calls regularly (and eventually was appointed to an important post) said the phone calls were sometimes made to ask if she had any interest in a job, sometimes to ask her to evaluate other names: "One caller ran thirty names by me—some very good. Most of the calls came through people I know, but I got calls on other people from people I didn't know. Sometimes I also got 'thank you for your interest' letters from agencies I'd never contacted. It was the era of the computerized grapevine!"

So, after all this negotiation, how much power and influence have women gained? It will be a while before substantive program changes that affect women will begin to show up—if they do at all. But still there are small indicators of changing times. Now and then, new Administration policies are announced by women instead of men. And women activists seeking policy changes have gained more access to Carter aides than ever before. Julia Graham Lear, a member of the Women's Coalition and the Federation of Organizations for Professional Women, said: "When we met with people like Dr. Elizabeth Abramowitz in the White House [she handles education and women's affairs on the Domestic Council], we were not rushed in and rushed out. They are willing to give us time, and these meetings are going on all over town."

The meetings are extremely important. Women are network-building through organizations like the NWPC and the Coalition for Women's Appointments, which many women in the Administration support. They are getting together through organizations like the Federal Women's Interagency Board that recently studied option papers that came out of Carter's reorganization effort. (The board made recommendations to resolve employment problems of federal women personnel.) They are meeting in the White House in Midge Constanza's office. And women representatives in Congress have formed a caucus.

Right now, for example, women in both the legislative and executive branch are focusing on the issue of battered women. Representatives Barbara Mikulski (D.-Md.) and Lindy Boggs (D.-La.) have each developed legislation. Administration women are also at work on the issue. Jan Peterson, an aide to Midge Constanza, has been holding meetings to stimulate discussion of the problem; Alexis Herman, head of the Women's Bureau at the Department of Labor, is pushing for funding of shelters for battered women who also need job skills; and at Justice's Law Enforcement Assistance Administration, Jean Niedermeyer is working on two programs involving battered women and abused children, one of which helps the family unit when an abuse occurs. "The thrust for the agencies getting together is not coming from the top," notes Joyce Skinner, director of Women's Policy and Programs Division at HUD. "It's coming from people at the program level."

Other changes favorable to women seem to be occurring at or near the top echelons of some of the agencies. HUD's Women's Policy and Programs Division will make sure women's concerns are respected in HUD's policies and procedures. It also serves as a consumer advocate for women. At the Justice Department, there's a new employment review committee under Civil Rights Division chief Drew Days and Civil Division head Barbara Babcock to monitor the advancement of women and minorities within the Justice Department.

Most important, affirmative action directives are still being issued from the White House. In August, to commemorate the 57th anniversary of the women's suffrage amendment, Carter ordered the heads of all his executive departments to reexamine their personnel policies expressly to eliminate discrimination against women. And noting that the Civil Rights Commission had recently reported that more than 3,000 federal laws still discriminate against women, he also called on the Attorney General "to coordinate all of the activities undertaken by the department and agencies to eliminate sex discrimination." Further, the Administration agreed last fall to set up a monitoring system in the White House personnel office to record for the first time how well the various departments are doing in hiring and promoting women and minorities. The figures are to be broken down by sex, ethnic origin, age, salary grade, and by department. At last report, the White House personnel office was having trouble collecting the data from the departments and there was no telling when it would be released.

Though slowly, the process of change has certainly begun. As one woman at HEW put it: "Carter has appointed a few feminists in visible positions. But five or six, or even twenty people, don't make that much difference. We don't have a critical mass yet." Nevertheless, among most women in Washington these days, there is a prevailing spirit of optimism—a feeling that the doors are opening and women are standing at the thresholds. Some have even come in. "I find there's a pleasant mood in town," Barbara Mikulski reported happily. "You walk into a meeting in one of the departments and now there's another woman there. You see each other, maybe you wink, and you know you're both glad to see each other there. We've arrived—and we're looking for each other." It's bound to make a difference.

Deciding the Budget

Every government, whether city, county, state, or national, operates under an authorized spending plan—a budget. Because budget documents are massive tomes, filled with figures, they are commonly thought to be dry, dull, and unexciting. But nothing could be further from the truth. Money is the lifeblood of an agency or a program: Its budget will determine how many people will work and what facilities will be available to them. The struggle for such allocations is a life-and-death struggle, a struggle over values. Should the available dollars go for police patrol or for amublance drivers or for a remedial reading program? The answer is not a matter of logic, but of preferences and priorities.

At the height of the financial crisis in New York City, bureaucrats were hard put to stave off severe budget cuts. To demonstrate their program's importance and to demonstrate the political costs of slashing their funds, they enlisted their natural allies—worker organizations such as fireman's union, client groups such as commuters, or neighborhoods, such as that around Gouverneur Hospital. As "Unmasking of the City Budget" illustrates the resulting city budget document reflected the relative successes and failures of the various contenders. "On Trying to Budge the Budget Cutters" shows that the preparation of the budget for fiscal 1980 reveals the same dynamics at work at the federal level. The representatives of special interest groups lobbied vigorously, and often with the active cooperation of the bureaucracy involved, to restore budget cuts that the president had proposed.

QUESTIONS FOR DISCUSSION

In what ways do the politics of a local budget differ from the politics of the national budget preparation?

In what respects are they the same?

Is it just or fair that special interest groups can influence the budget decisions of elected officials?

Is it possible to develop a budget process that is objective and fair to all groups receiving public services?

UNMAKING OF THE CITY BUDGET: A CASE STUDY

Maurice Carrol

Painstakingly, an $11-billion budget was constructed during the first six months of this year to meet the demands of the variety of groups have a claim on the New York City government. Painfully, for the first time in generations, that budget—tumbled into the red by the national inflation and recession—is now being dismantled.

Forecasts of vast deficits in the budget are forcing layoffs of the city workers, the closing of firehouses and day-care centers and cuts in the quantity and quality of services for New Yorkers. A crew of city workers drapes Christmas lights on an evergreen in City Hall Park one day and on the next, city workers walking past that tree learn that some of them will be laid off before the holiday.

That economic situation, in which the Beame administration at City Hall must choose which among promises it made only a few months ago it must now renege on, has focused attention on the process by which those promises were compiled in the first place.

What is the political input into the budget? How is it decided who will get what services? What politicians and special interest groups are most effective in getting what they want? Have political pressures imposed unwise financial decisions on the economically ailing city government?

There are those who believe that because a budget is expressed in numbers, it represents austerely arithmetical decisions.

"Nonsense," says David Grossman, who was Mayor Lindsay's last Budget Director. "The budget is a battle over resources—who gets what."

"Politics? Sure," says First Deputy Mayor James A. Cavanagh. "The politics of parties. The politics of establishments. The politics of unions. There are many, many forces."

Melvin Lechner, who is Mayor Beame's Budget Director, puts it this way:

"It's a balance. The supply of funds is limited. There are many, many demands for them. So in the context of how to allocate, a budget is a political document."

But as the Beame people tell it, the political implications in the current cutbacks were given no more than token attention.

"Oh, there's going to be screaming in the clubhouses," a City Hall worker said the other day as the Mayor, looking strained and unhappy, announced the latest list of proposed dismissals of civil servants and provisional workers, including some who got their jobs through political patronage. But the aide said that after arriving at the numbers to be dismissed, Mr. Beame, like the Budget Director he was, had apportioned the pain like the consensus politician he tries to be.

"He couldn't hurt just one agency, just one union, just one political organization," the aide said. "It had to be across the board to win acceptance."

But the pressures remain.

The Fire Department, for example, was ordered, as were all agencies, to pinpoint what would be needed to achieve an 8.5 per cent budget cut. It reported back that, among other things, 72 firehouses would have to be closed.

"So we had John O'Hagan (the Fire Commissioner) in," said Mr. Cavanagh, the No. 2 man in the Beame administration and a major architect of the current austerity program, "And we asked him what the Rand Institute, the consultants, had come up with. We've paid for a lot of studies by them on fire. Some of these houses were laid out when you had horse-drawn equipment. Were they still needed where they were?"

Mr. O'Hagan brought back his management reports, and the decision on the Beame staff's first-round budget trims was to close just eight fire companies at a saving considerably less than 8.5 per cent.

But even that was cut back when the firemen's union protested and threatened to stir up the communities that would lose their local firehouses. Just as it did in building its budget in the first place, City Hall had bowed to pressure, to an extent, in deciding how to cut back.

This year's tug of war involves an expense budget of $11-billion, which lists day-to-day expenses (cleaning the streets, buying paper clips, paying salaries) and which is supported by taxes and by state and federal aid, and a capital budget of $1.7-billion, a somewhat misleading list of hoped-for construction that is financed mostly by borrowing and that has been described by one jaded city official as an exercise in "spending money that doesn't exist for projects that will never be built."

Both budgets are for a July-through-June fiscal year.

The Beame administration is now cutting back on the expense budget. It has already imposed a temporary "freeze" on projects in the capital budget and has proposed a capital budget for next year listing practically nothing new.

In the expense budget the pressures cluster at these points in the time table:

The pre-budget psychological warfare, which prepares the public for new taxes and Albany and Washington for pleas for more aid.

The building-the-budget appeals from agencies and constituencies for kind treatment for their programs.

The top-of-the-budget tinkering with estimates of costs and tax yields.

The post-budget rearrangements as developments require a re-slicing of the proposed pie.

Pre-budget alarms were an annual feature of the John V. Lindsay administration. Without directly criticizing his predecessor, Mr. Beame has said that some of this amounted to crying wolf and that now, with a real crisis, he has a hard time making anyone believe him.

But whatever the finagling on the fringes, the bulk of the budget is effectively predetermined.

Dictating the division of almost all of the budgetary pie are pressures—political or whatever—that have produced collective-bargaining contracts with city workers and the uniformed services and their accompanying package of wages and fringe benefits; the state and Federal rules that decide eligibility and rates for welfare; the accumulation of city debt over the decades, which has to be paid back; the very structure of the New York government, with its unusually broad array of services (a tuition-free higher education system; a 35-cents-a-ride mass-transit system; a city-run hospital network whose emergency rooms have in vast areas replaced the traditional family doctor; a generous program of aid to cultural institutions) and the virtually uncontrollable cost of supplies.

"So you can change maybe 1 per cent" notes Matthew J. Troy Jr., the Finance Committee chairman of the City Council, who was a well-prepared interrogator at budget hearings in his days as a Council maverick. "But politically that can be as important as the other 99 per cent because somebody's breaking your neck to get it."

"It may seem small, but the ability to take care of the cosmetic stuff can make you look good in your district. It's taking care of your sewers, your trees, your potholes."

There is, for instance, a dogeared map of his Brooklyn district near the City Hall desk of Thomas J. Cuite, the Council's majority leader, that shows city facilities—libraries, parks and schools—that Mr. Cuite has helped to obtain or protect or maintain. It is a crowded map.

"My personal priority goes right to my district," Mr. Cuite said once, and the Lindsay administration, then in command at City Hall, was careful to take care of the man who put together the votes in the City Council.

Agencies tend to be solicitous of the needs of most legislators. Mr. Troy tells how, in his role as a budget specialist, he had built a friendly relationship with Donald Cawley, then the Police Commissioner. One Friday afternoon he found Martin Van Buren High School in his district in an uproar; a popular policeman assigned there was to be transferred on Monday. Mr. Troy was asked to prevent it.

"Geez, you know what a police transfer is like," Councilman Troy recalled. But he telephoned the Police Commissioner, informed him of what the neighbors wanted, and, he said, was told, "Tell them they got it."

Too cautious to put himself out on that sort of limb, Mr. Troy turned toward the protesters. "I've talked to the Commissioner," he said, "and I think—just possibly—we may be able to work something out."

At that moment, the tiny page box on the policeman's belt began to go "beep, beep, beep." The policeman telephoned headquarters. His transfer had been rescinded.

Another Councilman recalled that in 1969, when Mario Merola was waging a close election fight, "We put so much city construction into his district it damn near sank under the weight. He was the Mendel Rivers of the North Bronx."

"It's true," Mr. Merola, then the Council's Finance Committee chairman and now the Bronx District Attorney, recalled merrily. "I didn't become Council finance chairman to preside over the demise of the Bronx."

How did Mr. Merola, an organization Democrat, get what he needed from the independent Lindsay administration?

"Well, there's none of this quid pro quo business. None of 'You give me this and I'll give you that.' That's kid stuff. It's more of an attitude of getting along."

Neighborhood and special-interest groups have learned to play the budget game, too. Sometimes they win, sometimes they lose.

Recently, for example, Mr. Beame spent a few weeks facing down the trustees of the New York Public Library, who tried to reverse a reduction in city funds by threatening to close down library branches in three demonstration-prone neighborhoods. School officials had been winning with that sort of thing for years, but, in this case, Mr. Beame stood fast and the branches remained open.

In recent years, suggested a former Lindsay official, the black community had done particularly well, dominating poverty programs, manpower training and the like.

"And I'd say," he continued, "That commuters have been extraordinarily effective. New York City is the only place where there's such a significant difference between the income taxes paid by residents and those paid by commuters. Don't forget, a lot of the city's political battles are fought in Albany."

Historically, when a neighborhood wanted something, the squeakiest wheel would get the grease.

The officials now seem agreed that creation of the 62 decentralized community planning boards has tended both to diffuse and, to some extent, to equalize neighborhood voices.

"A lot depends on the capacity of the community board," said John Zuccotti, Planning Commission Chairman. But officials say it is not like the old days when there were wide differences in treatment of communities depending on their capacity to organize to bring pressure on government.

A Canarsie politician remembers, for example, that mushrooming white middle-class neighborhoods once developed a political sophistication that got for it almost all the schools that its population of young families needed.

"Now we're up to our elbows in schools," he said with a rueful laugh "And the kids have all grown up and they're busing the black kids in from East New York."

The tortuous history of the new Gouverneur Hospital on the Lower East Side is another classic example of pressure brought to bear on a budget in which effectiveness is the true practical test.

In 1956, hospital planners pronounced the old Gouverneur Hospital unfit and, according to then prevailing medical doctrine, they decided that a replacement was unnecessary; that bigger existing hospitals on the periphery of the neighborhood could absorb Gouverneur's patients.

The neighborhood fought back, however, and in 1961 Mayor Robert F. Wagner ordered a replacement built. It was to cost $7.8-million, but by 1972, when the building was finally finished the price had soared to $22-million. "But by that time," said a city planner, "health-care doctrine had caught up with the community and decided that neighborhood hospitals like that now were a good thing."

Such pressures are what the budget is all about.

The over-all size of the budget has, moreover, been a subject for some much-criticized political manipulation.

A "buy now, pay later" series of budgeting devices that ballooned through the Lindsay years have not been reversed by Mayor Beame. These gimmicks have helped put the city in its current "pickle" according to State Senator Roy M. Goodman, who heads the state commission studying the City Charter.

Mr. Goodman referred to the practice of putting into the capital budget, financed by borrowing, things that by any normal definition would be day-to-day expenses, financed by taxes—things like salaries, text-books, manpower training.

"It's like putting the milk bill into your mortgage," is the way one critical politician described this long-standing practice.

Another technique used to avoid cutting back too far or pushing taxes up too high is known as the optimistic pencil. Budget officials simply write down the estimated cost of doing things that City Hall wants done. They write up the predicted yield from taxes to bring the budget into legally mandated balance although they know that the balance is illusion.

Then these officials try hard to make what actually happens during the fiscal year match the numbers they have written. To the extent that they can't achieve that, they stack some of the bills on the mantelpiece until the next fiscal year arrives, hoping that things will get better.

City Hall says the accumulation of such actions under Mayor Wagner and Mayor Lindsay have contributed, in no small part, to the need for the current austerity program.

For all the compromises essential to manage the nation's biggest city and to operate the biggest governmental budget next to the Federal budget, the Beame administration says it is now determined to make, rather than defer, tough decisions.

It would be unusual in recent municipal history, but perhaps Mr. Beame, a man whose political identity is built upon fiscal expertise, is the only man who could have attempted it.

One City Hall politician put it this way:

"President Kennedy, a Catholic, could get the Government into birth control. Nixon, a hard-liner, could open up relations with China. For the city now, Beame is the right man in the right spot. He's doing something he hates to do—but he's doing it."

But even the Beame team appears shaken at the emotional hurt the cutbacks are causing.

Mr. Cavanagh listened impassively the other day when the Mayor announced the latest round of dismissals that included deferring the appointments of recruits just emerging from the Police Academy. Then, with a troubled frown, he said:

"Why does that bother me more—the kids coming out of the academy and expecting to go on the job—than firing some guy in

another department who's already working? I don't know. Philosophi-
cally you can't justify it. I don't know. It's just how I feel."

He shook his head and stomped back into his office to mull over
further fiscal steps to balance the city budget.

ON TRYING TO BUDGE THE BUDGET CUTTERS

Bruce Drake

Washington—It's starting all over again, as it does every four years
when a pack of people run for President. No sane candidate on either
side of the political fence will fail to say, at some point of his campaign,
at some stop on the hustings, that he's going to cut the waste in the
federal budget and get a grip on federal spending.

That's what candidate Jimmy Carter was saying in 1976 when he
told crowds about the wonders he would work with something called
"zero-based budgeting." And that was what the Carter administration
was saying in the winter of 1979 when, swept up by cut-the-budget
fever, its Office of Management and Budget issued a three-page hit
list of programs that they said should be scrapped in the name of
austerity.

The President proposed and the Congress disposed. Mostly,
Congress disposed of the no-dough recommendations. There were
about 80 programs targeted for extinction in this year of Proposition 13
and balance-the-budget mania, but the clear majority of them will
survive another year as an object lesson in how old programs never
die—or hardly ever fade away.

The ink is not quite dry on Congress' appropriations book, but
taxpayers will again be compensating beekeepers for losses when their
bees' little buzzers are felled by pesticides. They will pay again for a
Defense Department program to promote rifle practice among civilian
gun clubs. Taxpayers will again help build roads to lakes created by
flood control dams so that constituents of powerful congressmen can
go boating.

Not all the hit list programs were just small change or old standbys
either. On a grander scale, Congress is on its way to spending hundreds

of millions of dollars on military aircraft that the administration said was not needed. It is all but certain to fund a multimillion-dollar youth employment program in conservation that the administration called "a summer camp for middle-income kids." Congress refused to wipe out expensive programs in education aid and assistance for health professionals' schools that administration experts said have outlived their original purpose.

Here's a sampling of how things went: Out of 17 small programs marked for extinction in the Agriculture Department, from the West Indian Sugar Cane Root Borer Control Program on up, at least 15 will persevere. There were 12 grant programs for schools and colleges that the administration said served no great purpose any longer, but 12 will survive. There were seven pork barrel programs in transportation to be hit, and the ax missed at least five.

In some cases, the administration's own employees—the lobbyists employed by each cabinet department—worked to keep the very programs the White House wanted cut. In some cases, the administration made no real effort to knock out the programs because they were considered too small to justify using the manpower to fight them.

But mostly, on programs big and small, the hit list was a paper tiger because the administration, like its predecessors, was overwhelmed by special interest lobbyists—from military weapons contractors to well-organized nurses groups—who could focus all their energy on a single issue. And if it wasn't the lobbyists it was the members of Congress who brushed aside this year's austerity rhetoric when it came to the moment of truth on their own pet programs.

A symbol of all this was the Beekeepers Indemnity Program. Congress decided back in 1970 that beekeepers should be indemnified against the loss of bees that were poisoned while gathering pollen in fields that were poisoned by federally permitted pesticides. This year, to the dismay of the American Honey Producers Association and its Capitol Hill allies, the administration decided that the beekeepers now had enough experience to deal with the pesticide problem on their own.

The death knell for this economy move was sounded by Rep. Jamie Whitten (D.-Miss.), chairman of the House Appropriations Committee and the beekeepers' first line of defense. "Bees are essential to our food supply," declared the powerful Whitten. The declaration humbled Agriculture Department lobbyists who decided the better part of valor was not to offend Whitten. "Those guys sat down and played dead on this one," snorted a White House aide.

And so it went. The budget office proposed killing a half dozen pest-control programs for farmers costing up to a few million each. Congress ignored the recommendations. "Word gets around the farmers pretty fast when you even talk about ending one of these, like the range caterpillar or imported fire ant program," said an Agriculture Department aide. "No congressman wants to offend a lot of farmers over small programs like these. And I have to say the department didn't exactly stand up and fall over itself demanding that these things be scrapped."

Here are some more sorry anecdotes:

The administration said it was time to stop spending $300,000 a year for the Pentagon's Office of Civilian Marksmanship to run the National Board for Promotion of Rifle Practice, which lends or sells surplus guns and ammunition to junior rifle clubs. Congress created the program in 1902 after expressing concern that recruits for the Spanish-American War were rusty in their rifle skills.

The National Rifle Association, one of Capitol Hill's most vociferous lobbies, was enraged. Letters of protest rained down on Congressmen. Despite the official administration position opposing the program, an official in the marksmanship office said enthusiastically: "The mail was terrific." The board may get $97,000 more than last year.

The administration said that it didn't think the Marines needed a verticle [sic] takeoff and landing plane known as the Harrier. But while the commander in chief's budget office was saying "no," the Marines were up on Capitol Hill saying "yes." "They lobbied like hell for it," said a Senate Appropriations Committee staffer. McDonnell-Douglas, which would make the plane, lobbied like hell for it. It looks like Congress will appropriate about $180 million for its development.

There was the two-seat training bomber known as the A-7K, which the Air National Guard dearly wanted although one Hill weapons specialist called it a "completely outdated plane whose only selling point is that Air National Guard commanders can qualify to fly it." The National Guard is not an inconsiderable force in congressional military committees. Figure $100 million-plus here. But its manufacturer, Grumman Aerospace, liked it. Congress liked it. Figure $145 million.

The administration proposed no funds for an array of pork barrel transportation programs. A good example was a program called "access highways to certain lakes." Under this, $7.9 million was used last year to help build roads to lakes created by Army Corps of Engineers' dams so that locals could go boating and swimming.

No more money, said the White House budget office. The

House Appropriations Committee ignored that advice putting in $2 million for the upcoming year. It directed that one of the projects include a package of roads in Yalowbusha and Grenada counties in Mississippi. These happen to be counties in the congressional district of Rep. Whitten. Over in the Senate they had more time to mull the merits of this program and voted to add $7.65 million to it.

The administration wanted to end a $4 million program in the Commerce Department designed to "promote and develop fishery products"—much to the consternation of New England and Pacific Coast fisheries. When West Coast fisheries like a program, so does Sen. Warren Magnuson (D.-Wash.). Magnuson is chairman of the Senate Appropriations Committee. The program survived.

The administration also said that Commerce's U.S. Travel Service, which maintains offices in six foreign countries to encourage tourists to come here, served no useful purpose since discount air fares and the purchasing power here of foreign bucks were inducements enough. The travel industry thought otherwise. Sen. Howard Cannon (D.-Nev.) and Sen. Daniel Inouye (D.-Hawaii) are chairmen respectively of the Senate Commerce Committee and the Merchant Marine and Tourism subcommittee. They come from tourist-happy states. The Travel Services lives.

But there were bigger battles to be fought and they were fought with mixed success, each side claiming victory. One is an education program known as impact aid, which every President since Eisenhower has tried to cut back or end. Originally, impact aid was begun to assist school districts that had to handle an influx of new kids because of military bases that sprung up after World War II and the Korean War. The program cost $27 million in 1951.

Impact aid cost $816 million last year. School districts love impact aid because it is money without strings. Impact aid goes to schools in 432 out of 435 congressional districts and congressmen love impact aid because it makes them look like Santa Claus. The administration wanted to cut $288 million that was added to the program when Congress stretched it to cover districts in which there was so much as a federally assisted housing project. After a major battle with congressional supporters, powerful school groups and lobbyists for cities like New York, it looks like the administration will get a $52 million cut.

The other major battleground set by the administration was over a federal aid program to schools that train doctors, nurses and other health professionals—a program that the administration asserted was meant to cope with a shortage in these professions that no longer exists.

Arrayed against this effort to slice out about $110 million in such programs were the schools that benefited from this boost to enrollment and one of the most effective lobbying groups in Washington—the nation's nurses. "They filled the halls with white," moaned Hubert Harris, chief lobbyist of the Office of Management and Budget, as he recalled the legions of uniformed nurses who arrived here to do battle.

In the end, the administration got a reduction in spending to about $80 million for fiscal 1980. As with impact aid, OMB's Harris considers this a victory because, with both programs, it was the first time Congress agreed to any cut at all.

"We realized full well that a lot of things we proposed for zero funding we weren't going to get," Harris said. "But you have to force people to start looking at these things, and we did accomplish that."

Introduction
An Empty Building

Any seasoned bureaucrat will readily admit that bureaucratic decisions are often political decisions. Employees are hired to appease one or another influential individual; contracts are awarded to relatives of high officials; ex-officials become consultants at lucrative salaries. Complicity in such actions is not usually for personal gain but for the sake of keeping peace. One of the first laws of bureaucracy is "don't make enemies." As James Boren advises: "When in charge ponder. When in trouble delegate. When in doubt mumble."[*]

The case of tenants competing for limited space in Manhattan's Chinatown illustrates such behavior. The competing groups seem to have equally powerful allies, creating a stalemate that the bureaucrats are not willing to break. Rather than make the decision to let one group use the building, HRA bureaucrats leave it empty, apparently more interested in not making enemies. But a decision not to decide is a decision.

QUESTIONS FOR DISCUSSION

Should the bureaucracy have made a decision one way or another?
If a decision had been made, would the bureaucrat making that decision have become a political scapegoat?
Could this case have come to the media's attention through the efforts of a concerned bureaucrat?
How would you have handled this case?

[*] Laurence J. Peter, "Heralding a Man for All Bureaucracies," *Human Behavior* 6 (March 1977), p. 12.

AN EMPTY BUILDING IS SYMBOL TO AGED OF OFFICIAL INERTIA

Dena Kleiman

The ways of government are often mysterious, leaving baffled the un-initiated. So it is with the story of 115 Chrystie Street on the Lower East Side.

This is a story about a shiny new building for which the city pays $216,000 a year to rent, but which has been empty for the last two years—a five-story brick-and-glass monument to bureaucratic indecision.

The structure is vacant because the city cannot, or will not, decide between two tenants—two Chinatown centers for the elderly that, officials concede, are in desperate need of the space.

Rather than make a decision (the center has only enough space for one tenant), the city has bolted the building's front door, denying both groups access to its fresh-painted meeting rooms and expansive new kitchen.

Officials say that, until they can find another site in Chinatown so that both groups can be accommodated, neither will have access to 115 Chrystie.

"The idea is to find a site for each, rather than establish competition," said Howard S. Stein, deputy administrator of the Human Resources Administration.

The senior citizens groups, which are confined to grimy, poorly ventilated quarters and have looked to the building at 115 Chrystie as a source of hope for years, are embittered, frustrated and confused by the city's refusal to act.

They say they want the city to allow at least one of them to make use of the space.

"It gnaws away at you," said Charles Wang; managing director of the Chinatown Planning Council, which is the sponsor of one of the groups. "We need the space. We have a building. But neither of us can use it."

Edward Goon of the Hamilton Madison Golden Age Club, the other group, said: "They're just passing the buck. It's political bureaucracy."

The struggle for space at the building, which is situated in a section of the Lower East Side that, over the years, has become increasingly populated by residents of Chinese descent, began in 1972 when a dilapidated garage at 115 Chrystie Street was selected for conversion into a day-care center.

A complex series of developments followed, including the city's fiscal crisis, a lawsuit involving the city and the building's landlord, and a revised plan to use the building as a senior citizen's center. Since its completion in 1976, each of the senior citizens groups has said it has a unique claim to use the building. It is agreed, however, that both are in need of its space.

The Chinatown Planning Council operates its center for the aged on the third floor of an otherwise-abandoned building at 173 East Broadway, where there is no heat in the winter and where the kitchen consists of three rusty hot plates and several large kettles.

A hundred people eat hot meals at the center each day, but, since there is only water in the washroom, heavy pots of water must be carried from there to the kitchen. Washing and cooking are severely limited and the elderly take their used chopsticks home for cleaning.

The council, a private, nonprofit social agency, contends that it is entitled to the use of 115 Chrystie Street because it helped initially to secure Federal funds for its renovation and was over the years instrumental in its construction.

"We put in 10 years of our blood and soul in this building," Mr. Wang said. "We watched it being built brick by brick."

The Hamilton Madison Old Age Club, which is operated by the city's Department of Social Services, is situated at 50 Madison Street, where 250 elderly residents daily sit elbow to elbow at long, narrow tables. Since there is only seating for 84, there are three sittings for lunch, and, once members finish eating, they must leave the center to make room for others. Recreational space is virtually nonexistent.

"We are a city agency. It is a city building," said Mr. Goon, in explanation of why he thought his center was entitled to the new building. "The city promised the building to us."

(Officials in charge of the center, who are employed by the city, did not return repeated phone calls. A spokesman for the Human Resources Administration denied that either of the centers had been promised the building.)

Members from both centers pass the empty building frequently and stop to peer into its darkened entranceway, where a heavy chain has been looped between two smashed windows. Recently, workmen have been busy on its upper floors because the city has decided to install additional H.R.A. offices upstairs. The first floor and the basement, which includes the institutional kitchen, however, has been reserved for one of the groups.

A spokesman for the administration said that the building could not accommodate both groups, as the plumbing and kitchen facilities were only sufficient for one.

"It's a jigsaw puzzle," said a top City Hall official who is familiar with the case. "You can't give to one without the other. It is a whole power thing. It's not as simple as it seems."

Mr. Stein of the H.R.A. said: "They both desperately need space. We are trying to identify a second site within the Chinatown area so we will offer adequate space to both programs."

However, when asked when the second site might be located so that the vacant quarters could be put to use, Mr. Stein replied: "I'm afraid to give indications on that."

Introduction
Going Nowhere—A Story of Transitory Madness

Decisions to implement policy are usually made in small steps, incrementally, rather than through an all-encompassing, rational plan. Advocates of rational-comprehensive decision making hold that all consequences of a decision should be accounted for. Incrementalists argue that crisis pressures and deadlines limit the amount of time that can be devoted to analysis. The incremental approach constitutes "muddling through," selecting alternatives that are simply satisfactory and sufficient.

In muddling through toward approval of a transit system, Greenwich illustrates the rare case in which an incremental decision was aborted because basic questions *were* asked and the answers *were not* satisfactory. The per capital cost of the system was embarrassingly high.

QUESTIONS FOR DISCUSSION

Do government programs that begin without adequate scrutiny tend to persist and grow over the years without any better scrutiny?

How many individuals or communities would turn down "free" federal funds the way Greenwich did? Could Greenwich afford the luxury of doing so because it was an unusually rich city?

Does the Greenwich case indicate that making policy in bits and pieces may blind policymakers to the overall consequences of their decisions?

GOING NOWHERE—A STORY OF TRANSITORY MADNESS

Daniel Oliver

The stage was set . . . in Greenwich, Connecticut for a major rip-off of the taxpayers. If ever there were any doubts that federal programs tend to transfer wealth up the economic ladder, not down, they were demolished by the facts that emerged from the debate over a proposed public transit system for Greenwich.

Greenwich is the third—fourth—fifth—whatever—richest per capita town in the nation. Its disposable personal income is around $36,000 per capitum. The town is laced with private roads, private enclaves, private police. Greenwich—the name is synonymous with wealth. Even a garbage man has an unlisted phone number. Out of a population of 65,000 there are only 111 families receiving aid to families with dependent children.

But like a character in a children's story, some people were not happy: everything was not enough. They desired—a transit system. And why not? It was, after all, free. Milton Friedman, call your office.

Free! Zippity doo dah—or rather, zippity umta. For it is UMTA— the Urban Mass Transit Act of 1964—that makes such transit boon-doggles possible.

Under UMTA, the Federal Government—who?—will pay 80 per cent of the capital cost of a transit system, and up to 50 per cent of the operating costs. Funds for operating costs are channeled through a state agency—ConnDOT in Connecticut. ConnDOT pays 40 per cent of operating costs plus 50 per cent of any deficit, plus—not incidentally —the remaining 20 per cent of the capital costs. So of the start-up cost of over $1.6 million estimated for the Greenwich system, Greenwich was to pay: zero. Irresistible. And of the estimated annual operating deficit of $1,238,000 Greenwich needed to pay only $160,400. Irresistibilissime.

The problem started in 1974 when the town fathers created a Transit District to study whether the town needed a transit system. Many people had doubts about the project from the beginning but, assuming the idea would die a natural death, said nothing. That silence

Reprinted with permission by National Review. National Review Vol. 30, November 10, 1978.

lulled the committed transit supporters into overestimating the demand for a system and underestimating the opposition. Four years later, when the date for the Representative Town Meeting (RTM) vote was in sight, too large an investment of time and money had been made for the leaders to take a second look. Attitudes had hardened. Minds were made up.

AT HOME IN GREENWICH

And First Selectman (that's yankee for Mayor) Ruth Sims—a Democrat (the town's first in 72 years) who had a few months earlier won in a second election after tying the sleepy Republican incumbent in the first—had been very vocal in favor of the transit proposal. She hoped to ride the issue to a state job that doesn't have to be translated from the yankee.

Basically, the proposal called for 22 of the world's most expensive minibuses, at $55,000 each (foreign made, to make them feel at home on the roads with other Greenwich cars) and 26 bus shelters at $8,000 each—plus the regular transit system paraphernalia: one control room radio at $2,000; 22 vehicle radios at $1,250 each; 22 fareboxes, $250 each; and 12 system information stands at $500 each.

Initially—and perhaps finally—money wasn't the prime concern. This was Greenwich. The system was promoted, and debated, on other grounds: alleviating the traffic problem, doing something about the energy crisis, helping the elderly, the handicapped, and the "transit dependent." But with so much benevolence being offered, someone was bound to become suspicious.

Questions began to be raised. About alleviating traffic. Nature abhors a vacuum, and so do automobiles. Traffic grows to congest the space available for it. People in Westport, Connecticut, which had developed a transit system only a few years earlier, reported that their system had delayed traffic growth by only a single year.

Besides, to the extent the system would serve the "transit dependent"—i.e., people who couldn't drive—there would be no reduction in the number of automobiles on the road.

And who are these people called "transit dependents"? Some are handicapped people, but many are just children under driving age or without wheels. In Westport, 7 per cent of the non-commuter riders turned out to be children. The official study claimed that only 35 to 40 per cent of Greenwich non-commuter riders would be children. But some people thought that since Greenwich already has an extensive school bus system—with the normal school bus safety features, which the transit system minibuses would lack—an additional system was unnecessary. So it was really Greenwich mothers who would be the beneficiaries of the transit system—if they wanted their children independent, able to hang out downtown after hours. One taxpayer suggested that the federal government should provide a federal pool hall, and then the buses.

DEALING WITH THE FEDS

What about the elderly? "Elderly" in bureaucratese means anyone over 65. The elderly in Greenwich still play in tournaments. And the elderly probably don't want to ride buses crowded with noisy children.

The threat of federal controls was also raised. The Transit Directors tried to dispel the worries by pointing out that Greenwich already accepts about $10 million a year in federal grants and subsidies. But a sort of illegitimate federal bureaucracy, the Health Systems Agency, had recently suggested that the town's hospital might not be allowed to build its new wing—to be paid for entirely with private funds—if it didn't meet certain government criteria. And also that it might be required to transfer its pediatrics and obstetrics units to a Stamford, Connecticut hospital, which in turn would send alcoholism and mental disease to Greenwich. The citizens were justifiably suspicious of meddling bureaucrats and federal control.

Money? On close examination the cost turned out to be prohibitive. The Westport experience was revealing. An RTM member reported that in Westport the estimate of the deficit rose from an original guess of $20,000 to a later figure of $88,000, and a final estimate of $140,000. The actual deficit was $219,000, all told.

PLAYING THE NUMBERS

It was always difficult to determine how many people would benefit from the system. In the official handout it was estimated that in the first year there would be 1,448,000 "paid riders." And the two Transit Directors claimed that in the "initial years" of operation "2,607,000 passengers" would be able to ride the buses. Not bad for a town of 65,000 souls. Think what the Transit Directors could do with loaves and fish.

What they mean was "passenger-riders." If Jones rides twice a day, five days a week, 46 weeks a year, that's 460 passenger-rides, but only one passenger. The question is how many Joneses are there?

One can only guess, again by looking at the figures from Westport which has half the population of Greenwich. One estimate was that the Greenwich system would carry 540 commuter riders, and 1,700 other riders. Again, it's hard to tell how many of those passenger-rides are made by the same passenger.

If, as was the case in Greenwich, a system is being touted for its benefits to the "elderly and other (non-youth) transit-dependent" the question is, how many are there?—the answer leading to the per capitum cost the taxpayers are being asked to bear. The answer in Greenwich was that about five per cent of the riders, say 325, would be "transit dependent." If the town's share only of the operating deficit were divided among them, each would get $493. If the entire operating deficit were divvied up among them, each would receive $3,800—each year.

In the end, the town fathers decided there must be a better way and, just six days after the Proposition 13 victory in California, voted down the proposal for the public transit system.

Mrs. Sims has vowed to fight on—for all that free money. Her philosophy, and that of two or three generations of Americans, was expressed by the two Transit Directors:

> Perhaps the most unfortunate result of a negative vote on transit would be that over $1 million of our federal and state taxes—dollars not now available and allocated to the proposed transit system—would be spent somewhere else.

That philosophy has nurtured UMTA's growth from a little government giveaway group, which in 1965 distributed $60 million, to a swollen bureaucracy, which in 1976 shelled out $1.9 billion. And has encouraged the growth in federal spending from $118 billion in 1965 to Mr. Carter's coming $500-billion budget with its $60- or $100-billion hole. And the growth in the percentage of GNP that the Federal Government spends, from 17 per cent in 1965 to 22 per cent in 1976. A plethora of federal programs pervades the nation, busy transferring wealth as much up as down the downstaircase. That is why Proposition 13 Fever is spreading like plague on the politicians' houses.

The taxpayers' victory in Greenwich need not be seen as *sui generis* just because the townsfolk are rich. Notwithstanding their wealth, they understood: a) that however much the system appeared to be free, its cost would surface someday, on some tax bill in their mailboxes; b) that the system was not needed by the general population (or at least, that the case in favor of it had not been convincingly made); and c) that as a welfare measure for a limited group of people the system was unnecessarily expensive—and very likely not the best measure anyway. Such is the beginning of political wisdom. For the moment at least, Greenwich has decided not to be taken for a free ride. Ruth Sims, call Milton Friedman.

Introduction
The Assassins

A major trend in public administration was the movement away from the "neutrality" emphasis and toward the "politics" emphasis. Although early advocates of administrative neutrality had argued that administrators merely *implement* public policies, that assumption now seems naïve. We now recognize that values intrude on administration from many external sources and are also present in even supposedly "objective" internal decisions as to policy implementation. Bureaucrats are policymakers as much as any other participants in the process are.

The case of CIA assassination attempts poses the question clearly: Is the bureaucracy out of control? The administration ostensibly and overtly opposed a policy of assassination. But the CIA plotted to kill Castro, among others. CIA Director Helms pursued the proassassination policy that he interpreted as having implicit approval. Perhaps he was as disinclined to ask for clarification as the administration was to give it. Without an explicit policy, Helms could pursue a course he determined to be in the nation's interest. The administration could profit from CIA successes, at the same time denying that their activities were U.S. policy. Tragically, the result may have been a retaliatory pro-Castro effort to assassinate Kennedy.

QUESTIONS FOR DISCUSSION

Should bureaucrats be able to make decisions with potentially important political consequences?

Should bureaucrats take the initiative in requesting clarification of policy from their superiors, or should they assume that their superiors will initiate such clarifications if necessary?

How common is it for policymakers to commit themselves to one type of policy but hope that the opposite occurs? in school integration? in equal employment opportunity? in conflict of interest?

THE ASSASSINS

Daniel Schorr

Everything about assassination seems un-American. The word *assassin* comes from "hashish." The first assassins, almost a thousand years ago, were the "hashshashin," the "hashish-users", a fanatical Moslem sect in Persia who considered murder of their enemies a sacred duty. Violence may be, in the words of the black militant H. Rap Brown, "as American as cherry pie," but for most Americans political assassination was an Old World phenomenon of bomb-throwing Bolsheviks and Balkan fanatics. Even though four presidents fell to assassins' bullets and others were targets of assassination, the staff of President Johnson's National Commission on Violence concluded in 1969 that the general pattern was not one of conspriacy but of "freelance assassins in varying states of mental instability."[1] The wave of assassinations that cut down, in less than a decade, President Kennedy, Senator Robert F. Kennedy, Martin Luther King, Jr., Medgar Evers, and Malcolm X must have made many Americans wonder whether this alien aberration was becoming a feature of American life.

In the summer of 1975, there was the nagging suspicion that for *some* Americans, in some shadowy recess of government, the idea of assassination had long been a way of life. Because of this, Senator Church's committee, pushing on with the investigation of intelligence abuses from which President Ford had recoiled, found itself enveloped in tension. The CIA felt threatened by an assault on its deadliest secrets. The White House saw America's reputation in the world endangered. Senators found themselves walking a tightrope across an abyss of dark deeds plotted under two Democratic and two Republican presidents. And, if all this were not painful enough, they would end up with the nightmarish question of whether assassination cast upon the Cuban waters might somehow have returned to Dallas.

Under Presidents Eisenhower, Kennedy, Johnson, and Nixon the

[1] See Hugh Davis Graham and Ted Robert Gurr, "Violence in America—Vol. 1, Historical and Comparative Perspectives. A Staff Report to the National Commission on the Causes and Prevention of Violence" (Washington, D.C.: U.S. Government Printing Office, June 1969).

CIA had been involved, in varying degrees, in plots and coups against at least eight foreign leaders.[2]

In 1960, against Lumumba. He had threatened to bring Soviet troops into the Congo. Plans had been made, poisons shipped, access to Lumumba sought. But he was killed by others before the CIA plans could be realized.

In 1961, against the Dominican dictator Trujillo. His brutality had inspired fear of another Castro-style revolution. He was killed by Dominican dissidents, who had received American arms, though it was unclear whether these were the guns used.

In 1963, against Ngo Dinh Diem. His repressive actions had led to fear of an uprising in Vietnam. He was killed in a generals' coup, supported by the CIA, but without evidence that the United States wanted him dead.

In 1970, against General Rene Schneider, the Chilean army chief of staff. He had stood in the way of a CIA-supported military coup against Allende. The CIA backed a plan to kidnap Schneider, but apparently did not foresee that he would be killed when he resisted abduction.

By the time of the coup against Allende in 1973, the CIA claimed it had "separated" itself from the military plots against him.

There was evidence that some thought had been given, at various times, to the assassinations of President François Duvalier of Haiti and President Sukarno of Indonesia, both of whom died in the early Seventies of apparently natural causes.

The chief target was Fidel Castro of Cuba—the closest to American territory and the closest to America's trauma. Castro became the subject of much of the goings and comings of an extraordinary variety of witnesses before Senator Church's committee, which had moved, for the purpose, into the most secure hearing room on Capitol Hill—the windowless penthouse of the Joint Committee on Atomic Energy. Some of the activities surrounding the closed hearings are described in my journal: . . .

· *July 18:* Senator Church, at one of his regular posthearing briefings, says, "The agency [the CIA] may have been behaving like a rogue elephant on a rampage." Church, now obviously nurturing presidential dreams, would find life more comfortable if he could exonerate the

[2] The eight plots are described in the report of the Senate Intelligence Committee, "Alleged Assassination Plots Involving Foreign Leaders—An Interim Report," November 20, 1975 (Assassinations Report, hereafter AR), pp. 206–264, 13–70, 191–215, 217–223, 225–254, 4n.

Kennedys and pin all the assassination plots on Helms and his cloak-and-dagger band.

• *July 20:* On CBS's "Face the Nation," Senator Richard Schweiker, a Republican on the Intelligence committee, disputes Church on the "rogue elephant" theory. "I think it's only fair to say there was no direct evidence that exonerates presidents from assassination attempts. . . . It's hard for me to conceive that someone higher up didn't know."

• *July 22:* Lawrence Houston, retired CIA general counsel, while on Capitol Hill for testimony, agrees to be interviewed on film. He says that in 1962 he briefed Attorney General Robert Kennedy about the CIA-Mafia plots to kill Castro and that Kennedy's only reaction was that "if we were going to get involved with the Mafia again, please come to him first because our involvement with the Mafia might impede his drive against the Mafia in general crime-busting." Houston implies Kennedy didn't object to the assassination plans as such.

• *July 30:* Senator George McGovern, back from Cuba, holds a news conference to release a Castro book recounting twenty-four plots against him, all allegedly CIA-inspired, the last of them in 1971 when Castro visited Chile. Confessions of would-be killers are quoted, mostly Cubans. The weapons pictured range from dynamite to a gun hidden in a television camera. McGovern notes that many of these plots were hatched after President Kennedy's pledge, in return for Bay of Pigs prisoners, to avoid future violence against Cuba. McGovern says that either the CIA acted on its own or President Kennedy broke his promise. . . .

Nothing says more about what was wrong with the CIA—the James Bond role-playing, the loss of touch with reality, the intellectual incestuousness of professionals shielded by their secrecy from being held accountable—than the grand obsession with Fidel Castro. "We were hysterical about Castro at the time of the Bay of Pigs and thereafter," testified former Defense Secretary Robert McNamara.[3] Between 1960 and 1965 the clandestine services nurtured eight separate plots to kill him, with various mixtures of absurdity and ingenuity.[4]

They started, in March 1960, wanting not to kill Castro, but just

---

[3] AR, p. 142, n. 1.
[4] AR, p. 71, The CIA disclaimed credit for the twenty-four plots that Castro had told Senator McGovern about. In nine of those cases, the agency admitted "operational relationships" with some of the individuals, "but not for the purpose of assassination." AR. p. 71, n. 1.

his public image. In the next six months, as planning for the Bay of Pigs invasion proceeded, they discussed spraying Castro's broadcasting studio in Havana with a mood-altering chemical; arranging to get him to smoke a cigar soaked with a disorienting drug before delivering a speech; dusting his shoes with thallium salts, which was supposed to make his beard fall out and thus cause him to lose face, so to speak, with his worshiping citizens.[5] Speaking of worshiping, my favorite plot—nonlethal—was what someone in the CIA called "elimination by illumination." It was dreamed up by General Edward Lansdale, Robert Kennedy's coordinator for the hidden war against Castro. Never put into execution, the plan was to spread the word in Cuba of the imminent Second Coming of Christ, with the corollary message that Castro, the Antichrist, would have to go. At the appointed time, American submarines would surface off the coast, sending up star shells, which would presumably inspire the Cubans to rise up against Castro.[6]

More serious—though hardly less absurd—were the various plots on the life of Castro unearthed by the Senate Intelligence Committee.

· *The Accident Plot.* In July 1960, the Havana station chief of the CIA was startled to receive a message saying, "Possible removal top three leaders is receiving serious consideration at HQs," starting with Fidel Castro's brother, Raul. A Cuban agent was to be offered $10,000 for "arranging an accident." The agent, also promised a college education for his children in case of his own death, agreed to take a "calculated risk," limited to possibilities that might pass as accidental. The agent returned from meeting Raul Castro, reporting he had not been able to arrange the accident.[7]

· *Poison Cigars.* In October 1960, experts in CIA's Technical Services Division completed work on treating a box of Castro's favorite cigars with a toxin so potent that "a person would die after putting one in his mouth." In February 1961, the cigars were delivered to a contact in Havana. The files do not make clear whether any attempt was made to pass the cigars to Castro.[8]

· *Mafia, Phase One.* In September 1960, Robert Maheu, whose private detective agency was on CIA retainer, was asked to contact John Rosselli, involved with the gambling syndicate, and enlist his aid in an assassination plot. Rosselli agreed to go to Florida and recruit Cubans for the enterprise. To assist him, Rosselli brought in Momo Salvatore "Sam" Giancana, the Chicago-based gangster, and Santos Trafficante, the Cosa Nostra chief in Cuba. . . . A scheme evolved to have one of Trafficante's agents put a poison pill in Castro's drink. One batch of pills was rejected because they would not dissolve in water. A second batch was tested on monkeys and found effective. In March 1961, Rosselli reported that the pills had been delivered to an official close to Castro, his cooperation purchased by kickbacks from the gambling interests. The Cuban official reported, however, that he had lost his position before he could poison Castro's drink, and he turned back the pills with regrets. Another effort was made to administer the lethal pill through a contact in a restaurant frequented by Castro, but Castro stopped going to the restaurant.[9]

• *Mafia, Phase Two.* In the shake-up after the Bay of Pigs fiasco, a veteran clandestine operator, Bill Harvey, was assigned to develop an "executive action capability"—the disabling of foreign leaders, with assassination as a "last resort." In April 1962, Harvey reactivated the Rosselli operation, trying to get the same Cuban who had failed so ignobly before to try again with four new poison pills for Castro, pills that "would work anywhere and at any time with anything." The pills got to Cuba—along with guns and radios that the Cuban had asked for. A three-man team was slipped into Cuba to help "penetrate" Castro's bodyguard. The CIA had put a price of $150,000 on Castro's head. When nothing had happened by February 1963, Harvey called the whole thing off. . . .

• *Seashell and Diving Suit.* By early 1963, the CIA's assassination planners were called "Task Force W," led now by a legendary secret agent, Desmond Fitzgerald. They worked on the idea of creating an exotic seashell, rigged to explode, which would be deposited in an area where Castro usually went skin diving. When that proved impractical, the Technical Services people came up with a diving suit, dusted inside with a fungus that would produce a chronic skin disease, its breathing tube contaminated with tuberculosis germs. The idea was that James Donovan, who was going to Cuba for President Kennedy to negotiate the release of Bay of Pigs prisoners, would unwittingly present the diving suit to Castro as a present. Donovan was so unwitting that, on his own initiative, he presented Castro with a different diving suit.[10]

---

[9] AR, pp. 74–82.
[10] AR, pp. 85–86.

• *The Inside Man.* Starting in 1961, the CIA had been developing its most prized "asset"—a disgruntled official still close to Castro. By the end of the summer of 1963, having given up on the American underworld, the agency turned to him for an "inside job" of assassination.

His code name was AM/LASH. (His closest associate was, of course, AM/WHIP.) The real name of AM/LASH is Rolando Cubela Secades, a physician and army major (Cuba's highest rank), who had led the Castro guerrillas in the Escambray Mountains. . . .

A chillingly laconic CIA memorandum records, "Fitzgerald left the meeting to discover that President Kennedy had been assassinated. Because of this fact, plans with AM/LASH changed. . . ."[11]

In Dallas, President Kennedy lay dead from an assassin's bullet. In Paris, a high CIA official purporting to represent the president's brother (there is no evidence that Robert Kennedy knew) was meeting with a prospective assassin of Fidel Castro. In Havana, at the same moment, Castro was meeting with a French journalist, Jean Daniel, bearing a message from President Kennedy of his wish to explore ways of improving relations.[12] No Hollywood scenario could match the irony—and the madness—of this triangle.

How could such things be? Had President Kennedy been pursuing a "two-track" policy of offering Castro friendship while plotting his murder? Or were the cloak-and-dagger people, in Senator Church's words, off like a "rogue elephant" on a singular private rampage? The mountains of testimony and documents indicate that these things could be because the CIA—proceeding on what it claimed as previous "general authorization"—kept its incessant plotting secret, ostensibly to spare the White House embarrassment. The Kennedy administration, while exploring for ten months the idea of accommodation with Castro, had kept that initiative confined to a few trusted individuals, none of them in the CIA.

For CIA professionals, deceiving the US government was almost as natural as deceiving the US public.[13] The customary tactic was to tell higher authority of the operation in the past, not the one in progress. In May 1962, Robert Kennedy was briefed on Phase One of the Mafia plot, but not Phase Two—despite his demand to be told next time. In 1966, Helms told Secretary of State Dean Rusk in a memorandum that "the agency was not involved with AM/LASH in

---

[11] AR, p. 89.

[12] On the coinciding events in Dallas, Paris, and Havana, see: AR, pp. 72, 89, 174; SIC-V, p. 21.

[13] The following account of CIA deception of other government agencies is documented in: AR, pp. 153, 266–267, 268, 269, 150, 173, 131–134, 178, 89–90; SIC-V, pp. 77–80.

a plot to assassinate Fidel Castro." That, Helms admitted under Senate questioning ten years later, was "inaccurate." Despite the Kennedy assassination, contact with AM/LASH for the assassination of Castro was resumed a year later—and continued until June 1965, when it was ended only because it was finally judged to be compromised: the FBI had found out about it independently.[14] Yet when President Johnson demanded a report in 1967, Helms told him only about AM/LASH during the Kennedy administration, not about the revived plotting during his own administration.[15] Major Cubela had already confessed his role as a CIA agent at his public trial in Havana in March 1966, asking a death sentence ("To the wall! To be executed is what I want!"). He was sentenced to thirty years' imprisonment after Castro had opposed execution.[16]

Had the CIA been acting on its own volition, and then deliberately deceiving one president after another about its murderous activities? In extensive interrogation before the Senate Intelligence Committee behind closed doors, Richard Helms sought to explain and justify.

There was, he said, "intense" pressure by the Kennedy administration to overthrow Castro.

> I believe it was the policy at the time to try to get rid of Castro and if killing him was one of the things to be done in this connection, that was within what was expected. . . . Any of us would have found it very difficult to discuss assassinations with the president of the US. I believe we all had the feeling that we're hired to keep these things out of the Oval Office. . . . No member of the Kennedy administration was proscribed or ever referred to [it] in that fashion. . . . Nobody

[14] Although 1965 marked the end of anti-Castro plots as far as recorded in Senate reports, new charges were made by Castro in October 1976. Before a rally in Havana's Revolutionary Square, he blamed the CIA for an explosion on a Cuban Airlines plane in Barbados that had killed seventy-three persons, and asserted that the CIA had also renewed attempts on his life in retaliation for Cuban involvement in the war in Angola. Castro read what he described as the text of a message to a CIA agent in Havana asking for the itinerary of his proposed travels outside Cuba. The message, he said, was obtained through a double agent recruited ten years before by the CIA who had kept the Cuban government "fully informed."
He added that he was willing to end the usefulness of this agent because of the "value of revealing the conduct and activities of the CIA." Secretary Kissinger stated that "no one in contact with the American government" had anything to do with the sabotage of the plane, but the US government had no comment on the alleged message to Havana. (For Castro's statement, see the *Washington Post*, "Cuba Voids Hijack Post," October 16, 1976.)
[15] AR, p. 179.
[16] For Cubela's confession, see *The New York Times*, March 8, 1966. In fairness it must be said that Communist "show trials" were not taken seriously in those days. A *New York Times* editorial on March 7, 1966, said, "Premier Castro blames the United States Central Intelligence Agency, but that is a stock charge."

ever said that [assassination] was ruled out. . . . Nobody wants to embarrass the president of the United States by discussing assassination of foreign leaders in his presence.[17]

Every serving intimate has testified that President Kennedy did not want assassination, but somewhere amid all the winks and nods and euphemisms about "getting rid of" and "eliminating," something had gone off the rails. McNamara acknowledged a dilemma when he testified before the Senate committee. On the one hand, he said, "I know of no major action taken by the CIA during the time that I was in government that was not properly authorized by senior officials." On the other hand, every senior official he knew was opposed to assassination. So, he concluded, "I find it almost inconceivable that the assassination attempts were carried on during the Kennedy administration without the senior members knowing it, and I understand the contradiction that this carried with respect to the facts."[18]

All the talk did not change the fact that President Kennedy, in whose name the CIA had tried to kill Premier Castro, was dead—at the hands of an avowed admirer of Castro named Lee Harvey Oswald.

One investigation breeds another. The exposure of the plots to assassinate Castro raised new questions about the assassination of President Kennedy. Was there a connection? Why had the Warren Commission not been told about the anti-Castro plots? That became the subject of the final report of the Senate Intelligence Committee—actually filed by Senators Richard Schweiker and Gary Hart in June 1976, after the committee had disbanded. It unveiled a strange and sinister cover-up. . . .

A possible "Cuban connection" should have been a natural line of inquiry for the Warren Commission. After all, Oswald had been arrested in New Orleans in August 1963 for making a scene while distributing leaflets for the pro-Castro Fair Play for Cuba Committee. On a New Orleans radio program, he had praised Cuba and defended Castro. He had used the alias of "A. J. Hidell" because it rhymed with Fidel, his wife, Marina, testified.[19] Less than two months before the assassination, in late September, Oswald had visited the Cuban consulate in Mexico City and tried to get a visa. Staff lawyers Coleman and Slawson had emphasized in their report that "the Cuban government might have been involved" in the Kennedy assassination because it "had ample reason to dislike and distrust the government of the United States and the late President in particular."[20] There were,

[17] AR, pp. 148–150, 119–120.
[18] AR, p. 158.
[19] SIC-V, p. 91; CSR, p. 90.
[20] SIC-V, pp. 4, 24, 25: CSR, pp. 91–92, 94–95, 90.

however, powerful forces in government with disparate motives for playing down the Cuban connection. . . .

After the creation of the Warren Commission, Counterintelligence Chief James Angelton took over the CIA's part of the investigation in January 1964. To make the cover-up accident-proof, he sought to ensure that the FBI did not tell the commission anything the CIA was trying to hide. FBI documents reveal that Angelton contacted William Sullivan of the FBI, saying that "it would be well for both McCone and Hoover to be aware that the commission might ask the same questions wondering whether they would get different replies from the heads of the two agencies."[21] Angelton gave examples of what questions might be asked and how they should be answered:

1. Q. Was Oswald ever an agent of the CIA?
   A. No.
2. Q. Does the CIA have any evidence showing that a conspiracy existed to assassinate President Kennedy?
   A. No.

Angelton chose his team from his own counterintelligence staff, which was preoccupied with the Soviet Union and the KGB. There was no one from Fitzgerald's task force on Cuba. Exhaustively, the Angelton group analyzed Oswald's activities in the Soviet Union, and assiduously it stayed away from every Oswald link with Cuba. Indeed, as the Senate report noted with astonishment, AM/LASH, who still had access to high officials in Havana, "was never asked about the assassination of President Kennedy in meetings with the CIA in 1964 and 1965."[22] It could only be assumed that the CIA was afraid of what Cubela's answer might be. Angelton, who believed that all communist activities basically started with the KGB, would have loved to find a Russian conspiracy. . . .

The Warren Commission did not press the CIA for information about Oswald's Cuban associations, this despite the fact—or perhaps because of the fact—that one of its members was former CIA Director Allen Dulles, who knew about the early plots against Castro. Of thirty-four requests for information from the Warren Commission to the CIA, fifteen dealt with the Soviet Union, one with Cuba. That one asked about Jack Ruby's alleged visit to Cuba in 1959. In the Warren Commission, former Senator John Sherman Cooper told the Senate committee, no word was ever said about CIA anti-Castro plots. "The subject never came up. . . ."[23]

[21] SIC-V, pp. 31, 49n.15.
[22] SIC-V, pp. 57–59.
[23] SIC-V, pp. 60, 67.

CIA officials, such as Helms, who knew about AM/LASH, insisted in 1975 that there had been no reason to see any connection with the Kennedy assassination.[24] But in 1965, when the CIA finally gave up on AM/LASH, fearing that the operation had become too widely known and might blow up in its face, the counterintelligence officer of the task force on Cuba wrote this assessment for the CIA:

> The AM/Lash circle is wide and each new friend of whom we learn seems to have knowledge of plan. I believe the problem is a more serious and more basic one. Fidel reportedly knew that this group was plotting against him and once enlisted its support. Hence, we cannot rule out the possibility of provocation.[25]

By then the Warren Commission—to whom Helms had indicated that the case would remain open—had gone out of business.

"All the Government agencies have fully discharged their responsibility to coöperate," said this high board of inquiry, as it concluded:

> . . . no evidence that Oswald was involved with any person or group in a conspiracy to assassinate the President. . . .
> . . . no evidence to show that Oswald was employed, persuaded, or encouraged by any foreign government to assassinate President Kennedy. . . .[26]

The Warren Commission's confidence in 1964 that government agencies "fully discharged their responsibility to coöperate" sounded in 1976 like a melancholy travesty as the final report of the Senate Intelligence Committee concluded that "for different reasons, both the CIA, and the FBI failed in, or avoided carrying out, certain of their responsibilities in this matter."[27] The FBI mainly covered up the extent of its contacts with Oswald; the CIA worked assiduously to steer the Warren Commission away from any knowledge of its own activities in Cuba.

Would anything be different if the Warren Commission had not been so manipulated?

The commission might have probed the "Castro retaliation" theory and run up against lack of evidence of Cuban involvement. It might have investigated the alternate theory of the commission staff—that Oswald could have been programmed by anti-Castro exiles to simulate a pro-Castro assassination—and also run up against a blank wall. What the commission might have discovered was not evidence of a con-

---

[24] SIC-V, p. 71.
[25] SIC-V, p. 78.
[26] President's Commission to Investigate the Assassination of President John F. Kennedy, Final Report, September 1964.
[27] SIC-V, p. 2.

spiracy, but a clear indication of what set Oswald off. It probably could have wound up its historic mission less baffled about his possible motive, less mystified about when the assassination idea formed in his distorted mind.

Had the commission not been so completely sidetracked from every Cuban lead, it might have found what this reporter was able to find—buried in the commission's own files or later dug up in congressional investigations and from other sources.

Where the "Castro revenge" theory had run aground was on the lack of evidence that Oswald had any contact with anyone who knew about the CIA's secret plotting against the Cuban leader. But Oswald did not need to have such contact to reach the conclusion that Castro, his hero, was being threatened and that he, in turn, could become a hero in Cuba by responding to the threat.

Oswald, his wife Marina testified, was an avid newspaper reader. On September 9, 1963, Castro's *Associated Press* interview was printed on the top of page seven of the New Orleans *Times-Picayune*. It started this way:

> *Havana* (AP)—Prime Minister Fidel Castro said Saturday night "United States leaders" would be in danger if they helped in any attempt to do away with leaders of Cuba.
>
> Bitterly denouncing what he called recent US-prompted raids on Cuban territory, Castro said, "We are prepared to fight them and answer in kind. United States leaders should think that if they are aiding terrorist plans to eliminate Cuban leaders, they themselves will not be safe."

The interview was not mentioned in the Warren Commission's report. It was not simply an oversight. A staff member, Wesley J. Liebeler, had written a memorandum urging that attention be paid to it, but General Counsel J. Lee Rankin ruled against its inclusion on the ground that there was no evidence that Oswald had seen it. . . .

Nonetheless, the commission, without soliciting it, got further word on what had happened at the Cuban consulate. On June 17, 1964, J. Edgar Hoover sent, by special courier, a top-secret letter to Counsel Rankin. It said that "through a confidential source which has furnished reliable information in the past, we have been advised of some statements made by Fidel Castro, Cuban Prime Minister, concerning the assassination of President Kennedy." . . .

What the FBI learned through secret means in 1964 Castro described publicly, in more detail, three years later. In an interview in July 1967 with a British journalist, Comer Clark, Castro said that Oswald had come to the Cuban consulate twice, each time for about fifteen minutes. "The first time—I was told—he wanted to work for us. He was asked to explain, but he wouldn't. He wouldn't go into details. The second time he said he wanted to "free Cuba from American imperialism." Then he said something like, "Someone ought to shoot that President Kennedy." Then Oswald said—and this was exactly how it was reported to me—'Maybe I'll try to do it.'"

Castro said that he had not thought of warning the United States government because Oswald had been considered a "wild man" and was not taken seriously. "We didn't have any relations with the American government anyway," his interview continued. "If I'd taken it seriously I might have informed the United Nations or some other official agency like that. But who would have believed me? People would have said that Oswald was just mad, or that I'd gone mad. . . . Then, too, after such a plot had been found out, we would be blamed —for something we had nothing to do with. It could have been used as an excuse for another invasion try."[28]

When Castro said the assassination was "something we had nothing to do with," he may not have been quite accurate. It was likely that Castro had had an effect on Oswald that he did not realize or preferred not to speculate about. Former President Johnson, a year before his death, told columnist Marianne Means of his conviction that Oswald acted "either under the influence or the orders of Castro."[29] The "influence" may have been as simple as reading Castro's public denunciation of attempts on him and the warning of possible retaliation.

The possibility that Oswald acted on his own, inspired by Castro's statement, cannot today be proved, but it has the elements of the fortuitous and the lunatic that sometimes govern history. The "conspiracy," then, would have been a conspiracy of interlocking events— the incessant CIA plots to kill Castro, touching off something in the fevered mind of Lee Harvey Oswald.

It would be comforting to know that Oswald acted on his own— not as part of some dark left-wing or right-wing plot to strike down a president. It is less comforting to realize that the chain of events may have started with the reckless plotting of the CIA against Castro, perhaps in pursuit of what it thought to be Kennedy's aim. An arrow launched into the air to kill a foreign leader may well have fallen back to kill our own.

[28] *National Enquirer*, "Fidel Castro Says He Knew of Oswald Threat to Kill JFK," October 15, 1967.
[29] King Features Syndicate column, April 24, 1975.

Section IV
HUMAN BEHAVIOR

In the "management" phase of development in the field of public administration, the focus had been on the organization as a role structure. It was assumed that in exchange for a fair day's pay someone competent could always be found to fill any vacant slot in the organization. Money would be a sufficient motivator, setting aside personality, individuality, social interests, and so forth as irrelevant to job performance.

The Hawthorne experiments made it clear that that assumption was not valid. Subsequent research confirmed that people remained individuals, even in the workplace, and were affected and moved by many things, of which money was only one. As individuals, they could be "turned on" or "turned off" by their organizational role, depending on what it offered them and whether it treated them as mature, vibrant adults or as lazy dependent drones. It was revealed that people tend to join social groups on the job and these groups develop norms of their own to which the individual is expected to adhere.

Human behavior, therefore, must be understood to reflect not only organizational but personal and group pressures as well. A humane organization is structured around not only the task but its members and their human needs as well. The art of leadership inheres in getting people to work well for the organization by understanding and responding to their needs—by motivating them.

The cases in this section illustrate the relationship between the individual and the organization. They show how participation in an organization can turn people off—and turn them on. They explore just what behaviors some organizations reward today and what behaviors they punish. The influence of the group and of the leader are illustrated. Finally, we get a glimpse into the nature of the relationship between the governmental organization and certain types of people: the "organization man" in government, the businessperson, the professional, and the former activist.

Introduction
My Brief Career as a Bureaucrat

An unanticipated consequence of the bureaucracies we have established to serve the public is their disservice to their own employees. In place of incentives to produce, there are often—too often—pressures to be mediocre. Somehow, bright, eager new employees quickly receive messages not to work too hard, not to outperform their superiors, not to rock the boat. A lackadaisical attitude is often reinforced by the knowledge that nonperformers are seldom fired. To effect a reversal of these pressures, President Carter initiated major reforms of the federal Civil Service system in 1978, including provision for individual incentives and greater accountability. Similar programs are being instituted at the state and local levels.

But such reforms come too late, and perhaps too little, for "producers" such as James North, now by choice an ex-civil servant. Frustrated and then maddened by the inane behavior of his colleagues, his superiors, and even his superior's superior—all of whom obstructed his efforts to do his job—he still retained enough perspective to realize that their behavior was largely a product of the "system."

QUESTIONS FOR DISCUSSION

Is there incentive to operate government bureaucracies efficiently?
Are government organizations inherently unwieldy and unmanageable?
Can individual employees resist pressures toward mediocrity?
Can performance standards be developed for government?
Would you leave a government position as North did? Or could you tolerate
    problems until change slowly occurred?
The system affects behavior, and behavior reinforces the system. How can
    the cycle be broken?

MY BRIEF CAREER AS A BUREAUCRAT

James North

The first day I went to work as an economist for the Agriculture Department, I was assigned to a nine-by-twelve cubicle, to be shared with my immediate supervisor.

Bob Barnet had a PhD in economics, but was prouder of a pin he had just been awarded marking his 20 years of government service. Barnet showed me the ropes. Once through the technical details, he leaned back and, with the relish of a seasoned veteran, laid out his philosophy of how to succeed in the bureaucracy: please your boss, cover your ass and always be cautious. This isn't a university, he told me. I wouldn't be able to switch professors if dissatisfied, and I would never get away with challenging my superiors. Patience was the greatest virtue, not performance. The way to get ahead was not to outshine everyone else, but to do precisely what your superiors wanted, prove your absolute loyalty and meanwhile get to know everything you could about the bureaucracy's inner workings.

Barnet followed his own rules to the letter. He arrived early every morning—not to get any work done, but to peruse the desks of everyone else in the office, thus keeping one step ahead of his superiors. He would gleefully fill me in on his findings the moment I arrived, the first wave in a day-long deluge of chatter that made it impossible for either of us to get any work done. I listened to this man eight hours a day, five days a week. My life became a mind-numbing swamp of monologues—held up at my end by an occasional "oh?" or "really"—about who got what promotion, why it was undeserved, which employees hated each other and why. "That goddam Elizabeth," he would rant, "she's in there with Cobourn (his own boss) every day, pushing her way into everything. You know what she majored in? Art History. She doesn't do anything but dog work, but hell, Cobourn loves to have a good piece of ass around to play up to him." On occasion he would branch out into broader social issues, vilifying blacks, denouncing Arabs, ridiculing liberals. And when he really got going, he would unwind on the details of his adolescent sex life.

Bob's incessant jabbering meant, of course, that he did precious little work. His formal responsibilities were far broader than mine: to review and edit my written reports on price support levels, and to keep tabs on all developments affecting domestic agricultural production. I soon discovered that his idea of keeping tabs consisted of reading *Fortune* magazine and a few routinely distributed DOA circulars. As for passing on my analyses, he concentrated mostly on perfecting my painfully learned bureaucratic jargon.

So at a cost of $15,000 a year to the taxpayers, I slowly cranked out reports that Bob could have (and once had) written if he was not, at a cost of over $30,000 per annum, reading *Time* or disparaging some unsuspecting colleague.

Bob's own supervisor, F. D. Cobourn, posed no threat at all. Neither an economist nor a manager by training, Cobourn was a classic case of the Peter Principle: he had been promoted fairly rapidly until he hit a position he couldn't handle, and there he sat. An introverted man who had once apparently been a fair researcher and writer, he simply could not manage an office. He would grunt hello in the morning and then disappear into his office, where he spent his days rearranging the commas in our reports.

Another figure who came to play a daily role in my life was a $34,000-a-year systems analyst who was either reading the paper or wandering from office to office pestering the rest of us. Karl, Barnet explained with true venom, had been kicked upstairs into a deadwood slot rather than fired, and had almost nothing to do.

Then there was the commodities specialist with a passion for sailing, who would spend much of his day on the phone arranging weekend voyages. Whenever I dropped in with specific questions on his speciality, he would launch into a half-hour lecture on general economic conditions, arguing mostly his own political beliefs. Questions about a particular crop would be deflected into general explanations of the country's agricultural output. When I really pressed he would point me to his file cabinet, which contained all manner of classified documents supposedly too sensitive for me to see. One of my biggest headaches was what to do with the stacks of copies I routinely made of classified documents. If I threw them out, someone might notice; if I took them to be shredded, someone surely would.

Georgia Buck, a black secretary in the office, at least had a reason not to produce: revenge. Several years earlier she had been involved in an affirmative action suit, and since then she had been shuffled— "detailed," in bureaucratese—among several offices in the department. When I knew her she was on her fifth detail, felt very persecuted, and on the rare occasions when she was given anything to do, worked far below her capabilities. The climate of racism I witnessed at Agriculture was truly unnerving. Cobourn, Barnet and others did little to hide their disdain for affirmative action, often doing what they could to subvert it. "What do I have to do to get this guy hired," Cobourn would scream into the phone, "paint his face black?" Needless to say, such attitudes did nothing for department morale.

As the pleasure of my newfound financial security wore off, Bob Barnet and his incredible tongue began to drive me mad. In desperation, I did the unthinkable, going behind his back and forcing my way into a transfer to another office. My stock in the department plummeted, as expected, but at least I started getting some work done. Then came the real shocker. After several weeks of good old-fashioned productivity, Cobourn called me into his office. "Listen," he told me, "I have a political problem with your reports. I don't want you to take this personally, because you're doing a good job. But I can't justify the existence of these things in their present form. They're too comprehensive, and they're beginning to compete with those put out downstairs. He leaned forward. "All I really need is a quick and dirty job."

What was it with these people? They were all intelligent, potentially competent, as honest as the next guy. They had probably all entered government service with enthusiasm and dedication. Cobourn had been promoted rapidly, I was told; even Georgia, now so adamantly counterproductive, had once shown such ability that she had quickly become one of the highest paid secretaries in the building. But somewhere along the line they had all settled for far less than expected—and some had virtually embraced incompetence.

The odd thing was that most took no joy in their malfeasance. Sure, there were a few who delighted in petty corruption, but most were frustrated and dissatisfied. They felt, I realized, that theirs was the only rational course open, that the system demanded incompetence if they were to get along and get ahead.

But why? With my new instructions from Cobourn, I had plenty of leisure in which to ponder the question. The traditional explanations bandied about were threefold: that lacking a profit motive, there is no incentive to run government bureaucracies efficiently; that such organizations are, by size and character, inherently unwieldly and unmanageable; and that the comprehensive job security offered by the civil service system makes it impossible to fire incompetent employees.

There is probably some truth in the first two, though I suspect that not much capitalist zeal filters down into the bureaucracies of large corporations, and that many of them are just as bad. The third reason, however, is obvious and important: the federal bureaucracy is filled with people who should but can't be fired. The process is simply too time-consuming and tedious, involving hearing after hearing and appeal after appeal. It's much easier to kick someone sideways or even upstairs, shunting the problem to his next supervisor. Thus many an incompetent has received an unbroken string of promotions—and, in a nice twist, any boss who dares fire the slouch often draws a black mark against his or her name. If other managers could handle the employee, superiors wonder, why couldn't this one?

But none of these three factors, though they suggest why poor performance is *tolerated* in bureaucracies, really answered my question of why individuals so often *choose* to be incompetent. One answer is obvious: the pressure toward mediocrity is simply too enormous to resist. After all, to stand out one need perform only slightly better than the prevailing level of incompetence. To do much more is to play the fool—doing others' work—and invites the hostility of co-workers.

But that also doesn't get to the heart of the problem. Individuals may bend to the norm, but why has that norm been established? Why have so many made that choice of mediocrity? Looking around me during long afternoons with nothing better to do, I decided that one big problem is that so many bureaucrats are effectively *stuck*.

At first, government employees rise through the ranks with ease. But once they have reached the highest mid-level grade, GS-12, further promotion becomes difficult. Federal agencies are bulging with professionals in their early 30s who have already reached their career peaks. They have little incentive to excel, but lots of incentive to last through the next 25 years, after which they can retire on a full pension.

A few turn to private industry for advancement, but by the time they've invested five years in the bureaucracy and secured their $25,000 to $30,000 incomes, their marketability has eroded considerably. There is no "revolving door" for most bureaucrats, in part because of the low esteem in which they are held by the private sector, in part because so many gain only the most esoteric experience with their agencies. The system closes in around you.

Ambitious employees have two ways to get out of this trap, both of which tend to compound the problem. The first is to jump sideways as you jump up, finding high-paid jobs in other agencies that you often are only remotely qualified to fill. Most hiring officers prefer the relatively unqualified but established civil servant to the highly-qualified outsider, both because internal transfers avoid some of the complexities of civil service hiring and because all outsiders are unknown quantities.

The second road to glory—and mediocrity—is to join the ranks of management, jumping beyond the GS-12 level. This is typically accomplished by building a small empire. For lack of a better index, one's importance, and thus one's grade, is ultimately determined by the number of employees supervised, the number of publications issued, the number of projects undertaken. This of course leads to the creation of unnecessary work, but it certainly explains why employees with nothing to do are kept around.

Even more damaging than empire building is the fact that most who jump into management from, say, research, simply lack the temperament and training to make tough administrative decisions. Some are so obvious that their subordinates can operate more or less as they please. Cobourn, for example, never felt quite on top of Barnet's supposed field, so whenever Barnet scented danger he would simply invoke his expertise to cover for his lack of work. Secretaries and clerks are usually the only people whose performance is visible to the inept manager, so they often find themselves rebuked while professional misconduct goes undetected. An effective double standard develops, and morale suffers accordingly.

Even competent managers learn to keep their heads down and protect their flanks. They have no incentives to run a tight ship, and no way to fire incompetent employees. Perhaps most important, there are no real standards of performance demanded by the system, seemingly no way a middle manager's superiors can accurately measure the job he is doing. Advancement requires only that one sit tight, make no waves and quietly go about building one's empire.

Reaching this conclusion brought only limited satisfaction. It's nice to understand *why* you face 30 years of intolerable boredom and frustrations, but it hardly eases the pain. Two years after arriving, I'm about to leave.

When President Carter's Civil Service Reform Act finally passed, I asked a few of the old-timers if they expected it to have any impact. Needless to say, they didn't. It's sad, but I imagine their complacency is justified. On paper, the act does have some strong points: it makes firing employees easier; it links salary hikes for all managers in the GS-13 to 15 range to performance, not just length of service; it creates an elite corps of about 8000 managers ranking GS-15 and above, the Senior Executive Service (SES), whose members will be rewarded for outstanding performance with substantial cash bonuses but will have less job security than others; and it prohibits reprisals against "whistle blowers."

The emphasis on improving management is important. But I wonder—will encouraging competition among managers lead to more efficient government, or simply to more and better empire building? No new standards for what constitutes good management have been laid down, and in their absence, it's fair to assume the bureaucrats will continue to respond to old ones.

Even if some agency directors do develop an adequate system to determine who deserves merit awards, I doubt financial incentives alone will suddenly equip inept managers with newfound skills. Dead wood is dead wood, and apart from more elaborate annual performance appraisals, managers will be given no magic new tools to help supervise their subordinates. As for firing, most managers, by training and inclination, will continue to shun such strong medicine; it will always be easier to reorganize someone out of a job or simply neglect incompetence.

That is doubly true now that President Carter has proclaimed, as part of his anti-inflation program, that only 50 percent of outstanding vacancies will be filled. Hiring freezes, according to the old-timers I knew, are always counterproductive. They give employees even greater impunity than usual, because from a manager's point of view, an incompetent employee is better than no employee at all.

The new protection for whistle blowers, though also admirable, will affect only the few employees who witness gross impropriety. A few more GSA scandals may be exposed—an important goal, surely. But it is the commonplace, everyday abuses—hardly worthy of mention individually—that add up to such a stifling atmosphere, robbing employees of their motivation and self-esteem. Will the reform act change Georgia Buck's life, or Bob Barnet's? I just can't see it.

In fairness to President Carter, it is terribly difficult to alter individual behavior arising from long-standing and well-founded beliefs about how things operate. Just for *attempting* to shock the system out of its lethargy, the reform act is probably worthy of praise. But essentially, the act asks people to perform more productively without giving them any way, aside from firing people, to do so. It won't change much of anything. If I thought otherwise, I might stay on.

Introduction
Balancing Ideals and
Frustrations in the Bureaucracy

A worker will accept and keep a job only if the satisfactions outweigh its negative aspects, as seen from the worker's standpoint. What are the satisfactions of public sector employment? And what are the negative aspects? In the introduction that originally appeared with the following cases, the author sums up the attractions.

> For many people, government is where the action is. It's government employees who—in conjunction with the politicians and the courts— weigh the worth of laetrile and the safety of saccharin, build the cruise missile and decide where the Concorde will land. . . . Government job-holders often enjoy a degree of power they would never have attained on the outside. Mid-level civil servants are put in charge of millions— even billions—of taxpayers' dollars. . . . Civil servants also feel they are a part—however small—of something worthwhile. . . . [They are] part of the "good guys." The "good guys" are well paid. Professionals like doctors and lawyers may find private practice more lucrative than working for the government, and top government administrators don't enjoy the six-figure earnings of the heads of big corporations. But average government salaries are considerably higher than those in private industry.

The frustrations center in large part on the "red tape blues"—fed by regulations, restrictions, paperwork, and delays in getting approval for action—and the lack of reward for innovation.

Diane Sedicum of HEW finds deep satisfaction in working on a program she believes in. Edward W. Scott Jr. enjoys making decisions and achieving results in whatever program he is charged with. Barbara Cohn entered New York city government service in 1960 and still thinks of it as "temporary." Wayne Jacox wants a permanent career as a bureaucrat but is getting ready to leave his Illinois state job.

QUESTIONS FOR DISCUSSION

What additional satisfactions and frustrations can you see in a public service
career?

On balance, how does such a career appeal to you? What factors do you
consider important in attracting or discouraging you, personally, to a job?

Can an "idealist" survive effectively in the bureaucracy?

Do people seek employment in government for reasons of salary and fringe
benefits, or is public service a more important motivation?

Are the career patterns in these profiles typical of many government employees?

BALANCING IDEALS AND FRUSTRATIONS IN THE BUREAUCRACY

Caroline Donnelly

DIANE SEDICUM

On the face of it, Diane Sedicum, 32, is a classic bureaucrat, awash in
paper and wed to procedure. She is, however, dedicated to helping
people—in her case, getting money to the college and vocational school
students who need it most. As assistant to the director of the Division
of Basic and State Student Grants in HEW's Office of Education, she
gets $26,000 a year and a dreary windowless Washington office where
the air conditioning is a sometime thing.

One of Ms. Sedicum's primary responsibilities is to handle the
65,000 letters sent to the bureau each year. Many are from parents who
want to know why their youngsters didn't qualify for the $1.7 billion
the bureau is handing out this year to needy college students. A Los
Angeles widow, for example, complained that her son had received a
computer-printed rejection notice stating that his "eligibility index"—a

Profiles excerpted from "Balancing Ideals and Frustrations in the Bureacracy" by
Caroline Donnelly, MONEY MAGAZINE, August, 1977, by special permission;
© 1977, Time Inc. All rights reserved.

formula involving a family's income and assets—was too high. "Just who sets up this index?" she wrote plaintively. "Who's to help me and all like me who try to pull their own weight but keep getting pushed down again and again by the bureaucracy of it all?" Lately a lot of letters have come from "born-again" Christians who are ineligible but who hope the Carter Administration will make an exception for them. Ms. Sedicum takes all inquiries seriously. "I feel strongly about this program," she says. "It's like a child to me."

EDWARD W. SCOTT JR.

Ever since his first job as a clerk-typist in the Panama Canal Zone, Edward W. Scott Jr., 39, has been working for the federal government. Now he has risen almost to the top: as Assistant Secretary for Administration in the Department of Transportation, he makes $47,000 a year.

All of Scott's fellow assistant Transportation secretaries are political appointees. In fact, most were Capitol Hill confreres of Transportation Secretary Brock Adams, who was a Congressman before President Carter appointed him to the Cabinet. Scott, a relative outsider, had some quick catching up to do when Adams hired him last May. "I spent my first week figuring out how many people are wired to Adams and how tight," he says.

Born in Panama, Scott returned home after earning a master's degree and two bachelor's degrees, including one from Oxford; the clerk-typist's job was the only government position he could get. He climbed through the ranks, moving to the Internal Revenue Service in Detroit, then the Justice Department in Washington. He made his administrative reputation there, ultimately unveiling a plan to reorganize the entire department. Unfortunately, the plan was announced two days before Richard Nixon's Saturday Night Massacre, when the top ranks of Justice were upended. "The whole thing went down the drain," Scott says. "I was a superdisillusioned young man."

Scott switched to the Immigration and Naturalization service, a branch of the Justice Department that he says was a "hangdog, down-in-the-mouth, screwed-up mess." But working for a small stepchild of an agency can be "the most fun of all," he says, because you can make decisions on your own. Scott's last job at Justice was as Deputy Assistant Attorney General.

Eventually, Scott would like to head a government bureau. He says which bureau doesn't matter much: "I wouldn't care if it was the one that makes the park benches. I want to make the most park benches, the best park benches, the ones that last the longest and go into the most parks."

BARBARA COHN

Barbara Cohn, 40, New York City's deputy commissioner for rent control, steers clear of politics, although she is at the center of a political maelstrom. In a city where 75% of the families are renters, rent control is a perennial political football—and has become increasingly controversial in the current mayoral campaign.

Ms. Cohn's typical day is "hectic, nonstop." She frequently wakes up in the middle of the night to write notes to herself. Then she appears in her office at 8:30, often works through lunch, and stays until 7:30 at night. One evening recently her husband, Frederic Berman, a criminal court judge, appeared then to pick her up; she was still poring over reports. "Enough already," he said. "Let's go home." She left, toting a bulging red leather briefcase.

Growing up in a single-family house in Brooklyn, Ms. Cohn gave little thought to pursuing a civil service career, much less to a job overseeing rents in apartment buildings. "I wanted to be in the academic world," she says. So in 1959, after college and graduate school, where she studied sociology, she signed on as a $2,000-a-year lecturer at Brooklyn College. About a year later, she was lured off by a $5,150 salary to work as a researcher in the city planning department where, she felt, she could apply sociological techniques to real problems. She regarded the city job as temporary and always intended to return to academic life.

She never did; instead, she worked her way up through a series of civil service jobs, primarily in housing. Last spring she was appointed to her present job, which pays $31,000 a year; she is in charge of 600 city workers.

Still, Ms. Cohen isn't sure she will stay in government. "I've never thought this was my only option," she says. "I've gained great experience that might be transferred to the private sector."

After the election next fall, she might have to consider that option more carefully. Whatever happens to rent control, she might be asked to resign if a new administration takes over.

WAYNE JACOX

From a drab cubicle in the only unrenovated wing of the Illinois state-house, Wayne Jacox, 32, an analyst in the budget bureau, rides herd on millions of dollars spent by five agencies. His own salary: $18,500. "Friends ask me, 'Why the hell don't you get out of government and earn some money?'" he says.

Jacox, a graduate of the Maxwell Graduate School of Citizenship and Public Affairs at Syracuse, doesn't want to get out of government, although he wouldn't mind leaving the budget bureau. It is regarded as a model agency and training ground for people who want to move up in the state government. But he is in something of a rut there. He is assigned to housekeeping agencies such as the Department of General Services and the Department of Finance, rather than to the more glamorous regulatory and social welfare agencies. Although he had been in his job longer than any of his colleagues in the bureau, Jacox was bypassed last year for promotion; now he thinks he has little future there. And he feels stiff competition from younger colleagues with even more impressive academic credentials than his own, including some with Ivy League degrees.

Jacox's lack of enthusiasm shows. During the fall, bureau employees are required to work with missionary zeal, often all through the night, to prepare the governor's annual budget message. Jacox doesn't like the hours or share the zeal, which he describes as "boot-camp mentality and rah-rahism."

Most of all, Jacox would like to go home to Oregon, where his father was the purchasing agent for the city of Salem. A city manager's job appeals to him, as does a city manager's salary (typically $25,000 or $30,000 in a medium-size suburb). He also has his eye on a political appointment in Illinois—a coveted "special assistant" job in one of the agencies he oversees. But, he says, "I'm not a political leader in my election district. Sometimes that kind of thing counts."

Introduction
The Reward System

The behavior of a worker is shaped by many forces: the individual personality, professional standards, social group norms, and organizational policies. In general, individuals will undertake an action only if they believe that the action is feasible and that it will be rewarded. By rewarding the behaviors it wants encouraged and by punishing those it wants eliminated, the organization actively modifies the behavior of its members.

"Buying and Selling at the Pentagon" is a tale of two men who worked for the Department of Defense. A. Ernest Fitzgerald called attention to an outside corporation's cheating on a contractual agreement with the department. Malcolm Currie accepted favors from and gave preferential treatment to an outside corporate contractor. Fitzgerald was fired; Currie was promoted.

"What Does a Civil Servant Get for Turning Down a Raise?" is about Andy Bevas who, acting out of public spirit, turned down a raise from HEW and was punished for his pains.

QUESTIONS FOR DISCUSSION

Based on these cases, what conclusions would a reasonable worker arrive at concerning how to behave in an organization?

What can you deduce about organizational "values" from what an agency chooses to reward?

How does personality or professionalism interact with the organizational reward system in determining an individual's behavior?

What effect would published cases such as these have on an organization's reward system?

What impact might they have on an agency's effectiveness in influencing an individual's behavior?

BUYING AND SELLING AT THE PENTAGON

James Nathan Miller

On October 18, 1968, A. Ernest Fitzgerald, an obscure Pentagon cost analyst, received an invitation from Sen. William Proxmire (D., Wis.) to testify at a Congressional hearing about military procurement practices. The letter's envelope had been tampered with, and Fitzgerald later charged his superiors at the Department of Defense (DOD) with opening and reading his mail from Proxmire. Why would they have been watching his mail?

When the Air Force had hired Fitzgerald in 1965, he seemed ideal for his cost-analysis job. Formerly the president of a successful management-consultant firm, he was 39, smart, hard-driving, a firm believer in a strong military establishment.

But it wasn't long before he begain raising Pentagon eyebrows by questioning practices that everyone else took for granted. He complained about generals and civilian employes who, while overseeing defense contracts, solicited postretirement jobs with the companies they oversaw. He criticized the Pentagon practice known as "contract nourishment," by which weapons' specifications would be changed during the production run, thus freeing manufacturers from the original contract's price ceilings. He stated openly that he thought much of the waste he saw could easily have been avoided if the Pentagon had really cared about keeping costs down.

But Fitzgerald's biggest complaint had to do with the building of the Air Force's C-5A cargo plane by the Lockheed Corporation. While many Pentagon weapons contracts had involved huge cost overruns, the $3.4-billion Lockheed program, said the Air Force, was different. It was worded in ironclad overrun-proof language. If any overruns did occur, they would be paid for by the company, not the taxpayers.

By early 1968, however, Fitzgerald began to grow suspicious. When he asked Air Force officials and Lockheed executives to show him key cost records, they refused. And when he tried to check reports that Lockheed was seriously "flimsying" the plane's construction, he received an angry call from Pentagon brass warning him, in effect, to keep out of engineering matters.

Fitzgerald told his bosses he smelled a cover-up. By mid-1968, he was convinced he knew its dimensions: Lockheed was piling up a $2-billion cost overrun on the C-5A, and the contract's fine print contained loopholes that could require the government to pay the full amount. Furthermore, he said, the plane the Air Force would get for this increased sum would be defective. Yet the Air Force managed to convince Congress that everything was fine.

All of which explains why, in October 1968, Fitzgerald's bosses were watching his mail—and why, when he received Proxmire's request to testify, they ordered Fitzgerald to "stay away from the C-5A."

Proxmire, however, would have none of this. At a November 13 hearing, he asked Fitzgerald point-blank: Was it true that the C-5A was headed for a $2-billion overrun? Fitzgerald finally said yes, it looked that way—if no action was taken to head it off.

A few hours after Fitzgerald's testimony, a staff meeting of generals and high civilians was held at the Pentagon. One of the subjects discussed (as described in the meeting's minutes) was to decide on a strategy to counteract "Fitzgerald spilling his guts." The minutes concluded, "It looks bad . . . [we should] stand fast until we see if Proxmire makes statement. In meantime, prepare bland responses to have in hand." Though the Air Force did cloak the facts about the C-5A for many months, eventually these facts emerged:

The Air Force originally planned to buy 120 C-5As for $3.4 billion —$28.3 million per plane. It actually bought 81 planes for $4.5 billion —$56 million per plane. And the airplanes are unable to operate out of rough airfields as they were supposed to. Their predicted life span is a quarter of the time called for. To keep them flying, the Air Force will have to pay an additional $1.3 billion for improvements.

Overruns are commonplace on DOD contracts. In 1969, the year the C-5A dominated headlines, Congress's General Accounting Office reported that cost increases in 38 major weapons systems totaled $21 billion.

What has happened to Fitzgerald as a result of his testimony? In late 1969, after his name was out of the headlines, the Air Force fired him. But that wasn't all. Fitzgerald found himself blacklisted, unable to get a job in his old calling. In 1973, after a series of administrative appeals and lawsuits, the Civil Service Commission ordered the Air Force to reinstate Fitzgerald. But today his career is at a dead end. He has the job of his former assistant. He has already run up $500,000 in legal costs. And he is still suing to collect damages from the individuals who prevented his reinstatement to the Air Force in good standing, and for restoration of his old job or its equivalent. Ostracized by top Pentagon officials, he is currently assigned to look into the operation of maintenance depots.

A partial list of public figures involved in Fitzgerald's firing and its aftermath provides a disturbing insight into the reach of the military–industrial complex's influence in Washington:

- *Harold Brown, then Secretary of the Air Force*, who, about a week after the Proxmire hearing, called Fitzgerald in and told him he made "a damned poor Congressional witness." Shortly afterward, Fitzgerald's job tenure was canceled. It had been granted, Brown told Proxmire, as the result of "a computer error." (A personnel expert later admitted to Fitzgerald that it was the only such error in Air Force history.)
- *Brig. Gen. Joseph Cappucci, then director of the Air Force Office of Special Investigations*, who in 1969 conducted a probe of Fitzgerald's life, searching for evidence of conflict of interest or security violations. He found none.'
- *Alexander Butterfield*, an aide to President Richard Nixon, who made the following recommendation: "Fitzgerald is a top-notch cost expert, but he must be given very low marks in loyalty; and, after all, loyalty is the name of the game. We should let him bleed, for a while at least," (Nixon did nothing in Fitzgerald's behalf.)
- *President Jimmy Carter*, who during his campaign praised Fitzgerald and cited his firing as the kind of injustice that must never be repeated. As President, Carter has refused to intervene for Fitzgerald. The man he appointed Secretary of Defense— Fitzgerald's old boss Harold Brown—has refused even to grant Fitzgerald an interview.

Now, observe a very different Pentagon story: the career of Malcolm Currie, a former executive of the Hughes Aircraft Company, who joined DOD in 1973.

As director of Defense Research and Engineering, Currie supervised testing and evaluating billions of dollars' worth of weapons that manufacturers wanted to sell to Uncle Sam. The job made him one of the most influential and sought-after members of the military–industrial complex. Here are some of the facts later discovered about him:

- In September 1975 Currie, his daughter and a woman friend of Currie's were flown to Bimini in the Bahamas by the Rockwell International Company, a defense contractor, and spent the weekend as guests at a Rockwell-owned resort, in the company of Robert Anderson, Rockwell's president, and Mrs. Anderson.
- In October, Senator Proxmire started an investigation into defense contractors' entertainment policies. He was to learn that, at the time of the Bimini trip, a Rockwell weapon, the air-to-ground Condor missile, was finishing a series of tests under

Currie's supervision. Many DOD experts felt that the Condor had proved to be a waste of money—"A prime candidate for total cancellation," said one Assistant Secretary of Defense. Anderson's Washington lobbyists were then in the midst of a frantic behind-the-scenes effort to prevent this,* and Currie was one of the key officials on their target list.

· Memos subpoenaed by Proxmire indicated that during the Condor testing Currie had been feeding Rockwell's lobbyists information on Condor's future. One memo relayed advice from Curie on how to lobby the Senate Appropriations Committee in the missile's behalf. Another described a letter Currie had written to the Deputy Secretary of Defense making a case for the Condor. Currie insisted the memos were merely a self-serving attempt by company employes to impress their bosses with their inside connections.

Actually, none of these activities was unusual for a Pentagon weapons buyer. Such behind-the-scenes contacts between buyers and sellers of military hardware have long served as the mortar binding together the bricks of the military–industrial complex. Indeed, the Bimini resort was just one of five retreats used by Rockwell, discovered by Proxmire. On the Eastern Shore of Maryland, within a two-hour drive of Washington, the Senator's investigation revealed that five defense contractors—Rockwell, Northrop, Raytheon, Dupont and Martin Marietta—provided all-expenses-paid recreational facilities for personages ranging from a Secretary of the Navy and a former chairman of the Joint Chiefs of Staff to scores of generals, admirals and members of the Congressional Armed Services Committees. (Immediately after Proxmire's revelations, the companies closed the facilities.)

When Secretary of Defense Donald Rumsfeld learned of Currie's Bimini trip, he found himself in a dilemma. Currie had done nothing unusual in accepting favors from a defense contractor, so to single him out for punishment would be unfair. But with Proxmire's investigation of contractor entertainment bringing headlines, to ignore Currie's violation of DOD's official code of ethics would be politically unacceptable.

Rumsfeld took a middle course. On March 16, 1976, he wrote Currie saying that—while he was sure Currie was not guilty of any conflict of interest on the Bimini trip—Pentagon officials must avoid any conduct "which even appears to place them in a position of conflict." Thus, Currie was "severely reprimanded" and docked four weeks' pay (about $3500). Two months later, however, Currie was quietly

*Congress killed the Condor program in September 1976.

promoted, and given authority for all Pentagon weapons-buying decisions. (When word of the DOD promotion leaked to the press, it was canceled.)

How has the affair affected Currie's career? In February 1977, he retired from DOD to rejoin Hughes Aircraft as its vice president in charge of missile systems. (He was succeeded at the Pentagon by a former official of another defense contractor.) Two of the programs he supervises for Hughes—valued at an overall cost of $3.4 billion—involve weapons whose approval he recommended while in DOD.

Another arm of the Hughes organization, Hughes Helicopter, was awarded a $4-billion helicopter contract two months before Currie left DOD. The craft's development was endorsed by a Pentagon committe chaired by Currie.

(In his testimony before Proxmire's committee, Currie denied reports that while in his Pentagon post he had solicited defense contractors for employment. But he conceded that he knew "hundreds" of people at Hughes, and that "at a cocktail party someone might have said, 'Mal, when you get out of Washington someday we hope to see you!' But nothing more than that.") . . .

WHAT DOES A CIVIL SERVANT GET FOR TURNING DOWN A RAISE?

Barbara Kleban

"Just because you're paranoid," warns a poster in Andy Bavas' office, "doesn't mean they're not out to get you." It is a lesson the 49-year-old bachelor learned the hard way. Six months ago, as a $43,000-a-year, HEW-paid consultant at Northwestern University's Center for Urban Affairs in Chicago, Bavas decided he didn't need an upcoming $1,272 raise. "It is most gratifying to be appreciated," he wrote his regional director, "but it may well be that the money can be used more beneficially in some other way or simply not spent."

The reaction was swift. His incredulous boss wrote back saying

Reprinted with permission of *People Weekly*, Barbara Kleban, "What Does a Civil Servant Get for Turning Down a Raise?" in May 21, 1979 issue of People Weekly.

that it was illegal to turn down a raise and that doing so would subject the supervisor to prosecution. He suggested instead a contribution to the government. "Can you believe it?" shrugs Bavas. "Waste is so institutionalized, it's against the law to save the government money!"

That, alas, was not the end of it. Three months later Bavas was notified that he was being transferred to Philadelphia—and to a job paying nearly $10,000 less. Under HEW's reorganization guidelines, a salary reduction was justifiable. "But I regard the attempt to move me as punitive," says Bavas, who considers Chicago his home (and has gone for 16 years with Joyce Wiegand, administrative assistant to the managing editor of *Playboy*).

Bavas remembers a comparable instance in 1963, when he was fired from a janitor's job at a Sun Valley ski lodge after suggesting some time-saving efficiencies. But he insists he's neither a crusader nor an obnoxious do-gooder. "I'm as greedy and venal as the next guy," he says. "I just didn't need the raise."

Still smarting over the relocation order, Bavas has asked his lawyer to determine if any jobs for which he's qualified were filled by HEW in Chicago recently. However that battle comes out, the war, it appears, is already lost. Echoing W. C. Fields' famed epitaph, Bavas vowed from the start, "I'd rather resign than move to Philadelphia"— and effective this month, he did.

Introduction
The City Manager Builds
a New Life

Classical administrative theory assumed that the only thing that motivated people to work was money. That theory is still held by many managers today. Human behavior theorists, on the other hand, maintain that people are also motivated by many things: a desire to belong, to be part of an informal social group, to gain esteem and status. Beyond these needs, the most powerful motivation may be a desire to self-actualize—to do work that is personally meaningful or fulfilling.

William Donaldson would agree. An unusually successful city manager with an excellent national reputation, he has given up power and prestige, salary and status, in exchange for a job he loves—running a zoo. As Donaldson put it himself in a public administration newspaper article,

> The opportunity to preserve even a small number of species that are threatened with extinction comes only once, and unfortunately comes at a time when zoos are the most beleaguered. . . . If improved management in the form of the better utilization of human and fiscal resources makes it possible to preserve even a few more species from extinction, my management skills learned slowly over 25 years in local government will be well invested.*

QUESTIONS FOR DISCUSSION

Is Donaldson's behavior unusual?
Should all people, at least once in their lives, work at what they want to, rather than what they have to?
Did he leave because he was not good at his old job?
What job would you find sufficiently satisfying to work at for less money?

*Public Administration Times 2, No. 21 (November 1, 1979), p. 3.

A CITY MANAGER BUILDS A NEW LIFE AS PRESIDENT OF PHILADELPHIA'S ZOO

The Associated Press

William Donaldson relished his weekends. He would leave behind his worries as City Manager of Cincinnati for a few hours and visit his favorite place—the zoo.

A few months back, the head of Cincinnati's zoo told Mr. Donaldson, just as a joke, that Philadelphia's zoo was having some money problems and was looking for someone to head it.

If Mr. Donaldson had the conventional ambitions of most political animals, he would have laughed and forgotten the idea.

Instead, he left Cincinnati's most powerful government job, which he had held for four years, and in July took a big pay cut to become president of the zoo in Philadelphia. . . .

The decision by one of the nation's ablest city managers to turn zookeeper was not all that surprising to those who know him. He told a reporter two years ago, "I only came to Cincinnati because I heard they had a great zoo."

In fact, he numbered among his accomplishments as City Manager bringing an aardvark, a burrowing African mammal, to Cincinnati's zoo.

In a more recent interview, Mr. Donaldson said that he faced the same kinds of problems at the Philadelphia zoo that he grappled with in Cincinnati.

"The zoo had been unduly optimistic about its annual revenues since 1974," he said. "They were running a deficit which was the product of declining attendance. So we immediately reduced the payroll by 12 people."

City deficits are an old story to Mr. Donaldson, who was City Manager of Montclair, Calif., Scottsdale, Ariz., and Tacoma, Wash., before taking the top post in Cincinnati.

When he arrived in Cincinnati in 1975, he said, he found a bloated bureaucracy, a deficit of more than $10 million and city administrators who were not facing up to the city's dire straits. He quickly cut the city's labor force by 20 percent, but he still left Cincinnatians more satisfied with local government than before.

He also went a step beyond a policy of having the doors of his City Hall office wide open to all. He removed the doors.

And now, according to the city's latest financial report, Cincinnati enters the fiscal year 1980 with a $9 million surplus.

Besides trimming the staff at the Philadelphia zoo, Mr. Donaldson said, "We're now looking at what we ought to charge; sort of like what the airlines do, some days we should charge more, some days less."

He also wants to find ways to expose inner city youngsters "to our roots in the wilds."

How long does he plan to remain Philadelphia's zookeeper? "I don't know," he replied. "Until I get it the way I like it."

Was Cincinnati the way he wanted it when he left? The city's books are in better shape, he said, but he conceded that he had left behind a city with racial problems that flared recently.

He left those problems in the hands of another highly regarded City Manager, Sylvester Murray, a black official who had previously managed Ann Arbor, Mich., and a woman Mayor, Bobbie Sterne.

"But it's just great at the zoo," said Mr. Donaldson. "Can you imagine getting paid to look over the rhinoceroses and pat the birds every morning? I'm having a grand time."

Introduction
The City's Biggest Landlord

Organizations are made up of people—with needs, interests, and perceptions of their own. A central question for administrators is how all these people can be motivated to involve themselves in their work and perform energetically. According to Frederick Herzberg, a worker's output will suffer if wages, benefits, and social satisfactions are inadequate. Restoring them will not stimulate the worker to an enthusiastic all-out effort, however. That kind of energy is released only when people feel self-esteem and the satisfaction of self-actualization.

Chip Raymond, like many other public servants, could probably earn more in the private sector. Unlike many other public servants, he seeks out challenging tasks and throws himself into his work. Already at work at 7 A.M., he barely stops to eat, wrestling all day with a depressing and Herculean task because he derives satisfaction from his ability to "make a difference" in his city.

QUESTIONS FOR DISCUSSION

Is Raymond a realist or a dreamer?
Could lower-level positions in his agency also provide opportunities for self-actualization?
What does Raymond get out of his job?
What does his job take out of him in terms of physical wear and tear or stress on the family?
Can a job be too "challenging"?

THE CITY'S BIGGEST LANDLORD

Rinker Buck

He cuts a portrait of worldly success—every bit the man who seems to have everything.

Each morning, often as early as seven o'clock, the earnest, strikingly handsome young man who controls the fastest-growing real-estate empire in America leaves his apartment at 2 Fifth Avenue, turning east toward the downtown IRT. Chances are he's kept his wife up late the night before, ruminating over what to do with one of the 10,000 apartment buildings he manages all across New York. Now he's suddenly got the solution. Out comes the ubiquitous yellow legal pad; a felt-tip pen is pulled from its cap between his teeth. Dodging traffic, he scribbles his way across University Place. It is 7:05 A.M. and Charles V. "Chip" Raymond has begun the day's first memo.

You can take Lefrak, and Starrett, and even throw in a few holdings of Helmsley, Spear, and together they wouldn't come close to what Chip Raymond will someday call his own. Over the past year, his astonishing record of acquisitions has made heads spin from City Hall to Wall Street. No one can believe just how fast he moves; his ambitious plans, the sheer numbers involved, are staggering.

Before lunch one day last year, Raymond took over 750 buildings in Manhattan alone. For dinner on another, he gobbled up 1,000 more parcels in Brooklyn. Assorted financial bigwigs are concerned that so much real estate, so much power, could fall into the hands of one man, whom most of them had not even heard of a few months ago. So alarmed are observers at the City Planning Commission, for instance, they've taken the unusual step of issuing a report warning that Raymond's spreading domain will soon encompass over 16,000 buildings in all five boroughs, housing 250,000 tenants. That translates into a whopping 13 percent of this city's housing stock and more people, they say, than currently reside in all of Wyoming.

No matter—Scott Fitzgerald would have loved this guy. All the finishing touches he would have given the consummate tycoon are firmly in place. Son of a comfortable Rhode Island family, Raymond attended private schools and Syracuse University. He has a beautiful, independent wife, two healthy boys, and a house, where he summers, in Darien. For connections, he's got a brother working in the White House; for noblesse oblige, throw in an early stint as a John Lindsay aide. He sails—well enough to have placed in the Newport-to-Bermuda race and to have made the 1976 U.S. Sailing Team. He is tall—six feet four inches—has sandy-colored hair and dark-gray eyes. And as for the style that pulls this all together, most would call it, well . . . classic Yankee Wasp.

There's only one problem. Those buildings Raymond has been snapping up happen to be located on some of the most undesirable blocks in the world—properties big-name realtors wouldn't touch with a ten-foot wrecking ball. Raymond is, in fact, a civil servant, holding down what everyone agrees is the most taxing, no-win job in city government: deputy commissioner of housing in charge of a woebegone division called the Office of Property Management. His job is to manage the thousands of dwellings—block upon block of tenement slums in New York's worst neighborhoods—that the city seizes every year from slumlords who have failed to pay their taxes. Days that stretch anywhere from twelve to fifteen hours aren't long enough to cope with buildings that come to him in ungodly chaos, the product of years of landlord neglect and milking. The vast majority of these buildings need new roofs, new boilers, whole new floors. A full 40 percent of them were built before 1901, another 40 percent date back to before the 1929 depression. The best Raymond can hope to do with many of them is to level them before they fall down on the few squatters brave enough to remain inside. And in many of them, there are dozens of residents, justifiably bitter over what has happened to them and this city, all of whom must be either appeased or promptly relocated to better buildings. To put it simply, Raymond presides over the real-estate sinkhole of the century. He may just have the worst job in America.

"That sounds like Chip all right," says a cheerful, supportive Jan Raymond, who hasn't seen much of her husband since he took the housing job sixteen months ago. "He knew from the beginning that this was going to be a terrible job, but he took it anyway. You just can't separate the man from the challenge." Brooklyn City Councilman Leon Katz, chairman of the council's Government Operations Committee, which created the city's current In Rem Housing Management Program two years ago, puts it this way: "The guy is dynamic, he's competent, he's intelligent, and oh my God is that boy handsome—but I think he's probably going to have a nervous breakdown soon."

"I've worried about that myself sometimes," laughs Raymond, a veteran of ten years of city and state government jobs nearly as arduous as his current assignment. Raymond, who had made an "absolute" decision to leave city government before City Housing Commissioner Nat Leventhal asked him to take over the In Rem program, recalls, "A lot of people thought I was crazy to take this thing on; they said I'd be a burnt-out case myself in six months. Although it sounds pretentious to say so, I really thought I could make a difference."

Sixteen months and 10,000 buildings later, virtually everyone agrees on two things. Raymond has made a difference, but the toll, both physically and emotionally, has begun to show. "He's a lot more serious than he used to be," says Jan Raymond. "He worries more. I've never seen him put in such hours, and he brings the job home more. At cocktail parties, all he can talk about is the price of fuel, converting boilers from coal to gas, or insulation." Nat Leventhal, who has nothing but praise for Raymond's performance so far, nevertheless feels "the job has gotten to him more than he shows."

The city's current In Rem (in lieu of taxes) program dates back to 1977, when, as part of the charter-revision reforms that year, the City Council transferred the responsibility for seized residential buildings away from an overwhelmed and scandal-prone Division of Real Property, part of the Department of General Services. "Real Property was in a total shambles," recalls Katz, "so we decided to turn the whole mess over to Housing, which had the experience and willingness to deal with these buildings." But that was an election year, so the enormous problems associated with the transfer waited, like a ticking bomb, for the incoming Koch administration. At this time, there were 4,500 city-owned buildings, requiring over $20 million annually in upkeep. The city was collecting $14 million in rents of approximately $21 million due.

Raymond came on in May 1978, assuming command of a confused, disorganized army that would eventually include over 1,000 city employees, 2,700 building superintendents, and 400 handymen. He also had to assemble a team of management experts, piece together a multi-million-dollar budget of city and federal Community Development funds, and sort out the complex billing, repair, and maintenance procedures required to manage the largest single urban real-estate entity in America. Meanwhile, In Rem seizures were accelerating under a new city law that permitted the city to foreclose after only a year of tax arrears, instead of the previous period of three years. By last September, when the Office of Property Management finally assumed complete control, the number of In Rem buildings had climbed to 8,500. A third of the occupied buildings were less than 30 percent full—thousands were just abandoned shells, which means that vandals and thieves had already walked off with a good deal of the essential heating, plumbing, and electrical systems. Rent collections were running at less than 25 percent of bills due.

Raymond's buildings were, in short, in an advanced stage of collapse; maintenance was—and is—the biggest headache. "From the start," Raymond laments, "you have to assume that if a landlord hasn't paid taxes for three years he hasn't put a penny into that building either. I hate to say this at a time of fiscal restraint but, frankly, with $54 million in federal funds this year, and $108 million hopefully in the pipe for next year, we've got the resources to fix a lot of these buildings. The problem is I can't push the work through fast enough to catch up."

Indeed. Raymond's legions spend most of their time responding to thousands of requests for emergency repairs each week; in the last year his office ordered 50,000 open-market repairs from private contractors while completing 70,000 repairs with its own staff of handymen. Each open-market job—from the most complicated boiler repair to the glazing of a window—demands pre-inspection and audit visits, work orders, bids, payment approvals, and post-work inspections, as required by the city comptroller's accounting regulations. This involves months of paperwork for each job; contractors often must wait two to three months just to receive a final sign-off and payment for their work. By that time, very often, vandals have walked off with part of that new boiler, or broken in through the window, so around and around the whole paper chase goes again. "It's maddening," sighs Raymond, stretching his frame across two office chairs. "I've got some lady in East Harlem screaming at me because her toilet has just fallen through the ceiling. She's got a right to be mad, dammit, but before I can help her, I've got all this crap—this paper—to push around. That's what is frustrating. The job itself is fine."

It's understandable just why Raymond's hair has turned gray since he began this job. He runs his hand across his chin. Underneath a "tension" blemish on his cheek, the stubble of his beard now comes through perfectly white. But, to hear him speak, it is difficult to detect the level of anxiety he lives with every day. The burden of constantly making decisions that affect the lives of thousands of people only occasionally shows. He covers over a lot of grief with a steady banter of irreverent humor. And Raymond, who is used to keeping his emotions in check, nevertheless feels passionate about those buildings, as well as the people in them. This he expresses through a fascination with numbers, systems, and management details—the intricacies, for instance, of rerouting a broken sewer pipe across a city street. He has a McNamara-like mind for detail.

"In my more ridiculous moments," Raymond continues, "I worry about all the things that can go wrong out there. Think of it—90,000 toilets that could plug up, 50,000 walls about to fall down, a couple of thousand plumbing and electrical systems that might fall apart tomorrow. Just now, I'm obsessed with the 500 or more boilers that I know, good weather or bad, are about to blow their stacks. Those are my nightmares these days, literally."

It is Monday, July 30, a typical business day for Raymond. By 7:30, he's already at his desk at 75 Maiden Lane, answering mail, reading memos, routing flowcharts to a half dozen or more of his top deputies. At eight, his special assistant, Betsy Foote, comes in to review his agenda for the day. Ever since she came on four months ago, she's been trying to convince Raymond to cut down on the number of meetings he attends. She'd like him to give someone else the chore of personally reading the more than 30 letters of complaints from tenants that find their way to Raymond's desk every week. But Chip won't hear of it. "I've got to keep in touch, I've got to stay accountable," he tells her.

He'll continue to attend all those evening meetings with tenant groups too, he tells her. They're horrible sessions, really, during which angry tenants often jump up and down, scream, and hurl obscenities at Raymond. He went to the first one of these, in 1978, with a full entourage of his staff. But he saw how humiliating, how morally devastating the experience was for all of them. Never again, he decreed, would they have to attend if they didn't want to; now Raymond handles most of these meetings himself.

By nine o'clock, Raymond is reviewing with his legal staff a long list of proposed amendments to the city comptroller's billing and accounting rules that will help streamline his repair program.

For the next 45 minutes, before he's due at a meeting seven blocks away, Raymond has time to take a few calls, conduct an interview, handle a sudden crisis that can't be put off. His door is always open; assorted aides constantly drop by with pressing matters. "Chip," one of them calls from the door, "the OMO [Open Market Orders] tracking system? There's still a few problems, but I gather the earliest you can get together with the staff on that is mid-August."

"Christ, I hope not," Raymond replies. "I want to hear about that. Look, I'm supposedly taking Thursday and Friday off next week, but have Marie ink in some time for me to meet with you. Or the next week—wait—a minute, I'm supposed to be on vacation then. Oh, what the hell, tell Marie about it and I'll come down for it some day that week." It's a constant refrain: Over the next four days Raymond will whittle down his "week" of vacation to about 72 hours.

A few minutes later, he is bounding down four flights of stairs for his meeting, too impatient to wait for the elevator. Betsy Foote and two other aides have trouble keeping up. It's the Mad Hatter routine all over again out on the street. Raymond strides up Maiden Lane, turns right on Broadway, violating three Don't Walk signs at once as he crosses the triangle below City Hall Park. In and out of his teeth goes the felt-tip pen. Three pages of yellow legal pad are filled with notes to himself and others by the time he arrives at 349 Broadway.

It's a complicated meeting, full of bureaucratic angst, as the conflicting priorities of three separate agencies clash over matters large and small. . . .

Cooling down back in his office, Raymond eats a hamburger, a bag of potato chips, and a Coke . . . Between calls and more staff interruptions, he muses about himself. "All right, I guess I can explain just how I got into this mess. I grew up in Barrington, Rhode Island, where my father was in business. He was, I guess you could say, a pillar of the Barrington Congregationalist Church. I wasn't especially religious. You know—the typical problem-kid routine—I spent a good deal of my free time down at the Barrington Police Station. So they sent me off to Wilbraham Academy, which I somehow survived, and then to Syracuse, where I was to pursue a business education. Well . . . I flunked out."

Back at Syracuse a year later, Raymond moved over to the sociology department and began a new round of political and social activism that has shaped his attitudes and life ever since. By all accounts, it was Raymond's future wife, Jan, whom he met during his freshman year, who influenced his new activism. A close friend from their Syracuse days remembers, "Chip and Jan were the kind of people who headed south every summer for places like Selma, or north for the civil-rights marches in Chicago."

Later, Chip moved into and out of a couple of graduate programs, never really finding a comfortable place in academe. "I remember it so well now, the day I put my 'education' behind me. In 1969, I was in a graduate seminar at NYU. Some horseshit course on 'The Negro in Urban America' or something. I said to myself, 'This is boring. It's ridiculous. Here I am in a city with *millions* of urban Negroes all around me, and I'm wasting my time with someone who thinks I don't understand Ralph Ellison.' It was time to move."

Raymond went around to see Gordon Chase, then head of the Human Resources Administration under Mayor John Lindsay, who offered him the first of his string of no-win government jobs. The payroll division of the Neighborhood Youth Corps was in crisis, shaken by a scandal that included charges of widespread fraud, payroll padding, and no-show patronage jobs. Raymond, who had never taken an accounting course or laid his eyes on a payroll before, took over and kept the job for one grueling year. He ended up in the mayor's office by 1973, running the Lindsay administration's Single Room

Occupancy Task Force. Later he served as deputy administrator at the State Division of Criminal Justice and as deputy commissioner at the city's Department of Mental Health.

With a resume like that, Raymond should be comfortable with his current job, used to the kind of pressure it virtually guarantees. He's not. "I don't think I can take this for much more than another year," he says. "The job is just too much for any one man to carry too long. It's the first job I've had where I don't feel in total control. The problem's too immense."

It's now 2:15 and members of Raymond's staff are beginning to drift in for a meeting on the agency's contingency plans for the winter. Raymond is obviously at ease here, enjoying himself with his staff. Practically anything goes during these sessions; the most difficult decisions are made in an atmosphere of laughter broken by occasional moments of seriousness. Everything from calling in the National Guard to make Sunday oil deliveries to buildings to installing heat pumps and solar panels is discussed. Raymond is obviously one of those managers who like to experiment, a dreamer, sometimes, who views every crisis as an opportunity.

Slouched across his chair and part of the conference table, he points across the room with his foot. "Which one of you guys is going to find me a building for the heat panels?" Everyone groans. "No, seriously, these things are an interesting concept. We've got the money to buy a couple. Let's try them on a building or two and see what happens."

There was a time, not very long ago, when Raymond had neither dreams nor laughter to fall back on. Last winter, there was little time to plan ahead for emergency fuel deliveries and boiler repairs in buildings Raymond had just taken over, and a lot fell through the cracks. Last winter, a total of five people froze to death in Raymond's buildings. "It was the worst time of my life," Raymond remembers. "I have never been so depressed. The *Daily News* ran all these headlines saying that we'd killed those people; every night the TV stations were out there identifying a building that didn't have heat. I felt responsible. I was sure there was something we could have done to prevent those people from dying."

"He was close to tears," says City Councilwoman Ruth Messinger, who worked closely with Raymond last year. "Nobody in the press bothered to look into just how such a horrible thing could have happened, probably because Chip didn't offer any phony excuses. He took it all on himself and said it was his fault. And in a way, that was very good. He made everyone want to try harder and showed that those people out there weren't just abstractions. They were very real to him, and he cared."

And for as long as Raymond keeps this job, maybe longer, he'll probably never be able to enjoy a winter again. "I used to love the cold weather. I always tried to get away for a few weekends and ski. Now if I wake up in the morning and the temperature has dropped below 40 degrees, I'm depressed. All those idiot weather forecasters are like brothers to me now. That's all I do all winter, listen to weather reports."

Before Raymond takes a tour that afternoon of some of his buildings in Manhattan Valley and on the Lower East Side, there's still time to discuss the hardest part of this job. During a time of severe financial difficulties for the city, Raymond faces the task of moving whole bureaucracies, and mutually hostile constituencies, in directions none of them wants to go. All year, he's been under pressure from a skeptical, often misinformed City Council, the Budget Bureau, City Hall, and the Planning Commission, all of whom are beginning to fear that the burgeoning In Rem program will bust the city.

"Yes, it's an enormous program, costing the city millions," Raymond explains. "But first we've got to appreciate that this is something that's got to be done, and it's something that no other city except New York is facing head-on. Because this idea of city management is so new, people haven't really gotten used to the issues yet. They don't see what I've got to do to please everyone. If the Budget Bureau calls over and says, 'Hey—let's get serious about rent collections!' sure, I can do that, but then you're going to have a lot of angry tenants who can say, 'I won't pay—you haven't fixed the buildings yet.' Both sides are right, but I've got to decide."

Matters aren't made any easier by a testy Mayor Koch, who on several occasions has gone out of his way to antagonize the minority constituency in Raymond's buildings. During one televised appearance, the mayor told a group of In Rem tenants, "Pay your rent—or get out." During another, Koch recalled, "I grew up in a neighborhood where people didn't burn down the buildings in which they live." Utterances like these hardly make Raymond's job easier, as tenants presume the mayor is handing down official policy on the question. Asked about that, Raymond, not one to undercut his boss, says, "I've had more contact with him than any other mayor—and I've worked for three. Koch is a good mayor—very accessible and informed. If his style is combative, well, that's just his style. He's given me all the help I need."

Late in the afternoon, Raymond and a few of his aides head uptown, to visit one of his buildings along Amsterdam Avenue between 108th and 109th streets, where renovation work is under way. Before he left, Raymond had listened for over an hour to complaints about that block from community residents, who criticized him sharply for failing to evict tenants of illegal storefronts, for going slow on repairs, and for turning his back on prostitution and drug rings moving into the block. He was upset about these reports; now he'll have a chance to see for himself just what's been happening in Manhattan Valley.

The city car swings down from the 125th Street exit of the West Side Highway as Raymond points out his buildings. Whole blocks stand shuttered and gutted by fire, the only evidence left behind by slumlords who have long since skipped on their taxes and moved to Florida. You begin to appreciate just what's at stake here, just how much more will be lost if the city fails to act. "That's ours, that's ours —there, over there, see that block? It's all ours," Raymond says, as the car passes a building of walk-ups near 129th Street and Convent Avenue.

Arriving at Amsterdam and 108th, Raymond immediately steps upstairs, where a half-dozen handymen are renovating apartments, building new walls, installing plumbing. Downstairs, a boiler has just been repaired; basement windows have been sealed with cement and cinder blocks against vandals. He's relaxing again, enjoying the details, and wants to know about everything from stucco paint in one apartment to the cost of the new rising pipes he passes in the hall.

"This looks terrific—goddammit, I'm proud of you guys," he tells a group of handymen. "I've got to get out here more often, bring the mayor up here and see what you've done." In a few weeks the renovation will be finished, and residents from neighboring buildings will be consolidated into this one so that the same rehab job can be done next door. The block doesn't look nearly as bad as the neighborhood leaders had made it sound, but Raymond is far from content.

"So this may be something of a success story, the way we understand success. It's a building, at least, where it will be safe for people to live. But this ain't really where it's at—round the corner there's a *terrible* building. We've got to fix it."

It's endless. Raymond is back in the car, discussing with his staff what else can be done on the block. They pass that around a few times, until someone suggests that Raymond would be lucky to be fired—only then would his job be done. "They can't fire me," Raymond shoots back, already laughing at his own expense. "You think they could find someone crazy enough to replace me?"

Introduction
Neil Welch, Boat Rocker

In order to survive, an organization must perform its mission. And in doing this, the organization must be able to motivate its members by offering them, in exchange for their work, something that they want or need—whether salary, an interesting task, the satisfaction of belonging to a "team," or the opportunity to contribute to a valued goal. The leadership function, as Chester Barnard pointed out almost half a century ago in *The Functions of the Executive*, is to see that the needs of the task and of the personnel are *both* met. Leadership is the art of bringing human resources to bear on the organizational purpose. It involves taking a position as to directions and tasks as well as understanding and reaching people.

Neil Welch's takeover as new head of the FBI office in New York illustrates the institutionalization of a change in leadership. He redefines the objectives for his office and changes the procedures for achieving them. And he understands the importance of motivation: Although New York is not, in the eyes of most agents, a desirable assignment, Welch feels he can create a feeling of satisfaction by offering the highest level of motivation—the chance to do a good job.

QUESTIONS FOR DISCUSSION

How does Welch's interpretation of the FBI mission differ from that of some previous leaders?

What is his view of a more appropriate administrative structure than he found?

What motivators will Welch offer his workers?

How will he bring the satisfaction of individuals and the achievement of the organizational mission into alignment so that they reinforce each other?

Who are some people you would consider good leaders? poor leaders? Why?

NEIL WELCH, BOAT ROCKER

Anthony Marro

It is 2 P.M. in the Philadelphia office of the Federal Bureau of Investigation, and Neil J. Welch, the SAC (for special agent in charge), is returning from lunch. He is a tall, serious man who seldom smiles in official photographs, who has a reputation as a loner and a brooder, and who is sometimes, but never to his face, called "Jaws," a nickname given him by agents in Philadelphia because, as one of them put it, "he can really chew your ass."

He walks slowly through the office, his head bowed slightly, his brow furrowed; the look and manner those of Alabama's "Bear" Bryant walking off toward a locker room, his team trailing by seven points at the half. He stops at a desk, checks his messages, then turns to his secretary, arches an eyebrow, and grins.

"Did Mr. Hoover call?" he asks.

J. Edgar Hoover has been dead for six years, the power of his surviving lieutenants has begun to fade, and there have been major, even radical, changes in the organization that he built in his likeness and then ruled dictatorially for almost half a century.

The signs of change are everywhere, from the more liberal dress and haircut codes approved by L. Patrick Gray (who is still highly regarded by agents because he ended many of the petty harassments of the Hoover years) to the more rational priorities (a greater emphasis on organized and white-collar crime, a lesser emphasis on stolen cars and military deserters) established by Clarence Kelley.

Moreover, there are indications that this move out of the shadow of Hoover will continue under William Webster, the current director, and one sign of this, in the view of many agents, is Webster's decision —to the consternation of many of his senior officials—to send Neil Welch back to New York to take charge of the office and its 830 agents.

Even before Welch's arrival, agents who worked with him in the past predicted that he will make major changes both in the structure of the office and in the kinds of cases the agents will work on. They expect him to yank agents off the routine bank robberies, truck hijackings, and bad-check cases that now make up much of the work of the office and to concentrate their efforts more on the sort of sophisticated organized and white-collar criminal schemes that some local prosecutors have complained they shied away from in the past. They expect that far more agents will be thrown into investigations of on-going criminal conspiracies—such as the massive probe of waterfront corruption now in progress in New York and other East Coast ports —and pulled out of the routine investigations of stolen cars, military deserters, and thefts of government property.

"There are a lot of old-timers at headquarters who aren't happy" about Welch's assignment, one FBI official said recently. "Back when Hoover was alive, people in the field couldn't blow their noses without an okay from headquarters, and the people at headquarters liked it that way. That's why they never felt comfortable with Neil. They think he went off the reservation too often."

It is no secret that Welch has gone "off the reservation" many times during the 27 years he has been in the bureau, particularly while serving as SAC in Philadelphia, Buffalo, and Detroit. Part of the reason was that he never shared the enthusiasm of his superiors for surveillance of political dissidents and refused to commit large numbers of agents to the job of monitoring harmless Trotskyist groups.

"The SWP [Socialist Workers Party] was never of any interest to me," he says. "It was never worth spending time or money on, so far as I was concerned."

Part of the reason also was that he considered many of the bureau's top priority cases—particularly hunts for deserters, small-time bank robbers, and stolen cars—to be a foolish waste of resources, designed more to produce impressive-looking statistics than to deal with urban crime. "It wasn't so much that he was anti-Establishment as that he was anti-waste," says Joseph MacFarlane, a former assistant to Welch in Philadelphia, who is now a top official in New York.

Moreover, Welch argued that the whole headquarters structure, as it operated under Hoover, and to a lesser extent under Kelley, was built on a false premise—the mistaken notion that it was possible to exert supervision over day-to-day activities of agents from 300, or 3,000 miles away.

The structure, he wrote in a letter to the committee President Carter created to find a new director (and which subsequently picked Welch as one of its five candidates, the only FBI official on the list), was a "ponderous, ineffectual, costly bureaucracy, which does not contribute substantially to the essential work of the FBI."

For their part, the headquarters officials over the years made only grudging acknowledgments of Welch's successes, barraged him with an unusually high number of surprise inspections, and waited, in vain, to catch him in the sort of mistake or embarrassment that could result in his banishment to some backwater or in his outright dismissal.

In 1970, the attitude of these officials was summed up by John Mohr, then the number-three man in the bureau, who, when Welch was promoted to the larger field office in Detroit, after considerable success against organized-crime families in Buffalo, told him: "Detroit is yours because no one else wants it."

Mohr is retired now, as are many of the others, and Welch insists he is more interested in doing a good job in New York than he is in continuing old feuds. "I'd just as soon you stopped writing about sandbags," he said in a recent interview, a reference to a statement he once made to the effect that the bureau would be better off if someone put sandbags around the J. Edgar Hoover Building and disconnected the telephones.

Whatever Welch's current relationship with the new leadership of the bureau, the decision of Webster to give him the New York job (which carries a title of assistant director and which makes him one of the half dozen most important officials in the agency) is viewed by many agents as being of great significance.

For one thing, it puts the bureau's largest field office in the hands of a man who has a track record of devoting his resources to serious crimes, rather than to the petty, easily solved violations that many FBI offices pursued in order to generate the blizzard of statistics that Hoover used to snow congressional committees.

For another, it suggests that while Hoover surrounded himself with a coterie that included a truly stunning number of sycophants, Webster is willing to promote officials who are known to speak their own minds, and who aren't reluctant to debate with their bosses.

Moreover, the general assumption within the bureau, at least among agents, is that Welch is likely to change the New York office in dramatic ways, and likely to have a major impact on federal law enforcement in the city.

"This isn't some guy who's on his way to the elephants' graveyard," says one agent who has worked with him and who knows him well. "That office needs someone to motivate it, and Neil's done that every place that he's been." . . .

There are a number of things that set the New York office apart from most others, and one is the large number of agents who are anxious to leave it. Last year, a check of FBI records showed that nearly two thirds of the agents in the city had listed other offices as their "office of preference" and that of the 7,000 or so agents working elsewhere in the country, only 4 had expressed any desire to move to New York.

The chief reasons, most agents agree, are that agents are paid the same money no matter where they are based, and working in New York, particularly in Manhattan, involves higher taxes, higher living costs, and a brutal commute.

This desire to flee the city was illustrated several years ago when an agent there lost his FBI credentials and was punished with a "disciplinary transfer" to the Midwest. "People there began throwing away their credentials. They were throwing them down the storm sewers," one agent recalls. "The bureau couldn't transfer them all out—that's what they wanted—so they had to give them letters of reprimand instead."

At the same time, there are many agents who like the city, who find the work exciting, and who stay on, in part, because the quality of the cases is so good. "We've got the best organized-crime and white-collar-crime cases right here," one agent said recently. "This is where the best counter-intelligence work is too. The Trojan horse, the United Nations, is right down the street."

This mixture of the resentment that many agents have about being assigned to New York and the conceit that many others have that they're working the hottest cases around has given rise to what is known at headquarters as "the New York attitude." The phrase is used in many ways, but in general it is used to sum up the hostility and scorn that agents in New York tend to display toward their nominal superiors in Washington, particularly those who have spent little time out on the street.

The office itself is large, sprawling, and complex, with nearly 50 individual squads (bank squads, hijacking squads, check squads, and the like) and with operating divisions (criminal, administration, internal security, and intelligence) larger than many whole field offices. It is so big, in fact, that while many agents complain about attempts by headquarters to run it from Washington, others question whether it can be controlled effectively from anywhere, including New York.

During the last fifteen years, the New York office has been headed by two men, John Malone and J. Wallace LaPrade. Malone, who was assistant director from 1962 through 1974, is a distinguished-looking former firearms instructor who delegated much authority to his subordinates, acted largely as a symbolic head of the office, and was known to many of his agents as "cement head."

Some of Malone's critics insist that the nickname was fitting. "You'd say, 'Hello, John,' and he'd be stuck for an answer," says one. But others disagree, arguing that he was a competent administrator, a man of great bravery, and that the nickname grew mainly from a hearing problem that he had developed while a firearms instructor, and which he never tried to have corrected.

"He used to try to fluff his way through conversations when he couldn't hear what was being said," says one former colleague. "That resulted in some situations that were almost ludicrous."

He was followed in February 1975 by LaPrade, who was well respected by agents and federal prosecutors while SAC in Newark but who is still remembered in St. Louis for the time when, as SAC there, he took the stand during a trial and mistakenly identified as the guilty party a United States marshal who was sitting inside the rail.

LaPrade lasted just three years and was ousted four months ago by Attorney General Griffin B. Bell, who charged that he hadn't fully cooperated with an investigation of illegal break-ins by FBI agents in the early 1970s during a hunt for Weathermen fugitives.

Whatever their record for running the office—and the reviews are mixed—there are many agents who insist that Welch has better credentials than either Malone or LaPrade had when they took charge.

MacFarlane, the former Welch aide who now heads the administrative division in New York, argues that Welch's background makes him uniquely suited to steer the office toward the priorities set by Webster and Bell: organized crime, white-collar crime, and foreign counterintelligence.

"He's shown he can direct agents on long, complicated cases," MacFarlane says. "They may be the director's priorities, but they're Neil's forte."

Welch has been developing his "forte" for 27 years, through work as a street agent in Bangor, Maine; Boston; and New York ("That was back before headquarters acknowledged the existence of the Mafia," he says); and administrative jobs in Tampa, Florida; Jackson, Mississippi; Buffalo; Philadelphia; and Detroit.

In general, he is well liked by agents, respected by prosecutors, and disliked and distrusted by many of the survivors of Hoover's old guard. He has a reputation as a competent manager in an agency that has been plagued by notoriously inept management in the past, and as a maverick in an organization so given to caution that, under Hoover, a routine response to a letter from a congressman had to be approved by more than a dozen officials before it could be sent.

Welch is not without his critics. There are former prosecutors who complain privately that, at least in the past, he tried to undercut them both personally and professionally when he didn't share their enthusiasm for certain cases. There are officials at headquarters who insist he is too headstrong and too stubborn for a key job in an agency that requires a high degree of central control.

Moreover, some older agents and officials smolder at his criticisms of Hoover, saying that he wasn't as openly critical while Hoover was still alive. "It's easy to talk in 1978 about what a turkey Hoover was," one of them said recently. "But Neil wasn't so outspoken back in 1968. He may have thwarted some of the things Hoover tried to do in the area of domestic intelligence, but he took his money from this outfit; he didn't resign."

A former eagle scout who was born in St. Paul, Minnesota, and raised in Nebraska, Welch has a wife, Geri, two college-age sons, and almost no outside interests, save golf, a game for which he reportedly has no talent at all.

According to FBI agents who have worked with him and for him, he seldom gets upset about honest mistakes but is harsh with agents who don't produce because of laziness or inertia. He has a reputation in the field for personal bravery (he once rescued a woman and her child from an escaped convict and then talked the man into giving up his gun and returning to prison). He's also known for making quick decisions and then sticking by them. A favorite saying, according to several colleagues, is: "I may be wrong, but I'm never in doubt."

Welch's ability to rebuild an office and change its priorities can be seen in Philadelphia, which had only two agents working political-, labor-, and business-corruption cases when he arrived in 1975, but had, according to one newspaper account, "vast flotillas of agents investigating the deadly threat of feminism and women's liberation."

Within two years, he had turned that around, shifting 50 agents onto political-corruption cases ("I felt like a woodsman in a virgin forest," he says) and, in general, insisting that agents work significant cases—investigating bank-robbery gangs, for example—rather than just specific bank robberies.

People who have worked with Welch expect him to begin immediately to restructure the New York office and to direct it toward broader ongoing criminal conspiracies.

"The first thing he'll do is have his supervisors rate all the agents on a scale of one to five," says a former co-worker. "That way he'll know who his .340 hitters are and who his .240 hitters are. The heavy hitters, especially if they're young and not burned out, will be the shock troops; the others he'll try to recycle."

Welch himself is known to question the wisdom of a high priority on bank robberies, which for the most part are uncomplicated and easily solved, and which agents like to work because they're exciting and fun and because, if gunfire is involved, they can get a story on page 3 of the *Daily News.*

"The New York office leads the country in the number of bank robberies it handles," he said, "and there's good reason to think that the local police, or the Nassau County police, could handle them if we stepped out of the picture."

And as for a restructuring of the office itself, Welch says he's confident that the system in Philadelphia was good for Philadelphia, but isn't committed to imposing it on New York.

"I'm not going to go up there and change everything just to change things; I'm not going to be George Allen [the football coach] and lay a system on them that's totally strange.

"There are a lot of hardworking kids up there, and they're not a part of the bureau's past—they're its future. If there's a new system in New York, it will be one that we'll develop together.

"The cases are there, and good cases can be pretty big compensation for the taxes and the high cost of living and the other things. If the work is drudgery, you've got a morale problem. But I've found that if agents are working hard and are given good cases, the morale will take care of itself."

Introduction
Snow Report

When individuals join large organizations they become part of something vast and complex. Other workers are scattered about in different departments, often in different buildings, sometimes even in different cities. Higher-ups in the hierarchy may occupy different floors and be seen rarely, if ever, by those at the bottom. It is difficult for the individual to relate directly to such an entity. Instead, individuals receive much of their social satisfaction in organizations through membership in informal groups. They give the group their loyalty and receive from it recognition and the satisfying feeling that they "belong."

As the Hawthorne studies revealed, a group has its norms as to appropriate attitudes and behavior on the part of its members. These norms are enforced through sanctions, in the form of social and other informal pressures on deviant members. In general, groups serve the organization by providing social satisfactions and control. But it can also happen that the selfish goals of a group displace the goals of the overall organization. This condition is called "suboptimization."

Consider now the plight of the hero of "Snow Report." Pat Saunders is dedicated to the goals and norms of his organization, the Federal Bureau of Narcotics and Dangerous Drugs. But his work unit contains a powerful secret group, nicknamed the Ski Club, with interests, procedures, and norms that violate those of the organization. He is under pressure to conform. But he is too principled to do so.

QUESTIONS FOR DISCUSSION
Why would the Ski Club be called an informal group? What makes it a group? What makes it "informal"?
What does the Ski Club offer its members?
What does the Ski Club demand of its members?
What sanctions could it impose?
What should Pat Saunders do?

SNOW REPORT

Sylvia Schneble and Donald Freed

Duane G. knew everything there was to know about coke; knew he had a sucker pegged if he or she bought a gram for over $100; knew the best cuts—like Inositol, a vitamin B compound which had the reputation for preventing baldness and constipation, among other things. Never mind the telltale post-nasal drip.

Duane circled the block for the meet in his primer gray, '57 Chevy, too snow-billed to take heed of the half dozen cars tailing him. When he finally did, it was too late. Six unmarked cars screeched up and Duane jumped out of the Chevy and rolled between two parked cars.

"Hold it, you motherfucker!" yelled Special Agent (S/A) Stiles of the Bureau of Narcotics and Dangerous Drugs (BNDD) as he leaped towards him. Together with a Long Beach Police Department undercover man they slammed the hype against the wall and began their "interrogation." . . .

S/A Patrick Saunders, ace wiretap expert of the Intelligence Unit, watched helplessly from behind one of the surveillance cars. He didn't like what he saw. The P.D. took one side and Stiles the other—both ignoring Duane's pleas of mercy as they jammed his face against the wall, demanding to know where his connection was. . . .

"Hey, lighten up, guys. He's not resisting arrest. . . ."

Stiles ignored Pat, so the young, blond Irishman threatened to report the incident to the Bureau's Office of Inspection (OI).

The Office of Inspection was the internal wing of the BNDD which was designed to function as an investigative police force, known euphemistically as "shoofly." Inspection's task, on paper, was "to correct deficiencies in employee behavior and attitude. . . . Correct situations which interfere with efficient operations, maintain the high standards of government services, and maintain the public confidence in BNDD."

In reality, the OI was the ineffective watchdog for agents who stepped out of line. And right now Stiles was stepping out of line— way out of line. The beating continued. So Duane G. finally agreed to take them to the source. Inside the house, while gathering evidence, someone stole $400 of Duane's money from his dresser drawer.

That night after the case was locked up, Stiles told S/A Fezmire that Pat Saunders was going to implicate them in the beating and that Saunders had seen Stiles take the money out of the bedroom.

Nine months later Saunders was indicted on charges of embezzling the $400 from Duane G. To finger Pat, Stiles and Fezmire perjured themselves in court.

From Crawdaddy, June 1978.

At first, Pat had thought that the serious corruption of Bureau agents was what was being covered up at all costs. The cash involved was considerable; Jerry Laveroni, a Special Agent expert on organized crime, called it "the ground floor incentive plan."

Saunders got his first taste of big money the night a team of agents kicked in Abel Quadrelle's door. He and Agent Combs covered the bedroom. Combs may have been looking for narcotics but what he found was $10,000.

On the porch, afterwards, as the party was breaking up, Combs slipped Saunders $200. "Here's yours, the rest goes into the split." The split was the informal organization that controlled the cash flow. Veteran agents handled the money and never disclosed the totals involved. Dividends were usually paid according to whether you knew what had actually taken place; and if so, how much. Inclusion in the split was by no means automatic.

"If they think you're going to be loyal," Saunders wrote, "a team player sort of thing, then everything's cool. Then some guy'll say, 'Hey,' hand you some money, and if you take it, they figure you're one of the boys." . . .

Pat Saunders took two weeks off to analyze the events and what he deemed to be Bureau "horrors." Upon his return he went to see Assistant Regional Director Leo Bacerra and told him he had had enough. He was sick of the Bureau. He was quitting.

Bacerra looked pleased and shook Pat's hand. "Let bygones be bygones," he said "Don't say anything about anybody else and you'll be OK." He slapped Pat fraternally on the back. "Get yourself a new profession, kid." Pat resisted telling him where to shove it, and left.

As Pat was cleaning out his desk, two inspectors from the Bureau's Washington Office of Inspection insisted Pat follow them into the Conference Room. There, they locked the door. One of the Inspectors told Pat they knew Léo Bacerra and something called the "Ski Club" was involved in illegal activities and wanted Pat to cooperate with their investigation. If he did, they'd forget all about the charges against him.

"You're not going to forget anything because I didn't do anything," Pat said soberly. "I'll cooperate only if you're willing to do something about the corruption around here. I'm not going to let you intimidate me by saying you'll help me only if I cooperate."

The two inspectors looked at each other. They could bring formal charges against him, they warned. Pat stood his ground. He wouldn't cooperate under these circumstances and walked out of the room.

It was then that the late-night threatening phone calls began. A few days later Pat contacted Washington *Post* columnist Jack Anderson and said he wanted to talk to him about what he had seen and learned while he was an agent of the United States government and a member of the notorious Ski Club within BNDD's Region 14. Anderson said he'd be in L.A. in a week and would contact Pat then.

But he never did.

It was obvious to Pat that Anderson had been tipped off by some of his Justice Department contacts that Pat Saunders was about to be indicted; wasn't a guy to be trusted; to stay away from him. He's trouble.

With his defense attorney, Ronald Sherwood, Pat prepared witnesses for the trial: Duane G. and fellow agents Johnny Q. Sanchez and Steve Kenworth. A week before the hearings a doctor from the Metropolitan Hospital called Pat saying that Duane G. wouldn't be able to testify. He was in the hospital kicking a heroin habit. No way could Pat justify putting a hype on the stand. Pat's pal, wiretap tutor Johnny Q. Sanchez, was called to testify. He was suddenly transferred to Texas. S/A Kenworth was willing to testify about Stiles' reputation as a notorious liar; he too was "assigned" to Texas.

Sherwood told Pat he would lose the case because the Bureau would bring in supervisors to say Pat was lazy and uncooperative. He suggested Pat plead guilty to a misdemeanor. If he didn't and was found guilty, he could look forward to a maximum of ten years in prison.

"But I didn't do anything, goddamn it!" Pat seethed.

"Yeah, but that's not what their agents are saying," Sherwood countered.

"Why believe them instead of me?"

"Cause you're the misfit, for chrissakes. You're the troublemaker, an embarrassment to the Bureau 'cause you won't wear a suit, won't cut your hair—and you wear a peace button!" The attorney paused dramatically and looked hard into Pat's blue eyes. "Besides, kid," he said cryptically. "You know too much about the Ski Club. . . ."

Pat took the misdemeanor and a $1000 fine. That was before he found out that Ronald Sherwood was an ally of the Club. . . .

Jerry Laveroni was on his way to the Bureau's Office of Inspection when he pulled his car to a stop in front of the Federal Courthouse in Los Angeles. Some premonition deep in his guts warned him to watch out. Earlier, he had noticed a green souped-up VW (cut out in back for a Porsch engine) tailing him. A .38 slug cracked over his head, just missing his six-foot frame as he crouched low.

Jerry tried to get the license number but failed. The VW fishtailed through a red light and disappeared the wrong way down a one-way street.

Three days later Jerry walked into Bacerra's office and handed in his letter of resignation.

Bacerra scanned the letter behind the cluttered mahogany desk. "Laveroni," he grinned unctuously, "I don't blame you one bit. Keep in touch. Don't be a stranger." With that he turned his back on Jerry, pretending absorption in a stack of Bureau transmittals.

To Jerry, the "end" seemed anticlimatic. So this was it. At least he expected a drum roll, bells, something to herald his ten years of distinguished service in law enforcement. Slowly it dawned on him who had taken a pot shot at him: the mysterious, omnipotent, unforgiving "Ski Club." His knees were weak with a fear and rage that wouldn't leave him for years to come. . . .

Pat and Jerry knew about each other, that they were "dead men." The only way out, they decided, was to join forces and debunk the "narc" myth. . . .

By far the most powerful "group" was the unauthorized "Ski Club." The exact origin of the Club isn't precisely known, but it rose to power and infamy through internal politicking as early as the late '50s. It was headed by the scheming Leo Bacerra, the Club's progenitor and high priest. His power base rested on contacts in the upper levels of the Bureau. Desk burglaries of supervisors and tapping of BNDD workers' phones were common Ski Club tactics. Dossiers were built on dissenting and rebelling agents and supervisors alike, as well as competing political factions, for blackmail and extortion. . . .

At first Pat and Jerry rationalized that the Ski Club was comprised of the brightest and best of the agents, a southern California "old boy" gang of sorts that made the best cases, had the most fun, looked good, rose through the ranks fastest, and were immune from internal and external prosecution. A friend of Jerry's, who had also quit, told Jerry the BNDD reminded him

> of Hitler's regime. You have the regular army, that's the agents; and the SS, that's the Ski Club—then here on the outside, the Gestapo is 'Inspection,' each trying to get on top of each other. You know the old saying in the Bureau: 'If you got a rabbi, you're gonna make it.' Some big honcho back in Washington, a rabbi, who likes your act and protects you. In practice that means you better be prepared to cover your ass. Give them an opening and it's curtains.

Over the years within the narcotics bureaucracy, lines of support have caused cliques to form and lock horns over the choice governmental positions. Throughout its history as FBN, BNDD, and now Drug Enforcement Administration (DEA), the Los Angeles Office of Inspection has been one of the best bases from which to strike. Region 14 evolved two factions which spent great amounts of time and energy trying to discredit one another.

Said Jerry, "They can make a case on anybody. It's just a matter of how or where you stand, if they want to 'do' you or not."

By Pat and Jerry's time, the ferocity of the infighting had sky-rocketed. These were the Nixon years. Money was flowing easily from the Nixonian cornucopia, and the intra-agency brush war was escalating dangerously.

One sure promotion was "doing" another agent. There were those in the Bureau who made a career of building paper cases on fellow agents who had fallen from grace, through personal enmity or Club vendetta; reports were written, calls monitored, desks rifled, setups made, traps set—all waiting for the Big Slipup. Should the targeted agent commit the slightest offense, the sword of Damocles came down on his head.

An ounce of heroin in a desk, especially if you knew an ARD checked the desk, was an effective measure of control. Blackmail was the best defense. If you could bust your enemy, he would think twice about busting you. It amounted to a balance of terror. Jerry and Pat had seen fellow agents madly tapping each others' phones, breaking into each others' desks, trying to feed the losers into the jaws of Inspection. The warfare left little time for the pursuit of street criminals. The winners went public as Mr. Clean, and the losers were cast into the brimstone of "corruption." . . .

Said Jerry, "When the OI investigates you, you never know when the investigation ends. It was used to manipulate and control your future if you dared step out of line."

And Pat and Jerry had really stepped out of line.

The Ski Club was extremely well connected at the telephone company, where security men in Ma Bell's stable could get unlisted numbers for them at any time. But the phone company clamped down on the Bureau's agents from time to time, to avoid getting caught itself. An electronics wizard who made most of the phone company's equipment (later, for the CIA) gave illegal equipment to the "boys" at the Ski Club. . . .

It seemed the Ski Club could weather transitional storms from both the local Office of Inspection and HQ in Washington. The OI came down hard trying to derail the Club or make inroads into the rumors that the Club was alive and well and festering within the Region like a cancerous growth, controlling L.A. and major investigations throughout the United States.

L.A.'s Regional Director cried the blues about the Ski Club—which he feared. He couldn't run his Region because his hands were tied behind his back by Bacerra.

Remembers Pat, "One time, Harpo jimmied open [Regional Director Otis] Quinn's desk and found 700 Darvon capsules. Maybe it was a setup. After all of Quinn's hollering, yelling and finger-pointing, the Ski Club still marches on. . . ."

Bigger and more powerful than before.

Leo Bacerra no longer works for the Bureau. He's now in a high-level government position working for his cousin, a Senator for a prominent Southwestern state.

Introduction
The Rise and Fall of
Richard Helms

The "organization man" is often defined as an individual who has bartered his conscience for his security. He or she is a survivor, a faceless product of the necessity "to go along to get along." As civil servants, such people serve Democrats or Republicans, liberals or conservatives. They are cooperative, adept at stroking colleagues, studious in building informal links within the organization, protective of their subordinates. In short, they are successful bureaucrats.

Richard Helms, who was a bureaucrat in the intelligence community for 30 years, the last seven as director of Central Intelligence, was such an organization man. He improved his position quietly within the CIA over a period of years. Powers interprets Helms as a calculating bureaucrat, ever careful to dole out enough information to please and protect his superiors, but not so much as to jeopardize his position. He avoided policymaking, serving "one President at a time." His chief concerns were retaining his position and protecting his agency. When a congressional committee questioned him, he lied. In so doing, he protected an agency operation and its personnel. He also put himself above the law and betrayed the duly elected representatives of the people. "If public officials embark deliberately on a course to disobey and ignore the laws of our land . . . the future of our country is in jeopardy," said the judge in pronouncing the sentence of a $2000 fine and one year's unsupervised probation.

QUESTIONS FOR DISCUSSION

Why is Helms called the "perfect bureaucrat"?
Was Helms' behavior ethical?
Did he look on advancement as a game?
Was Helms seeking to serve the public interest?
How typical is Helms of bureaucrats in general?

THE RISE AND FALL OF RICHARD HELMS

Thomas Powers

Richard McGarrah Helms believed in secrets. Of course, everyone in the American intelligence community believes in secrets in theory, but Helms really believed in secrets the way Lyman Kirkpatrick believed in secrets. At one point years ago they were rivals in the Central Intelligence Agency. But they had certain things in common and one of them was a belief in secrets. They did not like covert action operations—subsidizing politicians in Brazil, parachuting into Burma, preparing poisoned handkerchiefs for inconvenient Arab colonels, all that sleight of hand and derring-do of World War II vintage which certain veterans of the Office of Strategic Services (OSS) brought into the CIA—because covert action operations had a built-in uncertainty factor. They tended to go wrong, and even when they succeeded they tended to get out. Too many people knew about them. You couldn't keep them secret; not just confidential for the life of the administration, like so many secrets in Washington, but secret, in Lyman Kirkpatrick's phase, "from inception to eternity."

As Director of Central Intelligence (DCI) from June 1966 until February 1973, Helms was as close to anonymous as a senior government official can be. In political memoirs of the period Helms is often in the index, but when you check the text he is only a walk-on, one of those names in sentences which begin, "Also at the meeting were. . . ." If it were not for a little . . . bad luck . . . Helms would be as faintly remembered now as Rear Admiral Roscoe Hillenkoetter or General Hoyt Vandenberg, two early DCIs. . . .

Helms' personal background was atypical of the CIA in two ways. He went to school in Europe (Le Rosey in Switzerland, a posh social institution with Mohammed Riza Pahlavi, later Shah of Iran, who also went) and he had no money of his own. The practical importance of this fact was that Helms, unlike many early CIA people, needed his job. He could not afford to resign if he got mad and he knew it. In all other respects—race, politics and social background—Helms was typical of the Eastern, old family, old money, WASP patricians who ran the great financial institutions, the Wall Street law firms, the Foreign Service and the CIA. . . .

If it had not been for Watergate, which opened up the American government like an archaeologist's trench, Helms would have retired and remained unknown by the general public. Even now he remains an elusive figure, despite dozens of congressional hearings. He does not give interviews, his friends are cautious in discussing him, his enemies found him hard to fathom even when they worked down the hall, and nobody connected with an intelligence agency really believes in letting facts speak for themselves.

This is not to say that Richard Helms was a retiring public servant, one of those gray men who washes his own socks. Far from it. He was personable and good-looking in a dark, brilliantined sort of way, and he got about a good deal socially. He even dated Barbara Howar, and he was never at a loss for a luncheon partner. But lunch was part of the job. The CIA lives on a kind of sufferance and it was Helms' job to see that the Agency's fragile charter survived intact. So he often lunched with the kind of men—Senators, senior government officials, important journalists—whose good will, whose trust, in fact, gave the Agency the freedom from scrutiny it needed to do its job.

One of the men Helms used to see regularly in this way was C. L. Sulzberger, the diplomatic correspondent for the *New York Times*. They would lunch at Helms' regular table at the Occidental and talk about Soviet strategic capabilities, Greece and Cyprus (in which Sulzberger took a special interest), why the North Vietnamese failed to stage an offensive during Nixon's trip to Peking, things like that.

"You know," Helms told Sulzberger once, "I tell you almost anything."

Helms reputation in official Washington—as opposed to his broader public reputation, which is more recent, more sinister and less precise—is that of an able, honest man, with the emphasis on honesty. The journalists who talked to him and the congressmen he briefed over the years trusted Helms implicitly. Even at the height of the war in Vietnam, when Lyndon Johnson was calling for "progress" reports as a patriotic duty, Helms would go into an executive session with Senator Fulbright's committee and tell them the bad news. Like Sulzberger, the senators convinced themselves that Helms told them just about anything. They did not grasp the extent to which he answered questions narrowly, or phrased himself exactly, or volunteered nothing.

But not even that covers it. There are some secrets you just flat-out lie to protect, and Helms knew a lot of them. Until he became DCI, Helms' entire career had been in the Deputy Directorate for Plans. He had lived through every bureaucratic battle in Washington and he knew the details of every operation abroad, not just the routine agent-running but Cold War exotica involving Ukrainian emigrés penetrating the "denied areas" of Russia, Polish undergrounds, counterguerrilla operations in Latin America, the acquisition of the Gehlen organization from Nazi Germany at the end of the war. The world looked quite different in the early years of the Cold War, and things that seemed demented or criminal now sometimes looked plausible then.

Helms knew every crazy, crack-brained scheme dreamed up over drinks late at night—or meticulously, in committee, where men were sometimes crazier still—and he knew what would happen if those things ever got out. It was bad enough having Jean-Paul Sartre and half of black Africa think the CIA had killed Lumumba. What would happen if the *New York Times* found out about secret drug testing, links to the Mafia, poison-pen devices . . .? Helms knew secrets which could wreck the whole CIA and leave the United States with a crippled intelligence agency, or no intelligence agency at all.

There is only one man with a right to ask questions about such things: the president. If the president were to ask, clearly and unmistakably, Dick, what about this story the CIA tried to kill Castro with the help of the Mafia? Is this true?

Helms would have to answer a question like that. But God forbid the president should ever ask. Once you begin to look into such matters there was no telling what you would find, or what would follow, or where it would end.

There is no way to rise to the top of a bureaucratic structure like the Central Intelligence Agency without a combination of ability and luck. Helms' abilities were narrow and conventional; he was a man of lean gifts. He was a first-rate administrator, for example, quite unlike Dulles, who would call for a briefing from one of his top men and then keep him waiting outside his office for an hour while he chatted on his intercom with Robert Amory, the deputy director for intelligence. Helms was also a great manager of men. He always dealt with people with what one colleague called a "perceptive courtesy," and it is easy to collect stories of Helms' consideration and regard where personal relations were concerned.

Helms knew a great deal about running agents, the most delicate work in the field of intelligence and, before the introduction of the U-2 and reconnaissance satellites, potentially the most valuable. But even this talent probably did not have so much to do with Helms' rise in the CIA as plain luck.

Some of his luck was of the traditional sort—being in the right job at the right time—but occasionally Helms' luck required something close to an act of God. His rise to the top of the Deputy Directorate for Plans (DDP), for example, required the departure of three men his own age and at least his equal in ability, who could have been expected to remain right where they were.

The first to go was Lyman Kirkpatrick, something of a protégé of an early DCI named Walter Bedell Smith. In the summer of 1952 Kirkpatrick, an ambitious man who was then Helms' immediate superior, came down with infantile paralysis during a trip to the Far East. Eventually he returned to the Agency in a wheelchair, but by that time he was no longer blocking Helms' path.

The second was Frank Wisner, a charming and intelligent Southerner of independent means who was the first head of the Deputy Directorate for Plans. In the fall of 1956, probably sparked by the Hungarian uprising which he witnessed from Vienna, Wisner suffered a nervous breakdown. Helms was appointed the acting DDP while Wisner was on leave, and then reappointed after Wisner suffered a relapse and permanently left the DDP in late 1958.

Helms was not alone in thinking Dulles would appoint him the next DDP after Wisner's departure.

He had been Wisner's deputy since 1952, he was widely considered a protégé of Dulles', and he had a group of CIA friends—one former colleague described Helms as a cardinal surrounded by his bishops—who were backing him for the job.

Dulles appointed Richard Bissell.

Helms was so disappointed that for a while in late '58 he even thought about leaving the Agency, or perhaps taking a post abroad. The foreign assignments were the most interesting in the CIA but they were off the upward path, away from the centers of bureaucratic power where careers are made and unmade. Helms' career seemed to have been unmade in late 1958 and if it had not been for some personal troubles (according to one of his colleagues at the time) he probably would have left the country. Instead, he accepted a job as Bissell's deputy.

The true explanation of Bissell's promotion was probably not so much Helms' failings as the fact that Dulles had great respect for Bissell's brilliance, and that he liked him. Dulles was a talker and storyteller, a man who liked knowing people, and who appreciated flair, energy, wit and imagination. Bissell had worked on the Marshall Plan before joining the CIA at Dulles' request in 1954, he was well-known on the Hill, he had a wide social acquaintance, and he was a man of ideas.

The first major assignment Dulles gave Bissell when he joined the CIA was to find some way of penetrating the so-called "denied areas" of Eastern Europe and Russia, something Helms and the clandestine foreign intelligence side of the DDP had largely failed to do. Bissell had come up with the U-2, which provided huge quantities of intelligence, and later he developed the satellite reconnaissance program, which produced even more. This was without question the CIA's greatest single achievement, an intelligence gain which has been directly responsible for the arms-limitation agreement reached with the Soviet Union by Nixon and Kissinger in May 1972. The Russians have always refused on-site inspections, and without satellite reconnaissance such arms agreements would have been impossible, because the sine qua non of trust—exact knowledge that an opponent is in fact keeping his promises—would have been lacking. After an achievement of that magnitude it is only natural that Dulles would have given Bissell the best job available, which turned out to be the one Helms thought he deserved. The result, equally naturally, was that Helms and Bissell did not get along.

One reason for their cool relationship—Bissell cannot remember ever having had a general conversation with Helms—was that Bissell was openly skeptical of the value of traditional intelligence agents. Even with Oleg Penkovskiy, who delivered more than 10,000 pages of documents to Britain's MI-6 and CIA between April 1961 and August 1962, Bissell was doubtful. "How do you know this guy is on the level?" he would ask John Maury, head of the DDP's Soviet division at the time. Maury pointed out that no intelligence agency in its right mind would hand over material of that quality solely in order to prove the bona fides of an agent. Later Penkovskiy's information would be of critical importance during the Cuban missile crisis when it showed, among other things, that the missiles in Cuba could hit every major city in the United States except Seattle. But Bissell was skeptical anyway and Helms resented it.

These and other differences created a little cold war within the DDP. "Take it up with Wonder Boy next door," Helms would sometimes say in answer to a request. His allies started what amounted to a whispering campaign against Bissell's professionalism where spies were concerned (he thought a lot of them were a plain waste of time and money) and his administrative ability, which was as erratic as Dulles'. He got results, as the U-2 showed, but his methods caused a lot of confusion along the way. The little war simmered just beneath the DDP's surface (Helms' secretary used to say, "Well, we all know Dick really should have been DDP") until the Bay of Pigs. At that time their differences—expressed bureaucratically, as always—reached a point of such heat that Helms came within a hairbreadth of being banished from Washington.

The basis of their disagreement was the old one—the distrust of the Foreign Intelligence specialists for covert paramilitary operations that balloon to such a size that the hand behind them can no longer be hidden. The Bay of Pigs was the biggest operation of all, expanding from a proposal for a limited landing of guerrillas to a full-blown invasion force with ships, an air force and well over a thousand fighting men.

Helms knew how to disguise and mute his role, which makes it difficult to reconstruct just exactly what he did to anger Bissell. As assistant DDP he had control of the money, the people and the directives going out to the field, all of which gave him a vantage from which to subtly impede, frustrate and harass the Bay of Pigs planning. One former colleague and rival "imagines" (CIA people often tell you things elliptically) that Helms must have tried to protect his own assets, refused to assign his best people to the project, advised those involved not to back it too strongly. Others say he discussed it quietly with the DDP's division chiefs, encouraged a consensus of doubt and opposition, argued (but not insistently) with Dulles that experienced operators doubted the CIA's role could be hidden and so on. He would not have said, "This is foolish and wrong," but he might have said it was unworkable, impractical, unwieldly, a threat to CIA assets built up over the years, and more properly the work of the Joint Chiefs of Staff.

It was arguments of this sort, at any rate, which Helms took to Robert Hilsman at the State Department. Early in 1961 he told Hilsman he did not know exactly what was going on, that he disagreed with what he knew, that Bissell was running off on his own without a word of advice from the Office of National Estimates (ONE) or Robert Amory, the Deputy Director of Intelligence (DDI). He told Hilsman he had argued with Bissell and Dulles without effect, and Hilsman, alarmed, "put in my two cents' worth with Rusk," also without effect.

Bissell, characteristically, says that to the extent he knew of Helms' opposition at the time he "probably" resented it. Others say he was angered by Helms' disloyalty in even raising the issue with CIA people like James Angelton, not to mention outsiders like Hilsman.

Whatever the exact cause of Bissell's anger, he went to Dulles early in 1961 and said he could no longer work with Helms. Dulles disliked personal conflicts of this sort but finally steeled himself and gave Helms a bleak ultimatum—London Chief of Station or resignation. . . .

As things turned out, Helms was not required to make the painful choice Dulles had offered him. On April 15th, 1961, the Bay of Pigs invasion was launched, and three days later it ended with the surrender of the entire surviving invasion force. It was not Helms who left Washington or the CIA, but Dulles (in November 1961) and Bissell (the following February). The new director, a conservative Republican businessman named John McCone, appointed Helms DDP.

Helms had reached the CIA's top level, and had even been mentioned for the first time outside the Agency as a potential Director, Hilsman having suggested to Rusk that Helms be appointed to replace Dulles. The suggestion didn't get anywhere—Kennedy had political problems on his right, and McCone's appointment served as a buffer— but Helms, all the same, was on the upward path. He was in charge of the CIA's most important branch, in a position of real authority for the first time, but he also was, as he learned, in charge of the secrets, and when Dulles and Bissell left the CIA, they left plenty.

The biggest secret, known to only a handful of CIA officials, was assassination. If it were not for a little-noticed Drew Pearson column on March 7th, 1967, the assassination plots might never have been revealed at all. But on that day, or soon after, President Johnson saw the story and two weeks later, in a White House meeting on the evening of March 22nd, Johnson personally asked Richard Helms about it. By that time Johnson had a preliminary FBI report on the matter and he apparently put his questions to Helms with a directness which could not be evaded.

Johnson told Helms he wanted a full report, not only about Castro but about Trujillo and Diem as well. On March 23rd Helms—however reluctantly, after years of resisting just such inquiries—asked CIA Inspector General Gordon Stewart to conduct an investigation.

Helms did not like covert action operations and assassination is the most dangerous of them all. Skeptics may say this was only a deceptive mask, when you consider all the operations with which he was involved, but the available evidence supports his reputation among CIA people as a foreign intelligence man first, last and always. He was skeptical of the underground stay-behind nets organized for Eastern Europe in the late 1940s and early 1950s; he was happy to turn over the Meo army in Laos and the pacification program in Vietnam to the Pentagon in the late 1960s, and throughout his career he was known as a man who would quietly discourage just about every covert action proposal brought up in his presence. . . .

If Helms was doubtful about the utility of most paramilitary and covert action programs, he was doubly skeptical of assassinations, which were hard to organize, harder to keep secret, and all but impossible to justify or explain away once revealed. But this does not mean that he opposed them in principle or refused to contribute to carrying them out. Either would have been out of character. Helms is often described by CIA people as a "good soldier," by which they mean someone who will argue with a policy until it is adopted, but not afterward. Assassination plans did not originate with Helms, and he did not encourage or push or support them with energy, but there is no record that he ever opposed one either, and he had been Director of Central Intelligence for five years before he issued an explicit order that assassination was forbidden. Helms' private policy on assassination was purely pragmatic, but for a while more effective: he tried only to keep them secret.

There are only three known plots by the CIA to deliberately kill specific foreign leaders—an Iraqi colonel, Patrice Lumumba and Fidel Castro. The first plot did not get very far. The plot against Lumumba was extensive and energetic but superseded by events when Lumumba was abducted by his Congolese enemies and murdered by them, probably on January 17th, 1961, according to a United Nations investigation conducted at the time. The plot, or plots, against Castro were first proposed in late 1959 and were actively pursued from 1960 until 1965 when Lyndon Johnson, preoccupied with the Dominican Republic and Vietnam, called off all covert action operations against Cuba.

The ultimate responsibility for the assassination plots is uncertain. It is hard to imagine that Dulles, DCI during the initiation of all of them, would have acted without at least indirect authority from the president. But Dulles, and the presidents he served, are dead, next to nothing about assassination is mentioned in the minutes of official meetings, and the aides of Eisenhower and Kennedy still swear their men would never stoop to murder.

Richard Bissell told the Senate Select Committee that he assumed Dulles was acting with presidential authority, and that he, Bissell was certainly acting with Dulles' authority. While Bissell was DDP Helms remained in the background. A CIA intelligence officer asked by Bissell to take over the faltering Lumumba plot in October 1960 protested vigorously and went to several CIA officials, including Lyman Kirkpatrick, the Inspector General, and Helms. Kirkpatrick went to Dulles and protested that the plan was absolutely crazy. Dulles thanked him for his opinion. Helms simply listened to the intelligence officer's protest, told him he was "absolutely right," and did nothing else whatever. He did not protest to Bissell, Dulles or Kirkpatrick, and when he was asked about it by the Senate Select Committee 15 years later he conceded it was "likely" he had discussed the Lumumba plot with the intelligence officer asked to carry it out, that the officer's version of their conversation was probably correct, but that he did not remember anything else about the plan or what happened to it.

The plots to kill Castro were far more extensive, beginning with a plan in 1960 to retain two Mafia figures, John Rosselli and Sam Giancana, both of whom were later murdered after the assassination story finally got out. Their interests in Cuban resorts and gambling casinos gave them a private motive for killing Castro, not to mention the $150,000 offered them by the CIA. Helms apparently had nothing to do with the early stages of the plots, but after the departure of Dulles and Bissell he inherited Operation Mongoose, an anti-Castro effort which had the strong support of the Kennedy brothers.

Later plots sometimes bordered on the bizarre and included one plan to give Castro a poisoned wet-suit for skin diving, and another to place a gorgeous but booby-trapped seashell on the ocean floor where Castro liked to go diving. When the CIA's operational officers in charge of the Castro plots came to Helms he routinely approved their plans for contacts with the Mafia or the provision of poison-pen devices and sniper rifles to a dissident member of Castro's government —whatever, in fact, those in charge of the plots thought they needed— but he does not appear to have believed the plots were going anywhere, and he deliberately avoided telling John McCone, the new DCI, anything about them.

Despite this initial evasion when Helms became DDP he only narrowly managed to keep the facts from McCone three months later, in May 1962, during a complicated wiretap case involving the FBI, the CIA's liaison with the Mafia, Robert Maheu, and the attorney general. After an initial briefing, Robert Kennedy requested a written memorandum on the CIA's involvement in the matter and one was submitted on May 14th, 1962. The memorandum, with Helms' approval, admitted an early CIA-Mafia plot to kill Castro but deliberately left out the fact that the assassination attempts were still going on—Rosselli, in fact, had been given poison pills only a few weeks earlier—and implied that the operation had been terminated "approximately" in May 1961. Despite the involvement of many high CIA officials, Helms again managed to avoid telling McCone anything about it.

Helms dealt with Bobby Kennedy and McCone in the same way. He would tell them nothing about assassination plots if that were possible, and he would minimize them if he had to say something. The last thing he would admit was the fact they were continuing, because that would incriminate him.

Bissell, among others, said that Helms' characteristic way of dealing with an inherited operation he didn't like was to cut off its funds, ask skeptical questions, delay its paper work—in effect, to starve it to death quietly. To kill it quickly would only make enemies of its supporters. Helms seems to have treated the ongoing assassination plots in precisely this way, letting them die of their own inertia, and perhaps thinking that if one somehow worked—if some Havana busboy really did manage to slip botulin into Castro's beans—well, who would object? Whatever the truth, there is no question Helms did everything he could to keep it to himself. . . .

There are many . . . examples of Helms' continuing and determined effort to conceal or minimize the CIA's attempts to carry out assassinations. In 1966 Dean Rusk somehow learned of one of them, but Helms denied it flatly in a memo which he later admitted was "inaccurate." In 1964 Helms avoided all mention of anti-Castro plots in front of the Warren Commission (as did Allen Dulles, a member of the commission, and J. Edgar Hoover, who had by this time a fairly complete knowledge of the Giancana-Rosselli plot).

But on March 22nd, 1967, Helms was asked a question by President Johnson which he could not evade. He ordered the CIA's Inspector General to make a full investigation and over the following nine weeks the IG did so. When he first began to receive sections of the IG report on April 24th, 1967, Helms' reaction must have been one of queasy horror. Everything was there, every plan to shoot Castro or poison him or blow him up; the CIA's provision of arms to the men who eventually assassinated Trujillo in the Dominican Republic in 1961; the CIA's intimate foreknowledge and encouragement of the coup which resulted in Diem's assassination in 1963; the continuing Castro plots and Helms' efforts to hide them from John McCone; the fact that the CIA had gone on trying to kill Castro after Johnson became president, and did not finally give up the attempt once and for all—so far as we know—until 1965.

Helms read the report as it came in and then, on the day it was completed, May 23rd, 1967, he ordered Gordon Stewart to destroy every piece of paper connected with the investigation, every last interview and internal memo and working draft. Stewart did as he was ordered. By that time—it is not known exactly when, but it was between April 24th and May 23rd—Helms had already gone to see Johnson to tell him the secrets which he, Helms had been trying to suppress since the beginning of the decade.

Johnson was apparently shocked by what he learned. He later told a journalist that "we had been operating a damned Murder Inc. in the Caribbean." He even concluded that Castro must have arranged Kennedy's murder in retaliation for the CIA's plots to kill him. "I'll tell you something that will rock you," Johnson said to Howard K. Smith, the television newsman, before leaving the White House 18 months after Helms' briefing. "Kennedy was trying to get Castro, but Castro got to him first."

The IG's report makes no such bald claim, but then again Johnson did not see the report. Helms gave Johnson an oral briefing instead, leaving out a great many details—it is not hard to guess which ones— and halting his account in 1963—the year Johnson took over. Even *in extremis* as he was, responding to a direct presidential request, Helms managed to keep some of the secrets.

The president is the sun in the CIA's universe. The cabinet secretaries all have constituencies of their own, with interests which sometimes conflict with the president's, but the Central Intelligence Agency and its Director serve the president alone. If he does not trust or value the CIA's product, then the paper it produces ceases to have meaning or weight in government councils and the Agency might as well unplug its copiers, since it is talking only to itself. The first duty of the DCI, then, not by statute but as a matter of practical reality, is to win the trust, the confidence and the ear of the president. Allen Dulles had Eisenhower's but lost Kennedy's. John McCone had Kennedy's but lost Johnson's, and Richard Helms was close enough to the top during McCone's tenure to watch it happen.

There are various explanations for McCone's failure with Johnson. He irritated Secretary of Defense Robert McNamara with frequent pleas for support in intelligence community battles with the Defense Intelligence Agency. He irritated Johnson with his skepticism about the president's War on Poverty. He once said, for example, that he had some poor relatives himself, but what they needed was a little hard work, not another government program. Johnson was not amused. Far more important, however, was the fact that McCone slipped out of phase with Johnson on Vietnam.

Throughout 1964 and 1965 McCone argued that the United States should neither bomb the North nor send troops to the South unless the president were willing to bomb heavily and send a lot of troops. But Johnson was preoccupied with the politics of the war; he wanted to slip around his critics by moving slowly. McCone argued that it was better to do nothing than too little, touching the president's rawest nerve, the soft point in his consensus.

In the past McCone had talked privately with Kennedy once a week, a source of great bureaucratic authority. Now McCone found it hard to see Johnson at all, even in groups. He was pointedly dropped from the Tuesday lunch, Johnson's main foreign-policy-making group, and he was told the president was no longer reading the CIA's paper. McCone never quite knew why he couldn't get along with Johnson but for one brief moment, when Johnson invited him to fly up to New York on the presidential plane for Herbert Hoover's funeral, McCone hoped that perhaps he was getting through at last. One CIA colleague said McCone was as happy with his invitation as a kid with a new toy, but it turned out to mean nothing. Johnson apparently had assumed that since Hoover was a conservative Republican, and McCone was a conservative Republican, it was only right to take one to the funeral of the other. Early in 1965 McCone told an aide, "I've been trying to get Johnson to sit down and read these papers [Soviet strategic estimates] and he won't do it. When I can't get the president to read even the summaries, it's time for me to leave."

The search for McCone's successor lasted for months before

settling improbably on Johnson's prominent supporter and fellow Texan in 1964, Admiral William F. Raborn Jr. Raborn had a reputation as a management whiz and was the father of the Polaris program and champion of the PERT system—Program Evaluation Review Technique. Raborn's tenure as DCI was unhappy and short. He did everything wrong, such as calling up the CIA's Office of Current Intelligence during the Dominican crisis to ask how all the secret agents were getting along. The OCI was amazed; didn't Raborn understand need-to-know? The OCI didn't know any more about secret agents than the Department of Agriculture. "Sorry," said Raborn. "I get confused by all these buttons on the phone."

The principal beneficiary of Raborn's failure was Richard Helms, appointed by Johnson as Raborn's Deputy Director of Central Intelligence. In the spring of 1966 Johnson told reporters on one of his walking press conferences about the White House grounds that Raborn had been only an interim choice. He, Johnson, always told Raborn to bring Helms with him when he came to the White House because Helms was being groomed for the DCI's job. In June he got it.

Under Johnson and Nixon the central preoccupation of Helms' tenure as DCI was Vietnam, and its theme was the contradictory demand it placed on him for intelligence which accurately reflected what was happening in Vietnam, but which at the same time did not challenge the president's right—perhaps willingness is a better word, since who gave him the right?—to do as he liked in Vietnam. McCone told Johnson he was going about things in a way bound to fail. McCone was right. Johnson got rid of him. Helms did not miss the point. He provided Johnson and, later, Nixon with information which was as factually accurate—for the most part; we shall note some exceptions— as the CIA could make it. But the CIA phrased its questions in a narrow way, and Helms himself, during six and a half years as DCI, apparently never once told a president or anyone else that American policy was not working and was not going to work. He stood on punctilio. The CIA is an intelligence-gathering, not a policy-making body. Helms did not presume to advise on policy. Pressed, he would give an opinion, but he was never insistent, his fist never came down on the table, his voice did not rise. Dulles once told a friend that Helms had two great qualities: he knew how to keep his mouth shut, and he knew how to make himself useful. Helms, like the Agency he directed, was purely an instrument, and the two presidents he served found him useful.

It is almost impossible now to determine what Helms, himself, thought about Vietnam. "We just can't fight this kind of war," one colleague remembers him saying in a staff meeting, "not against a fanatically committed bunch of guys who don't need anything except a bag of rice on their backs." Helms had a fairly realistic idea of how we were doing, in other words—the CIA never said we were winning, unlike Walt Rostow, who always said we were winning—but Helms had no objection to the war. He thought the choice of enemy was fine, the choice of a means to fight him something else again. . . .

The CIA was right about a lot of things involving Vietnam under Johnson and Nixon. It warned Johnson that bombing North Vietnam's oil-storage system in 1966 would not cripple Hanoi's war effort. It warned both presidents that bombing would never by itself break Hanoi's will to resist. It warned Nixon in 1972 that mining Haiphong harbor would only mean the diversion of military supplies to the rail lines from China. But the CIA was sometimes wrong, too.

In May 1971, for example, the CIA told the White House that the North Vietnamese did not have sufficient reserves in Laos to put up more than light resistance to a South Vietnamese foray across the Ho Chi Minh Trail. It turned out they had reserves aplenty. More than 600 American helicopters were hit. A hundred were shot down outright, and the South Vietnamese came back in wild disorder holding on to the helicopter skids.

. . . Some of the CIA's errors, however, were not quite so honest. It is not that they constitute outright lying or deception, but rather a degree of cynical weariness, an overrefined sense of audience, a realistic caution about telling certain men things they don't want to hear.

By temperament and from an instinct for survival Helms shrank from battles; he would argue but not insist, and after a lifetime of softening differences in the interest of bureaucratic peace, compromise had become part of his nature. On major issues he began speaking only when spoken to, and when Nixon or Kissinger had decided to go ahead and do something, like invade Cambodia, Helms backed right out of the way. . . .

Helms was a participant in many of the meetings which led up to the invasion. He did not argue against the invasion, and he did not show the paper in Indochina prepared by the ONE to Kissinger or Nixon, who had been steeling himself for his decision by watching the movie *Patton*. Later Helms explained that there was no point in doing so; the president had his mind made up, and it would have been unfair to the analysts, since they had not known about the invasion plans when they wrote the paper. Instead, on the evening of April 29th, Helms returned the paper to the ONE with a note saying: "Let's take a look at this on June 1st, and see if we should keep it or make certain revisions." June 1st was the date by which Nixon had promised to withdraw all American forces from Cambodia.

Richard Helms often said he only worked for one president at a time, and until January 20th 1969, that president was Lyndon Johnson. But a time came when it was not easy for Helms to know where his allegiance to Johnson ended and his allegiance to Richard Nixon began. His relationship to Nixon was to be distant and elusive, perhaps the strangest of his life, and it began on the same note of Byzantine intrigue and divided loyalty with which it ended almost exactly four years later.

Helms first met the president-elect officially at the White House on Monday, November 11th, 1968, when Nixon paid a courtesy call on Johnson and received routine briefings from top administration officials. Most of them knew they would be leaving the government, of course, but Helms was in a somewhat different position as DCI and he hoped for reappointment. Sometime that week Helms was invited to come to the Hotel Pierre, Nixon's transition headquarters in New York, where he met first with John Mitchell and then was taken into Nixon's suite for a private conversation.

Nixon told Helms he would be reappointed as DCI, and of course Helms thanked him, but!—Nixon made quite a point of this—Helms was not to tell anyone. This was to remain secret until Nixon chose to make a public announcement. Helms agreed, and after he returned to Washington he told only a few old friends of his tentative reappointment, stressing the need for silence. They couldn't understand Nixon's insistence on absolute secrecy; they tried to guess his motives. Rumors spread in intelligence circles as time went by without an announcement. Nixon had been clear enough with Helms, however; he was going to be reappointed. Surely there was no problem, unless . . . well, there was one thing, one possible problem known to Helms and a few others, and Ehrlichman was to say later that if Nixon had known about it, that would have been the end of Helms.

During the last weeks of the 1968 election campaign Johnson's representatives at the preliminary peace talks in Paris were slowly working out an agreement with the North Vietnamese for a complete bombing halt in return for expanded peace talks among all interested parties, meaning the Vietcong as well as Saigon. On October 16th Johnson felt he was close enough to an agreement to call the candidates—Humphrey, Nixon and George Wallace—to ask their forbearance on the question of the war. Nixon agreed along with the others but later told his aides he was suspicious that the whole thing was a bit fishy, a bit too convenient in its timing. Then Nguyen Van Thieu in Saigon began to drag his feet; he didn't like the agreement, it gave away too much for too little and he didn't want to sign it. A reasonable enough position from his point of view, but Johnson was in no mood to see the reasons of a man standing in the way. Now *he* began to smell something fishy, to find Thieu's resistance a bit too convenient in its timing.

On Thursday, October 31st, Johnson announced a bombing halt on television, giving Humphrey an immediate lift in the polls, but then on Saturday, November 2nd, Thieu announced in Saigon that he would not take part in the expanded peace talks in Paris. On the same day a Johnson-ordered FBI tap of the South Vietnamese embassy in Washington picked up a call to an official from Mrs. Anna Chennault, the Chinese-born widow of the founder of the Flying Tiger Line in the Far East. She told the official to urge Saigon to hold off until after the election, when it would get better terms from Nixon.

When Johnson learned of Mrs. Chennault's call he was furious. On Sunday he called Nixon and denounced her meddling; Nixon denied any knowledge or involvement.

What Nixon did not know was that Johnson had asked Richard Helms, as well as the FBI, for an investigation of the matter, and that while he, Nixon, was telling Helms he would be reappointed as DCI, the CIA was gathering material in Saigon and Paris in an effort to determine why the South Vietnamese had been balking, and whether or not there had been collusion with Nixon or any of his representatives. George Carver had tried to reason with Walt Rostow at the White House, saying Thieu just didn't like the agreement, and that he wasn't doing anything the U.S. wouldn't do in a similar situation. Rostow wasn't having any; the White House wanted answers.

Helms, it is said, was not happy with the order to investigate possible Saigon-Nixon collusion for obstruction of the peace talks. It was a legitimate request, and one the CIA was in a position to answer, at least insofar as it could be answered by CIA files or by its agents and electronic surveillance in Paris and Saigon. But the target was the man who had just been elected president, and who was about to reappoint Helms as DCI.

As it turned out, the investigation was far from thorough because Saigon agreed to join the peace talks the week after the election. Johnson cooled down, and he had time to reflect. What, after all, would be the next step, if Helms or Hoover told him that Nixon had been behind the delay? It was better not to know than to know and do nothing. But while the investigation lasted Helms did his part, according to one colleague, for the reason he so often cited when the interests of one president clashed with another's: he worked for only one president at a time.

On December 16th, 1968, Nixon announced the reappointment of J. Edgar Hoover as Director of the FBI and Richard Helms as Director of Central Intelligence.

. . .

At 10 A.M. on the morning of Monday, February 5th, 1973, Senator J. William Fulbright of Arkansas called the Senate Foreign Relations Committee to order in Room 4221 of the Dirksen Senate Office Building for the purpose of considering the nomination of Richard Helms to be ambassador to Iran.

THE CHAIRMAN: Mr. Helms, we are very pleased to have you this morning. Would you for the record just state what you have been doing the last 10 or 15 years?

MR. HELMS: I was working for the Central Intelligence Agency, Mr. Chairman.

THE CHAIRMAN: I am glad for it to come out at last. This has all been classified. I think this is the first time you have ever appeared before this committee in open session, isn't it?

MR. HELMS: That is correct, sir.

THE CHAIRMAN: In all these years.

MR. HELMS: All these years.

THE CHAIRMAN: Are you sure we were wise in having them in executive sessions?

MR. HELMS: Yes, sir. . . .

THE CHAIRMAN: Are you under the same oath that all CIA men are under that when you leave the Agency you cannot talk about your experience there?

MR. HELMS: Yes, sir, I feel bound by that.

THE CHAIRMAN: You feel bound by that, too?

MR. HELMS: I think it would be a very bad example for the Director to be an exception.

. . .

As so often before, Helms was telling the truth. There can have been few senior government officials who more completely won the trust of congressmen. In a speech before the American Society of Newspaper Editors in April 1971—one of the rare public speeches of his CIA career—Helms said. "The nation must to a degree take it on faith that we too are honorable men devoted to her service."

The senators at that hearing in February 1973, three days after Helms left CIA headquarters at Langley, Virginia, for the last time, took him to be just such an honorable man. They knew how often he had gone out on a limb, even jeopardizing his career, to tell them what he took to be the truth. At a private briefing of the Foreign Relations Committee in May 1969, for example, Helms and Carl Duckett, of the CIA's Directorate for Science and Technology, had directly contradicted certain claims by Melvin Laird, the secretary of defense, concerning the Soviet Union's huge new missile called the SS-9, claims also made by Kissinger, Nixon's special assistant for national security affairs.

The result in the White House was cold fury, so much so that it was a subject of general speculation in Kissinger's office whether Helms could survive as DCI. One staff member remembers thinking that if it had not been for Helms' reputation for integrity throughout government circles, he would have been sacked.

The Senate Foreign Relations Committee trusted Helms to tell them the truth about the SS-9, but it wasn't traditional intelligence questions the senators had in mind when Helms testified on February 5th, 1973, and again for two hours in executive session two days later. On those occasions they wanted to know about things like the CIA's clandestine army in Laos, reports of CIA involvement in the Chilean elections of 1970, a CIA program to train U.S. police departments in the right way to keep intelligence files, the CIA's alleged involvement in the heroin traffic in Southeast Asia, liaison troubles with the FBI, CIA support of Radio Free Europe, a rumored report of CIA involvement in a "1969 or 1970" White House plan to keep track of the domestic antiwar movement, and especially about the CIA's involvement in the Watergate break-in. . . .

The members of the Senate Foreign Relations Committee had a lot on their minds that day in February 1973.

At the beginning of the second session Senator Fulbright said, "I think Mr. Helms, in view of the nature of these questions, it would be appropriate that you be sworn as a witness, which is customary where we have investigative questions. Would you raise your hand and swear. Do you solemnly swear to tell the truth, the whole truth and nothing but the truth, so help you God?"

Helms raised his hand. "I do, sir," he said.

On that day, as on so many similar days since, Helms testified truthfully only about matters of small consequence, or about things which had already become known. If he were asked about things which were still secret he would not betray them, not then, not ever, not to anyone.

The Watergate and Church committee investigations uncovered a great deal about Nixon, the CIA and the secret history of the last 20 years before they finally came to a halt, but as far as I know, no one ever learned anything from Helms. He testified on more than 30 separate occasions, sometimes in open hearings, more often in executive session, but the secrets which emerged did not come from him. During his testimony in February 1973, he did not tell the Foreign Relations Committee about the aid to E. Howard Hunt in 1971, or about his meeting with Ehrlichman and Haldeman on June 23rd, 1972, when he was asked to scuttle the FBI's investigation of Watergate funding. He did not mention the Ellsberg break-in, although he certainly ought to have known of it by that time, and he flatly denied CIA attempts to overthrow Allende even though one of the senators present, Stuart Symington, knew a good deal about it. He did not mention the Huston [sic] domestic intelligence plan or Nixon's request through Ehrlichman for certain CIA files which might discredit the Kennedys—files which Helms finally handed over to Nixon himself with the observation that he worked for only one president at a time. He did not tell them what explanation Nixon gave for his dismissal, if any, or suggest who might have been hired behind the Watergate break-in. Helms was, then as later, the least forthcoming of witnesses.

There are three reasons why Helms kept the secrets. Obviously, the first is that he was at the heart of a lot of them; candor would amount to self-incrimination. Helms was protecting himself.

The second is that the secrets to which Watergate led threatened to wreck the CIA by shattering that complacent trust in the Agency's honor and good sense, without which it can have no freedom of action. If Congress once insisted on real oversight of the Agency's operations the secrets would begin to get out and the CIA would be hobbled. Helms was protecting the Agency.

The third reason is harder to explain. The history of the CIA is the secret history of the Cold War. Over the last 30 years one-half of the CIA only answered questions—sometimes not—but the other half . . . did things. . . . The things it did were not all as bad as bribery, extortion and murder, etc., but they were all the sort of things which cannot work unless they are secret. If a foreign leader is known to be on the CIA's payroll he ceases to be a leader. Who would believe in the anti-communism of a newspaper which could not publish without CIA funds? How can it be argued that Allende is a threat to American security when it is known that ITT is a principal advocate of his removal? There is a chasm between what nations say and what nations do, and the CIA—or the KGB, or MI-6, or Chile's DINA, or Israel's Shin Bet, as the case may be—is the bridge across the chasm.

The CIA's belief in secrets is almost metaphysical. Intelligence officers are cynical men in most ways, but they share one unquestioned tenet of faith which reminds me of that old paradox which is as close as most people ever get to epistemology: if a tree falls in the desert, is there any sound?

The CIA would say no. The real is the known; if you can keep the secrets, you can determine the reality. If no one knows we tried to kill Castro, then we didn't do it. If ITT's role in Chile is never revealed, then commercial motives had nothing to do with the Allende affair. If no one knows we overthrew Premier Mossadegh, then the Iranians did it all by themselves. If no one knows we tried to poison Lumumba, it didn't happen. If no one knows how many Free World politicians had to be bribed, then we weren't friendless.

So it wasn't just himself and the CIA that Helms was protecting when he kept the secrets. It was the stability of a quarter-century of political "arrangements," the notion of a Free World, the illusion of American honor. Only Helms would not have admitted it was an illusion, perhaps not even to himself. If no one knows what we did, he would have thought, then we aren't that sort of country.

During his final week as DCI Richard Helms destroyed his personal records. On January 16th, 1973, Senator Mike Mansfield mailed Helms a letter asking him to preserve all materials relating to Watergate. Helms testified later that he checked everything carefully but one allows oneself to doubt.

It doesn't take much wit to guess why so secretive a man with so secretive a profession would destroy his records. If it wasn't Nixon's curiosity which Helms feared, it was the prying of the Senate, of the Watergate grand jury, of the press and even of history. Like Lyman Kirkpatrick, Helms thought secrets should be secret "from inception to eternity."

Businessmen in the Bureaucracy

Motivating people to carry out their assigned responsibilities is a problem in any organization: government, business, sports, voluntary groups, and so on. A common image of the private sector is that employees must "shape up or ship out." In sports, players who do not perform are benched, released, or traded. But in government, which lacks clear indicators of performance, employees have many means by which to frustrate executives who exercise leadership—trying to improve their performance or redirect their energies.

Although the "business model of administration" has been touted to the public sector for a century, the experiences of business people who joined the Carter Administration highlights the more complex problems of motivation in government. While Sidney Harman had some success in improving motivation at the Department of Commerce, James Joseph feels constrained by a loss of flexibility, an absence of cash awards, an inability to fire incompetents and the power of the bureaucracy to "wait you out." Jay Solomon encountered major bureaucratic–congressional alliances in asserting his authority. A. Vernon Weaver encountered similar bureaucratic–press coalitions.

A closer insight into Jay Solomon's perceptions is provided in "In Washington, 'No One Is Responsible for Anything.'" He finds that, in government operations, responsibility is not fixed, costs are not considered, half the employees are incompetent, and stalling on new polices is commonplace.

QUESTIONS FOR DISCUSSION

Are these cases typical of problems business people would encounter in any government?
Would cash incentives help improve performance?
Is meaningful work as important as cash in improving performance?

If you were a businessperson, what are the most important two things you would do to improve the civil service?

Is it as easy as it seems to remove bad employees in business, or do unions and friendships interfere?

FOR BUSINESSMEN IN THE BUREAUCRACY, LIFE IS NO BED OF ROSES

Caroline E. Mayer

. . . "In business, I was a hard-working executive—or so I thought," says Sidney Harman, 60, under secretary of commerce. "But now, my old intensive schedule seems like a cakewalk."

The former chairman of the board, president and chief executive officer of Harman International Industries, Inc., a manufacturer of high-fidelity equipment and side-view mirrors for automobiles, Harman was brought to the federal government because of his innovative ideas on how to "humanize" the workplace.

Having launched bold programs to improve the morale and productivity in some of his factories, Harman was eager to try similar experiments within the sprawling Department of Commerce, which employs 40,565 people scattered in 1,600 different locations around the world.

To find out how employes felt about their jobs, Harman spent the first few months at Commerce as a clerk performing routine tasks. He found that many workers were indifferent to their jobs, because he says, "they failed to feel like an integral part of the process." Harman adds: "One clerk who produced statistics for a monthly report that he never saw told me he felt like a replaceable part on an assembly line."

To boost morale and make employes feel like part of Commerce's large and diverse community, Harman encouraged workers to start an interdepartmental newsletter, which has now become a vehicle of complaints about unpopular work rules. For the 178 employes in the office of publications, Harman also launched a work-improvement experiment that features staggered work hours and training programs for those who want to qualify for better jobs.

In his 18 months in office, Harman has discovered that even a top-level official can get discouraged in the federal government.

As the second-highest official in the department, Harman's job is often frustratingly vague.

Besides functioning as a stand-in for Commerce Secretary Juanita M. Kreps, Harman is responsible for the department's day-to-day operations. His role in policymaking is very limited, because most of the recommendations approved by Kreps come from assistant secretaries below Harman. "He's like a vice president," remarks one colleague, "a standby with no specific sphere of interest."

Harman's workdays are long, beginning at 7:30 A.M. and, if he is lucky, ending "as early as 8 P.M." Often, he works well past 10 in the evening.

"More than the long hours, it's the pace which I find difficult to adjust to. I constantly have to fight to get breathing time—time where I can reflect on the consequences of my actions. I'm a captive of my schedule, and the only moments I can steal for contemplation are on the weekends."

As a vice president for corporate action at Cummins Engine Company, a leading producer of high-speed diesel engines, James A. Joseph believed that the federal government had far too many employes.

So when Joseph assumed his post as under secretary of interior, one of the first things he did was reduce the size of his staff.

Just as he was complimenting himself on his ability to function with a smaller staff than his predecessors had, Joseph was requested by Congress to testify on the Alaskan oil pipeline. Needing a detailed briefing, he asked to see Interior's Alaskan-oil experts, only to discover that they were the very people he had let go.

That experience, says Joseph, 43, made him quickly appreciate the size of the bureaucracy. "From the outside, it looks like there are far too many people in government. But from the inside, when you discover all the technical responsibilities that you have, you realize you need a large staff."

Joseph's goal has now shifted to making the government run more efficiently—a difficult task, he says, given the strict civil-service rules.

"An institution is what it rewards," says Joseph. "But I don't have much flexibility to reward people for outstanding performance. You can give your people good assignments, but you can't give them bonuses. And, there is little I can do if I don't like people's work. I'd have to document their incompetence in ways for which I don't have time."

Nevertheless, Joseph says, "you can't operate without the cooperation of the permanent bureaucracy. In the private sector, when you give an order, it gets done quickly. But in government, an order often gets lost, sometimes because of competing priorities, and sometimes because the nature of the bureaucracy allows things to get lost. Other times, it's because people disagree with your orders and decide they can wait you out. You have to remind folks you were serious."

According to Joseph, his greatest frustration is "the amount of time it takes and the number of people involved in making a decision." He laments: "To get a policy implemented, you need to win approval from the department, the administration and Congress. You have to make so many compromises with so many power centers, that by the time you get it through Congress, what started as an initiative you felt strongly about doesn't look at all like what you wanted."

When shopping-center and real-estate developer Jay Solomon came to Washington to head the General Services Administration, he thought that his job would be easy enough to permit him to spend most of his time promoting one of his favorite causes—making federal buildings more accessible and inviting to the public.

But soon after Solomon assumed his post, a series of newspaper reports revealed widespread fraud in the GSA, the government's construction and housekeeping agency. Upon hearing allegations of graft, contract favoritism and payment for nonwork, Solomon promptly pledged to reassign, demote or dismiss any employes who "betrayed the public trust." He appointed a special counsel, well known for his probes of organized crime, to scrutinize the agency's expenditures. He also took the politically daring step of firing his deputy administrator, Robert T. Griffin, a close friend of the Speaker of the House, Thomas P. "Tip" O'Neill. Although Griffin was not implicated in any of the scandals, Solomon dismissed the 35-year GSA veteran because he felt that agency employes were following Griffin's orders instead of his.

While the firing of Griffin earned Solomon the enmity of O'Neill, it won him new respect among several other members of Congress who had expected little from the 57-year-old millionaire.

Says one congressional aide: "Solomon started out fiddling with his pet projects. But when he saw GSA crumbling from all the scandals, he took a hard-nosed business approach to clean up the agency. When he saw that his orders were not being carried out, he had the nerve to fire a politically well-connected deputy."

Solomon finds it difficult to be a businessman in government. "In business, you can get people with the skills you need whenever you want them. But here, it's difficult to bring in new blood. Out of the 35,000 employes in GSA, I was able to appoint 25. That's not much to help and serve me."

The GSA chief remarks: "You have to learn to operate in an atmosphere where the bureaucracy sees people like us come and go. That's a hard atmosphere in which to do business."

Robert H. McKinney, a Naval Academy classmate of President Carter's [sic], almost failed to become chairman of the Federal Home Loan Bank Board.

Consumer groups opposed his appointment because, they argued, as chairman of a major Indianapolis saving and loan association, he was an important member of the industry that he was supposed to regulate. Civil rights groups also opposed his nomination, charging that his savings and loan was insensitive to the housing needs of inner-city blacks. . . .

On the job for a little over a year, McKinney, 52, has since won over most of his critics. Not only has he become one of the toughest regulators that the FHLBB has had in years, but he has also issued strict rules to force mortgage lenders to make more loans on homes in poor sections of cities.

In the eyes of many Washington insiders, the bank-board chairman is one of the few businessmen who has succeeded in taking hold of his agency and charging ahead.

But the job hasn't been an easy one, McKinney says. "Government is much more difficult to run than a business. It's almost impossible to make it more efficient.

"You can't reorganize a government agency and set up a chain of command so that the chief executive officer has more time to deal with major problems. You have to deal with what you have.

"Most government executives have far too many people reporting to them. It is difficult for me to see the 29 officials, who report to me every day, especially when there are so many demands on your time. No matter how well you plan your day, it always gets out of kilter because there are so many uncontrollables."

McKinney's major gripe: "how long it takes to do things here. Because you have to get different viewpoints and a consensus on your decisions, it takes 200 percent longer to accomplish anything. But then, the results of that decision might be better since so many people were involved."

A. Vernon Weaver, 56, head of the Small Business Administration, does not bother to hide his frustration with running a government agency.

Dealing with civil-service employes, Congress and the press poses new and difficult problems for the former president of the Union Life Insurance Company of Little Rock, Ark.

"My biggest surprise here," says Weaver, "is how government is ruled by leakage. Employes use the press and Congress to accomplish their goals instead of meeting the issue head-on in an honest fashion. I know that if I make a decision against someone, that person will be on the phone to Congress and the press within an hour. It astounds me how reporters are willing to take as gospel anything that a low-level employe says. They never check with me to see if it's true.

"At the average company, I would report to only one person— the chairman of the board. Here, in addition to the President, I must report to 535 people. Dealing with Congress takes over 40 percent of my time.

"In business, I wouldn't have to show up for a week, and everything would run smoothly. In government, I can be gone for just a day and I come back to emergencies. It's difficult to organize well enough to let the ship sail for a few hours alone."

IN WASHINGTON, "NO ONE IS RESPONSIBLE FOR ANYTHING"

Q. *Mr. Solomon, as a businessman who has returned to private life after serving in Washington, how do you rate the federal government on overall efficiency?*

A. The federal government has a lot to learn about efficiency. The process just won't allow it. For one thing, the government lacks accountability. No one is responsible for anything. When I first came to the General Services Administration and had a problem, I'd say, "Now, bring me everybody who's accountable for this." I'd turn around and find 17 people in the room. A business is never run that way. There is always somebody who is responsible. He may delegate authority, but he always knows what is happening.

There's another problem: The government never monitors its actions. Once an official decides to do something, he rarely looks at his decision three or six months afterward to see if it is being carried out and is achieving its purpose.

Q. *If the federal government were a profit-making organization, how long would it last?*

A. It wouldn't last long. One problem is that it's hard to organize the government like a profit-making company. When I tried to reorganize my office to make it more efficient, I found that the law barred me from making certain changes. I couldn't eliminate some duplicate, unnecessary positions, because they were mandated by legislation.

Another reason why the government could never be a profit-making organization is that it has the attitude that service is more important than price. Certainly service is important. That's why we're here: To serve our bosses. But the government should be able to provide it in a more cost-effective manner. It should consider prices. But many officials in government never think about price.

Q. *How does the caliber of the average government worker compare with that of people in private industry?*

A. I can only speak of employes of GSA, which is the government's procurement, development and business arm. The caliber and training of its employes are not professional. There are a lot of dedicated people there, but dedication alone doesn't mean that you have the professional talents needed to run a business. Only about half of the agency—most of them employes who are already at the top—could go on the open market and land jobs with private industry.

Q. *Are there many incompetents in top-level federal jobs?*

A. Definitely—much more than in private industry. Many of them rise through favoritism, some through political appointments. The "buddy system" runs rampant in Washington. There are a lot of people who have risen to executive positions and then appoint friends to high-level jobs. In some instances, we found that people created jobs for friends when there was never any need for the positions.

Many employes rise just by their longevity. At GSA, there are people who have been around for 35 and 40 years. They should be gotten rid of. You can't stay in a job like that for that long and be efficient. You've got to bring young people into the government: That's its future.

One thing the government does well is to give opportunity for training. There are programs at Harvard and other business schools. But the problem is that after these people go to the schools, they come back to the bureaucracy and get buried there.

Q. *Can you get rid of incompetents in government?*

A. It's hard. The civil-service system doesn't allow it. So you try to encourage incompetents to retire, or you move them to unimportant jobs where their incompetency can't show up. Under civil-service laws, you can't fire them unless you can make an ironclad, watertight case against them. That's a pretty tough thing to do without opening yourself up to court cases and a lot of criticism.

Q. *Are federal employes overpaid for what they do?*

A. Some middle and lower-level employes are overpaid. That

happens in all businesses. When you have millions of employees, not all of them are going to be good.

But the majority of high-level employes—those in executive positions—are underpaid. Take myself, for instance, I was the chief executive officer of a 5-billion-dollar business—bigger than Sears, Roebuck. I was paid $52,000 a year. In private industry, that job would command a salary of at least $250,000 a year. The commissioner of GSA's public-building services is paid $47,500. In private industry, he could earn $150,000.

Unless the government raises salaries for high-level employes, it can't expect to keep attracting good people unless they are wealthy and can afford to take time off to come to Washington. The secret is to bring people in who are dedicated to do a job. Until the people of the United States—and especially the business world—understand that, you'll never beat the game.

Q. *Did you find much loafing on the job in Washington?*

A. Yes, I did. I found a lot of people did not have enough to do. And that's largely because many of the jobs were not created out of necessity but rather out of friendship. The federal government can be cut back easily—maybe by as much as 25 percent.

Q. *Is it true that career bureaucrats frequently refuse to carry out top-level policies and stall until elected officials give up or leave office?*

A. Absolutely. It's horrible—everything you could possibly imagine. A government employe who is there for a long time thinks there is only one way to do business: The way he has been doing it all his life. He has seen jokers like me come and go. Our average life in the government is only 2¼ years. So he says: "Well, he'll come and make some rules. The next guy will change them all. Why should I go to the effort?"

Q. *Don't these employees have a point—that constant changes can be disruptive and harmful to government efficiency?*

A. Change is good. It keeps you from getting complacent, from doing the same thing routinely. Every organization needs to take a new look at how it operates every few years. That's the only way to respond to the modern world: To be aware of technology that can improve efficiency and save money.

Q. *Do bureaucrats really waste more time and money on red tape than businessmen do?*

A. They spend an awful lot of time writing letters. A letter can start at the level of a secretary, and by the time it gets to the administrator to sign, it could have gone through 23 different hands—and still have errors in it!

Bureaucrats like to be very verbose. In one recent incident, GSA sent a congressman a 5½-page reply to a question that could have been answered in one sentence. The congressman told me: "Bull! I never got my answer."

But, still, I'm not sure there is more paperwork in government. There are an awful lot of memos that float around business, too.

Q. *Business complains that government is the cause of its paper-work headaches. From what you have seen, do you agree?*

A. Absolutely. One day I wanted to emphasize how many forms we required business to fill out for us. I wanted to pile all our forms on the stage in our building—as high as they would go. But the building engineers wouldn't let me. They said the weight of the forms would have been too much for the stage.

Q. *Would it help government become more efficient if some federal offices were moved to other parts of the country?*

A. Yes. Washington is overbuilt and overstocked with federal employes. I'm a great believer in dispersing the federal government because I think that the rest of the country should share some of the wealth that the federal government has to spend. I don't believe that every mission must be close to the White House or Capitol Hill.

Q. *Does the government waste any more money on consultants and studies than private business does?*

A. I don't know about private business, but I'd hate to tell you the number of consultant studies I found at GSA that were sitting on the shelves. We paid millions of dollars for them, but they have never been used.

Q. *GSA has been accused of massive waste and corruption. Is this an isolated occurrence, or do you believe there is a lot of wrongdoing going on at other agencies?*

A. I suspect that what you find in GSA you would find elsewhere. The head of the General Accounting Office and the assistant attorney general have said there may be 50 billion dollars of fraud and waste in the federal government. I believe them.

We're not the only agency that has authority to build buildings and procure merchandise and services for the federal government. We're only a small part of the government's construction budget: Only 6 percent of the total in 1977. Out of the procurement budget, we account for less than 2 percent.

Q. *Aside from setting policy, President Carter promised to let his agency chiefs run their own departments. Did you experience any interference from the White House?*

A. None whatsoever. But I don't think that's necessarily wise. I don't think the heads of federal agencies should be allowed to make all the decisions on how their agencies should be run. The President or one of his advisers should be more closely involved in decisions to make sure his policies are carried out. Agency heads need responsibility, yes, but you need a thread through the whole thing that the President can pull and say: "Let's do this. This is my policy." That's the way it is in private business: Someone must be the final decision maker. . . .

Q. *Did Congress interfere in your management decisions?*

A. No. In fact, Congress understands GSA better than anybody else in government. I hear that, in the past, congressmen did interfere by forcing GSA to hire their friends. It was the dumping ground for political appointments. But that's not true any longer.

Q. *Based on your own experience, would you recommend that business executives try a tour of government service?*

A. Without any question. I considered what President Carter gave me as a real privilege. I've gotten knowledge that is beyond my belief.

I've learned that, as a businessman, you have to stay on the backs of people in Washington. You have to pay attention to them and be vocal and consistent with your criticism. They don't hear from business people often enough. I tell businessmen now: "Don't let Washington do anything to you. Go up there en masse and holler!"

Q. *If you knew a businessman who was entering a federal post, what advice would you give him?*

A. Don't let yourself be taken in by the bureaucracy. Keep yourself independent. Keep saying, "I'm from the private sector." Don't join the bureaucracy; fight them. Remind yourself that you are going back where you came from.

Introduction
Professionals Can Buck the Boss, If They Know the Ropes

The organizational role of the technical expert is a special one, whether in a staff or line position. Technical experts are usually "cosmopolitans" with a special commitment to their skills and a primary identification with their professional peers. Their professional values may conflict with bureaucratic claims for loyalty and adaptability. As a result, they often find it difficult to play the roles required to compete for organizational success and power. These "cosmopolitans" stand in contrast to "locals" who identify themselves with the organizational group and stress loyalty to the organization.

Glenn Greenwald, a chemist for the North Miami Beach Public Utilities Department, is a "cosmopolitan." His superiors felt he owed loyalty and obedience to legitimate organizational authority. But as a chemist he perceived a stronger, professional responsibility for public health. It was his misfortune to be placed in a situation in which he could not honor both loyalties.

QUESTIONS FOR DISCUSSION

When professional and organizational norms clash, which should take precedence?

How can experts be protected from formal sanctions by the organization?

Can they be protected from informal pressures and sanctions?

What kind of mixed loyalties might bureaucrats from other professions feel?

PROFESSIONALS CAN BUCK THE BOSS, IF THEY KNOW THE ROPES

Rosemary Chalk and Frank von Hippel

On Aug. 23, 1977, Glenn Greenwald, a chemist in the Public Utilities Department of the City of North Miami Beach, Fla., was called to 800 N.E. 182d Terrace by a resident who complained that the water coming out of the tap tasted, smelled and looked peculiar. Greenwald agreed, and his tests showed that the water contained an abnormally small amount of free chlorine.

Laboratory analysis completed the next day revealed coliform bacteria in the water sample, and Greenwald decided that action was needed. Unable to find his supervisor, he asked his department head for an immediate flushing of the water distribution system in the area. Such flushings are accomplished by opening a neighborhood's fire hydrants, usually at night, but—trusting Greenwald's judgement—the department head ordered immediate action.

Greenwald's supervisor was irate when he learned of the flushing: he doubted that the action had been necessary; he feared that the residents of the affluent neighborhood where it had taken place might become unduly alarmed. He told Greenwald that he should consider resigning if he could not work through channels.

But the contamination problem had not been resolved by the flushing, and—in contrast to his superiors—Greenwald continued to believe that there was a potential health hazard. He wanted to continue tests and officially to advise residents of the house not to drink their tap water until further notice. His supervisors agreed to the continued testing but refused to authorize the official notice.

On the third day after Greenwald had first visited 800 N.E. 182d Terrace, a teenage resident asked him why the testing was still going on. Greenwald explained about the contamination problem, and he suggested that the family not drink the water until the problem had been cleared up. Later that same day, when the chemist told his supervisor and department head of this conversation, he was summarily discharged for insubordination.

Greenwald promptly took his case to the city's Civil Service Board, which three months later upheld his firing. Then he took his case to the US Department of Labor, appealing under the employee protec-

From Technology Review, June/July 1979.

tion section within the Safe Drinking Water Act of 1974. The relevant part of this legislation states that "No employer may discharge any employee or otherwise discriminate against any employee . . . because the employee has . . . participated . . . in any . . . action to carry out the purposes of this title."

The Labor Department's administrative law judge who heard the case agreed that Greenwald's discharge was indeed a violation of the Safe Drinking Water Act, and the judge went on to observe that "to punish or discriminate against a chemist for recommending a procedure which, at worst, would be a precautionary step would be to demand that all subordinates at all levels remain silent if so instructed until harm has occurred or is imminent." But Greenwald's was an empty victory. His complaint had not been filed within a 30-day statutory limit contained in the Act, so the judge recommended to the Secretary of Labor that the appeal be dismissed.

Glenn Greenwald's experience in exercising his professional responsibility highlights a serious dilemma for modern scientists and engineers. Early assessments of adverse impacts of science and technology on society are often made by professionals working within large organizations, but such organizations are usually eager to avoid what they describe as "premature" disclosure of concerns which may later prove to be insubstantial. Furthermore, such concerns typically involve value judgments as well as professional judgments, and this complicates their analysis.

The tension between an organization's concern to control its own affairs and the public's interest in knowing of possible hazards is mirrored in a tension of loyalties within its professional employees.

Scientists and engineers are expected to be loyal to their organization's management, and they are so instructed by their professional societies; in its "Guidelines of Professional Employment for Engineers and Scientists," Engineers Joint Council writes that "the professional employee must be loyal to the employer's objectives and contribute his creativity to those goals." But as professionals—and in recognition of their special expertise—engineers and scientists are also given special responsibilities for the protection of the public. The "Engineer's Code" of the National Society for Professional Engineers states, for example, that "the engineer will have proper regard for the safety, health, and welfare of the public in the performance of his professional duties. If his engineering judgment is overruled by nontechnical authority, he will clearly point out the consequences. He will notify the proper authority of any observed conditions which endanger public safety and health. . . . He will regard his duty to the public welfare as paramount. . . ."

Ordinarily these expectations do not conflict. Occasionally, however, as in Greenwald's case, an issue cannot be resolved within organizational channels, and an employee is moved by feelings of professional responsibility to make sure that his concerns are heard by higher levels of management or responsible outside individuals. The employee is said to have "blown the whistle" when, without support or authority from his superiors, he independently makes known concerns to individuals outside the organization. . . .

Unfortunately, most managements see dissenting employees as challenging the legitimacy of management's authority, and "whistle-blowing" is taken as a challenge to the credibility of the organization as a whole. Dissent therefore provides the ingredients for a confrontation between a technical expert and his management, and for most employees this is an intimidating prospect.

Yet, as the case of Glenn Greenwald shows, "whistle blowing" does in fact occur in the U.S. today, and no engineer or scientist can assume that he or she is immune to the pressures and dilemmas out of which it may arise.

However, the dissenter is not the only one who has something at risk when dissent is ignored by management. Technical dissent is often an "early warning" signal of real problems that may escalate into serious issues for the enterprise if not dealt with early and effectively. We are all familiar with cases when safety-related automobile design defects have been left uncorrected and resulted in lawsuits by injured parties, in massive automobile recalls, and ultimately in adverse publicity.

The suppression of professional dissent can have another damaging effect on the organization, too: it can strain the loyalty and morale of employees who otherwise would care enough to do their jobs well and creatively. . . .

Inside Outsiders

The activist movements of the 1960s spawned thousands of "outsiders" dedicated to forcing government to be more socially responsible. Rather than "sell out" to the establishment by taking well-paying jobs in business or government as their parents did, they went to work for lobbying groups, poverty programs, and consumer alliances. Some of them have now been given their chance for power by the Carter Administration: A number of sub-Cabinet positions have been filled by young activists. And many are finding that they now receive criticism from their former friends and allies. They face a dilemma. To achieve their purposes within the bureaucratic setting, they must work to acquire broader support and must move through recognized procedures. This requires patience and a willingness to compromise, qualities that are synonymous to many activists with "selling out."

Carol Foreman and Joan Claybrook ("Cool Carol and the Dragon Lady") find that "they have to take more balanced views as regulators than as shake-'em-up activists."

A public interest lawyer, an environmental lobbyist, a social activist clergyman, and a former NAACP lawyer are among the "Six Who Help Run a Government They Spent Years Trying to Change." They, too, find that a need to deal with complexities and a need to be even-handed make the job different from the work they did as partisans.

QUESTIONS FOR DISCUSSION

Can workers who have been co-opted remain true to the special interests they represented?

Should they?

What are the advantages of bringing such people into the administration?

Explain how these cases illustrate the saying, "Where you stand depends on where you sit."

Are these people being corrupted by power?

COOL CAROL AND THE DRAGON LADY

It seems hard to believe, but a Ralph Nader lieutenant now bears the chief responsibility for U.S. auto safety as head of the National Highway Traffic Safety Administration. As if that were not enough, the consumerist who once sued the Agriculture Department over its beef grading and food-stamp rules is now Assistant Agriculture Secretary for Food and Consumer Services, overseeing the same grading of meat and food-stamp programs.

These two regulators, Joan Claybrook, 41, and Carol Foreman, 40, were among Washington's most feared and revered consumer interest lobbyists when they, along with other activists of the 1960s and 1970s, accepted sub-Cabinet positions in the Carter Administration almost two years ago. Now both are in the news: Claybrook for engineering the recall of 7.5 million Firestone "500" radial tires, and Foreman for ordering cutbacks of nitrites in bacon because they are suspected of being carcinogens.

Claybrook's appointment to NHTSA was greeted with cries of "Astounding!" and "Appalling!" from automakers in Detroit, where she was known as the "Dragon Lady." Her past days as a lower-level Government aide and then as Nader's chief lobbyist and director of his Congress Watch had shown her to be extremely zealous on auto safety. Foreman, who headed the Consumer Federation of America, provoked outcries from farm commodity producers when she became Assistant Agriculture Secretary. Each woman continues to be criticized, but now by Nader as well. He has charged that Claybrook is "a disaster" and that Foreman has "sold out" to the food industry. In interviews with *Time* Washington Correspondent Eileen Shields, both women denied the roundhouse charges but added that they have to take more balanced views as regulators than as shake-'em-up activists.

Claybrook, a Baltimore-bred divorcee who delights in being called feisty, is proud of the record 12.9 million auto-safety recalls that her agency originated in 1977 and the 8.9 million so far this year. After long and bitter negotiations, she got Firestone to give in to the recall of 7.5 million of its "500" radial tires, which had a high level of defects. She says she expects the company to agree further this week to proceed with the recall "as expeditiously as possible," to produce an extra 400,000 replacement tires a month, and to run TV ads telling customers that a recall is under way.

Not all of her battles have ended in victory. She tried and failed to persuade her boss, Transportation Secretary Brock Adams, to make air bags mandatory in all new cars beginning in 1981 but had to settle for a 1982 to 1984 deadline. Claybrook later lost out even more embarrassingly in her attempt to tighten braking standards for tractor-trailers. She was testifying before a congressional committee on her opinion even as Adams was disagreeing with her at a press conference.

Automen do not fault Claybrook's intelligence, but they complain that her agency shoots from the hip and uses the media to publicize charges that are not retracted with the same fanfare when proved incorrect. They criticize NHTSA for yielding to pressure groups, for failing to measure costs against benefits, and for lacking enough competent staffers. Undaunted, Claybrook aims next to get the automakers to improve seat belts and to scrap their spearlike hood ornaments, which she considers dangerous.

Carol Foreman also thrives on controversy and, like Claybrook, works twelve hours a day. She is aggressive and serious, as could be expected of a woman who once lobbied for Planned Parenthood while in a visibly advanced stage of pregnancy. The mother of two children, Foreman is married to a vice president of the retail clerks union. She looks more like an editor of a fashion magazine than a tough Government regulator, and she strikes visitors as calm and relaxed. Soft, gentle music plays in her office because, she says, "it calms the wild beasts who are in here all the time."

Today Foreman manages a staff of 13,000 and a staggering budget of $9 billion, which is largely spent on nutritional and food-stamp programs. Foreman has control of drafting specifications for almost all federal food purchases, including those of the Pentagon and the Veterans Administration. She has taken steps to reduce the sugar, salt and fat content of school breakfasts and lunches; proposed a regulation that would remove Super Donuts and other fortified pastries from school breakfast programs; successfully lobbied for a law banning junk food in school vending machines; helped to persuade Congress to drop requirements that food-stamp recipients pay some cash, thereby making the stamps available to 1.5 million more people.

The Agriculture Department, Foreman argues, used to cater solely to the interests of food processors and big farmers, and her goal is to make it "the people's department" that Abraham Lincoln had envisioned. The processors and many farmers complain that she is hurting agriculture, in part because she is calling for service restrictions on food additives and for more detailed product labeling. Nebraska Republican Congresswoman Virginia Smith, expressing a view common in the farm belt, protested: "Carol Tucker Foreman, one of agriculture's biggest enemies, is at work right now discrediting the meat industry and causing the public to lose confidence in American farm products." The meat industry has sued to block her order that nitrite levels in bacon must be sharply reduced, from 150 parts per million now to 40 parts per million next year. Still, Nader found the order too weak and roasted her for caving in to the food industry.

Foreman laughs off the criticism and is happy that she enjoys the confidence of Agriculture Secretary Bob Bergland as well as of her friend Joan Claybrook. On Foreman's 40th birthday Claybrook gave her a gift: a spiky cactus plant. It was festooned like a Christmas tree, with candy, chewing gum and junk food that Foreman had just proposed banning from sale during school lunch hours. Today only a few of the trimmings remain on the tree. The rest, reports Foreman, have been eaten by her sugar-loving staff.

SIX WHO HELP RUN A GOVERNMENT THEY SPENT YEARS TRYING TO CHANGE

. . . *Carol Foreman,* the new Assistant Secretary of Agriculture for food and consumer services, took the job with some misgivings.

In her previous position as executive director of the Consumer Federation of America, she had taken part in several suits against the Department of Agriculture. Now she is managing some of the very agencies she had been suing. . . .

Ben W. Heineman, Jr., executive assistant to Health, Education and Welfare Secretary Joseph A. Califano, Jr., had to remove himself from a suit against HEW upon taking his current job.

Until 1975, when he joined Califano's old Washington law firm, Heineman had been a public interest lawyer with the Center for Law and Social Policy to Washington, where he specialized in criminal corrections and the rights of mental patients.

Heineman has been astounded by the speed with which important decisions are made in Government.

"It's clear that, within HEW, something that will be litigated for years is often decided within a matter of two hours," he says.

Working for HEW is "very different" from public-interest law. Heineman has found.

"When you work for the public interest, you try to be a strong advocate," the Government lawyer explains. "You push your client's interest as hard and fast as you can, but when you work for the Government, you try to be as fair and evenhanded as you can."

Heineman, who is 33 and married, is being paid $46,423 a year in his new post.

He finds himself keeping long hours these days, including weekends, but he says: "We have this optimistic, perhaps naive, hope that we'll soon have things under control."

Joe B. Browder, formerly one of Washington's top lobbyists on environmental issues, says that surprisingly little has changed in his daily routine since he joined the Interior Department as a top specialist in land and water issues.

He says that he has not put in less than a 12-hour workday since joining the Department at an annual salary of $39,419. Browder notes, however, that he put in similar hours at the Environmental Policy Center in Washington, which he helped to organize.

Browder, 39, says that his biggest surprise since joining the Administration is that he is enjoying his work. "I knew it would be challenging and rewarding, but I didn't know it would be this much fun," he explains.

Although Browder has been at odds with various policies of the Interior Department over environmental matters during the years, he has no doubts about his ability to work with the Department's career bureaucrats.

"I don't feel like a token citizen by any means," he asserts. "There are a lot of good people who have been here for years, and more are coming in."

Browder says that he is excited about the kinds of people being brought in by the new Administration, not only the environmentalists, but also consumer advocates, public-interest lobbyists and civil-rights activists.

"What is important is not any particular interest that we represent, but that we represent a whole kind of thinking that was excluded by the previous Administration." Browder emphasizes. "What is happening is a real opening of Government to people who don't represent a party line."

The Rt. Rev. Msgr. Geno Baroni, a new Assistant Secretary at the Department of Housing and Urban Development, is a longtime social activist who wants to help local organizations around the country set up programs to attack their city's problems.

"There are a lot of things that people can do to help each other without waiting for Government," says Monsignor Baroni, "We'd like to increase those kinds of activities."

As a start in his $50,000-a-year job, Monsignor Baroni plans to step up efforts to involve volunteer organizations, religious groups and others in solving housing problems in their communities. He argues that inner cities need intensive care.

A founder of the National Center for Urban Ethnic Affairs, a nonprofit group based in Washington, the Catholic priest is a veteran of the civil-rights movement and more recently the battle to preserve ethnic neighborhoods.

The 46 year old cleric, son of an Italian immigrant coal miner, holds that ethnic values are important.

"People live in neighborhoods," he explains. "People get identity from them. I hope to be part of the policy team in terms that will relate to the revitalization of the city."

Drew S. Days III, the first black to head the Justice Department's civil rights division, has found it difficult to please anybody in his new job.

State and local officials around the country want the Carter Administration to ease up on civil-rights enforcement, but Day's former colleagues in the rights movement demand that enforcement be stepped up.

Before joining Justice at $50,000 a year, Days, 35, was a lawyer with the New York-based NAACP Legal Defense and Educational Fund, Inc., where he handled many school-integration cases. He assures doubting civil-rights advocates that, in his new role, he fully intends to enforce the law, but he says he will do it in a conciliatory way.

"I've found that this job requires one to be sensitive to a number of situations," Days says. "These matters are complex, and my style is to look before I leap."

The new Justice official says that he would not press for extensive busing or other massive desegregation measures unless there is proof of intentional racial segregation throughout an area's entire school system.

Days, who supervises 200 lawyers at the Justice Department, says that his overriding concern at present is a growing resistance among State and local officials to the federal role in civil-rights enforcement.

"I don't think that is a particularly healthy trend, and it is not one that I would accept without a fight," declares the former civil-rights lawyer.

Joan Claybrook, the new head of the National Highway Traffic Safety Administration, worked for 10 years at various federal jobs before joining Ralph Nader's consumer aid movement.

"I was prepared for what I found," the former Government critic says "I don't hold much of a brief for bureaucracy. I'm asking an enormous amount of questions about why things are done the way they are and whether they could be done better some other ways. They're not used to that around here. Some have found it refreshing. Others feel threatened by it."

In her new job, Claybrook, 39, is responsible for the highway-safety program—one of her prime concerns when she was serving as executive director of Nader's lobbying organization, Congress Watch. . . .

Section V
PROGRAM
EFFECTIVENESS

In the days of Frederick Taylor, life changed slowly and the environment within which an organization functioned could be more or less taken for granted. The years since Taylor have seen rapid change. Population mushrooms and institutions grow from the corner candy store to the McDonald's food chain. The town dump and the river no longer suffice for the removal of waste products.

Such rapid change has meant less predictability in the life of governmental agencies. Worker skills and expectations change. Technology changes. Neighborhoods and cities change, and client needs are constantly changing. The policies, programs, or procedures that were appropriate even five years ago may no longer suit an agency's clientele today. What all this means is that it is not possible today to develop slowly the "one best way" and then continue to use that way without question. Instead, activities must be constantly monitored and questioned in terms of their effectiveness.

There are many standards by which the effectiveness of a public organization's performance can be judged. Is it doing its job? Is it creating unintended side effects or producing unanticipated impacts? Is it responsive to the public? Is it fair to all, or does it favor certain groups, inadvertently or deliberately? Does it keep within its proper bounds of authorized activity?

Given the current tax revolt, citizens are asking more than ever just what they are getting for their tax dollar. The cases in this section illustrate the need for attention to the question of the effectiveness of policies and programs. Some agencies fail to do what they should; some do things they should not; some create unintended problems. This section also explores some of the mechanisms for controlling against the misuse of administrative powers: the "inner check" that keeps the individual from doing what is wrong, the sunset laws that mandate periodic evaluation and weeding out of programs, and the "whistle-blowing" phenomenon of the seventies.

Introduction
Grim Legacy of Nuclear Testing

Unintended consequences can flow from the sum of policies set by many different decision makers in different agencies. Serious but unintended effects can also result from decisions made in one agency (with respect to its area of expertise). New drugs are approved, which later turn out to have dangerous side effects. A child support program turns out to tempt teenagers to seek pregnancy as a way of achieving financial independence. The desire to retain social security tempts senior citizens to "live in sin" rather than remarry.

In the period following the development of the atomic bomb, nuclear weapons were refined and tested. Unaware of the danger, the Department of Defense ordered military men into close proximity with nuclear explosions. Only much later did we discover an unintended effect of the nuclear testing program—diseases killing and disabling men who were serving their country. The bureaucracy is reluctant, however, to admit that mistake. Perhaps they are afraid that claims could run to billions of dollars; perhaps they are afraid to admit that their employer could have been wrong.

QUESTIONS FOR DISCUSSION

Given what was known about the dangers of nuclear radiation in the 1950s, was the Department of Defense negligent in protecting the health of its personnel?

To the military mind, was exposure to nuclear radiation an acceptable and necessary risk?

Do we tend to count the advantages from a government program without subtracting the losses?

Are we now more aware of the possible negative consequences of government policies—such as urban renewal and energy development?

Would government be unable to act if all the possible consequences of action had to be explored first?

GRIM LEGACY OF NUCLEAR TESTING

Patrick Huyghe and David Konigsberg

"They told us we would be the closest human beings outside of Hiroshima to a nuclear test," Martin Simonis says, recalling the events of a spring morning in 1955. As he and 12 other United States marines were ordered into a narrow trench, an atom bomb sat on a steel tower just over a mile away, ready to unleash its fury on the desert floor. Simonis was at the Nevada Test Site, where for four years the Atomic Energy Commission had been exploding nuclear weapons and the Pentagon had been testing the mettle of its men.

Simonis clearly remembers the moments before the blast: "They had a loudspeaker on a tripod next to the trench. I assume it was connected to the concrete bunker next to us. They started the count-down and they told us all to hug each other, dog fashion. When it got down to 30 seconds, they started counting by seconds."

One hundred and forty-five miles to the east, in the small resort town of St. George, Utah—and in other hamlets and ranches that dot the rangeland and cedar forests around the test site—some residents awoke early to catch a glimpse of another "nuclear sunrise." Few were worried about the radioactive clouds that might drift overhead in a few hours; they had been repeatedly assured by A.E.C. officials that their health was not being jeopardized.

When the bomb exploded, Simonis recalls that "it was like having 50 flashbulbs go off in your eyes, followed almost immediately by an earthquake. We were told to get up, and as we did, we could see the fireball. It was like a tidal wave of flame boiling and coming at us. They had tanks and some houses built—I guess to see what would happen in a blast—and we could see the tank turrets ripping off and the houses disintegrating. Then they told us to get down and the actual blast hit us. It caved in the trench all over us. We dug our-selves out and, before long, we had all gotten quite ill—we felt nauseous almost immediately."

Thirty minutes after the destruction was complete, Simonis says, helicopters picked the men up. As they returned to Desert Rock, the provisional military camp through which thousands of troops passed to and from nuclear detonations, people in the surrounding areas began their daily business; by now the bomb had become routine.

Martin Simonis sits in a lawyer's office now. The 45-year-old systems analyst from Sterling Heights, Mich., is worried. He suffers from an overabundance of calcium in his blood, and every six months, doctors check him for signs of leukemia. He says he has been in the hospital 10 times in the last four years, once for surgery on his parathyroid. "When I get the fever," he says, "it's like having a heart attack."

Simonis first came to suspect in 1976 that his condition was linked to the bomb. "A doctor tried to find out where in the devil I got something that would throw my blood off at my age. He kept asking me whether I'd gotten my teeth extensively x-rayed, or my thyroid. I told him I was in an atom-bomb blast. I guess that rang a lot of bells."

Martin Simonis says he cannot afford his medical bills, which average $4,000 for each hospital visit. When he brought his problem to the Veterans Administration, an official, he claims, "just laughed." Simonis believes he had no choice but to sue the United States Government. He is an angry man, and he is not alone.

The United States atmospheric atomic-bomb testing program lasted more than 17 years. Between July 16, 1945, and Nov. 4, 1962, 181 nuclear devices were detonated in the open air at Pacific and Southwestern test sites. An estimated 400,000 military and Atomic Energy Commission personnel—and an undetermined number of civilians living near the sites—were showered with radiation. They were told that the risk of injury was virtually nonexistent, that the tests were under strict control and that radiation dosages were too low to cause any harm. It is now apparent, however, according to the documentary record that has surfaced only recently, that the truth fell short of these assurances. that accidents occurred; that warnings concerning potential health hazards were ignored; that unfavorable scientific studies languished; and that fallout figures may have been manipulated by officials to support contentions that risks were negligible. Coming at a time when links between even small doses of radiation and a variety of cancers have become strongly suspect, these revelations have created a mood of concern and anger among those civilians and veterans who may now be suffering as a result. Moreover, the lesson of such revelations has not been lost on those who live near the crippled Three Mile Island nuclear power plant, whose reactions last month to official pronouncements of safety were frequently tinged with suspicion. Said one man who grew up in southern Utah in the 1950's and now lives near the Pennsylvania nuclear facility, "I have a sense of *déjà vu*."

As of April 9, some 600 damage claims had been lodged by residents of Nevada, southern Utah and northern Arizona against the Department of Energy (which has absorbed the A.E.C.). These claims, which represent roughly 275 individual disorders, seek damages totaling more than half a billion dollars. At the same time, more than 400 former military men have sought compensation from the Veterans Administration. Still other veterans, wary of a compensation system that has turned down 92 percent of bomb-related radiation-injury claims since 1967, have taken their cases to the courts.

The Carter Administration, which had nothing to do with decisions surrounding above-ground testing, has nonetheless found itself in a potentially explosive dilemma, involving billions of dollars in possible damages—because the claims that have already been filed in no way reflect the number their success might spawn. The fact that few, if any, civilians or soldiers were followed up to determine what effect their exposure had has made any individual claim difficult, if not impossible, to prove or disprove. But as demands for redress grow, and as evidence mounts that the tests were not as safe as they were claimed to be, the Administration is under intensifying public pressure to resolve the matter quickly and justly.

The relationship between American servicemen and the testing program began three weeks before Hiroshima with Trinity, the very first atomic bomb blast. Patrick Stout, an Army counterintelligence agent for the Manhattan Project, viewed the detonation, and two months later, as the driver for project director Brig. Gen. Leslie R. Groves, accompanied a group of reporters to ground zero, supposedly to prove that it was safe from radiation. To emphasize his point, Groves ordered Stout into the bomb crater, where the young soldier remained for a half-hour. Stout died of leukemia 22 years later. In testimony before the Board of Veterans Appeals, a medical expert estimated that his overall exposure may have approached 100 roentgens, an overdose of some magnitude. . . .

Documents show that the A.E.C. understated local exposure to radiation. For example, off-site monitoring by the Public Health Service reveals that in 1953 four tests dropped more radiation on the St. George, Utah, area than the A.E.C. claimed for the entire first eight years and four months of testing. The A.E.C. also released "average" figures to the public, thereby ignoring a fact that was known back in 1945—that radiation accumulation, like that of snow, varies.

As far back as 1953, it also appears that A.E.C. officials began a record of decisions that, critics say, stifled, reinterpreted or discredited a number of studies that might challenge the agency's assertions that all was well. That year, sheep grazing north of the test site suffered a mysterious illness, and some 4,300 of them died. While an A.E.C. scientist concluded that radiation was "at least a contributing factor," the report blamed malnutrition.

In 1965, Dr. Edward Weiss of the United States Public Health Service (P.H.S.) completed a study in which he found "excessive" leukemia deaths in two Utah counties close to the Nevada Test Site. While he did not blame the testing for this excess, he noted that all the victims had lived in the area for extensive periods of time, and that he could find no other apparent causative factor. A.E.C. officials attacked the study, objecting that the size of the study group was too small. The study was not published for 14 years until it turned up as a result of a Freedom of Information request.

During this episode, the Government entertained the possibility that it might eventually be held liable for alleged fallout-related injuries. "What," a White House aide asked the P.H.S., "would be the Federal Government's liability for any clinical effects possibly due to radiation" should a proposed follow-up to Weiss's work find such effects? Twelve years later, a claim for veteran's benefits would beg the same question.

Paul Cooper was one of more than 3,000 soldiers who watched a 44-kiloton blast named Shot Smokey and marched over the still-hot earth toward ground zero. In 1977, he lay in a Salt Lake City hospital, dying from leukemia and fighting for compensation he believed the Veterans Administration owed him.

Cooper drew attention from the press, and his case touched off a probe by the National Center for Disease Control (C.D.C.) into leukemia incidence among Smokey participants. The center quickly found a statistically significant higher number of victims than expected. Shortly afterward, the Defense Department began the arduous task of piecing together a clear picture of the tests from sketchy, ill-kept and frequently missing service records—this in preparation for more studies by the National Academy of Sciences. And in the early months of 1978, a House subcommittee under Paul Rogers, at that time a Florida Congressman, poked about the cobwebs of troop-and-test history and found plenty of horror stories. . . .

Orville Kelly of Burlington, Iowa, . . . has been gathering evidence to support his claim since 1974. But his case clearly illustrates the difficulties faced by atomic-test veterans in seeking relief from the V.A. for radiation-related claims.

From November 1957 to November 1958, Kelly commanded Japtan Island, which lay about seven miles across a lagoon from the Enewetak detonation site. During a four-month period, he says, he and his men observed 22 installments of Operation Hardtack I, from a beach on Japtan Island. Four of the shots were a megaton or better.

Kelly says that the safety precautions set by the task-force command seemed oddly lax; he recalls being warned only against eating the sea life and the coconuts. Thirteen years after his discharge, on June 15, 1973, Kelly, then a weekly newspaper editor, was diagnosed as suffering from lymphocytic lymphoma—cancer in the lymph system. He applied to the V.A. for a disability pension the following year, but his claim was turned down on the ground that evidence of his cancer had not appeared at the time of his discharge in 1960—a decision that ignored the possibility of latency, which in radiation-induced cancers can last, some say, up to 30 years. In 1978, Kelly reopened his claim, having accumulated more evidence, but again he was denied. He is currently appealing that ruling.

Veterans Administration officials point out that claims proceedings are not "adversary" proceedings. Reasonable doubt is decided in favor of the claimant. Moreover, a veteran who is turned down at the regional level may take his case to the Board of Veterans Appeals (B.V.A.), which, as a "last chance," says board chairman Sydny J. Shuman, "tempers justice with a little humanity." Many veterans claim, however, that institutional barriers to proving radiation-related cases—even to within the boundaries of reasonable doubt—are formidable indeed.

"All the information I need must come from D.O.E., D.O.D. and their civilian contractors," Kelly says, describing this as "something equivalent to a prosecuting attorney's asking a defense attorney for information with which he can convict a suspect."

A look at V.A. records for the last 12 years shows that the nearly 300 bomb-related claims now pending before various V.A. boards do not face encouraging prospects. Since 1967 (when the V.A. began keeping tabs on radiation cases), only 19 out of 231 such claims have been approved.

Lacking firm scientific guidelines on which to judge radiation cases, the V.A. prefers to find that symptoms related to the disease in question appeared during—or within one year of—service. Only when "pinned to the wall," as one V.A. official puts it, is the possible latent radiation issue ever considered.

Decisions on the regional level show that a veteran's records *must* reveal excessive exposure or evidence of symptoms during or shortly after service. On the B.V.A. level, five cases have been allowed on evidence that exposure records probably understated actual exposure. However, since the Cooper case inspired the bulk of bomb-related radiation claims, only one case has been approved by the B.V.A. on this basis. That case involved Donald Coe, a constituent of Representative Tim Lee Carter, Republican of Kentucky, an incisive questioner at the Rogers hearings.

"The door has slowly closed," Kelly says, "now that the Government has realized the magnitude of the problem." As a result, many veterans with illnesses they believe are linked to the bomb have not filed V.A. claims, or have chosen not to appeal unfavorable rulings. Kelly, seeking another forum in which to promote his cause, has founded a fledgling National Association of Atomic Veterans. Still others have gone to court, even though their chances of finding redress there may be nonexistent. . . .

One such action is already wending its way through Federal court in Philadelphia. There, the wife and children of Army veteran Howard Hinkie, and a genetic counselor, have filed a class action asking that all atomic-test veterans, doctors and genetic counselors be warned that genetic defects in children—something the Hinkies have been plagued with—may be cropping up as a result of the bomb tests.

Steven Phillips takes the legal possibilities one step further. "One of the Government's defenses here has been, 'We don't have the data, so we don't know if it's dangerous.' I don't think it would be inappropriate to bring a suit forcing the Government to start collecting data on Vietnam veterans with respect to things like Agent Orange." Agent Orange, a widely used defoliant during the Vietnam War, is now suspected of being highly carcinogenic.

"This is probably the cleanest environment in the United States —no industrial pollution whatsoever," says former Secretary of the Interior Stewart Udall as he traces a 200-mile arc across a map of the Southwest with his fingertips. The arc cuts across Nevada, southern Utah and northern Arizona, marking off a wedge of mountains, valleys, and grazing land that fans out north and east of the Nevada Test Site. During the testing period, says Udall, 25,000 people lived there. Most of the area's longtime residents are Mormons, who eschew the use of alcohol, tobacco and coffee. They are rural folk, and as such, they would be expected to have exceptionally low cancer rates. Yet they claim to have experienced a rash of cancers in the last two decades and Stewart Udall says he knows why. "These are the only people in the world who have lived for years with contamination in the food chain, who were irradiated repeatedly for years. On this planet, they are a unique group of people."

In a pamphlet handed out to local residents in 1955, the A.E.C. thanked them for their uncomplaining acceptance of their role as "active participants in the nation's atomic testing program." Indeed, they had believed those who insisted that the detonations would not harm them. "That was in the days of yore," says Irma Thomas of St. George, Utah, "when we believed everything the Government told us."

At 72, Mrs. Thomas has watched the rise and fall of the atmospheric testing program—and has witnessed what she believes is its legacy. Within a one-block radius of her home, she says, 29 people have had cancer and eight have died from it. In her own family of nine, her husband has cancer and her daughter's blood count is abnormal. "We didn't any of us believe that the Government would do this to us," she says.

Mrs. Thomas was one of the few St. Georgians who, as far back as the early 1960's, was concerned about fallout. As time went on, she began to notice what seemed to be abnormally high numbers of cancers around her. In 1978, she conducted an "informal survey" and discovered that more than 200 people who had lived throughout the test period in town had died or were suffering from cancer (in 1960, the town's population was just over 5,000). "These were just people I knew or knew about," she says. "It just dumbfounded me."

Last summer, the Committee of Survivors, a group of Nevada, Utah and Arizona residents, began filing some 600 claims against the Department of Energy. Grasping the inherent problems of proving causation in individual cases, the Committee attorneys decided to build a case by establishing a higher incidence of disease in a limited area. (This method was illustrated when, two months ago, a University of Utah study was released. Dr. Joseph L. Lyon, co-director of the Utah Cancer Registry, found that children born during the most concentrated period of weapons testing are two and a half times more likely to die of leukemia than those born before or after.) This, says Udall, "will enable us to discuss with the Government the total picture, whereas the veteran must approach the window as an individual." . . .

Stewart Udall views the history of the atmospheric test program as one in which people became trapped by their own assumptions. "They could not pay off the sheep farmers or the parents of the children who died of leukemia without admitting they were wrong in the beginning," he asserts. "All they could do was deny and deny."

Perhaps because it had nothing to do with above-ground testing, the Carter Administration, Udall says, has shown an apparent willingness to bring out the incriminating facts. Indeed, when President Carter ordered the H.E.W. report last year, hopes ran high that both the Government's past mistakes and the apparent dangers of even low-level radiation would be fully acknowledged. Representative Tim Lee Carter, for one, predicted "an admission that our services made a mistake—that they did in fact risk the lives of many men and that cancer has resulted in many cases from this."

When the preliminary report was released in March, however, it contained no such admissions. Recent radiation studies had raised "serious questions," it said, but their results were "not yet conclusive"; meanwhile, although "it is likely that a very small number of claimants . . . may have cancer related to radiation," it concluded, the only feasible modification to current methods of judging radiation-related claims is "refining the criteria used to define" them. That refining will depend on scientific studies now underway, the first of which—the Center for Disease Control's Smokey probe—will take at least another year. The question of whether civilians and veterans *now* claiming to have been injured because of atmospheric testing should, as a public handwashing exercise, *now* be compensated was essentially sidestepped.

Introduction
A City Speaks Its Mind about Federal Red Tape

Although the growth of government bureaucracy has slowed to almost zero, the growth of regulation has caused a blacklash of resentment. As a society we have decided to seek safe workplaces, compliance with tax laws, documentation of eligibility for federal aid, and so forth. But as individuals, we resent the burdens of the requisite paperwork and oversight. That "backlash" seems to be gathering momentum.

Kingsport, Tennessee, is the heart of an area where pioneers set up the independent state of Franklin from 1784 to 1788, and which refused to join the confederacy during the Civil War. Unlike most communities, Kingsport turned away from most of the "Great Society" programs of the 1960s and continues to look on federal funds with a "jaundiced eye." Its citizens' feelings highlight the frustrations with big government that many of us sympathize with but which few of us express so clearly.

QUESTIONS FOR DISCUSSION

Are the views in Kingsport held as strongly in your community?

Which of the Kingsport complaints do you feel are justified? Which are unjustified?

What federal regulations could we afford to eliminate?

What unnecessary information do individuals and businesses provide on federal forms?

Has Washington made any significant progress in reducing the burden of regulation?

Are the "burdens" of regulation as much a local and state problem?

A CITY SPEAKS ITS MIND ABOUT FEDERAL RED TAPE

Lawrence Maloney

MANUFACTURING

"Unless they threaten to fine us or put us in jail, I won't fill out a form."

Visitors in Kingsport can't miss the Mead Corporation paper plant. The sprawling buildings, steep smokestacks and piles of logs waiting for processing are only a couple of blocks from the heart of downtown.

Certainly, few Government inspectors have bypassed the mill, and their visits have brought some big changes to the 55-year-old plant that employs 1,150 area residents.

For the most part, Foster Park, industrial-relations director and a veteran of 35 years with the company, sees the merits of many of the changes. Yet he observes:

"It's the uncertainty about the investigations and the extent to which Government inspectors can apply the edictorial aspect of the law that bothers me. You develop a complex about Big Brother in trying to prove you're not guilty."

One of the biggest turnabouts has been in hiring practices. Feeling pressure from the Equal Employment Opportunity Commission (EEOC), the plant has opened up more jobs to minorities and hired women at about the same pace as men since 1973.

The problem, according to Mr. Park, is that the union seniority system prevents promoting such employes at a fast enough pace to please EEOC.

It takes three full-time people, plus a part-timer, about three weeks to prepare the annual affirmative-action plan that EEOC requires. That wouldn't be so bad, says Mr. Park, but the company must re-assemble the employment information in an entirely different form for the General Services Administration (GSA), which also reviews Mead's hiring record because the company sells to a prime Government contractor.

Probably the biggest worry over Government rules concerns a new proposal by the Occupational Safety and Health Administration (OSHA) that would force companies to lower the maximum noise level in factories to 85 decibles.

For the Mead plant in Kingsport, that measure would mean an added investment of more than half a million dollars. Just recently, the mill sank 6 million dollars into two precipitators to cut down on air pollution.

Despite all the effort, Paul Lacy, the plant's health and benefits specialist, contends that it's almost impossible to comply with all of the Government standards, especially the "hundreds and hundreds" of OSHA rules.

In fact, there are 4,400 safety rules, covering 800 pages in the Code of Federal Regulations.

Says Mr. Lacy: "We had one OSHA inspector here for five days and he found 42 violations. We corrected these, but I'm sure he could come back next week and find 42 more."

Across town, at the Kingsport Foundry, many of the same frustrations exist, but the small family-owned company has fewer people to contend with them.

William E. Ring III, president, figures it would take him about an hour and a half each to fill out all of the Government forms sent to him.

"I've just about given up," he says. "Unless they threaten to fine us or put us in jail, I won't fill out a form."

The foundry had to drop a training program for veterans in January because employes refused to provide the information needed for Veterans Administration forms.

There have been no problems with the 1974 federal pension law which has dramatically increased the reporting requirements for business. The company retirement plan is administered by an insurance company. Says Mr. Ring: "If we had to handle the pension ourselves, we'd probably be like the many companies that dropped the plan after the federal law was passed."

Gardner Hammond, company treasurer, is annoyed by many of the forms sent to manufacturers by the Commerce Department, most of them seeking information on materials used and the items produced. He notes that such forms are constantly changing and that the custom products that his firm produces don't fit neatly into Government categories: He adds: "If everyone has the same trouble we do, the statistics gathered from these forms aren't worth the paper they're written on."

The foundry also has had its problems with safety and environmental rules. It recently spent $150,000 on special booths to cut down on the noise in its grinding operation. Another $250,000 has been spent on a device to catch fly ash from the melting furnace. For that installation, the company had to spend an extra $5,000 to get early delivery on structural steel in time to meet a State deadline for air quality, a fruitless investment because delivery of the pollution-control device was delayed.

What bothers Mr. Ring is that, after all the effort to comply with federal and State standards, the company's accident rate has actually increased since 1970. There have been some problems with employe morale, too, because the company has had to threaten people with dismissal for not complying with new safety rules. It's OSHA's normal practice to fine an employer, even if a worker willfully violates a rule.

As for the future, Mr. Ring sees "little hope" for putting a lid on the growth of regulation—"not unless Congress passes some wild law that would force agencies to justify their existence."

MINING

"Our safety record is worse now than before all the new standards."

Getting mine operators from coal fields in the Kingsport area to talk frankly about Government regulation isn't easy. Barely 50 miles to the north, in Letcher County, Ky., 26 men were killed in two March explosions at mines operated by the Scotia Coal Company.

The memory of that disaster is still fresh in people's minds, and because mine safety is such an emotional issue, operators know that most complaints they voice will fall on deaf ears.

William Thomas, a health and safety director for the Westmoreland Coal Company, which operates 10 mines in nearby southwestern Virginia, insists that he's "100 per cent" behind most of the provisions of the 1969 federal law, which set up the Mining Enforcement and Safety Administration. He contends that the law's requirement of tougher standards on roof support, dust control and ventilation was sorely needed.

Still, he estimates that the many new rules have cut per-hour coal production by at least 25 per cent and added "tremendously" to the price of coal.

Charles Tosh, mine superintendent for the Apache Coal Company, a small Kingsport-based firm that sells coal to Westmoreland, believes that prices may have tripled because of regulation. Yet he, too, refuses to condemn the new standards. He adds: "Sure, we could probably boost production by 50 per cent, if we went in there and mined it any way we could get it. But we'd also have a lot of people killed or maimed."

One of his men, Lacy Winebarger, a miner for 36 years, affirms that the mines are "much safer than they used to be." He adds:

"I really don't know what else they could do."

Privately, however, companies complain that some of the regulations offer no real protection to miners and merely add to costs. They say that the 1969 act was "hastily formed" and that many mine inspectors are less knowledgeable than the operators they're supposed to be monitoring.

There's a feeling, too, that the emphasis on combing mines for violations takes away time that inspectors used to give to training—something that operators say is needed badly today when so many young men are taking mine jobs.

Says one operations chief: "Our safety record is worse now than it was prior to the act."

Mr. Thomas of Westmoreland asserts that a few of the new rules have added to injuries. He points to the metal-roofed canopies required in many mines. The canopies, which cover the continuous-mining machines and the shuttles that transport the men, are supposed to protect miners from cave-ins. However, the height of many shafts is less than 3 feet, and the men sometimes strike their heads on the canopies as they ride along the bumpy mine floor or, in trying to avoid that, they will move their heads to the side of the car and be injured by mine walls.

Mr. Tosh of Apache says that his company was required to spend $50,000 to construct a banked berm along a dirt road leading down from one of its mines. The purpose is to stop a runaway coal truck, yet the mine superintendent contends that the berms are useless.

"You couldn't get a driver to take a truck up against that berm for anything," he says.

Others are upset by a new federal proposal, already passed by the House, that would award automatic black-lung benefits to miners with long years of service, even if medical evidence shows no trace of that respiratory disease.

Criticism is also leveled at the string of permits and environmental standards that operators believe make the nation's goal of doubling coal production by 1985 "almost impossible to meet."

Virginia operators don't face as much paper work as companies in States such as West Virginia and Pennsylvania, which have long-established mining departments. One Pennsylvania operator, complaining of overlapping State and federal standards, says that he had to get 40 permits to open one major mine.

Still, there's the feeling that the State of Virginia is requiring more and more reports, and that the tougher standards are discouraging people from getting into the business.

One Westmoreland engineer, who specializes in quality control, complains that the Environmental Protection Agency, which prescribes pollution controls, and the Federal Energy Administration, which has been urging more use of coal, "seem to be working for two different countries."

He argues that federal air-quality standards should be modified until more economical technology can be developed to cut down on sulphur dioxide emitted from coal-burning power plants.

Mr. Tosh agrees that more coal has to be burned to save on gas and oil. But he sees a good deal of inconsistency in public attitudes.

"The Government worries about the levels of sulphur in the air," he says, "but people do more harm to themselves when they smoke a cigarette."

To a great extent, retailers here have learned to live with the long agenda of Government-related tasks that they're required to perform. Among them: the collection of State sales taxes, the withholding of employe wages for Social Security and income taxes, and the parade of reports on taxes, unemployment compensation, safety and other matters.

It's the future that they're really worried about. There are fears that the growing controls will not only place a greater burden on their operations but will limit the kinds of products that they can offer to consumers.

Wallace Alley, owner of a Plymouth dealership on the outskirts of the city, believes that rising prices, resulting from more regulation, will force many car buyers to settle for models that they really don't want. . . .

It's his feeling that too many of the safety devices added to cars in recent years have been adopted without proper testing. He cites the seat-belt interlock system, which has been discontinued because of large public protest.

The heavier bumper and door-frame systems, also required in the name of safety, have not only added to costs but have hurt fuel economy, Mr. Alley asserts. He insists, too, that parts and maintenance costs are up, because of engine modifications brought on by tougher federal standards on air quality.

"What we have in Washington are unqualified agency people playing God and ignoring the facts in the name of protecting the consumer," he says.

More low-keyed in his criticism of the bureaucracy is the owner of Sobel's men's store, a fixture in downtown Kingsport for 53 years. Says Norman Sobel: "Regulation costs us a tremendous amount of energy, and that's disturbing, because we could be doing other things. But we have to remember that we created the monster in the first place."

It's his view that businessmen too often use government at all levels as a scapegoat for their own shortcomings.

Still, even Mr. Sobel worries that a continuing growth in Government rules could "cut into profits."

He's upset, too, with some specific standards, such as the minimum-wage requirement, which keeps him from hiring more young people "because they're not going to pay their way at first." He'd also like to add a pension plan for his employes, but remains "totally confused" by the federal pension laws.

Pharmacist Carl Marcum, who owns a small drugstore that sits in the shadow of the community hospital, has hired an accountant to handle most of the paper work in his business. However, he can't farm out the many Government forms connected with the dispensing of drugs. A pharmacist has to handle that.

With the passage of the Controlled Substances Act of 1970, prescription drugs were classified under several schedules, each with specific regulations on record keeping and labeling, as well as on the number of refills permitted.

As a result, Mr. Marcum estimates that he spends about 15 per cent of his time with paper work relating to federal drug controls. He adds that the Substances Act not only has boosted the price of drugs but also has clamped controls on many medicines that have no possibility of being abused.

"When a woman calls me up at midnight and wants some paregoric for a sick baby, I'm now not allowed to give it to her, unless she has a prescription," he observes.

Marcum's Medical Arts Pharmacy is typical of the traditional corner drugstore. People come in and greet Mr. Marcum by his first name and ask what to buy for a cold or fever blister.

Mr. Marcum wonders how long his kind of small, personal establishment can stay in business. He's worried that even more small druggists will be undercut by the chain stores and will "fall by the wayside" if the Federal Trade Commission forces pharmacists to post their prices. The Supreme Court recently ruled that drug prices can be advertised.

In his way of thinking, the consumer would be the loser because the chain stores are not prepared to give enough personal service. He points out that Marcum's offers 24-hour service, delivers free and keeps a record on drugs dispensed to each family to help them with tax and insurance forms.

Asks Mr. Marcum: "What price can you put on all that?"

Cham Percer and Bill Greene are the president and the chairman of the two-year-old Bank of Tennessee, now operating in temporary quarters while work goes on next door on a new building.

What they're finding is that government rules are one of the biggest roadblocks in making a fledging bank grow. . . .

Mr. Greene says the paper-work burden is "astronomical."

"For every 10 million dollars in deposits, we need another two people just to handle all the State and federal forms," he says, "and that eats up our capital. Much of this information could be gathered by government bank examiners."

Mr. Percer adds that, when the Bank of Tennessee was first formed, a veteran of 30 years in the industry was called in to serve as president. He left after one year, saying he was "too old" to keep up with all the changes, particularly the government rules.

Says Mr. Percer: "The Government has set up federally insured financial institutions as policing agents, and we don't feel that is our role."

He's particularly disturbed about a new Federal Trade Commission rule that could leave lenders holding the bag when there are defects in products bought under installment contracts covering purchases from car dealers, appliance stores and other retailers. He believes the measure may lead to a tightening of credit.

Mr. Greene points to other problems caused by mushrooming safety and environmental requirements. He explains that a bank, after lending a company money initially, sometimes feels compelled later to make additional loans for the purchase of safety or pollution-control equipment—even though the company may be having a tough time just paying off the first loan. The alternative is that a firm might be shut down by the Government, depriving people of jobs and jeopardizing the original loan.

"It used to be that when a company came to a bank for a loan, you would look at its cash flow and track record," he recalls. "Now we have to say, "Has EPA been to see you yet and what's the price tag?"

The bankers have no arguments with the system for examining banks. They find the federal and State inspections valuable, and they're opposed to current proposals to consolidate the agencies that supervise banking. Says Mr. Greene: "That idea is typical of the feeling that Washington can do it all."

They insist, however, that many of the regulations on banking should not be applied uniformly across the nation but to specific areas where most of the abuses take place.

Notes Mr. Greene: "Someone up there in big Government thinks banks are making a lot of money. But if they keep encroaching on this industry, there's no way we'll have enough capital to support the nation's growth."

Doing Business with the Government

The activities of agencies can produce unintended results, which have to be taken into account along with the intended impacts. It is important, in judging programs, to add up both all the benefits and problems (intended or not) that result for its members.

In order to accomplish their missions, many federal agencies require information from businesses. Such data range from tax and social security reports to hiring and safety information. The demands from any one agency may be enough to make a manager grumble. The cumulative effect of all the demands from many agencies becomes a tremendous burden of paperwork. That was not, however, an objective on anyone's part. Furthermore, as Ed Richard contends in "A Small Businessman's Nightmare," the burden falls more heavily on small businesses such as his, putting them at a disadvantage compared with large businesses. Sometimes businesses even fold under that avalanche of paper.

W. F. Numrich describes "The Frustrations of Building for HUD": delays, paperwork, regulations. The ultimate frustration comes from the official justification for it all: "That's the way we operate!"

QUESTIONS FOR DISCUSSION

What portion of the information that the government collects is actually used?

Would our public services be as effective with 50 percent less paperwork on our part?

Could we make do with less data if it were collected on a sampling basis?

Are there any incentives for bureaucrats to reduce onerous paperwork or regulations?

Why do the same requirements fall more heavily on small businesses than on big businesses?

What are the specific complaints of Mr. Richard? Mr. Numrich? How might
they be alleviated?
How do these agencies find out about the effects of their policies?

FEDERAL PAPERWORK: A SMALL-BUSINESS MAN'S "NIGHTMARE"

Michael C. Jensen

MAPLE HEIGHTS, Ohio—Ed Richard, president of Magnetics International Inc., a small manufacturer of motors, magnets and generators,
glared at the mound of Government forms on his desk. "It's become
a nightmare," he said. "We're spending hundreds of thousands of
dollars to keep the Washington bureaucrats happy."

With rising anger, the 41-year-old Mr. Richard ticked off 56
weekly, monthly, quarterly and annual forms his company must file:
to the Internal Revenue Service; the Federal Trade Commission; the
Commerce, Treasury and Labor Departments; the Securities and Exchange Commission; the Federal Reserve Board; the Occupational
Safety and Health Administration. . . .

Small companies such as Magnetics International are among the
loudest complainers about Federal paperwork, but are hardly alone.
The Dow Chemical Company recently reported that it spent over $186
million last year on Federal "regulatory costs," an increase of 27 percent in a single year. Who bears the cost? The consumer, according to
Paul F. Oreffice, president of Dow U.S.A.

Government reports, businessmen complain, are too often confus-
ing, redundant, self-perpetuating and outmoded. The civil servants who
order and process the reports, they say, can be rigid, authoritarian,
harassing, hostile and uncommunicative. Consequently, stories of bureaucratic nit-picking abound.

The Scottdale Savings and Trust Company of Scottdale, Pa., for
example, said it once answered some questions on a Government report
with the word "none." The reports were returned, the bank said, with
a request to insert "-0-" instead of "none." . . .

[Paperwork] is particularly severe at small companies like Magnetics International, where a 15-man, all-purpose office staff spends as much as half its time, by Mr. Richard's estimate, serving the Government instead of the company. With sales of only $20 million a year and profits of $1.5 million, Magnetics International cannot afford the platoons of attorneys and accountants that giant multibillion-dollar corporations hire to cope with the Government's demand for information.

Mr. Richard recounted with distaste his running battle with the Federal Trade Commission over a mandatory quarterly report form containing 39 questions about Magnetics International's sales, securities, assets and liabilities.

The fight started late in 1974, Mr. Richard said, when he received a letter from the F.T.C.'s division of financial statistics that began: "Your company has been introduced into the F.T.C. financial reporting program. . . ."

Then came this line: "The mandatory filing of the quarterly form enclosed is required by law (15 U.S.C. 46) without exception."

"I was upset for two reasons," said Mr. Richard. "First, it was another report. Second, it didn't even say please."

At first Mr. Richard resisted, firing off letters to his Congressman, the Small Business Administration, even the White House. But he received what he characterized as threatening phone calls. "They threatened court action if I didn't complete it, and even implied imprisonment." Finally, he gave in and now files the report routinely.

"The Government bullies people," Mr. Richard complained. "Those people are working for us, but the way they came on, it was as though I was working for them."

The Government, of course, defends most existing paperwork as vital to individual programs and broader informational systems. According to William H. Sprunk, a certified public accountant and former corporate controller who now serves as assistant director of the F.T.C.'s bureau of economics, the form that Mr. Richard found so offensive is one of the mainstays of national economic analysis.

"It's been in existence since 1947," he said, and is the sole source of quarterly corporate profit data for gross national product calculations.

A dozen lawsuits are currently being prepared or pressed by the Government to compel reluctant concerns to join the 15,000 companies already filing the report. "We've never lost one," said Mr. Sprunk.

Although Mr. Richard said the F.T.C. report was particularly distasteful, he rated tax forms as his No. 1 paperwork nuisance. The Chamber of Commerce of the United States said its surveys showed that most other small-businessmen felt the same way. . . .

Another agency that is frequently criticized by business is the Occupational Safety and Health Administration, which requires companies to keep a log of industrial deaths and accidents.

While criticism of Government paperwork is hardly new, some executives contend it is only beginning to receive the high-level attention it deserves—from business and elected Government officials. . . .

THE FRUSTRATIONS OF BUILDING FOR HUD

W. F. Numrich

Construction is my livelihood. I am an engineer by training. I have been president of my own construction company for 10 years.

Under what is known as the 236 program of the Housing & Urban Development Dept.—a program that subsidizes mortgage interest for middle-income families—I built Pinewood Village in Parkersburg, W. Va. Pinewood Village consists of 125 apartments, from one to four bedrooms, and it was completed in 1975 after 18 months of construction.

The Pinewood Village story begins early in 1972, when HUD authorized the West Virginia Housing Development Fund (WVHDF) to hold a competition to see who would be authorized to build this project. The fund selected a panel of three judges. Five developers submitted proposals. Our proposal received every vote. Of course, I was elated. I had never built a housing project before.

My elation was short-lived. My proposal had been submitted on June 1, 1972. I had proposed that construction be started in September, 1972. When HUD accepted my proposal, its officials informed me that my starting date was a bit optimistic. They felt it would take until November, 1972, to process my application.

The director of the West Virginia Housing Development Fund said: "Walt, consider yourself lucky that they agreed to a November starting date. No other proposal has ever been processed in twice that time."

Well, this one was not processed in twice the estimated time, either. November, 1972? It took the agency until November, 1973, to process my proposal.

Meanwhile, I was reminded that a Davis-Bacon minimum wage-rate determination must be made for all federally funded construction projects. The Davis-Bacon Act was passed in 1931, during the Depression, when unemployment was in the range of 25% to 30% and the building trades unions were suffering. Their unemployment rate was higher than the average, and they were affiliated with the AFL, which had lots of political influence. They got Congress to adopt the principle that any federally funded project must pay "prevailing wages." The Davis-Bacon section of the U.S. Labor Dept. determines what the prevailing wages are. In other words, it sets the minimum wages to be paid on each project.

Parkersburg, in the mid-Ohio Valley, is highly industrialized, and the building trades unions are strong. (In my opinion, they also have excellent craftsmen.) Housing in West Virginia, however, is traditionally built with nonunion labor. Union rates are double those of nonunion labor. On federally funded projects using union construction labor, the Davis-Bacon minimum wage determination can be perfunctory: The union rate is frequently used. But in the Pinewood Village project, the Davis-Bacon section had to make a field survey to determine the minimum wage rate by finding out what workers on nonunion construction projects in the area were getting.

The person making a field survey goes around to construction projects in the area and talks to the workers building houses or apartments. He establishes their crafts—carpenter, plumber, sheet-metal worker, electrician, and so on. He finds out what they are being paid. When he feels that his survey is ample, he determines the minimum wage from the data he has assembled. If 30% or more of the workers in a craft are being paid the same rate, this becomes the minimum wage. If no rate scores as much as 30%, the average is used. Since nonunion housebuilders pay their craftsmen according to ability, the 30% rule is rarely invoked. The average usually prevails.

The method is fine if the person making the field survey is objective. If he is not, he can make the figures come out to suit him. If he wants a high rate, he can tear up his low samples.

The first Davis-Bacon wage-rate determination for Pinewood Village was issued on July 26, 1973. It was an objective survey. It closely correlated with a private survey made for me by a labor consultant.

On Oct. 2, 1973, a new wage-rate determination was issued by Davis-Bacon. I made some rapid calculations. My costs would be increased by roughly $80,000. I called the head of the Davis-Bacon section area headquarters in Pittsburgh.

"What the hell is going on?"

"Someone from the Parkersburg Building Council called and asked for a new determination."

Building trades councils are local organizations consisting of one representative from each of the construction unions. Although union wages have nothing to do with the Pinewood Village project, the government had put through an increase in my minimum wages because the unions asked for it.

I called the director of the West Virginia Housing Development Fund and told him that I wanted to submit for an increase in the cost of building Pinewood Village. He said: "Two things, Walt. You have already been delayed a year. This will cause a further delay. Besides that, your project is going to be the best in all West Virginia. The quality you are building into this project we like, but it is approaching the top limit established by HUD. The $80,000 additional may throw it over and get the project declared 'unfeasible.'" His advice was: "Go through with the project and then submit a change order asking for an increase after the job is completed and you can precisely establish how much this is costing you. WVHDF will recommend that the change order be approved."

I respected the director, and I bought his argument. "Unfeasible means that a project will not be approved by HUD and therefore will never be built, and I didn't want to take a chance that that would happen. Initial closing documents were signed on Nov. 15, 1973. We started construction the next day.

One thing that the Davis-Bacon wage determination had done was eliminate all helpers' rates for the major trades—carpenter, sheet metal, and so on. On Dec. 2, I requested that the HUD office in Charleston have Davis-Bacon establish helpers' rates for all crafts. Housebuilders use as many helpers as they do craftsmen. My letter was never answered. By the grapevine, I heard that HUD had called Davis-Bacon and had been told to ditch my request because the AFL-CIO didn't want any helpers' rates.

About halfway through the project, the government made a field survey and found a helper carrying a piece of sheet metal. He was listed on the payroll as a laborer. The government issued an order that this man must be paid retroactively the full difference between sheet metal and laborer scale. According to the government, if a man carried a piece of sheet metal, that was adequate proof that he was a qualified sheet-metal worker. The man received a windfall check for $2,500. But, of course, we had to lay him off because he was not qualified as a sheet-metal worker.

When Pinewood Village was substantially completed, I documented the increase in labor costs due to the second Davis-Bacon wage-rate determination and submitted a request for a change order. HUD denied it but said: "You can submit it again if you wish."

After construction was totally completed, I submitted the request again. I felt that, by trying a second time, I could get it reviewed at a higher level of HUD than the Charleston office, which had turned down the first request.

The second request was denied. I asked who reviewed it, and they told me: "The same people who reviewed your first request." If I had known that, I wouldn't have wasted my time. The same people would have to admit that they made a mistake the first time if they approved it the second time. What kind of review is that? They say, "That's the way we operate."

I believe this story only because it happened to me. If you don't believe it, I don't blame you.

Introduction
Tower Warning Was Ignored, Group Charges

Every organization has its mission. The people in the agency and the tasks they perform should add up to the effective accomplishment of that mission. The most basic question about organizational effectiveness is: Is the agency doing its job? The failure of individuals to do their jobs will undercut bureaucratic effectiveness, as will poorly designed procedures and inadequate controls that permit breakdowns in communication, decision making, or execution to go unnoticed.

The mission of the federal Occupational Safety and Health Administration (OSHA) is to keep workers safe from hazards as they carry on their jobs. But 51 workers in West Virginia died on the job when the scaffolding around a tower they were building suddenly collapsed. They had been working on that scaffolding for more than a year after an OSHA inspector had warned in his report, and in no uncertain terms, about the inadequacy of the repairs that had been made by field mechanics instead of qualified engineers:

"This situation should be promptly rectified. . . . This special scaffolding is engineered to perform a specific function in a given manner utilizing specific parts; unauthorized substitutions could result in disastrous consequences."*

QUESTIONS FOR DISCUSSION

What apparently went wrong inside OSHA?
How was the situation made public?
What are the advantages and disadvantages of having problems of agency ineffectiveness made public?
Was there criminal negligence on the part of the contractors or OSHA? Should anyone have gone to jail?

*Staten Island (NY) Advance, May 11, 1978. p. 17.

TOWER WARNING WAS IGNORED, GROUP CHARGES

Robert Morris

WASHINGTON—A federal agency failed to heed warnings by its own officials about a cooling tower scaffolding that collapsed and fell 170 feet, sending 51 men to their deaths at St. Marys, W. Va., a public interest group said Wednesday.

Health Research Group, a Ralph Nader-founded organization, said that an inspection by the Occupational Safety and Health Administration 13 months before the accident occurred found that unsafe repair methods were used on the scaffolding after it had arrived badly damaged at the site of Monangehela Power Co.'s Pleasants plant.

The organization said it had obtained an in-house memo documenting the inspection, which took place in March 1977. An investigator for the Health Research group, Robert Stulberg, said that the memo, which questioned the safety of the scaffolding, was either ignored or misinterpreted by at least three OSHA officials.

Stulberg also said that Research-Cottrell, the company contracted to build two cooling towers at the $667 million plant, had been cited for 71 safety violations in the last six years at sites other than St. Mary's. Six were considered serious and three involved hazardous scaffolding, Stulberg said.

Phillip Coco, a spokesman for Research-Cottrell, refused to answer questions regarding the group's report and said a statement would be issued later.

Two days after the April 27 tragedy, David Rhone, OSHA regional administrator, said the agency's investigation of the collapse had virtually ruled out the likelihood that any fault in the scaffolding had caused the accident.

Rhone could not be reached for comment Wednesday.

Nothing in the group's report indicates what caused the accident, Stulberg said, but it raises the question: "Could vigorous enforcement of the Occupational Safety and Health Act have prevented the deaths of these workers?"

He said the group's investigation points to shortcomings and a lack

Reprinted with permission of The Charleston Gazette, Robert Morris, "Tower Warning Was Ignored, Group Charges," in The Charleston Gazette, Vol. 110. No. 112, May 11, 1978, pp. 1, 2A.

of communication in the agency. In recent years, OSHA has been criticized repeatedly as a bureaucratic maze in dealing with occupational safety.

According to Stulberg, the OSHA inspection apparently was part of the agency's review of a request by Research-Cottrell for a "variance" on federal standards. The request was made because the type of scaffolding used by the company was found to be in violation of federal standards and the company had hoped to be exempt from some of the regulations if other safety measures were incorporated, he said.

Stulberg said the inspection came after a memo was issued by John K. Barto, chief of OSHA safety programming, who reported "a lack of evidence" that the scaffolding met federal requirements that it be capable of handling four times the maximum intended load.

Barto's memo also said that only one stair tower led to the scaffolding, meaning the men would have had to move 500 feet to escape the structure.

The inspection had been conducted by Walter Wilson, who later passed his report to Rhone, Stulberg said. Rhone, when interviewed by the group, said: "I don't remember anything coming to my attention that would indicate a need for compliance inspection," according to Stulberg.

Stulberg said Wilson's report indicated that repair on the type of scaffolding used by Research-Cottrell should have been done by experts familiar with the structure. Instead, the report said, it was cut and welded by field mechanics with insufficient knowledge of the scaffolding's construction.

Stulberg quoted Wilson's report as saying: "Unauthorized substitution could result in disastrous consequences."

In an interview with the public interest group, Wilson said mechanics told him that the scaffolding had arrived with "things missing, broken and bent," according to Stulberg.

The inspection took place while the scaffolding was being used in construction of the first cooling tower, now completed. Research-Cottrell has said that the same scaffolding was used on the second tower, where the accident occurred.

Interviews with other OSHA officials resulted in denials that Wilson's report was their responsibility, Stulberg said. He also said that documents had been removed from OSHA's files after the accident occurred.

Stulberg said that in January, Research-Cottrell's variance request was denied, but the company continued to use the scaffolding in violation of federal safety standards. In the meantime, he said, an amended application was prepared.

"In effect, legal tactics were used in order for the company to avoid complying with federal standards," he said.

The group has sent its report to Eula Bingham, assistant secretary of labor and head of OSHA, and has asked for an independent inquiry into the matter.

Introduction
Field and Stream Annual
Dumb-Dumb Award

In the ideal-type bureaucratic model of Max Weber, an organization is a role structure that is rationally designed to accomplish some societal undertaking. The people in it leave their feelings and values outside the door, so the theory goes, and become impersonal, rational role actors. The total organizational enterprise is subdivided into specialized parts or subunits (departments, divisions, etc.), and each unit functions rationally in terms of the overall goal according to theory. As critics of the Weberian model have pointed out, however, the actual functioning of a real-life bureaucracy leads to situations of "goal displacement," where members treat the rules as if they were major ends in themselves; sometimes they take goal displacement to the point of "suboptimization," regarding their departmental interests as more important than broader organizational goals.

The U.S. Army Corps of Engineers has the mission of tending to the nation's rivers. It builds to facilitate river transportation and to prevent destruction from flooding or other causes. According to *Field & Stream* magazine, which reflects the interests of fishermen, the Corps of Engineers has already built "most all the truly useful projects." To preserve itself and the jobs of its members, the corps has suboptimized —it has continued to build even where building destroys rivers. In recognition of this, *Field & Stream* presents the U.S. Army Corps of Engineers with its annual Dumb-Dumb Award.

QUESTIONS FOR DISCUSSION

Who (including insiders and outsiders) has an interest in seeing the Corps of Engineers' activities continue?
Who is on the other side?
What should the army or the Department of Defense do about the corps?
What should be done with any bureaucracy when it has essentially accom-

plished its mission: Let it continue (like the Corps of Engineers)? Give it a new task (like the March of Dimes, which turned to birth defects when polio was licked)? Phase it out (as Sunset legislation might provide a mechanism for)? and so forth.

FIELD AND STREAM ANNUAL DUMB-DUMB AWARD

George Reiger

Last year we decided a theme was the best approach in making our annual Dumb-Dumb Awards. There are so many knaves and fools involved with resource exploitation and management in this country that to attempt to list them all by name would take a magazine the size of the Greater Los Angeles telephone directory.

Last year's awards were distributed among those federal bureau-cracies whose internecine rivalries were helping destroy marine re-sources. This year the theme is water projects. Although the Bureau of Reclamation and the Tennessee Valley Authority each designed or attempted to finish cost-detrimental and environmentally destructive projects, top honors for duplicity and sheer incompetence in the realm of public works must go to the Army Corps of Engineers for their unparalleled mismanagement of the riverine resources of the State of Missouri.

Our story begins in 1931 when the Union Electric Company con-structed Bagnell Dam to provide cheap electricity for central Missouri. The project also created much-needed jobs during the Depression. In time, by impounding the Osage River to form Lake of the Ozarks, the dam guided the future economy of the region toward tourism and retirement.

There were the usual social impacts of any sudden change to the landscape: Real estate prices soared as speculators made profits at the expense of people who had lived on or near the river. Additionally, and contrary to myth, sons and daughters who had previously gone away to uncertain futures in Kansas City and St. Louis did not now stay at home working as gas station attendants and hotel maids. Wandering spirits will always roam, and the assurance of local jobs has never had much to do with keeping young people in the nest.

Still, for the era and the region, Bagnell Dam produced many more benefits than liabilities. Tourists came to see the lake; local businesses

From *Field & Stream*, January 1979.

thrived. An old Rand McNally guide suggests Lake of the Ozarks is a success because "drowned towns beneath its surface intrigue visitors." (Footnote: If so, one wonders why federal officials have not suggested "reviving" inner cities by drowning them and then arranging glass-bottom-boat tours for the apparently endless supply of tourists who go in for "drowned towns." In addition, downtown Detroit or Miami would make an excellent artificial reef for recreational fishing.)

As time passed, the Army Corps of Engineers saw and envied the popularity of Lake of the Ozarks. Like movie moguls who believe in the power of positive sequels, the Corps' engineers began designing a rerun upstream just where the Osage begins to disappear into the lake. This was shortly after World War II when the Corps was fresh from its triumphs overseas, the economy had evolved from Depression to optimism, and the era of recreational projects had begun. Their thinking may have been that with a dam already in place even further upstream at Osceola, the Corps could oversee the conversion of the Osage from a river into a series of lakes, bringing new forms of recreation to the area, and enabling the district commander, not God, to determine when and where water would flow.

In addition, another dam would almost certainly deal a deathblow to the largest and most important self-sustaining population of paddle-fish on earth. The Corps' war on free-flowing water, and therefore on paddlefish and sturgeon, goes back many decades and involves most of the rivers running through the heartland of America. Gradually the Corps had eliminated or severely reduced natural reproduction of these valuable relicts until only the Osage stood between continued well-being and functional oblivion for paddlefish.

Thus, in the early 1950's, point men from the Corps infiltrated Benton County in Missouri with claims that a dam at Kaysinger Bluffs would eliminate floods, provide a constant water level for recreational benefits, and improve water quality downstream in Lake of the Ozarks. The good people of Warsaw saw themselves sitting at a crossroads between two reservoirs, collecting money from tourists on all sides. Even though the paddlefish run, which up until then had been the principal spring attention for thousands of visitors, would be wiped out, and even though much of the area's agriculture would be drowned, a glorious financial future based on water skiers seemed worth the losses. Thus, in September 1954, Congress gave Kaysinger Dam the green light.

The Corps immediately began distributing pork. By 1962, with so much money spent and so little actual construction done, the Corps found itself with a project whose annual expenses would soon exceed its alleged annual benefits. And this in a day when environmental costs weren't even reckoned.

Thus, Corps accountants did a little juggling with numbers and decided that by adding hydropower as a benefit the Corps could still spend over $20 million annually on Kaysinger Bluffs and make it appear as though the boondoggle would pay off in the long run. Of course, hydropower would eliminate the constant water level benefit, and a lot of perfectly good farmfields would alternately be flooded and left as mudflats, but such are the prices of Progress.

The work dragged on, and by the mid-1960's major opposition began to mount. Biologists had taken another look at the paddlefish situation and were no longer sure they could artificially maintain the species at anything approaching natural reproduction levels—certainly not as cheaply as the Osage had been doing for free for untold aeons.

Other citizens were no longer sure they wanted to trade good hunting in the bottomlands for a huge mud puddle, especially where fluctuating water levels would sustain little wildlife in the sterile zone below the high-water marks in the reservoir.

On its side, the Corps felt its work was being maligned. After all, the Corps does its dam-dest to be decent businessmen and politicians. The least civic leaders can do in return is to keep any opposition under control.

Construction continued to wallow along with mounting resistance until 1969 when the Army Corps finished a flood-control project in Cedar County to the south. The engineers so badly miscalculated the stream capacity below Stockton Dam that the agricultural lands the dam was supposed to protect from flooding were washed away with the first big rainfall. Additional "benefits" at Stockton included the destruction of fishes and aquatic habitat, severe erosion, bank sloughing, turbidity, water pollution, and curtailed recreation. Local residents sued the Corps.

Naturally the people in Benton County were alarmed and reviewed their own project. They found some disturbing details. For starters, part of Warsaw would be flooded. Furthermore, since fluctuations in water level would kill all protective vegetation and contribute to the sloughing and sliding of banks, other business and residential structures in town might have to be abandoned for safety reasons.

The Corps acted surprised: "Oh, didn't you boys know you would lose part of your county seat? You say our public relations people promised you all pleasure and no pain? Well, we don't know anything about that. We're only engineers doing what's best for the nation. Next time you should hire a lawyer to read and explain all the fine print."

Benton County didn't wait for a next time. They got some legal advice and the support of various state conservation groups. The Corps was forced to "ameliorate the situation," and this, according to Charles

Davidson of the Missouri Conservation Federation, is how "amelioration" works:

"For $2.5 million the Corps plans to dredge and fill the area between Warsaw and the river and construct a boat ramp and a boat harbor. This won't do anything to "ameliorate" the real problem—to lessen the effects of the fluctuation or reduce the turbidity or the velocities, or the damage to the river and its occupants—but it will fit into Warsaw's comprehensive plan and the Corps is gambling that it will calm the home folk. An open-and-shut bribe, a keep-quiet, don't-rock-the-boat crumb."

However, by 1973, such multi-million dollar "crumbs" were being discussed in an atmosphere of triumph and condescension by Corps officers. For just about the time conservationists' opposition to the Kaysinger Bluffs Dam had become strongest, former President Harry S. Truman died, and an anonymous public relations genius recommended rededicating the dam to Truman's memory.

State leaders immediately began rallying vox populi around the memory of Missouri's most illustrious politician, and the social and environmental issues of the project were trampled in a patriotic stampede. A vote against the Truman Dam soon became the moral equivalent of opposing public education or supporting communism.

Four years ago, the Corps even gave state fishery biologists a crumb by promising that before the Truman Dam was closed, the dam at Osceola would be opened so paddlefish, which would otherwise be trapped between that obstruction and the Truman Dam, could move upstream into free-flowing waters to spawn. This was supposed to happen at least one spring spawning run in advance of the Truman Dam, but the biologists should have known that a pledge from the Corps is not much better than a politician's campaign promise made to gain time or a favorable opinion. The Corps simply does not like to open a waterway once it has been closed.

As the next construction phase drew nigh, when the paddlefish would no longer be able to move past the Truman Dam site, the Osceola structure upstream was still intact. State biologists, some of whom knew something about explosives from their military days, began muttering about blowing the dam themselves. Then in 1977 it was learned that a lack of rain had so lowered the river that paddlefish would be unable to get through several shallow areas below Osceola, even if the dam wasn't there. At this point, the Corps specialist in charge of notching dams finally arrived, and the Osceola dam was notched for the benefit of surviving paddlefish that may be interested in spawning in the future.

Now for the denouement: As background you should know that in

1972, the Corps published a detailed analysis of the deadly "gas bubble disease" in fishes caused when water passing over a spillway or through a turbine becomes air saturated, and nitrogen concentrations from the atmosphere are then passed along to the fish. A related disease in people is called "the bends," and it is equally fatal. More significant, the Corps report went on to describe how dams can be constructed to prevent this disease from occurring.

Last spring, when the dam was still more than a year from completion, fish downstream began dying by the hundreds, then the thousands, then the tens of thousands. Initial reaction from the Corps was: "We have no idea what is happening; the fish in the river aren't our responsibility."

Within days the Missouri Department of Conservation determined the fish were being killed by nitrogen bubbles in their bloodstreams and vital organs, and that the water-diversion outfalls of the Harry S. Truman Dam were the culprit. The Corps then made a statement summarizing its traditionally indifferent attitude toward fishery resources. After assuring the public that the kill would taper off when water levels went down, or when warm weather arrived (or when there were no more fish in the river?), the District Engineer, Colonel Richard L. Curl, characterized the disaster as "an unexpected natural phenomenon."

By Memorial Day, over 300,000 fish of thirteen species were dead or dying. By the time the kill added another 100,000, even hardy channel and flathead catfishes were belly up in the shallows. On June 6, the state's Conservation Commission brought suit.

The case is still not settled. Missouri says the kill cannot be termed "natural" because it would not have occurred if there had been no dam. The Corps insists fish are not its responsibility. Besides, states shouldn't sue the federal government.

The value of the lost fish is at least $168,000. But how do you put a price on the recreation lost, or the fact that the river will take years to heal itself, though with the Corps still "modifying" the river, the Osage may never get a chance to recover.

In anticipation of the Truman Dam's completion, the Missouri Department of Conservation had pulled out the stops on artificial propagation of paddlefish and stocked over 5 million fry, including 180,000 advanced fry between 10 and 12 inches. This achievement was, of course, devastated by the gas bubble disease. Biologists wonder whether they will again match such a stocking effort—or whether they should try so long as the Corps is in charge.

Who is the ultimate victim? None other than you, dear reader. Whether Missouri wins or loses its case, taxpayers will find their wallets a little lighter. Whether the shame is at Warsaw or Stockton,

Missouri, or dozens of other poorly conceived and ill-starred sites around the nation, the Army Corps of Engineers continues to use your money to destroy fish and wildlife resources by degrading fish and wildlife habitat.

During the Depression, the Corps was an idealistic and not insignificant force in helping restore economic health to the nation. During all the early decades of this century, the Corps, by and large, built wisely and always well in logical locations to provide protection against spring floods or service to riverine and coastal transportation.

However, a generation of Americans went to war in the 1940's and came home changed. The Corps was affected more than most. It returned as the largest and most powerful agency on earth. Rather than shell-shock, it suffered from arrogance and acute bureaucratitis. No matter that most all the truly useful projects were built before the war. There was water. There were eager Congressmen. The Corps kept building.

The world turns, but the Army Corps of Engineers has not turned with it. The nation elected a President who, last October, vetoed a classic pork-barrel bill that would not have been given a second look ten years ago. The nation elected a House of Representatives that sustained the President's veto even though an aging circle of Senators led by Robert C. Byrd of West Virginia insisted the $10.2 billion public works proposal was essential to creating jobs.

Surely there must be less objectionable ways of creating jobs than destroying America's rivers. Merely giving $40 to every man, woman, and child in this country would be cheaper, generate more employment, and be far less harmful to our environment than plowing $10.2 billion into pork.

It is significant that of the 138 members of Congress who supported Jimmy Carter in his condemnation of the public works bill, 109 had been elected to office since Watergate. The times are a-changing, administrators of the Corps, and unless you learn to base your budget and promotions on essential maintenance and not on doubtful new projects, you may alienate an entire nation that still respects your skills and original purpose.

As an aid to your education, FIELD & STREAM, with sincere and profound disgust, presents you with this year's Dumb-Dumb Award.

The FBI

Unfortunately, an emphasis on program effectiveness may eclipse concerns of process. But we must remember that one of the basic differences between democracy and dictatorship is concern with the means as much as with the ends of government. In the United States we have established codes of ethics, often written into the law, that require that public services should be provided honestly, openly, fairly, and without discrimination. In short, we expect our bureaucrats to act within the law, not as a law unto themselves. We are willing to accept some ineffectiveness as the price of freedom.

But in their zeal to accomplish their goals, agencies can and do misuse their powers. They act as if the end justifies the means. One target of such criticism is often the FBI. As the following cases reveal, it has repeatedly exceeded its legal powers. The "Martin Luther King, Jr." case documents a campaign of illegal harassment that grew out of its director's personal biases and his subordinates' desires to accede to his wishes. In the "Stakeout" case, agents committed a series of illegal acts with the complicity of their superiors. Even if they had obtained useful information—which they did not—their actions impinged on everyone's freedom. As the "Double Entry" case reveals, the director himself oversaw a system for keeping records of illegal activities out of the official FBI files. Such documents went into Hoover's "Personal Files." Break-ins, such as those that occurred in the "Stakeout" case, were filed in the Personal Files under "B"—for "Black Job."

QUESTIONS FOR DISCUSSION

Are illegal governmental activities ever justified?
Does the FBI now act strictly within the law?
What legitimate reasons can you see for keeping records out of the official files of an intelligence agency? what illegitimate reasons?

Which reasons do you think were operating in this case?
Does the President have a right of access to complete FBI files?
Do members of Congress? Why?

THE CAMPAIGN TO DESTROY MARTIN LUTHER KING

David Wise

Perhaps the most shocking example of the FBI's abuse of power was its campaign of unrelenting surveillance and harassment of Martin Luther King, Jr. Hoover set out to destroy King by using the full powers of the FBI against him. Various theories have been offered for Hoover's motive, and a combination of circumstances may have been involved. Hoover was enraged when King criticized the FBI. The FBI's stated rationale for bugging and tapping King was to uncover "Communist" influence on the civil rights leader. Nor was Hoover pleased with King's growing success in the use of nonviolent confrontation. The police dogs of Birmingham snarling and ripping at black men and women in the summer of 1963 created a bad image for law enforcement. "We Shall Overcome" fell harshly on Hoover's ears.

William Sullivan, the assistant director of the FBI under Hoover, said that Hoover's view of blacks was the root cause of the campaign against King. "The real reason was that Hoover disliked blacks," Sullivan told me. "He disliked Negroes. All you have to do is see how many he hired before Bobby came in. None. He told me himself he would never have one so long as he was FBI Director.[1] He disliked the civil rights movement. You had a black of national prominence heading the movement. He gave Hoover a peg by criticizing the FBI.

Reprinted with permission from *The New York Review of Books*. Copyright © 1976 Nyrev, Inc.
[1] After Robert Kennedy became attorney general, he asked Hoover how many black agents the FBI had, Sullivan testified to the Church committee. Hoover replied that the Bureau did not categorize people by race, creed, or color. That was laudatory, Kennedy said, but he still needed to know how many black agents there were in the FBI. Hoover had five black chauffeurs in the Bureau, Sullivan said, "so he automatically made them special agents." In 1975 there were 8,000 FBI special agents, of whom 103 were black—still far below the percentage of blacks in the US population as a whole.

And King upset Hoover's nice cozy relationship with Southern sheriffs and police. They helped us on bank robberies and such, and they kept the black man in his place. Hoover didn't want anything to upset that relationship with law-enforcement authorities in the South." . . .

The FBI's fear that King might become a black "Messiah" was expressed in precisely these words in a memo from headquarters to field offices on March 4, 1968, one month before King's death. The memo said one of the goals of the FBI's counter-intelligence program (COINTELPRO) against "Black Nationalist-Hate Groups" would be to prevent the rise of a "messiah" who could unify, and electrify, the militant black nationalist movement. Martin Luther King might "aspire to this position," the memo added. "King could be a very real contender for this position should he abandon his supposed 'obedience' to 'white, liberal doctrines' (nonviolence) and embrace black nationalism."

Just before King's march on Washington in August 1963, Sullivan and Hoover began an exchange of memos about the degree of communist influence among blacks in the civil rights movement. Sullivan, who had earlier reported to Hoover that he saw no communist threat in King's movement, soon told Hoover what he knew Hoover wanted to hear: ". . . we regard Martin Luther King to be the most dangerous and effective Negro leader in the country." The FBI had begun surveillance of King's civil rights activities during the late Fifties. In January, 1962 the FBI warned Attorney General Robert Kennedy that one of King's senior advisers was a "member" of the Communist party, and later that year a formal FBI investigation was opened into alleged "Communist infiltration" of King's movement. The FBI bombarded Robert Kennedy with memos warning of King's continued contacts with the adviser and with a second associate who the FBI said had strong ties to the Communist party. In February 1963, after the FBI warned that King would be meeting with the two advisers, Kennedy wrote a note to Assistant Attorney General Burke Marshall: "Burke—this is not getting any better."

The FBI's avowed concern over communist influence on King centered on the figure of Stanley Levison, a New York attorney long close to the civil rights leader. In his 1971 book *Kennedy Justice,* Victor Navasky reported that Robert Kennedy gave his approval to tap King after receiving FBI reports charging that Levison and Jack O'Dell, a member of the staff of King's Southern Christian Leadership Conference, had "Communist" backgrounds. By Navasky's account, both President Kennedy and Robert Kennedy warned King about Levison and O'Dell in June, 1963, and King then agreed to sever relations with the two men. O'Dell was eased out of the SCLC, Navasky wrote, but King after a time resumed his friendship with Levison. According to Navasky, who cites information from

"Kennedyites," this convinced Hoover that King was under communist control and led him to increase his pressure on Robert Kennedy to approve the wiretapping of King.

If a few communists or former communists had been associated with King, there would have been nothing illegal about it. But in fact, King and the SCLC had an explicit policy that no communist or communist sympathizer could serve on the staff of the SCLC. The FBI's charges against King have never been substantiated.

In an interview with *The Washington Post* in December, 1975, Levison said "I was never a member of the Communist Party. I did know some people who were. . . . Particularly in the 1930s and 1940s you scarcely could have been an intellectual in New York without knowing some." Levison said he was a victim of "guilt by association." The final report of the Church committee notes that two FBI reports "which summarize the FBI's information about Adviser A"—Levison is not named—"do not contain evidence substantiating his purported relationship with the Communist Party." The Church report also noted that on April 14, 1964, the FBI's New York field office reported that King's adviser "was not under the influence of the Communist Party."

When O'Dell resigned from the SCLC in July of 1963, King accepted his resignation with a letter in which he said, "As you know we conducted what we felt to be a thorough inquiry into these charges and were unable to discover any present connections with the Communist Party on your part." But King said he was accepting the resignation in order to avoid any public impression that the SCLC and the civil rights movement had any communist ties; the movement, King said, could not afford to risk "any such impressions."

The FBI's warnings that King had "Communist" advisers placed both President Kennedy and his brother in what they felt was a vulnerable position. The administration was closely identified with King and had publicly defended him. The president did not want him tarred as a communist; on the other hand, if the administration failed to act, the FBI might leak the charges to the press, which could damage not only King but the Kennedys. They feared, in short, that Hoover would blackmail them.

According to Congressman Andrew Young, who had been an aide to King, after King met with the president in June 1963, the civil rights leader quoted Kennedy as saying "there was an attempt [by the FBI] to smear the movement on the basis of Communist influence." By Young's account, the president had also warned King: "I assume you know you're under very close surveillance."

The following month Hoover sent Robert Kennedy another memo charging that King was affiliated with communists. Courtney Evans, the FBI's liaison man with the Justice Department, described

Kennedy's reactions: "The Attorney General stated that if this report got up to the Hill at this time, he would be impeached."

One way to determine if Hoover's charges about King were true, of course, was to tap his telephone. Evans testified that Robert Kennedy raised the question in a meeting with him in July of 1963. Evans had told Kennedy that King traveled a great deal and that he doubted that "surveillance of his home or office would be very productive." Evans also suggested that if a tap on King ever became known, it could have unpleasant repercussions. "The AG said this did not concern him at all; that in view of the possible Communist influence in the racial situation, he thought it advisable to have as complete coverage as possible." Evans advised Kennedy he would check into the possibility of a wiretap, but within a week, on July 25, Kennedy informed Evans that he had decided against tapping King.

But early in September, Sullivan recommended to Hoover that the FBI wiretap King. This was only a week after Sullivan had admitted to Hoover that he had been sadly mistaken in failing to perceive the communist threat in the racial movement. Hoover approved, although he scrawled he was still "dizzy over vacillation" about the degree of communist influence in the civil rights movement.

On October 7, Hoover formally requested Robert Kennedy's approval of wiretap on King's home and office, citing "possible Communist influence in the racial situation." On October 10, Evans and Kennedy took up the question of Hoover's request. This time, according to the FBI memo of their meeting, Kennedy approved the taps on King "on a trial basis, and to continue it if productive results were forthcoming." On October 21, Kennedy told the FBI that by a trial basis he meant thirty days, after which time the taps would have to be evaluated before any decision was made to continue them.

But the tap installed on King's home in Atlanta remained in place for a year and six months, until April 1965.[2] In addition to the tap on King's home, the FBI wiretapped his hotel rooms in Los Angeles and Atlantic City, and SCLC headquarters in both Atlanta and New York. The longest tap, on the Atlanta office, lasted two years and eight months, from November, 1963, until June, 1966.

Three years later Hoover charged that the impetus to tap King had come from Robert Kennedy. By then Robert Kennedy had been assassinated. But his associates claimed that the pressure to tap King had come from Hoover, and that Kennedy had gone along with it to disprove FBI suspicions of King's alleged communist ties. William

[2] Asked whether it had been re-evaluated after thirty days, as Kennedy had instructed, Courtney Evans told the Church committee, "I have no personal knowledge in this regard but I would point out for the information of the committee that the assassination of President Kennedy occurred within that 30-day period and that this had a great effect on what Robert Kennedy was doing."

Sullivan, who headed the FBI division that handled the wiretapping, supported the version of Kennedy's friends when I talked to him. Asked whether the idea of tapping King came from the Attorney General or from Hoover, Sullivan told me, "Not from Bobby. It came from Hoover. He sent down a memo. He wanted King given the full treatment. The whole impetus came from us." He added, "I do know that Bobby Kennedy resisted, resisted, and resisted tapping King. Finally we twisted the arm of the Attorney General to the point where he had to go. I guess he feared we would let that stuff go in the press if he said no. I know he resisted the electronic coverage. He didn't want to put it on."

In December 1963, after Sullivan had agreed that King was "the most dangerous and effective Negro leader in the country," a meeting was convened at FBI headquarters in Washington to plan the FBI's war on the civil rights leader. Among the tactics and subjects discussed was whether black FBI agents in the Atlanta area might be used, and how many would be needed, and whether TELSURS and MISURS (telephone and microphone surveillance) might be used against King's associates. The agenda drawn up for the meeting asked:

> What are the possibilities of using this [electronic surveillance]? Are there any disgruntled employees at SCLC and/or former employees who may be disgruntled, or disgruntled acquaintances? Does the office have any contacts among ministers, both colored and white, who are in a position to be of assistance, and if so, in what manner could we use them?

Do we have any information concerning any shady financial dealings of King's which could be exploited to our advantage? Was this point ever explored before? And what are the possibilities of placing a good looking female plant in King's office?

There were twenty ideas in the FBI agendas.

After this meeting the FBI began bugging King's hotel and motel rooms, in addition to wiretapping his telephone conversations. The first bug was placed in the Willard Hotel, a block from the White House, when King stayed there in January 1964. In all, the FBI bugged sixteen of King's hotel rooms in Washington and six states.[3]

---

[3] The FBI bugs were placed in King's hotel rooms in Washington DC, Milwaukee, Honolulu, Los Angeles, Detroit, Sacramento, Savannah, and New York City, between January 1964 and November 1965.

New York and Miami police, and probably others, bugged King—even in church. Andrew Young testified before the Senate intelligence committee: "We found a bug in the pulpit in a church in Selma, Alabama, in 1965. . . . We took it out from under the pulpit, taped it on top of the pulpit, and Reverend Abernathy called it 'this little do-hickey,' and he said, 'I want to tell Mr. Hoover, I don't want it under here where there is a whole lot of static, I want him to get it straight,' and he preached to the little bug."

Although Robert Kennedy approved the wiretaps, it is not clear that he ever knew of or approved the FBI's use of bugs against King. When asked by the Church committee whether Kennedy had ever authorized the bugs or been told about them, Courtney Evans replied, "Not to my knowledge."[4] Kennedy received FBI memoranda based on the King bugs, but not so labeled; it is possible, however, that he guessed or suspected from reading the reports that the information in them came from hidden microphones.

On January 8, 1964, two days after the FBI began bugging King's hotel rooms, Sullivan wrote a memo to Hoover. The time was approaching, he wrote, to take King "off his pedestal and reduce him completely in influence." But if the FBI succeeded in that objective,

> the Negroes will be left without a national leader of sufficiently compelling personality to steer them in the proper direction. This is what could happen, but need not happen if the right kind of a national Negro leader could at this time be gradually developed so as to overshadow Dr. King and be in the position to assume the role of the leadership of the Negro people when King has been completely discredited.
>
> For some months I have been thinking about this matter. One day I had an opportunity to explore this from a philosophical and sociological standpoint with [name deleted] whom I have known for years. . . . I asked him . . . if he knew any Negro of outstanding intelligence or ability. . . . [He] has submitted to me the name of the above captioned person. Enclosed with this memorandum is an outline of [deleted] biography, it will be seen that [deleted] does have all the qualifications of the kind of a Negro I have in mind to advance to positions of national leadership.
>
> I want to make it clear at once that I don't propose that the FBI in any way become involved openly as the sponsor of a Negro leader to overshadow Martin Luther King. If this thing can be set up properly without the Bureau in any way becoming directly involved, I think it would be not only a great help to the FBI, but would be a fine thing for the country at large.

Hoover, pleased, replied, "I am glad to see that 'light' has finally, though dismally delayed, come to the Domestic Intelligence Division.

---

[4] On March 30, after Nicholas Katzenbach had become attorney general, he required that the FBI seek prior written approval of the attorney general before planting any bugs; later that summer Katzenbach gave Hoover permission to move without advance approval in "emergency circimstances." The Church committee obtained from FBI files four memos stating that King's hotel rooms in New York City had been bugged in May, October, and November of 1965, with approval after the fact. Althought Katzenbach conceded that each memo "bears my initials in what appears to be my handwriting," he professed to have no memory of reading or receiving them. Under questioning, however, Katzenbach declined to characterize them as forgeries.

I struggled for months to get over the fact that the Communists were taking over the racial movement, but our experts here couldn't or wouldn't see it. H."

By the fall of 1964 the FBI's campaign against King had become full-scale war. For months the Bureau had been bugging King's hotel rooms, and now it began to whisper stories to reporters in Washington about alleged sexual activities of the civil rights leader. King, the FBI told reporters, had cavorted with women in his hotel rooms; explicit details were available to newsmen willing to listen to the FBI's *Decameron.* The purpose of the FBI whispers was to publicize stories that King, whose power rested upon his moral authority, had a lively extramarital sex life, which the FBI considered inconsistent with his public reputation and his profession as a minister. The FBI coupled those stories with its usual unsupported claims that King was under complete control of the Communist party.

Rumors circulated in Washington that the FBI had offered to let trusted reporters either see the transcripts of the bugging of King's hotel rooms or listen to the actual tapes. In 1976 Benjamin Bradlee, the editor of The *Washington Post,* said that he had been offered a transcript of a King tape by Cartha D. (Deke) DeLoach, assistant director of the FBI, in the fall of 1964. At the time, Bradlee was chief of *Newsweek's* Washington bureau. "The circumstances involved a cover story we were doing on Hoover." Bradlee told me "I had finally succeeded in getting an interview with Hoover. It was to be me, Jay Iselin, and Dwight Martin from New York. On the morning of the interview we all had breakfast together to plan the interview, and then went back to the office around nine-thirty. The phone rings and it's DeLoach. Martin is not acceptable to the Director. In an act I regret, we [Bradlee and Iselin] went over alone. We went in and saw Hoover and asked one question and he talked for thirty minutes."

According to Bradlee, the interview was worthless. Afterward, Bradlee said, he met alone with DeLoach, who had promised to explain why Martin was barred.

> He [DeLoach] showed me the file. He said Martin's wife had been under some suspicion. It turned out to be his ex-wife, who was apparently an Oriental. During World War II she had seen a lot of military people. Since she worked for a Chinese tailor, it wasn't surprising—her customers were military people.
>
> [DeLoach] offered a transcript of Martin Luther King. No, I said, I did not want to see it.

It was made clear to Bradlee that the transcript was from the bugging of King's hotel rooms. "I said I thought it was a tape. I know of a journalist in Atlanta who heard the tape." But, Bradlee said, "it was a transcript he was offering, and I had the impression that he had the transcript on his desk next to the file on Dwight Martin's ex-wife. He kind of hustled it—saying King made unpleasant references to the Kennedy family." Asked whether the alleged remarks by King referred to Jacqueline Kennedy, Bradlee replied, "Yes."[5]

According to Iselin, in the cab going back to the *Newsweek* office Bradlee told him that DeLoach's conversation had been along the lines of "What do you think of a black man fooling around with white women?" Iselin told me: "Ben was offered the tapes. I remember my slack-jawed astonishment. We obviously declined to have anything to do with it." Bradlee, Iselin recalls, said the tapes had been described to him as "based on the bugging of hotel rooms of King. They would get white girls in the rooms . . . that sort of thing."

In October, *Newsweek* gave a large party to celebrate the opening of its new offices on the twelfth floor of an office building a block from the White House. Attorney General Katzenbach was there, and Iselin remembers needling Katzenbach and Burke Marshall, the assistant attorney general in charge of the Civil Rights Division. What kind of operation were they running, peddling smut, he asked them.

Katzenbach said that at the *Newsweek* offices Bradlee told him that the tapes he had been offered were "from hotel rooms and involved sexual activities. . . . Bradlee said DeLoach had offered interesting tapes, with a leer."

Katzenbach described the incident to the Church committee, without revealing the names of Bradlee and Iselin. He testified that he had been dismayed "and felt that the President should be advised immediately." He flew with Burke Marshall to the LBJ Ranch, where he told Johnson of his conversation with Bradlee, warning "that this was shocking conduct and politically extremely dangerous to the Presidency. I told the President my view that it should be stopped immediately and that he should personally contact Mr. Hoover."

Katzenbach said he got the "impression" that Johnson would do so. The president, Katzenbach said in an interview, "sat in a rocker by the fire and pretty much listened. He didn't comment one way or the other. But I had the distinct impression that he was going to do something about it to stop it."[6] Back in Washington on Monday,

---

[5] Since it was well known that Bradlee had been a close friend of the late President Kennedy, he assumed the derogatory reference of Jacqueline Kennedy was mentioned in an effort to pique his interest in looking at the transcript. That, he said, is what he meant by saying that DeLoach had "kind of hustled" the transcript.

[6] But the FBI did not stop spreading rumors to reporters about King's alleged extramarital activities. If Johnson did speak to Hoover, there is no record of it; what evidence does exist suggests that LBJ was annoyed not with the FBI, but with Bradlee for talking to Katzenbach. According to a memo by DeLoach of

Katzenbach said, he was told by one or two other newspapermen of similar offers by the FBI.[7] The same day, Katzenbach said, he confronted DeLoach. "He rather angrily denied it," Katzenbach said. "I didn't believe him."

When I interviewed DeLoach, he disputed the accounts of Bradlee, Iselin, and Katzenbach. DeLoach said he had arranged an interview for Bradlee with Mr. Hoover. The day before, Bradlee said he wanted to bring the man who would write the story. When he asked to bring the additional man, Mr. Hoover said have a file check. As a result of the file check, Mr. Hoover said he did not want to see the man." DeLoach added, "At no point did I ever offer Bradlee the transcripts or to play the tape." DeLoach also denied that Katzenbach had questioned him about making such an offer to Bradlee. "Absolutely not," he said. "He did not ask about the transcript."

On November 18 Hoover met with a group of women reporters in Washington and pronounced King "the most notorious liar in the country."[8] Hoover specifically criticized King for telling his followers not to bother to report acts of violence to the FBI office in Albany, Georgia, because the agents were Southerners who would take no action on civil rights violations. Hoover claimed that "70 percent" of agents assigned in the South were born in the North.

Hoover's astonishing attack on King received extensive coverage

December 1, 1964, Bill Moyers told him Johnson had heard that a newsman (Bradlee, whose name was deleted from the memo as published by the Senate intelligence committee) was "telling all over town" about the FBI bugging King. Moyers said "the President wanted to get his word to us so we would know not to trust" the reporter, DeLoach wrote.

[7] Various reporters were apparently offered transcripts of the King bugs by the FBI. David Kraslow, chief of the Washington bureau of the Cox newspapers, said that an FBI source had telephoned him—he thought it was late in 1964 or early in 1965—to offer a transcript of an interesting tape. Kraslow then was a reporter for *The Los Angeles Times* in Washington. Kraslow said the FBI official began reading from a purported transcript showing King allegedly participating in a sex orgy. Kraslow interrupted the FBI man and said he did not wish to listen to any more. He declined to identify his FBI source.

In February 1976, Paul Clancey reported in *Quill* magazine, a journalism trade publication, that James McCartney, while a reporter for the *Chicago Daily News*, had been offered a photograph by an FBI official supposedly showing King leaving a motel with a white woman. Clancey also said that Eugene C. Patterson, while editor of the *Atlanta Constitution*, had been approached by an FBI agent in Atlanta and offered similar material.

[8] The FBI's top public relations man was unhappy at Hoover's comment. "I was with Hoover at the time," DeLoach testified. ". . . I passed Mr. Hoover a note indicating that in my opinion he should either retract that statement or indicate that it was off-the-record. He threw the note in the trash. I sent him another note. He threw that in the trash. I sent a third note, and at that time he told me to mind my own business."

in the press and on television. In contrast, the prurient stories that the FBI had whispered to the press about King's sex life were not achieving their purpose for nobody would print them. Hoover apparently decided to take a more direct approach. On November 21, three days after Hoover's remarks to the women journalists, the FBI mailed an anonymous letter and tape of the King hotel room bugs to King and his wife Coretta.

The letter said:

> King, there is only one thing left for you to do. You know what it is. You have just 34 days in which to do it. This exact number has been selected for a specific reason. It has definite practical significance. You are done.[9]

The letter was mailed three weeks before King was due to receive the Nobel prize in Oslo, on December 10. Since it was accompanied by a tape which the FBI considered compromising, the letter could be interpreted as an invitation to King to kill himself. Apparently that is how King construed it, for Congressman Young told the Church committee that when King received the tape and the letter, "he felt somebody was trying to get him to commit suicide."

William Sullivan told me that he had, on orders from Hoover, arranged to have a tape mailed to Mrs. King. He said he received the order from Hoover's assistant, Alan H. Belmont.[10]

> Belmont called me. We met at his request and he said Hoover and Tolson wanted certain tapes sent to Coretta King. I objected, not on moral grounds, but on practical grounds, I said, "She'll know immediately that the FBI made the tapes."
> Belmont said King has been critical of Hoover and Hoover wants to stop that, and the tapes will blackmail him [King] into stopping. And Belmont said he was going to have the tapes sanitized so that Mrs. King will not know that they came from the FBI. He said, "I'll arrange to have the tapes selected and I'll have them sent to you in a box."

---

[9] Who wrote the letter was a matter of dispute. The text quoted at the Church committee hearings was, according to the FBI, found in the files of William Sullivan some time after he was forced out by Hoover. Sullivan claimed that the draft was a plant written by someone else and placed in his files to embarrass him.

The significance of the "thirty-four days" was not clarified by the Senate intelligence committee. But from November 21, the date the tape was mailed, it would have been exactly thirty-four days to Christmas Day.

James B. Adams, deputy associate director of the FBI, testified he could not "find any basis" on which the committee staff had concluded the letter was "a suicide urging." That annoyed Senator Church:

THE CHAIRMAN: It is certainly no Christmas card, is it?

MR. ADAMS: It is certainly no Christmas card.

[10] Sullivan testified he was told by Belmont that Hoover wanted the tape mailed to Mrs. King to break up her marriage and diminish King's stature.

In due course, Sullivan said, the box arrived, and he had the impression the tape it contained was "a composite of three tapes."

Had the FBI put together a composite in order to select what it considered the most damaging parts of the various hotel room tapes to send to Mrs. King? "Probably," Sullivan told me, "but I understood it was to sanitize, to disguise the FBI origin. Perhaps it was a composite of more than three tapes, I don't know." The work was done by the FBI laboratory, the same one proudly shown to the thousands of tourists who visit FBI headquarters each year in Washington. "I think Belmont called the lab," Sullivan said. "I don't know how it was done.

"Hoover called me on the phone and said he wanted it mailed from a Southern city. I picked an agent who was a very close-mouthed fellow; I picked him because I knew he wouldn't talk about it. I never told him what was in the box. I told him what the assignment was, 'Take this down to Tampa and mail it,' and he did. He came back and told me it had been done. I never discussed it with Hoover afterward. He never mentioned it to me."[11]

With the Hoover-King controversy now threatening to undermine King's leadership and endanger the civil rights movement, other black leaders urged King to meet with the FBI director. King, the Reverend Ralph Abernathy, and other SCLC leaders met with Hoover and DeLoach in Hoover's office on December 1. Precisely what was said is not clear. DeLoach has described it as "a very amicable meeting, a pleasant meeting between two great symbols of leadership." Hoover, he said, told King that "in view of your stature and reputation and your leadership with the black community, you should do everything possible to be careful of your associates and be careful of your personal life, so that no question will be raised concerning your character at any time."

This is supposed to have been said at a time when the FBI was bugging and wiretapping King's hotel rooms—as King now knew, since he had received the tape—and leaking stories about King's sex

---

[11] Although the whole purpose of the exercise was to mail the tape to Coretta King, the FBI agent who went to Florida told the Senate intelligence committee that he had mailed it to "Martin Luther King, Jr." on Sullivan's instructions. Andrew Young said the tape was received at SCLC headquarters in Atlanta and later sent to King's home.

The tape, regardless of the FBI's motive in sending it, apparently had very little effect. In an interview in the *New York Times* on March 9, 1975. Mrs. King acknowledged to correspondent Nicholas Horrock that she had listened to such a tape. "I received a tape that was rather curious, unlabeled," she said. "As a matter of fact, Martin and I listened to the tape and we found much of it unintelligible. We concluded there was nothing in the tape to discredit him." Mrs. King also said that she and her husband realized the tape had been made covertly and "presumed" it had been done by the FBI.

life to reporters. For the moment, Hoover's blackmail techniques seemed to work. A subdued King said after the meeting that he and Hoover had reached "new levels of understanding."

The tape, the apparent suicide letter, and the attempt to impugn King's moral character were the most vicious aspects of the FBI's campaign. But the FBI's harassment of King reached as well into pettier matters. According to Frederick Schwarz, the Church committee's counsel, the FBI in 1964 sought to block Marquette University from giving King an honorary degree "because it was thought unseemly," since the university had once granted an honorary degree to Hoover. Later that year the FBI learned that King planned to visit Pope Paul VI. John Malone, the head of the FBI's New York office, was dispatched to see Cardinal Spellman to persuade him to intervene with the Pope and prevent the audience. Malone thought he had succeeded, but the Pope met with King anyhow. "Astounding," Hoover wrote on a memo. "I am amazed. . . ."

Four years later King went to Memphis to participate in a strike of city garbage workers. The FBI campaign had not abated, for on March 28, 1968 the FBI drafted a blind memo—bearing no FBI markings—for distribution to "cooperative news media." "The fine Hotel Lorraine in Memphis is owned and patronized exclusively by Negroes," the memo said, "but King did not go there." Instead, King was staying at "a plush Holiday Inn Motel, white-owned, operated, and almost exclusively white patronized." The purpose of the proposed planted news item, the FBI documents said, was "to publicize hypocrisy on the part of Martin Luther King." Hoover signed the FBI memo, "Okay, H."

It was not established whether the memo was sent to the press, but King did change hotels. He went home to Atlanta, and when he returned to Memphis the following week, he moved into the Lorraine. Standing there on the balcony outside his room, he was shot and killed on April 4, 1968. James Earl Ray, a small-time escaped convict, pleaded guilty to the crime a year later and was sentenced to ninety-nine years in prison. But whether he acted alone or was part of a conspiracy remains an open question.

When the Church committee disclosed details of the FBI's campaign against King, including the "suicide" letter, questions were publicly raised about whether the FBI's actions against King could conceivably have extended to complicity in his murder. On November 26, 1975, Attorney General Edward H. Levi ordered a review of the FBI's investigation into the death of Martin Luther King.

Conducted by J. Stanley Pottinger, head of the Justice Department's civil rights division, the review found "no basis to believe that the FBI in any way caused the death of Dr. King," or that the FBI's investigation of his death had been less than thorough. But the study concluded that "the FBI undertook a systematic program of harassment of Dr. King in order to discredit him and harm both him and the movement he led." Although Pottinger found no evidence of FBI complicity in King's death, he said it was "possible" that a more detailed survey of the files would reach a different conclusion.

On April 29, Levi announced that an expanded investigation and a review of some 200,000 FBI documents on King would be conducted by a task force under Michael E. Shaheen, director of the department's Office of Presidential Responsibility. Levi said the new investigation would be asked to determine whether "the FBI was involved in the assassination of Dr. King" and whether the FBI's actions against King require "criminal prosecutions." A Justice Department spokesman said recently that the task force was expected to report "by January 1."

On September 17 of this year, the House of Representatives voted to establish a select committee to investigate the murders of President Kennedy and Martin Luther King, Jr., and empowered it to inquire into other assassinations as well. In its final report, the Church committee concluded: "The actions taken against Dr. King are indefensible. They represent a sad episode in the dark history of covert actions directed against law abiding citizens by a law enforcement agency."

ANATOMY OF A STAKE-OUT

The Case That Cracked the FBI

Judy Gumbo Clavir
A.K.A. Judy Cleaver
       "Gumbo"
       Judith Lee Hemblen
       FBI File #834–226–G

and Stew Albert
A.K.A. Stewart Edward Albert
       Stew Alpert
       Stu Alpert
       FBI File # (unknown)

Stew Albert is walking barefoot in the Catskill Mountains. It is December 4, 1973, Albert's thirty-fourth birthday, and the day is unusually warm. Albert and Clavir have recently left behind the

From Crawdaddy, February 1978.

paranoic walls of New York City and purchased a compact, out-of-the-way log cabin. They are no longer activists in the New Left, which appears to be disintegrating from a combination of murder/suicide, FBI-CIA attacks, and its own internal self-hatred.

Albert and Clavir are at peace. The sun shines, the stream bubbles, the last of the autumn birds chirp in bare branches. Relaxed and happy, they are glad to be alive in their private world.

They are not aware that on the road at the bottom of the hill, the New York office (NYO) of the Federal Bureau of Investigation watches their every step, conducting a round-the-clock stake-out of their personal Garden of Eden.

II

From December 4, 1973, to December 13, 1975, the FBI and its secret "Weather fugitive" unit will commit numerous criminal acts against the persons and property of Clavir and Albert. This federal conspiracy to violate their civil rights will include: burglary of their house; theft of objects from their house (subsequently sent to an FBI laboratory for "testing"); copying by U.S. Post Office employees of addresses of every letter they send or receive; monitoring of their bank balance on a regular basis; installation without court permission of an electronic listening device "in the home" for a period of 17 days; placing of a homing device on their car in August and December, 1975. The FBI watchdogs will follow Clavir to and around the college campus where she is employed as a sociology professor. They will copy down the license plates of guests who visit the couple's cabin and, in some cases, will follow their visitors home.

The federal government, sources close to the government and the FBI itself will eventually admit these transgressions as a result of a lawsuit which Clavir and Albert launch against FBI Director Clarence Kelley. Clavir and Albert will receive "eyes-only" files kept on them by government agencies. The files are heavily censored prior to their release, with names and whole paragraphs detailing FBI motivation whited out. Nonetheless, certain startling facts emerge.

Who are Clavir and Albert to deserve such attention?

At one time, the Federal Bureau of Investigation seemed committed to the belief that Clavir and Albert were responsible for the bombing of the U.S. Capitol Building in Washington, D.C., in March of 1971. In fact, Clavir and Albert were in Washington when the explosion went off. Together with a group of other activists, they were editing a newspaper which would urge people to attend the upcoming Mayday antiwar demonstrations. Their work completed, they had left Washington the day after the big blast.

Just outside Philadelphia, the suspects' car was stopped.

"Get out of there with your hands up," boomed a loudspeaker. Shotgun barrels stared. Four shaky individuals emerged from the Volkswagen and were spread-eagled against the hood. This was no ordinary traffic violation. The G-men and Army Bomb Disposal Unit searched the VW and found nothing more dangerous than a bald tire.

When Clavir and Albert returned to New York City, they were tailed constantly for two weeks and then subpoenaed to a grand jury. Nothing came of this investigation. . . .

One year later, when the couple moves to the mountains, the FBI moves with them. . . .

In the dead of winter, agents from New York visit Hurley rarely, leaving surveillance activities to their Kingston counterparts. These local agents drop in every week or two on the Hurley post office. There, two middle-aged women hand them a carefully copied list of names of every person who has corresponded with the couple, and every person the pair have written to. . . .

In a small, somewhat wealthy town like Hurley, where FBI agents have been acquaintances and neighbors for thirteen years, the thought of not cooperating with the authorities does not cross these women's minds. No one needs to request authorization for "mail covers" which, when they are legally administered, have time limitations set down in the post office rule book. No sanctions are placed on upstanding citizens who merely comment on small-town gossip.

The harshest post office caper is copying down messages found on the back of post cards. As far as the couple can tell, however, their letter mail remains sealed.

The local agents also make it their business to check periodically with the Kingston Trust Company to obtain ongoing reports of the ups and downs of the couple's bank balance. Again, the local bank is happy to comply, and the files show fortunes dipping to an ebb of $0.27 in January of 1974. The FBI's interest is in large transactions, which indicate to their minds that Clavir and Albert might be turning over vast sums to fugitives. The files show no such withdrawals.

The bank also provides the FBI copies of every check Clavir writes. A bank official walks to the local FBI office to deliver the evidence personally. . . .

In the course of this intensive surveillance, just what does the FBI learn about the threateningly subversive activities of Clavir and Albert? It turns out that the subjects lead a relatively conventional life. . . .

Sensible secret police would abandon surveillance attempts that consistently yield no meaningful data. But someone in Washington is convinced that the subjects must be up to something—why else would they have moved to a place where spying is so difficult. . . .

The lower-level field agents are under heavy pressure to draw some incriminating evidence from this bottomless well of ambiguous information. These operatives can't even accurately evaluate what data they do have because they have been ordered by their bosses to find evidence of illicit activity. When a year of relentless gumshoe work yields no substantial results, the FBI makes the decision to burglarize the cabin.

Burglaries are felonies, even when the second-story men are government bureaucrats. (The break-in is never specifically mentioned in the FBI documents, but the Justice Department admits that an "electronic listening device" was installed in the Clavir/Albert cabin for a 17-day period, from November 1 to November 17, 1974. Later, when the burglary comes to light, a very reliable source will inform the couple that as well as installing the device, the FBI agents also searched their house, ransacked their garbage and photographed all their notebooks and documents.) . . .

These extracts from the files of the FBI are concrete evidence of a prolonged criminal attack on Judith Clavir and Stew Albert. The pair is now suing the government for damages and relief. . . .

Clavir and Albert still live in the cabin on top of Hurley Mountain. Nature's seasons continue to evoke an inspiring and diverse beauty but now the foliage is more than lovely, it is also potential camouflage for police. The forest, through no fault of its own, has lost its innocence. . . .

DOUBLE-ENTRY INTELLIGENCE FILES

Athan Theoharis

. . . The Code of Federal Regulations of 1976 stipulates that "with particular regard to the formulation of basic Government policy, Federal officials are responsible for incorporating in the records of their agencies all essential information on their major actions."

. . . In memorandums of April 11, 1940, November 15, 1941, March 1, 1942, January 16, 1943, March 9, 1943 and November 9, 1944, FBI Director J. Edgar Hoover advised bureau officials (both those in Washington and Special Agents in Charge of field offices) how to

Reprinted with permission of The Nation, Athan Theoharis, "Double-Entry Intelligence Files," THE NATION, in October 22, 1977, p. 393

prepare for submission to headquarters memorandums that were not to be retained and filed in the FBI's general files. These communications were to be typed on pink paper (later blue) the better to keep them separate from white-paper memorandums which, on receipt by Washington, would be given a serial number for filing purposes. In part, Hoover's reason for setting up this color code had been to reduce paper work. A deeper purpose, however, was to enable FBI field offices to convey sensitive information in writing to the FBI Director or Washington headquarters without running the danger that a retrievable record would thereby be created. His April 11, 1940 memorandum identified documents to be destroyed as including those "written merely for informative purposes, which need not be retained for permanent filing." The March 1, 1942 instruction more specifically identified these as including memorandums "prepared solely for the benefit of the Director and other officials and eventually to be returned to the dictator [of the memorandum] to be destroyed, or retained in the Director's office."

In 1942 the bureau instituted a "Do Not File" procedure for all field-office requests for authorization to conduct break-ins, along with the documents that formally approved these requests. Such papers were not to be given serial numbers, nor to be filed under the appropriate case or caption category. Whenever Hoover or his headquarters staff deemed it advisable to destroy them, they could vanish without a trace. An internal bureau memorandum of July 19, 1966, from William Sullivan to Cartha DeLoach (both men at the time were assistants to the Director) describes in detail the Do Not File procedure. To prevent excessive recourse to break-ins—which Sullivan characterized as "clearly illegal"—and to make sure that sufficient care was taken to prevent their discovery, prior written authorization from the Director or assistant director was required for all such crimes. Under normal procedures, of course, this would create a retrievable record, and the Do Not File device was invented to avoid that hazard. In September 1975 Congressional testimony, former FBI Assistant Director Charles Brennan conceded that this was indeed one purpose of the Do Not File procedure. It would also enable the bureau to comply with court disclosure orders, since witnesses could affirm that a search of FBI records had been made and no evidence uncovered of illegal government activities.

The recent discovery of this separate file keeping raises additional questions about the FBI's way with its records. In the course of reviewing the "Official-Confidential" files formerly retained by Hoover in his personal office, the staff of the Senate Select Committee on Intelligence Activities came across the Sullivan-to-DeLoach memorandum mentioned above. Mark Gitenstein, the staff counsel who made this find, then noticed that a caption, "PF," had been crossed out in the upper-right-hand corner and the notation added that, in November 1971, the document had been transferred to Hoover's Official-Confidential files. Further investigation established, first, that "PF" stood for Hoover's "Personal Files"; second, that this document, along with seven other documents, had been transferred from the "B" entry in the Personal Files ("B" for "Black Bag" jobs or break-ins) to Hoover's Official-Confidential files and, third, that shortly after his death in May 1972, Hoover's Personal Files had been sent to his home. There, following Hoover's instructions but allegedly after first reviewing the voluminous Personal Files to insure that they contained no official documents, the FBI Director's personal secretary, Helen Gandy, destroyed them. In her December 1975 testimony, Ms. Gandy maintained that she had found no other official documents. . . .

Obviously, a Do Not File procedure allows those concerned to deny knowledge of the extent and nature of recognizably illegal or "sensitive" activities, and other recent disclosures suggest that such separate filing procedures were not confined to break-ins. Thus, Sullivan's 1969 reports from Paris to Washington headquarters on his surveillance of nationally syndicated columnist Joseph Kraft were sent under the Do Not File procedure. In addition, despite Atty. Gen. Nicholas Katzenbach's 1966 requirement that all requests for authority to wiretap be submitted in writing and the names of those subject to such surveillances be included in a special file (an ELSUR Index), the wiretap records of the seventeen individuals (White House and National Security Council aides and reporters) tapped between 1969 and 1971, allegedly to uncover the source or sources of national security leaks, were not placed in this Index or filed with other FBI "national security" wiretap records. (Nor were the 1972 wiretap records on Charles Radford, a lower-level military aide suspected of having leaked National Security Council documents to the Joint Chiefs of Staff, included in the ELSUR Index or filed with other FBI "national security" taps. And FBI reports on its surveillance of Anna Chennault in October/November 1968 were "protected and secured" to insure that they would not be discovered and thereby affect that year's Presidential race.) Accordingly, when Sullivan told Asst. Atty. Gen. Robert Mardian in July 1971 that Hoover might use these taps to blackmail the President, Mardian, after consulting with Nixon, transferred the tap records from the FBI to the safe of White House aide John Ehrlichman. Because they were not listed originally in the ELSUR Index, there was no record either that these files had been transferred or that the wiretaps had been carried out. . . .

During the pretrial hearings in the Judith Coplon case, the FBI's extensive and illegal use of wiretapping was revealed because Federal

District Judge Albert Reeves ruled that certain FBI reports be submitted as evidence. Hoover then devised yet another filing procedure. In Bureau Bulletin No. 34 of July 8, 1949, he ordered that "facts and information which are considered of a nature not expedient to disseminate or would cause embarrassment to the bureau, if distributed" were henceforth to be omitted from agent reports, but detailed in the administrative pages that accompanied these reports. Normally, agents employed administrative pages to highlight investigative findings or to outline future investigative efforts. Because those pages could be kept separate from the reports, Hoover's order would allow the FBI to conduct questionable or illegal activities, and profit from their findings without risking disclosure during trial proceedings or even without responsible Justice Department officials ever learning of them.

This need to prevent discovery of illegal FBI investigative activities had also led Hoover on October 19, 1949 to advise all Special Agents in Charge how to hide the fact that the bureau was conducting an extensive "security index" program. It predated passage of the McCarran Internal Security Act and was partially based on a secret directive of August 3, 1948 from Atty. Gen. Tom Clark. The FBI, however, began to compile additional indexes—a Communist Index, a "Detcom (Communist Detention) program" and a "Comsab (Communist Saboteurs) program"—without the Attorney General's direction or knowledge. To guard against discovery of this program by the press and the Congress—as well as to prevent the Attorney General from discovering the bureau's independent extension of his authorization—Hoover advised SACs: "No mention must be made in any investigative report relating to the classifications of top functionaries and key figures, nor to the Detcom or Comsab programs, nor to the security index or the Communist Index. These investigative procedures and administrative aids are confidential and should not be known to any outside agency."

Then, when the FBI after February 1958, began to receive copies of letters illegally obtained through the agency's closely guarded mail cover/intercept program in New York City, similar filing procedures were set down, as described in a November 26, 1962 memorandum. Copies of intercepted mail were to be destroyed (if of no value) or filed in a secure area, separate from other FBI files. Such copies were also not to be included in the subject's case file, although a cross-reference would permit retrieval. When significant information found in this intercepted mail was sent on to FBI field offices or other divisions, it was to be paraphrased to disguise the source. Agents in Charge of this project in New York were specifically warned not to disseminate the obtained information outside the bureau and not to cite it in any investigative report.

Are there other FBI files? Obviously, this question cannot be answered definitively. When interviewed by David Wise, author of *The Police State,* William Sullivan claimed that John Mohr (then an FBI assistant director) had removed "very mysterious files" from Hoover's office after the FBI Director's death. These were "very sensitive and explosive files," Sullivan maintained, and not all of them were located by Atty. Gen. Edward Levi when he found "164 such files in the Justice Department."

Nor were these separate filing procedures and the attendant document destruction confined to the FBI. The CIA's drug program documents were destroyed in January 1973. Also, during the September 1975 Congressional testimony, CIA Director William Colby affirmed that the agency's recordkeeping practices made it impossible to reconstruct past CIA activities involving the production and retention of highly poisonous toxins: "Only a very limited documentation of activities took place"; the desire for compartmentation involving sensitive matters "reduced the amount of record keeping." . . .

Are these separate file-keeping and destruction procedures merely aberrational practices that have now been abandoned? Unfortunately, in the absence of proof to the contrary we must assume that they may be continuing or might be resumed. It is unlikely that before 1975 responsible, informed citizens would have accused the intelligence agencies of such practices, and if they had, few Americans would have taken them seriously. Furthermore, recent testimony under oath by intelligence officers and their responses to document requests during the first intensive Congressional inquiry into the practices of the intelligence community have raised additional questions about the intelligence agencies' file-keeping practices.

Thus in 1975, FBI Director Clarence Kelley during a press conference, senior FBI officials testifying before Congress, and FBI memorandums responding to specific inquiries of the Senate Select Committee all affirmed that FBI break-ins during domestic security investigations had ceased in 1966, and that the exact number of such past FBI break-ins could not be provided because, thanks to the Do Not File procedure, written records did not exist. In 1976, however, in response to a court order involving a damage suit brought against the government by the Socialist Workers Party, the FBI not only produced break-in documents but these documents disclosed that FBI domestic security break-ins continued after 1966 and as late as July 1976.

In addition, William Colby testified in September 1975 that the CIA could not be fully responsive to the Senate Select Committee's queries concerning the CIA's drug programs and specifically its toxin program. Not only had documents concerning the CIA's general drug programs been destroyed in January 1973, but the agency's desire for compartmentation of sensitive materials had "reduced [the] amount of record keeping" and thus there had been "only a very limited documentation of [the] activities [which] took place." But in July 1977, contradicting Colby's assertions, CIA Director Stansfield Turner advised the Senate Select Committee that documents pertaining to the CIA's past drug program had been discovered after "extraordinary and extensive search efforts." These, Turner reported, had been found in retired archives filed under financial accounts. The newly discovered documents showed that CIA drug testing on American citizens had been more extensive than had been disclosed in 1975. . . .

The intelligence agencies' record-keeping practices in the recent past show their bureaucrats to have felt themselves above the law. Rather than being bound to respect legal or constitutional limitations, these officials decided that the law could be safely circumvented, first by exploiting popular and Congressional tolerance for secrecy, and then by devising elaborate filing procedures to prevent discovery. What is needed for a return to government by law, and not by men, is to create safeguards against the tendency of intelligence agency officials to decide for themselves, and secretly, what national policy shall be. Central to this is the need to reaffirm the people's "right to know" as much about national security as it does about economic policy. . . .

The Tax Revolt

The passage in June 1978 of California's Proposition 13, the "Jarvis-Gann Initiative," suggests a redirection to state and local government. Whether that redirection is toward enhanced productivity or gross cutbacks in service is as yet unclear. Subsequent to the passage of Proposition 13, a Gallup Poll indicated that sympathy with the "tax revolt" was widespread. Initiatives or legislation with similar intent have been proposed in a majority of other states. Although 57 percent of the public (nationally) favored a Jarvis-type cut, the vast majority did not believe that their communities are providing too great a range of services. That is, the American taxpayer seemed to want it both ways—lower taxes and ample services. Only improved government efficiency would satisfy that want, and the Gallup poll showed that most Americans believe it can be done. A *Los Angeles Times* poll, after the vote, found that 70 percent of those supporting "13" thought they would get by without cuts in services.

Is there really enormous "fat" in government? Ferndale, California, has apparently coped with "13" without damaging cuts in services. ("Proposition 13 Comes to Ferndale"). Mayor Stan Dixon feels that the community just "tightened up." But over the long run, Swanbrow suggests that problems may be building up: The quality of education may suffer and public employees may become disgruntled over low raises.

In larger cities, where services are not provided on a voluntary basis as often happens in smaller communities, the quality of life may already be on the decline as "San Francisco Feels Impact of Tax Cuts" shows.

QUESTIONS FOR DISCUSSION

What services does your local bureaucracy provide you?
What services does your state bureaucracy provide you?

What services does the federal bureaucracy provide you?

In what ways is a budget cut a valuable instrument for fighting waste and inefficiency? At what point does it become harmful?

Do taxpayers tend to seek only cuts in services to "others" (welfare, recreation, schools, etc.)?

Should the budget pinch go "across the board" to all services or to selected services?

If the taxpayers are not willing to pay more taxes and yet nobody is willing to suggest eliminating services, what can be done to deal with the situation?

PROPOSITION 13 COMES TO FERNDALE

Diane Swanbrow

When California residents went into the voting booth last year and came out triskaidekaphiles, the message that taxpayers had had enough became the nationwide electoral theme of the year. At the same time, there was much criticism and documentation of the fact that the resulting spending cuts hit the poor and minorities extra hard, both in terms of government jobs lost and social programs killed or cut back. But it is also true that the middle-class majority that supported Proposition 13's new limits was itself going to feel an impact. It has been a year since the trimming began. What do people feel? POLITICS TODAY decided to seek a partial answer by looking at life in one small town. We chose Ferndale, California (elevation 50; population 1,410) and dispatched a reporter who filed this story:

A few days after the passage of Proposition 13, Mayor Stan Dixon called a meeting of the Ferndale City Council. "I think we should start by cutting back with ourselves," he said. The five council members talked it over for a few minutes, then voted to stop paying their own salaries. The major had been receiving $15 for each meeting, the councilpersons $10. They also voted to stop reimbursing themselves for any expenses.

Dixon, 40, moved to Ferndale when he was in the eighth grade. His wife is a native, fourth generation. Dixon holds a full-time county social services job in Eureka, twelve miles away. He has heavy circles under his eyes but is tan and wiry. He is a long-distance runner.

"Ferndale's in pretty good shape," he says, one year after the passage of Proposition 13. "We haven't had to dip into our reserves this year; it's still about $200,000. We just had to do some tightening up."

Instead of giving the city's five full-time workers—three policemen and two maintenance men—a 9 percent pay increase, the city gave them 5.4 percent. That means that the chief of police, for example, received a raise of $44.28, instead of $73.80, bringing his monthly salary to $864.28.

The Ferndale Library hours were reduced from 49 to 29 per week and its book-buying budget was cut. But the library has not been too badly affected, thanks to a local custom that deserves to catch on everywhere. "When someone dies in Ferndale," says the part-time librarian, "a lot of people donate books instead of sending flowers. We put a nice memorial bookplate on the inside cover."

The heat in City Hall is turned on now only for special occasions, so the part-time city clerk shivers in her office with a small electric heater.

The city's 35 streets are still remarkably clean. If chuck-holes are not filled in as quickly as they once were, no one in town complains.

The move that saved most of the money, says the mayor, was abolishing the city's two-year-old Parks and Recreation Department— whose annual budget had been running between $5,000 and $6,000. Many approved of killing the department for reasons having little to do with Proposition 13. "You start adding a Parks and Recreation director to a little town and before you know it, he's got himself a couple secretaries," says Bruce Russell, publisher of a free weekly in the area, the HUMBOLDT LIFE AND TIMES. "Then he needs a proper office building, a fancy recreation center." With plenty of salmon and perch in the nearby Eel River, the Humboldt County Fairgrounds right in town, and a winning high school football team—the Wildcats—to cheer for, a formal recreation program seemed superfluous to many residents. Says Ferndale Fire Chief Lee Tomasini, "If people can't figure out how to entertain themselves around here, then they're fools who don't deserve to be entertained.

By taking these steps, Mayor Dixon believes the city was able to reduce expenses by about as much as it lost through Proposition 13— approximately $8,600. And cutting back on expenses made more sense to the Ferndale government than accepting state grants and aid. For one thing, the state has a maximum cash surplus that a town it helps is allowed to have. "We would have had to spend $23,000 of our reserve to get about $8,000 in Proposition 13 bail-out money." says Don Slocum, city clerk for 25 years. "So the council decided not to go along with it. We don't much go for the state telling us what to do around here."

The spirit of self-reliance is strong in Ferndale, encouraged by location and preserved by the character of the people. The northwestern California city lies five miles off the Redwood Highway at the foot of a mountain called the Wildcat. Some 75 percent of its residents were born there, half are second generation, and perhaps 150 people are descendants of the town's first settlers—the Shaw, Francis, Russ and Williams families. Those early settlers were sheep and cattle ranchers, lumbermen and dairy farmers. So are most Ferndale residents today.

"It is right and proper to have everything around the dairy house clean and sweet as circumstances permit," wrote a resident named Richard Johnson back in 1881. His advice is included in a history of the town, WHERE THE FERNS GREW TALL, compiled and published as a class project by the Ferndale Union High School students, Class of '77. And Mr. Johnson's century-old charge is still followed, judging from Ferndale's appearance. Along Main Street, the Victorian buildings are neatly, though perhaps too preciously, painted. In City Hall, the wood floors are free of scuff marks, shining. Citizens are proud of their one-square-mile city, the westernmost incorporated city in the contiguous 48 states. Did you know that the tallest lighted Christmas tree in the world is right here in Ferndale? people say. Did you know the Bank of America branch in Ferndale once had the highest per capita accounts of any branch in the United States?

In fact, there was a time when Ferndale was so prosperous and its dairies so productive it was called "Cream City." In May 1899, the Excelsior Creamery took in 1,054,619 pounds of milk from area dairies, producing from it 44,504 pounds of butter. Some of the profits the Holsteins and Jerseys provided were used to build ornate homes— "Butterfat palaces." But on the whole the dairymen were thrifty. All the creameries in the area operated hog farms, fattening the animals with waste skim milk. Animals and people had to pay their way. To identify and weed out unproductive cows, the farmers formed the Ferndale Cow Testing Association in 1909. Eight years later butterfat production per cow had increased by 50 percent. In Ferndale, prosperity has always depended upon culling the herd.

Lee Tomasini, 44, is a short man with thick black hair, black eyebrows and mustache. He was born in Ferndale and has lived there all his life, serving for 25 years on the volunteer Fire Department before becoming the chief just last year. "I voted for Proposition 13," he says, "My feeling is, something had to be done about taxes. But I work for the county road department, and I've gone two years now without a raise." Tomasini starts fishing in his pocket and says, "Lemme show you something. I carry this around with me 'cause people don't believe it when I tell 'em what I make after 22 years with the county."

The check stub he holds shows that his gross pay every two weeks is $597.14, and his take-home is $341.97.

To supplement his county income, Tomasini moonlights cleaning chimneys. On the front lawn of the Main Street home where he lives with his wife and three children, a hand-lettered sign says LEE (MARY POPINS) THOMASINI. Both names are misspelled. "Some of the guys started callin' me Mary Poppins 'cause I started sweepin' chimneys about the same time the movie came out," he says. From his work as a chimney sweep, Tomasini makes about $1,100 a year. From his job as Ferndale's fire chief, he makes $1,600.

The fire district Tomasini is in charge of stretches west to the ocean, east to the Eel River, up the Wildcat and down past Grizzly Bluff, and the district has its own budget. Before Proposition 13 passed, the Fire Department had ordered a new $68,000 Howe pumper that can handle 1,250 gallons per minute. They paid for it in cash. But the Fire Department budget was reduced by $14,000 this year, and Tomasini worries how they'll be able to save money now to purchase new or replacement equipment. "This other pumper's goin' on 28 years old, and we need two new tankers," he says. "We gotta pack our own water for country fires."

While most reductions were made this year simply by not buying equipment, Tomasini also had to drop 11 men, bringing his volunteer force down to 47. The men received no pay, of course, but the city had to carry costly compensation insurance on them. With about 50 fire calls a year to answer throughout the district, Tomasini worries about the effect of fewer men on his department's response time, a point of considerable civic pride. "By the time the whistle's winding down time, there's an engine ready to roll," he says. "It's a matter of one, two minutes. Even at night, I'd say it takes three minutes at the most. Usually there's two, three guys at the bar right down the street."

Joe Lewis, 28, chief of the Ferndale police, sits at his desk inspecting the sketch for a new police department emblem that he intends to present at a council meeting later that night. "We're trying to change the image of the police force," he says. "This new design is a lot better." The pencil sketch shows a gazebo surrounded by delicate fern fronds. The emblem presently on Lewis's uniformed arm shows a bear that looks like an anteater.

With clear blue eyes and an engaging smile, Lewis himself is perhaps the most convincing symbol of a pleasant, friendly police force. His department consists of two cars and three men—with one of the city maintenance men keeping his eyes on things in the early morning before the first shift comes on duty. "We don't have a high crime rate here," says Lewis. "We did have a church burglary last January."

Although the size of the police force is small, the attitude of Ferndale citizens help maintain order. They seem to assume responsibility for bringing offenders to justice, as the following item from the weekly FERNDALE ENTERPRISE of May 3, 1979, illustrates: "The lawns at the City Hall, Humboldt County fairgrounds and Ferndale Elementary School were damaged by a car. Anyone having any information is asked to call the proper authorities and it will be kept strictly confidential." And sure enough, a man who lived near the school called the next day with a description of the car.

The police department budget was not reduced because of Proposition 13, but Chief Lewis does what he can to keep expenses down. For example, he sometimes does not return calls from Los Angeles because they would be long distance calls. And by rebuilding the city's older police car instead of replacing it, he hopes to save the city almost $5,000.

Barking dogs and farm animals that offend fastidious neighbors are Lewis's major problems, as well as drunk and disorderly conduct. In all cases, the policy of the Ferndale police is to handle matters as amicably as possible. "If someone really drunk is trying to drive, first we try to reason with them, get them to call a friend to take them home," Lewis says. "If they won't, we offer to drive them home ourselves. But if they just won't calm down, and if we feel they're too drunk to drive safely, we have to arrest them. We try to avoid it wherever possible, though. See, we don't have a jail here. So we have to take them all the way into Eureka."

Neither of Ferndale's two schools looks run-down despite the fact that each lost $50,000 from their separate budgets as a result of Proposition 13. In the 375-pupil grade school, hallways and classroom floors are carpeted and windows are covered with color-coordinated shades. In the 260-student high school, the new gymnasium is spotlessly clean. But both schools have been forced to make staff and program reductions in the wake of Proposition 13.

Oscar Sequist, who is superintendent/principal of Ferndale Elementary, laid off a part-time art teacher, dropped insurance for school board members, and eliminated summer school and vocal music. The largest saving was effected by dropping an early childhood education program that employed four teacher's aides. "I was just as glad to see it go," says Sequist. "It didn't seem to be improving test scores any." As a result of these reductions, plus an increase in state bail-out funding, Ferndale Elementary will start the new school year with a reserve of $80,000.

Ferndale Union High School, on the other hand, will start the next school year in the red. "I can't blame the mess we're in entirely on Proposition 13," says Charlie Lakin, superintendent/principal of

FUHS. "Declining enrollment and bad fiscal management had a lot to do with it." The head maintenance man and two teachers have been laid off already. Another teacher has resigned, three have told Lakin they are looking elsewhere, and "the best new teacher I've seen in years makes so little he's eligible for food stamps," says Lakin. "None of my staff has had a raise in two years." The reduction in teachers caused the school to drop chorus and band this year, and next year courses in photography and gunsmithing are going.

The reason that Ferndale's two schools are in such dissimilar situations is that they are not merely separate schools but autonomous school districts. Together, they have 635 students. "It's ridiculous," says Charlie Lakin. "I mean, we're less than a mile down the road! And when you mention consolidation, people start shouting 'Local control!'" When the subject is mentioned to Oscar Sequist, he says with a satisfied chuckle, "It drives them crazy at budget time." . . .

SAN FRANCISCO FEELS IMPACT OF TAX CUTS

Wallace Turner

As California's local governments move into the third budget year after Proposition 13's property tax cuts, their confident paradeground stride has begun to resemble a ragged stagger.

Nowhere are the problems of municipal poverty worse than in San Francisco. The interior of the spectacular City Hall is marred by dirty paint; public parks now seem always to have shaggy lawns; libraries are closed longer and longer each day; permit processing is six months behind.

Public employees seem to be in running conflict with the city government or the school district, which are separate entities. The schools were hit last fall by a protracted strike of teachers. About 500 termination notices, required under state law if dismissals are to come for economy reasons, are to be given to teachers next week, and this is expected to exacerbate the relationships. . . .

Taking San Francisco as an example of the effect on city and county government, the state this fiscal year provided about 17 percent of the general fund budget. And even with that big contribution, and after lopping about 5,000 employees (17 percent) off city payrolls, a budget deficit of about 16.8 percent looms for the fiscal year beginning July 1.

"What is so frustrating to those of us familiar with what has been happening is that, because the schoolhouse doors are open, most people think it's business as usual and everything is just fine," said Wilson Riles, the California Superintendent of Public Instruction. "They couldn't be more wrong."

In the first two years of budget limitations, Mr. Riles said, the schools cut back on secretaries, janitors, school buses, and maintenance. He said that "every attempt was made to protect the classroom, and I applaud that."

But now more cuts have to come. In San Francisco, the school board has announced that it intends to eliminate all elementary school librarians, shorten the school day by one period, and cut out many high school electives in foreign languages, advanced English and science.

A plan to retain some elementary music teachers by public contributions is in the works. Mr. Riles said that such plans disturbed him because they showed the truth of his belief that "when you make cuts in services, you're not going to cut the affluent, you're going to cut the lower class and the poor."

For San Francisco's city-county government, the only such combination in California, the major financial crisis here this spring is a budget deficit of $112 million if services are to be maintained at their level of the last two years. This totals about 16.5 percent of what the board of supervisors has to spend in the general fund, but that is only a part of the problem.

Ray Sullivan, budget officer for Mayor Dianne Feinstein, said that about half the general fund budget went for public safety purposes, such as the police, firefighting and the courts, and the city's general hospital. These are almost impossible to cut, he said, which means that the cuts must come from the operations of some 50 city programs, ranging from parks through social services, city attorney, registrar of voters and the like.

So the Mayor's proposals have been to cut $28.7 million and to raise money by higher public transit fares and increases of some fees and use charges. However, the Board of Supervisors has resisted this, and no action is being taken while the deadlines for the new budget move even closer.

"Proposition 13 is really coming home to roost this year," Mayor Feinstein said. "If this new tax cut comes, we must prepare to lay off thousands of employees, and then the city cannot provide the services that San Franciscans expect and need."

Dealing with Fraud and Waste in Government

Critics of government often complain that fraud and waste are pervasive problems. The Government Accounting Office and the Department of Justice have estimated federal fraud and waste at $50 billion a year, about 10 percent of the federal budget. The estimate indicates the magnitude of the problem, one that government is relatively inexperienced in solving.

Two federal agencies have taken action. "Uncle Sam's Fraud Hot Line" reveals how the Government Accounting Office, a congressional agency, has instituted a hot line that is producing thousands of leads, capable of saving potentially millions of dollars. "Horror Story at GSA" indicates how the General Services Administration has begun reversing decades of neglect, using auditing and inspection procedures to go after blatant misconduct among its own employees—and revealing perhaps the largest scandal in government history.

QUESTIONS FOR DISCUSSION

Are you personally aware of fraud and waste in government at any level?
Is a fraud hot line ethical?
Does an open approach to fraud undermine confidence in government?
To what extent were GSA's problems a function of its use as a political dumping ground? Would merit appointments have resulted in better management?

HORROR STORY AT GSA

Carl T. Rowan and David M. Mazie

A contractor paints a third-floor corridor in the Pentagon and bills the General Services Administration—the all-purpose agency that manages property, buys supplies and handles dozens of other administrative chores for the federal government—for 500,000 square feet. A year later, 70 percent of the same corridor is painted by a different contractor. This time GSA pays for 1,065,000 square feet.

A woman who works for the U.S. Office of Education swaps her GSA credit card—good for purchases in government supply stores—for a free parking space. The parking attendant then uses the card to obtain $40,000 worth of merchandise, which he turns around and sells.

A GSA store manager in Baltimore accepts $6646 in gifts—color TVs, liquor, jewelry—from a supply firm. In return, he okays invoices stating that the GSA received supplies worth $15,000—goods the supply firm never sent.

These are but a few examples of the corruption and mismanagement found throughout GSA. Fraud, waste and outright thievery are "a way of life" in the agency, says Jay Solomon, who in two years as GSA administrator vigorously pursued investigations and reform. Vincent Alto, former special counsel for the GSA, has labeled the situation there "probably the biggest scandal in the history of the federal government, both in terms of money and in the number of federal employes involved." Although no one knows the exact extent of the crime, it appears to have added up, over the years, to several billions of dollars.

It's ironic that GSA should emerge as a symbol of scandal and ineptness in Washington. The agency was established 30 years ago on the recommendation of the Hoover Commission to provide more efficient, cost-effective administrative services to the federal government. Instead of each government agency buying its own supplies and managing its own office space, such tasks were to be centralized in the GSA.

Today, with 35,129 employes and a $5-billion annual budget, GSA would rank among America's 50 largest industrial firms. It owns 250 buildings and rents space in another 7500, making it the country's largest real-estate operator. It maintains 85,000 vehicles, operates a buying service and a chain of 71 self-service stores, manages an $11.5-billion stockpile of strategic materials, and keeps important records in its national archives.

Yet, almost from the start, its goal of efficiency has been elusive. GSA quickly gained a reputation as a dumping ground for political cronies second only to the Post Office. As far back as 1955, a *Fortune* article called GSA "Washington's most durable mess." For several years the *Washington Post* has reported irregularities and questionable practices at GSA. A handful of the agency's own employes have stepped forward with stories of illegalities and mismanagement. But, through it all, GSA kept doing "business as usual."

Things began to change in April 1977, when Solomon, a 57-year-old builder and developer from Chattanooga, Tenn., took over as GSA administrator. Spurred by revelations in the press, and by grand-jury investigations in Washington and Baltimore, Solomon launched an all-out inquiry. The Internal Revenue Service and FBI joined the investigation, and the Justice Department created a task force to coordinate the overall effort.

Finally, in 1978, subcommittees in both Senate and House began hearings on GSA activities. And before long a litany of horror stories covering virtually every aspect of GSA's operations came pouring forth. Among them:

• *Inflated contracts.* The most explosive testimony at the congressional hearings came from Robert Lowry, president of a Washington painting firm. He admitted taking part in "systematic bribery" of GSA officials for several years. According to Lowry, a cozy group of contractors would decide whose turn it was to get the next GSA contract for maintenance work on a building. At that time, contracts of $2000 or less could be awarded by individual building managers under an informal bid system. So the contractors would submit pre-arranged bids—say, of $1980, $1960 and $1925—for a $300 job.

What was in it for the manager? Lowry cited lavish lunches, parties, paid vacations, cash, and call girls. "Fraud became the rule, not the exception," testified Lowry, and accounted for "60 to 70 percent of the actual cost" of GSA maintenance contracts in the Washington area.

• *Phony Purchases.* GSA's self-service stores were also a prime target for fraud. Designated employes of government agencies, supposedly buying items for their offices, used the stores as one big grab bag. In the fall, for instance, government workers would bring their kids into the stores to pick out back-to-school supplies. Around Christmas, government offices suddenly seemed to need vast amounts of brief-cases, desk sets and other "giveable" items. One employe of the Arms Control Agency charged up $373,754 worth of Polaroid film, enough to take several hundred thousand more photos than his agency needed.

In one especially well-organized scheme, an office-supply firm, Hilles Associates, arranged for GSA employes in the Baltimore-Washington area to pick out TV sets, rings, watches, microwave ovens, clothing and other expensive items from local stores and charge them to Hilles. In return, Hilles was paid $1.7 million between 1974 and 1977 by GSA for supplies never delivered. The GSA stores then overcharged their government customers to cover up for the goods not received. Twenty-two persons—19 GSA store managers, one regional manager and two top officers of Hilles Associates—were convicted in this scheme, and eventually 27 of 30 store managers in the Washington-Baltimore region were removed.

• *Poor management.* A study by the General Accounting Office estimated that GSA wasted up to $2.2 billion over nine years by paying more for common items like typewriters and tape recorders than ordinary shoppers in local discount stores. At the same time that GSA was paying top dollar for non-competitive purchases, it was getting bottom dollar for goods it sold from strategic-materials stockpiles.

GSA's real-estate ventures were especially costly. For example, in 1976 the agency leased an eleven-story Washington office building so remotely located that it took the GSA nearly two years to find a tenant. The decision to rent the building was made when Arthur F. Sampson was GSA administrator. Sampson later went to work for the man who owned the building.

In all, during the period between September 1977 and April 1979, 97 persons were charged in connection with GSA misdeeds. Seventy-nine of them either pleaded or were found guilty; the other cases are still pending, and more indictments are expected as investigations continue in Hawaii, Texas, New York and other places.

How did corruption at GSA get so out of hand? The answers, as pieced together by GSA officials, investigators and others close to the scene, include:

• *Political cronyism.* One of Solomon's most bruising battles involved Robert T. Griffin, 61, protégé of House Speaker Thomas P. "Tip" O'Neill (D., Mass.). Griffin spent 29 years at GSA and was the agency's No. 2 man, in charge of day-to-day operations, when Solomon arrived. Solomon fired him in July 1978 because he felt Griffin represented the "old way" of doing things and was undermining Solomon's authority. President Carter backed Solomon. But after an outcry from

O'Neill, Griffin was quickly given a new $50,000-a-year job at the White House, working on trade and anti-inflation programs.

At least GSA was bipartisan. In 1970, it leased the Gateway Center office building in Philadelphia for 20 years for $52 million. The building project had been sponsored by the former law partner of Sen. Hugh Scott (R., Pa.), then Republican leader in the Senate, and worked out by Robert L. Kunzig, a former Scott aide who became GSA administrator in the Nixon years.

• *Bad organization.* "GSA was one of the most poorly organized agencies I'd ever seen in my life," says Solomon. Mid- and low-level employes, in effect, ran the place, making $5-million purchase decisions without any supervisory review. A "buddy-buddy" system—the same people, in and out of government, doing business with one another over the years—thwarted truly competitive bidding. Persons involved in hanky-panky often escaped punishment, while those who had the courage to report abuses were likely to be ignored, demoted, transferred or fired. As a result, employes and those doing business with the agency felt they could get away with almost anything. For example, last October, in the midst of Congressional hearings on GSA, almost daily headlines in the press, and mounting indictments, a painting contractor in Washington, D.C., offered a $5000 bribe to a GSA inspector to get him to pay for two coats of paint when only one had been applied. He was turned in.

• *Poor self-policing.* In mid-1978, when the current investigation was in full swing, GSA had only 90 auditors to check its operations, one-fifth the number the agency felt it needed. Rep. John Burton (D., Calif.), chairman of the House Subcommittee on Government Activities and Transportation, reported that only 11 of 16,000 GSA procurement contracts were audited in a two-year period. And until the scandal broke, Congress and the Department of Justice did not actively monitor GSA or pursue their own investigations.

Solomon did much to change GSA procedures and organization during his two years in charge. Dozens of employes were reassigned, scores of others admonished. The GSA auditing team was doubled, and inspections were stepped up. An Office of Inspections with a full-time inspector general was created to check out work and determine whether what was paid for actually was done. The management of self-service stores was tightened up. A system of checks and balances was also instituted so that the same person can't award a contract, inspect the work and then sign the check.

But GSA remains a troubled agency, resistant to change. There have been hints that former high-level people in GSA and Congress knew about fraudulent acts, even if they didn't take part. Further-more, doubts exist as to how determined the Carter Administration and the Congress are to see that change occurs. Solomon left last March 31—and no one seems quite sure why. Apparently his style or his actions—notably the Griffin firing—caused concern, and he was nudged out before his work was done.

His successor is Rear Adm. Rowland G. Freeman III, a 37-year Navy veteran. Freeman has a reputation as an expert in procurement, but his World War II combat duty may come in more handy. As White House Press Secretary Jody Powell observed, the GSA's top job "requires as much a policeman as a manager." Working with Freeman as the new GSA inspector general is Kurt Muellenberg, former head of the Justice Department's organized-crime section.

To help them make GSA an efficient, honest agency will require an all-out effort. Specifically, GSA needs: (1) Reorganization, tighten-ing and modernization of management; (2) a strong and independent inspector general's office; (3) more and better auditing, with the means to follow through on reports; (4) new laws closing the loop-holes in purchasing regulations and making punishment more certain for wrongdoers; (5) closer supervision by Congress.

What happens at GSA is vastly important to the nation. A lot more is on the line here than pilfered film, credit-card frauds or call-girl bribes. As President Carter observed when speaking of cor-ruption in government: "We are concerned with more than saving dollars, crucial as that is today. We must continue to restore and rebuild the trust that must exist in a democracy between a free people and their government."

UNCLE SAM'S FRAUD HOT LINE: A HIT WITH ANGRY TAXPAYERS

U.S. News & World Report Staff

Thousands of Americans are finding that blowing the whistle on federal waste and fraud is as easy as picking up the telephone.

And people are doing precisely that—calling a toll-free hot line operated by the General Accounting Office, the investigative arm of Congress.

The hot line, set up six months ago to receive citizens' tips on wrongdoing, already is producing results. New "inspectors general" are checking into more than 3,500 telephoned leads, and at least a dozen cases are being considered for prosecution.

The flurry of activity has been sparked by the more than 9,000 calls handled so far by the GAO, and by hundreds of other tips received by 14 federal agencies with hot lines of their own.

"By the time I returned from a news conference announcing the hot line, the phone was ringing—and it's been ringing ever since," says Harold L. Stugart, director of the GAO's fraud task force.

GAO officials believe that public enthusiasm for the project reflects concern about federal waste and fraud, which are believed to be costing taxpayers billions of dollars each year.

Tipsters using the GAO hot line have made an array of allegations ranging from the illicit collection of small federal-benefit checks to illegal awards of large government contracts. The hot-line number is (800) 424-5454 except in the Washington, D.C., area, where it is 633-6987.

Among the hot-line-inspired probes that have proved successful so far—

- The Department of Health, Education and Welfare has recovered $138,000 that it improperly paid to a contractor.
- Federal housing officials halted a scheme by applicants for urban-renewal funds to inflate land values and thereby obtain excessive federal aid.
- The General Services Administration imposed stiff controls on employee use of federal credit cards for gasoline purchases after callers cited abuses.

The GAO's hot line grew out of a study by the agency last year concluding that "the government's economic-assistance programs, amounting to about 250 billion dollars annually, are vulnerable targets of fraud and related white-collar crimes."

The line was set up to funnel information from citizens to newly established "inspector general" offices in 14 federal agencies. Simultaneously, each agency created a separate line for employees to use in reporting abuses.

GAO officials who screen the calls say about one third offer tips that are worth pursuing. Of the remainder, some are referred to state and local officials, others are merely requests for information and still others are too vague to be acted upon.

More than 60 percent of the callers refuse to give their names. One reason: Many are civil servants who fear retaliation from superiors or colleagues.

That worry may be justified, because federal workers are frequent targets of the complaints. Callers accuse them of taking bribes, purchasing unneeded supplies, claiming overtime pay when they did not work the extra hours and a host of other offenses.

But well over half of the accusations are against recipients of federal funds—individuals, corporations and nonprofit groups. "The federal employee isn't doing all the ripping off of the taxpayers," says one GAO official.

The Agency is checking hundreds of reports that federal grants are being spent improperly. More common are charges that citizens are cheating on taxes or breaking the rules in obtaining welfare, Social Security, veterans' aid, food stamps or other federal benefits.

Such cases are so numerous that federal authorities often must refer complaints to the state agencies that disburse much federal aid.

Allegations leveled over the hot lines sometimes sound plausible at first but in the end fail to turn up evidence of wrongdoing. One caller informed the Veterans Administration that a man was drawing disability benefits even though he was working. Investigators discovered, however, that the veteran earned only $1,500 a year in intermittent jobs and thus was eligible for aid.

"The accuser just didn't know all the facts," says Don Nelson of the VA inspector general's office. "But even in cases like this, callers are usually reasonable. When the situation is explained to them, they end up having more faith in government."

Often, however, a citizen who sees something amiss can alert officials to a real problem. General Services Administration officials cite a typical case: A charge that a federally owned car was used to transport personal goods.

The agency discovered that an employee of a firm that was repairing the vehicle had used it to help a relative move. The firm accepted the blame and reimbursed the government $10.

More important than the money involved, say GSA officials, is the deterrent effect of such probes. "We're treating all cases as serious because we don't want them to happen again," an investigator explains.

The hot lines are not uniformly popular. "We've had complaints that encouraging people to inform on each other is a Gestapo tactic," notes one federal official. But defenders insist that the telephone service is a valuable tool in the drive against misspending.

Says the GAO's Stugart: "The volume of our calls shows that there was a crying need for something like this. Civil servants and private citizens didn't know where to go with their complaints. The public has been demanding accountability, and we're helping them get it."

Introduction
Regulate the Regulators

The establishment or elimination of an agency is accomplished through legislative action. But legislatures generally act only in response to powerful pressures. Those who agitate for a new agency or program usually find getting it authorized and funded a tough, uphill battle. Once established, on the other hand, an agency builds support from its staff and special clientele. It tends to persist, as long as no politically powerful effort gets under way to kill it. And, in general, few people care enough about eliminating an ineffective or unimportant program to make that effort. So we see phenomena such as the persistence to this day of the tax-supported U.S. Board of Federal Tea Tasters.

As a way of making it easier to get rid of the ineffective agency, the State of Colorado pioneered in passing a "sunset law" at the urging of the citizens' organization, Common Cause. In Colorado an agency now automatically goes out of business at the end of a given period, unless the legislature acts specifically to renew or modify it. Colorado's model has now been adopted by many other states.

QUESTIONS FOR DISCUSSION

Why has "sunset" been successful?
Why didn't the impetus for "sunset" come from within the executive branch?
Why didn't it come from the legislature?
Would "sunset" be a good idea at the national level? for municipalities?

REGULATE THE REGULATORS

Irwin Ross

Rarely has this nation's public been more disillusioned with government. Citizens of all political persuasions see government as wasteful, out of control, prey to all sorts of special interests. Last April, a poll by Louis Harris & Associates revealed that 71 percent of Americans believe that they "do not get good value from their tax dollars."

But solutions are not easy. Hence the national attention that has focused on Colorado's imaginative approach to curbing the excesses of government—by way of a "sunset law" passed two years ago. Over a six-year cycle, 39 state regulatory agencies would go out of business unless the legislature voted to renew their tenure. Colorado's law was the first in the nation. Since then, 28 other states have enacted sunset laws of one kind or another. Most of them, however, have been too recently instituted to have produced significant results.

The Colorado law has already achieved an impressive track record. Three regulatory agencies have been abolished; two have been consolidated; one has been incorporated into another state agency; eight others have been reformed. "Sunset has clearly been a success," says Gov. Richard Lamm.

The law came to Colorado because of widespread dissatisfaction with regulatory agencies. Lawyer Craig Barnes, for example, spent an agonizing time before the Public Utilities Commission pressing the case of a client who wanted to start a Jeep-tour service in a small town in the Rockies. Under Colorado law, the PUC regulates both "fixed utilities" (electricity, gas, telephone) and transportation —everything from railroads to intrastate trucking to sightseeing tours.

Barnes's client needed a certificate of "convenience and necessity" from the commission before he could go into business. This involved a monumental legal effort, for the Jeep-tour operator already in the area opposed the newcomer's application. The client spent $4000 to support his application—and then failed to get his certificate. To Barnes, the nagging question was: why was the state involved in the first place? Moreover, why was it necessary to license barbers, hairdressers, landscape architects and even shorthand court reporters? All too often licensing merely restricted entry and thus restrained competition.

Barnes concluded that the regulators themselves had to be brought under control. In 1975, he proposed a plan at a board meeting of the Colorado chapter of Common Cause, the national "citizens lobby." Adapting a concept that had been occasionally suggested in the past, Barnes proposed that regulatory agencies come up, on a rotating basis, for periodic review by the legislature. If their existence could not be justified, "the sun would set on them." Common Cause began to mobilize support for the proposal throughout the state.

The idea quickly gained bipartisan backing in both the Colorado senate and house, and became law in 1976. Under the act, one third of the state's regulatory agencies are subjected to the sunset review process during each two-year session of the legislature. If the law-makers decided not to continue an agency, it has one year to wind up its affairs before it expires. The legislature has a third option, how-ever. It can modify the operations of an agency—change its com-position, consolidate it with another agency, increase or diminish its powers.

The goal of sunset is not merely to get rid of unnecessary agen-cies, but to promote reform. The legislature, of course, always had the power of review, but in the crush of other business it tended to skimp on its oversight functions. Unless there was some glaring problem, it left well enough alone. Sunset forces the legislature to deal with these policy issues. Significantly, the law places the burden of proof for continuance on the agency and its supporters. The prem-ise is the less government, the better.

The first agencies, 13 in all, were up for review in 1977. In preparation, the state auditor's staff and the Department of Regula-tory Agencies (DORA)—the umbrella agency that supervises all of the regulatory boards and commissions subject to sunset—each con-ducted a performance review of every agency and produced reports for the legislators.

The legislative review process was parceled out to various stand-ing committees, which held public hearings. Then the fun began. Seeking to avoid the death sentence, the agencies found all sorts of reasons to justify their existence, and in many cases mobilized bands of constituents to lobby legislators.

But the case against some of the boards proved devastating. The Athletic Commission, to cite one sorry example, had long outlived its usefulness in regulating boxing and wrestling; by 1976, there had not been a professional boxing match in the state for two years. As for wrestling, about 25 professional matches took place a year. But these were carefully choreographed "exhibitions," not true sporting contests; hence there was no compelling public interest in elaborate rules and regulations designed to ensure fair matches. The legislature voted to abolish the commission.

The Board of Registration of Professional Sanitarians also got the ax. It was doing a decent job giving exams and licensing inspectors of sewage-disposal sites and water-treatment plants. But the chore could just as well be handled by the state and county health departments, for which almost all the sanitarians worked. So the board was allowed to expire.

The activities of the Board of Shorthand Reporters, controlled by the court reporters themselves, were judged to be restrictive, limiting entry into the field and thus restraining competition. So the legislature abolished the board, transferring the licensing function to the state court administrator's office.

Sunset lopped off a bit of bureaucratic deadwood by combining the Board of Barber Examiners and the Board of Cosmetology. The board that regulated "life-care" institutions—homes for the aged to which the elderly turned over their savings in return for future care —was reorganized to include a majority of public members rather than industry representatives. There was also a drastic overhaul of the law involving the Racing Commission, to prevent its members from owning interests in Colorado race tracks, and to keep management of tracks out of undesirable hands.

The sunset process also stimulated reform of the Insurance Division, which oversees the operation of a $1.4-billion state industry. The commissioner, a civil servant who was a power unto himself, and who came from the industry, now reports to a six-person board that can hear complaints and reverse his decisions. As state senator Dick Plock, Republican majority leader, puts it, "The board basically gives the people a vote."

There was never any question of abolishing the PUC, the utilities commission that gave Barnes's client so much trouble. DORA and other critics simply felt its scope was too broad and they argued for significant renovation. The review process didn't achieve all that they had hoped on the first round, but it did succeed in deregulating a few transportation businesses, including haulers of sand and gravel, as well as companies that truck only their own goods. "Even though this was only a minimum change, we got our foot in the door," says Gail Klapper, DORA's executive director.

While no single reform has been earth-shaking, the sum total of all this legislative activity is impressive.

Can even more benefits be achieved by expanding the sunset approach to agencies outside the regulatory field? Quite possibly, but caution is needed. Six states have already decided to apply sunset review to all or almost all government agencies. Such an all-inclusive approach may be overly ambitious. Colorado's experience indicates that for sunset to be successful, it must be a painstaking process. If a legislature attempts too much, it may end up reviewing nothing adequately.

The sunset law is no panacea. Nonetheless, it is one of the most useful tools around to streamline government, improve its efficiency and make it responsive to the governed. Colorado deserves applause for leading the way.

Introduction
Power on the Potomac:
Whistle Blowing in the Plutonium

Many bureaucrats are content to adhere to rules and regulations and to follow customary procedures without question. It is personally the easiest path to follow, the least likely to "make waves" or earn disapproval. Some bureaucrats, however, exhibit an "inner check." This keeps them from following the customary path if that involves acting illegally, misrepresenting, or behaving in any way that they know is wrong.

Clifford Smith had that "inner check." A high-level career bureaucrat, a careful man, Smith was not a radical. But he was an honest bureaucrat who could not accede to the formal pressure to go along, to paper over problems of nuclear regulation.

QUESTIONS FOR DISCUSSION

To what did Smith object?
What do you feel motivated him to balk at the usual procedures?
How would bureaucrats remaining at NRC explain his case?
Could he have stayed at NRC? under what conditions?

POWER ON THE POTOMAC: WHISTLE BLOWING IN THE PLUTONIUM

David Burnham

Go down Soapstone Drive and turn right on Blue Smoke Trail and right again on Checkerberry Court. There, among the tall trees and deep shadows of Reston, is the home of Clifford Vaughn Smith Jr., one of the most unlikely whistle blowers ever to step from the gray ranks of Washington officialdom.

Clifford Smith is a careful man with a hard job.

His formal title sounds big: Director, Office of Nuclear Material Safety and Safeguards, Nuclear Regulatory Commission. His actual responsibilities are even bigger: coping with radioactive waste and designing safeguards to prevent terrorists and unstable nations from getting their hands on plutonium and highly enriched uranium from which they could make atomic bombs.

The job is located in the middle of a political minefield. Clifford Smith's $50,000-a-year slot is one of only five at the Nuclear Regulatory Commission where the holder serves at the pleasure of the Commission without any civil service protection. The insecurity of the position is doubly difficult because the Commission, itself pulled by powerful and sometimes conflicting forces generated by the powerful atom, frequently cannot make up its mind about the simplest questions.

A little more than a year ago, in the midst of an uncertain bureaucratic muddle that is Washington at its worst, Clifford Smith made a personal decision to challenge the established procedure in a way that made the Carter administration extremely uncomfortable.

Smith concluded that he did not know, and under the existing rules was unable to find out, whether some of America's closest allies had strict enough procedures to protect the nuclear supplies that American business and most of the federal government were anxious to sell.

His decision, almost completely unnoticed at the time, resulted in allegations that his action might undermine the entire system of international nuclear controls, and charges that he was damaging America's balance of payments position.

Reprinted with permission of The Washingtonian, David Burnham, "Power on the Potomac," *The Washingtonian*, December 1978, p. 69.

The 47-year-old Smith is a cautious man, an engineer who has moved regularly to more important jobs. Chief water engineer for the Commonwealth of Pennsylvania at age 28. Johns Hopkins for a PhD in environmental engineering and radiological studies. Pacific Northwest regional administrator for the Environmental Protection Agency. A short stay with a large engineering company. Then, in December 1976, to the Nuclear Regulatory Commission.

Smith is a conservative man. Even though his wife and her family were driven from South Carolina in the thirties because the Ku Klux Klan objected to an uncle's effort to register black voters, even though he himself was restricted to black cabs and restaurants and schools while growing up in a segregated District of Columbia, Smith is uneasy about programs setting aside jobs for minorities.

> I have some difficulties with affirmative action. . . . If I get out and get a big job, rather than assume he got it because he was qualified, the first thing they assume is he got it because he is black.
>
> And so I worry about affirmative action. I think that at some point people have to make it on their own. I made it on my own. I've always felt that the only thing I could do was to be the best damn engineer-administrator I could, and in whatever small way contribute to people's understanding that you have to look at people as individuals. I am not a card-carrying civil rights activist.

Smith also is a reticent man. No news conferences. No public letters of protest. No leaking of documents to the press. When asked a question, the tall, grave man answers quietly.

What, he was asked, prompted him to challenge the Nuclear Regulatory Commission's established method of considering an application to export plutonium or highly enriched uranium? More specific, what were his objections to the procedure under which he, as director of the Office of Nuclear Material Safety and Safeguards, was asked to sign a statement concurring in the approval of each individual export application?

"I've always had a problem with the bureaucracy in government —things have a way of perpetuating themselves without anyone really asking why," he replied.

At the time Smith became safeguards director, his predecessor as director of the NRC's safeguards office had concurred in the granting of about a hundred export licenses.

"On this particular issue, back sometime in July or August of 1977, we were having some disagreements and I simply asked the question on what basis do we concur? Jerry Page, my deputy, said, 'Cliff, our concurrence means—' well, no one really knew what it meant."

The next obvious question was how the Office of Safeguards, in this case Clifford Smith, could give an assurance when its only source of information was a United Nations agency which by international agreement was forbidden from disclosing the safeguard arrangements of individual nations to anyone?

But the problem was more than just the lack of specific information. Sometime in 1977, the staff of the International Atomic Energy Agency prepared a secret report summarizing its ability to insure the reliability of the world's nuclear safeguard systems. It remains to this day the only authoritative analysis of international safeguards, their implementation and their effectiveness.

The report opens with an optimistic assurance that no uranium or plutonium was stolen in the past year. But the report then concedes that the international system would not be able to detect the theft of these materials within the time period it would take to make an atomic bomb. The system, according to the UN's own standards, was not working.

"Well," Clifford Smith continued, "it finally came out that all we were saying when we concurred to an export was that the receiving nation was a member of the International Atomic Energy Agency. And I said, 'What do we know about IAEA safeguards?' . . .

"I became concerned that my concurrence might mean that the Commission thought everything was okay. I felt it was incumbent upon me to bring that to the Commission's attention so that it was unmistakably clear what the situation was."

On September 19, 1977, Smith wrote the NRC's Office of International Programs that his office could no longer give the Commission any assurances about nuclear safeguards in other countries.

Clifford Smith, the careful, conservative, experienced manager, acknowledges that his worries were motivated by personal, as well as public considerations. His personal concerns might be viewed as petty, the bureaucrat protecting his backsides; or noble, the official assessing his responsibilities.

He recalls that at about the same time he was discussing with his staff the implications of concurring with the export applications, he had gone to a congressional hearing where a colleague was sharply questioned about why he had signed off on a particular matter.

"I became concerned that if I went up on the Hill and they asked me why I had concurred that I would be unable to give a sensible answer. So I wanted that cleared up with the Commission."

Passing the buck? Or a courageous act? Whatever the perspective, the Commission, at least parts of it, was not pleased with Smith's questioning of established procedure. The problem, as noted in a November 22 memorandum of the NRC's general counsel, was not that the lack of concurrence would mean an end to nuclear exports, but that it would add to the personal responsibilities of the individual NRC commissioners.

As a legal matter, the memorandum said, the NRC can grant an export license "notwithstanding its ability to determine the adequacy of safeguards to be applied to that export." But because the Commission's determinations must rest on facts, the "strongly held views of a staff component charged with expert responsibility for an area cannot be lightly disregarded."

Despite the legal ruling that the Commission could go on approving licenses if it so desired, one commissioner complained to Smith that the problem he had raised would result in a reduction in America's nuclear exports and thus contribute to the United States' balance of payments problem.

Smith recalls telling the complaining commissioner that his particular responsibility was safeguarding nuclear materials, not solving the balance of payments problem. "I had my sphere, the Commission had its sphere, and the President had his." Smith said. "The question of safeguards, my responsibility, is only one aspect of the overall decision of whether a specific export may be in the interest of the United States."

But the heat was on. In addition to the complaints from the NRC commissioner, Clifford Smith heard whispered criticism from the State Department. His stomach started kicking up. "I thought for a while I had an ulcer but the doctor said I just had an overactive tummy," he said.

On December 28, Clifford Smith formally requested that the simple statement of concurrence by the Office of Nuclear Material Safety and Safeguards be replaced with very different language:

> NMSS wishes to inform the Commission that it has not received information which permits it to make an independent conclusion as to the effectiveness of IAEA safeguards as applied (name of country), but assurances have been provided by the executive branch that exports would not be inimical to the interests of the United States.

Clifford Smith's formulation, though phrased discretely, was uncomfortably close to the little boy's announcement that the king was naked. It raised a key question that remains unanswered.

If the United States relies on the International Atomic Energy Agency to assure itself that the safeguards are adequate in nations receiving United States nuclear materials, and the IAEA issues a report concluding that the safeguards are not effective, what should the United States do? Should the U.S. insist on its own investigation of the nuclear safeguards in each of the recipient nations?

These questions were discussed during a closed Commission

meeting on January 24 that was attended by Louis V. Nosenzo, the deputy assistant secretary of state for Nuclear Energy and Energy Technology Affairs. A censored transcript of the meeting was later placed in the Commission's document room.

Mr. Nosenzo said he was worried that if the NRC reported to Congress about the safeguard weaknesses acknowledged by the IAEA and by Clifford Smith's decision not to concur in approving export licenses, it might prompt congressional demands for the United States to obtain independent verification of the safeguards employed by each nation.

The public discussion of these problems, Mr. Nosenzo argued, would be "divisive" and "would tend to undermine the credibility of the agency [IAEA]. And I think that it is not in anybody's interest to do that."

The Commission, however, chose to ignore Mr. Nosenzo's advice. On February 2, letters were sent to the House and Senate acknowledging that the IAEA had reported that the application of its safeguard controls "does not necessarily assure that adequate material control and accounting measures are applied in all cases."

The Commission letters to Congress, which were not made public at the time they were sent to Capitol Hill, added that "it is therefore possible that the NRC could approve the export of nuclear materials to countries in which the IAEA is having implementation problems without the NRC knowing it."

Clifford Smith's Office of Nuclear Materials Safety and Safeguards has not concurred in any of the thirty export applications to come to the Commission since his decision to challenge the rules. In only one case, involving India, was an export license application not approved. And even in this case, the Commission's negative decision was subsequently overridden by President Carter. Thus, the United States has gone on approving the shipments of highly enriched uranium to such nations as Mexico, Indonesia, and the Philippines, as well as Germany, Canada, and France.

So Smith's challenge has had little effect so far. Discouraged by this and other struggles within the NRC, Smith has accepted a job beginning January 1 as vice president for administration at Oregon State University.

True to his careful, conservative self, Smith is loath to describe the lessons learned during the last months in the Nuclear Regulatory Commission. Pressed by a visitor, however, he somewhat reluctantly offers his judgment.

"I think one of the problems we have sometimes is that the responsible people don't want to look directly at the issues," he said.

"So there is pressure down the line not to say anything or take any steps that make it difficult for the people up above."

One official sympathetic to Smith's challenge is a bit more optimistic. "What Cliff did is to make it a little harder for the establishment types to keep up the facade that everything is okay. The sad thing is that it illustrates how rare it is for Washington officials to do what they should be doing every day." . . .

Clifford Smith stood up. It was 1:30 on a Sunday afternoon and the Redskins were playing football on television.

"My youngest daughter didn't want to move out to Oregon but I won her over with the promise that she can have a horse," he explained as we walked to the door and shook hands. A large red and white FOR SALE sign was stuck in the lawn in front of the house on Checkerberry Court. Though the football game was on television, Clifford Smith's little game in Washington was over.

Introduction
The Price of Blowing the Whistle

Bureaucracies are often so large and complex that it is difficult for an outsider to understand their workings. Often the subject matter is so highly technical that laypeople cannot make judgments about decisions. The first to see a problem may be a bureaucrat in middle management—someone who knows the organization and knows the field, someone who is high enough up to see the overall picture but not so high as to have a stake in the decisions already made. One way to remedy a perceived problem is to work through channels. But when the channels are unresponsive, an increasing number of officials are willing to leak information to the media and even to risk their careers by going public, by "blowing the whistle." In fact, the risk is almost always career-fatal, for the bureaucracy will certainly and quietly protect itself—shunning, transferring, demoting, ignoring, even firing the "culprit."

"The Price of Blowing the Whistle" tells the stories of some whistle blowers and their fates. Dr. Stanley Mazaleski, "an exceedingly earnest man who believes in God, the Constitution and conservative government," paid with loss of employment, mounting debt, a strained marriage, and loss of his friends for the "crime" of complaining about how slow his agency was in acting to protect factory workers exposed to dangerous chemicals. On the other hand, Dr. John Nestor and Al Louis Ripskis delight in their role of gadfly in the name of public well-being.

QUESTIONS FOR DISCUSSION

In what other policy areas have whistle blowers been ignored with tragic consequences?

Are the oversights that are underscored by whistle blowing also common in more routine areas, in cases with important but less dramatic consequences, such as inadequate housing, poor education, unsanitary food?

Could Weber or Taylor have foreseen the whistle blower? Why?

In what ways is whistle blowing a constructive force? In what ways does it hold a potential for damage?

THE PRICE OF BLOWING THE WHISTLE

Helen Dudar

In the spring of 1974, Dr. Stanley Mazaleski, a government scientist, began complaining about the sluggish pace at which his agency had set about designing safety standards for industrial workers exposed to carcinogenic chemicals. The following winter, Mazaleski's criticisms were leaked to the newspapers. Within a few months he was fired. And last May, after a two-year fight for reinstatement, he won a court decision ordering the Public Health Service to hold a new hearing. It was a modest victory, just enough to allow his attorney to try to open negotiations with the agency. After a while, the lawyer called with the report that he had been in touch with the agency's general counsel to no avail. "They said you're guilty," he told Mazaleski. "Guilty of what?" Mazaleski asked. "I don't know—they just said you're guilty."

Mazaleski's belief in his righteousness is whole and complete. He is driven by a fearsome persistence and by a myopic refusal to acknowledge that the system can possibly be as "unfair" as it has so far been to him. He is a "whistle blower"—a rather casual term for a risky business. Mazaleski belongs to a haunted little tribe of Federal employees who have transgressed against the bureaucracy—who, having seen something seriously wrong in a Government operation, made a noise about it.

The penalty for going public, for telling Congress or a reporter or even a superior a few steps up the chain of command can be harsh. Mazaleski lost his position at an agency hearing which he was not even invited to attend. A more sophisticated way of dealing with the over-zealous bureaucrat is to have his job abolished. If the dissident is too well known to be dismissed, he can be "promoted" into another section of the agency where his expertise is useless. If he is obscure but likely to make a public fuss, he can be effectively immobilized by demotion to a lesser, lower-paying job where his expertise is also wasted. On the other hand, it may be decided that his behavior has been erratic. In that event his superior may insist that he consult a psychiatrist in the expectation that he will be found to be unstable and thereby eligible for a disability discharge. Of course, he can refuse to submit to an examination. But then he may be fired for insubordination.

Theoretically, a bureaucrat who testifies before Congress is automatically protected from reprisal. Firing him is literally a crime. In practice, the system is "unenforceable," according to an aide for a powerful Senator. "What would you have the Senate do when a Pentagon employee testifies and is punished?" he asked. "Hold the Secretary of Defense in contempt?" A bureaucrat with a dismissal slip is entitled to a Civil Service hearing, but there the cards may be stacked, too.

The bureaucracy is a Goliath, and the machinery available to enforce its will is immense. Moreover, its will often extends far beyond its boundaries. A civil servant who has lost a post in a conflict that reached the press usually becomes unemployable. Advertised jobs in other Federal agencies prove to be illusory the day he applies; promising offerings in private enterprises that are dependent on the kindness of Government agencies vanish overnight. It takes merely a phone call to a former boss to learn that the applicant is considered just a trifle hard to get along with. . . .

Stanley Mazaleski's wife, Charlotte, tells him he can't win; his adversary is too powerful. Sometimes, Mazaleski thinks she may be right, but he can't give up. He really believes that "the truth will out." It has been more than two years since he was fired from his $17,800-a-year job with the Public Health Service, and his life is a shambles. A Ph.D. in preventive medicine, he could not find work in his field for 17 months. For a period, he worked nights as a security guard near his home in Monrovia, Md., and his teen-age daughter, eldest of his four children, took a job in a Hot Shoppe to help support the family. Last winter, money was so short that the family lived mostly on potatoes, which Mazaleski, a farm boy from Pennsylvania, had grown in the garden. The debts have piled up, and his creditors are pressing for payments he cannot make; the bank is threatening to foreclose the mortgage on his four-bedroom house; his marriage is desperately strained; friends have fallen away and relatives in Government service who are apparently nervous about their social connections exclude him from family gatherings.

In January, Mazaleski finally found work in Washington with the Environmental Protection Agency, but it is temporary and likely to end any day now. He writes letters incessantly to officials in and out of

Government, beseeching help which never comes.

A large, genial, sad-eyed man, Mazaleski went to work for the National Institute of Occupational Safety and Health, a P.H.S. agency, four years ago. His job was to write reports on a variety of dangerous and possibly carcinogenic chemicals used in industry and to develop standards, required by new legislation, for protecting the health of workers exposed to these materials.

Before the year was out, Mazaleski was in trouble. He insisted, against considerable resistance by the medical authorities over him, that the chemical cadmium may cause prostate cancer. A year later, the professional literature proved him right. He said the industry should be required to keep medical records for 20 years on workers exposed to chloroform, a suspected cause of cancer and birth defects; over his protest, the N.I.O.S.H. management reduced the period to a worthless five years. He filed a grievance against a supervisor who had dealt rudely with him. He complained to superiors that evidence he needed for his work was being withheld. He wrote letters to Congressmen bemoaning delays in setting safety standards, delays that probably made life easier for industry but surely imperiled the health of millions of workers. His criticism found its way into the *New York Times* early in 1975.

In March 1975, he was fired for "marginal and substandard performance" and for "insubordination." Mazaleski's fate, said Albert R. Lauderbaugh, a senior P.H.S. official who tried to help settle the affair before it reached the firing stage, was "an almost classic example of management's reaction to an internal critic." Mazaleski's former boss, Dr. John May, insists, "His charges have no validity whatsoever. He was fired because he didn't do his job."

What is so bewildering to Mazaleski is that he had spent a lifetime doing the right thing. When the Korean War began, he was about to enter college and he gave up a scholarship to enlist in the Navy. After four years of service, he came home and worked hard on his father's farm, spending six years in evening studies to earn a college degree. He has always been a popular and successful student. He is 44, an exceedingly earnest man who believes in God, the Constitution and conservative government. Sitting in a cramped little office we had borrowed for the interview. I wondered aloud whether Mazaleski was the kind of householder who regularly hung out the American flag on patriotic holidays. Yes, yes, he did. And on Veterans Day, he related, he always took the family on a pilgrimage to Gettysburg National Park. Abruptly, Mazaleski's eyes filled with tears and for several minutes he could not talk.

. . . "I get a kick out of outfoxing the bastards. Where else could

I be such a son of a bitch and be on the right side?" If there is an ideal position from which to pursue whistleblowing as a steady avocation, Dr. John Nestor occupies it. For 16 years, he has been bedevilling the Food and Drug Administration, which employs him. Since he is a bachelor, there is no family to worry about. He has a crusty self-assurance reminiscent of all the authoritative older-doctor roles Lionel Barrymore used to play. Rude, abrasive, difficult, obstreperous, rigid, inflexible—Nestor has been called all that and more. He will obligingly recite the complaints, observing that none of these flaws is as grievous as the official mendacity he sees all the time.

Nestor, now nearing 65, went to work for F.D.A. in 1961 as a reviewer of drugs for heart and kidney ailments. Nestor was not at F.D.A. long before he concluded that the agency was and had always been the captive of the industry it is supposed to regulate and so he has testified in numerous appearances at Congressional hearings.

In 1972, Nestor was "promoted" into the F.D.A. Office of Compliance—which oversees industry compliance with agency rules—an activity for which he had neither the appetite nor the experience. He has been kicking and fussing ever since. Three years ago, he and a dozen other F.D.A. employees appeared at a hearing before an inquiry conducted by Senator Edward Kennedy and offered testimony charging the agency with corrupt practices in drug approval and with the harassment of dissident employees. The complaints have been investigated, most recently by a special panel which delivered a 766-page report last April. It concluded that the charges were accurate. It also said that officials had lied. The report said Nestor was owed a formal apology, payment of his legal costs and a new position where his talents would be used. He is still waiting.

Nestor is an assiduous leaker. What he knows and what other agency employees feed him (Ernest Fitzgerald calls them "closet patriots") finds its way steadily into the files of Congressional investigators, consumer advocates and media folk. "Let me tell you," he commented over a beer, "the Freedom of Information Act hasn't opened up the Government. The duplicating machine has. I have kept very busy."

Al Louis Ripskis, a slender, mild-mannered bachelor of 40, now has the routine job of program analyst at the Department of Housing and Urban Development. "Paper-shuffling," he calls it contemptuously. The job has no psychic rewards, a dreary state of affairs for a man who went to Federal housing 16 years ago with more idealism than was good for him. But Impact fills the need.

Impact is a "leaksheet," a neatly mimeographed, $5-a-year report of almost everything that can go wrong at one public agency. Ripskis writes it with the help of anonymous regional correspondents, and on publication morning, before he signs in for work, he is to be found brashly hawking it on the sidewalk in front of H.U.D. Its subscribers include H.U.D. employees, some high agency officials he hopes to alert to the latest criticism, muckraking reporters in and out of Washington, the Office of Management and Budget and the Library of Congress. The H.U.D. Secretary gets one free. Ripskis says he is out of pocket about $3,000 a year on production costs.

In five years of publication, he has chronicled mismanagement, incompetence, waste and stupidity at his agency, assembling in print the kind of details that rarely get beyond the gossip hour around the water cooler. He flashily reported that a new housing project in Minneapolis lacked adequate elevators but had a brothel and that a high-ranking H.U.D. official seldom traveled anywhere without his mistress. In recent years, he has nagged at H.U.D. for its neglect of the lead-paint problems in housing. In the middle of President Ford's drive against inflation, Impact was reporting that H.U.D. Secretary Carla Hills had spent $82,000 for new air-conditioning for a conference room.

Born in Lithuania, Ripskis spent four years in a D.P. camp in Germany, and remembers it all: the dirt, the crowding, the lack of privacy. As a refugee in America, he lived in Chicago tenements. Out of school, Ripskis got a job with the Public Housing Administration in 1961, planning to stay no longer than two years. "It was to be my own domestic Peace Corps effort." But he began moving up the bureaucratic ladder and he was full of widely admired and widely ignored ideas for making public housing look more like homes than barracks. In 1965, after H.U.D. had become the umbrella agent for housing, Ripskis's innovative approaches carried him to Washington into a key task force called Social Concerns of H.U.D. The notion was that this time the Government was really going to build human concerns into public housing. Ripskis remembers that period as a wonderful time. The group, he says, wrote a wonderful report. And, in the end, it was interred wherever good Governments reports go to die.

That and the fate of a H.U.D. co-worker laid the groundwork for Impact. The newsletter's predecessor was Quest, an in-house underground journal published by a friend who, as a result, was briefly exiled to Alaska. Setting out on his own soon after, Ripskis planned the way with canny caution. "I have managed to survive with a minimum of harrassment, and it was not by accident. The critical choices came in the beginning. If they decide to fire you at the start, it's hard to reverse the bureaucracy once it gets rolling. But I started muckraking and kicking up a lot of publicity, and I became well known, so the department knew it would be bloody if they canned me."

Ripskis's modest success is instructive. The whistleblower must not only be strong and knowledgable, but exceptionally careful. Most people who wind up in the fraternity begin almost accidentally, expecting gratitude and encountering, instead, a stone wall of either indifference or hostility.

Some people have mused that the hazards were so great it might be sensible for the public-spirited bureaucrat to stay on the job, stay anonymous and simply "leak for life." That choice, of course, is made daily by hundreds of middle-management employees who become regular and protected sources for reporters and Congressional investigators. It's one way to serve the public interest without pain and intense public drama. What would recent American history have been for example, without those grand panjandrums of whistleblowing, Daniel Ellsberg, who xeroxed the Pentagon Papers, and Victor Marchetti, the first to tell us how the C.I.A. really works.

On the other hand, nothing about this activity guarantees it will fill a real need or gain wide public support. One of the celebrated whistleblowers of the early 1960's was Otto Otepka, the chief of security at the State Department who earnestly believed that subversives held down Government jobs in his agency. He leaked confidential loyalty files to the Senate Internal Security subcommittee, which was still pursuing "Reds" in Government. Otepka was demoted, wire-tapped and harassed in other illegal ways. In that case, it was not the advocates of free speech or open government who came to his support; Otepka found his modest constituency in the John Birch Society.

As it stands now, the civil servant who squawks is apt to be regarded at worst as a Judas, at best as a foolish aberration. One of the main priorities of the I.P.S. Project for Government Accountability is to institutionalize whistleblowing, to create a climate where it is easier and even commonplace for a public servant to deliver up to the public details of waste and deceit in his agency.

"We don't want saints and heroes," says Ralph Stavins, an I.P.S. fellow who heads the project. "We want this made automatic and procedural."

The I.P.S. literature on the subject includes a flashy red-white-and-blue brochure with a cover exhorting Federal workers to "Point Out Illegality, and Waste." Its final words are from one of President Carter's campaign speeches. Ten days before the election, Carter declared, "I intend to seek strong legislation to protect our Federal employees from harassment and dismissal if they find out and report waste or dishonesty by their superiors or others. The Fitzgerald case, where a dedicated civil servant was fired from the Defense Department for reporting cost overruns, must never be repeated." . . .